SCARECROW AREA BIBLIOGRAPHIES
Edited by Jon Woronoff

Bibliography of African Literatures

Peter Limb
and
Jean-Marie Volet

Scarecrow Area Bibliographies, No. 10

The Scarecrow Press, Inc.
Lanham, Md., & London

SCARECROW PRESS, INC.

Published in the United States of America
by Scarecrow Press, Inc.
4720 Boston Way
Lanham, Maryland 20706

4 Pleydell Gardens, Folkestone
Kent CT20 2DN, England

Copyright © 1996 by Peter Limb and Jean-Marie Volet

British Cataloguing-in-Publication Information Available

Library of Congress Cataloging-in-Publication Data

Limb, Peter.
Bibliography of African literatures / by Peter Limb and Jean-Marie Volet.
p.   cm. — (Scarecrow area bibliographies ; 10)
Includes bibliographical references and indexes.
1. Africa—Literatures—Bibliography. 2. Africa—In literature—
Bibliography. I. Volet, Jean-Marie, 1947– II. Title. III. Series
Z6514.C7A38   1996   [PN849.A35]   016.8088'9866—dc20   96-870 CIP

ISBN 0-8108-3144-9 (cloth : alk. paper)

☉™ The paper used in this publication meets the minimum requirements of
American National Standard for Information Sciences—Permanence of
Paper for Printed Library Materials, ANSI Z39.48–1984.
Manufactured in the United States of America.

CONTENTS

EDITOR'S FOREWORD

This book is the first in a new subseries of bibliographies of world literature. It deals with African literatures. Future volumes will cover Arabic, Slavic and other major traditions, but none of them is likely to have such a broad spread given the astounding diversity to be found within Africa. There are significant established authors in the more than fifty countries in North Africa and sub-Saharan Africa where they write in one of the various indigenous languages and/or those of the former colonial powers (English, French, Portuguese, etc.). Contemporary authors have adopted all of the existing genres and developed some of their own. Thus the primary task was to bring order into this mass of authors, titles, and literatures. That task has been solved admirably with an amazingly clear and simple structure.

The more demanding task was to fill out these categories so as to help readers to find works relating to the various authors and their writings. While some are already quite well-known, others are less familiar, or possibly unknown to the general public, yet they deserve to be considered. Finding out who wrote what, in which language, and which genre is no easy matter in any circumstances, but much harder in the case of African literatures given the paucity of reference material. Yet, this bibliography manages to provide an abundance of books by African authors, books on authors, anthologies, bibliographies, and other resource details. In so doing, it fills an important gap and makes one of the most interesting and vigorous literary traditions more accessible. Henceforth, it will be much easier for newcomers (and afficionados) to get to know Africa's literatures.

The *Bibliography of African Literatures* is due to the dedication of two researchers living on the other side of the world. Peter Limb, a librarian at the University (Reid) Library of the University of Western Australia, has long been interested in African cultures as well as African history and politics. Among other things, he compiled an annotated bibliography, *The ANC and Black Workers in South Africa, 1912-1992*. Jean-Marie Volet, a research fellow at the Department of French Studies of the same University, has written extensively on Francophone African literatures, including a book, *L'Idée de pouvoir chez les romancières d'expression française de l'Afrique sub-saharienne.*

Jon Woronoff
Series Editor

ACKNOWLEDGMENTS

A number of specialists on African literature offered suggestions about different aspects of the bibliography. We wish to thank: Bernth Lindfors in Texas; Albert Gérard in Liège; Virginia Coulon and Jean Michel Massa in France; Derek Wright in Darwin; Gareth Griffiths, Tony Simoes da Silva, Beverley Ormerod, and Taiwo Sanusi in Perth; Lilyan Kesteloot in Dakar; Nicolas Martin-Granel in Brazzaville; Pius Ngandu Nkashama in Leiden; Uzo Esonwanne in Windsor, Ontario; Nora-Alexandra Kazi-Tani in Algiers.

We wish to record the assistance of many "net-cruisers" on African groups on the Internet (such as Igbo--Net, soc.culture.berber, soc.culture.somalia, Ethiolist, Malawi-net, Sudanese-Net, and others), including: Meseret Mulugetta at Harvard University; Nadia Benakli at Princeton University; Hsen Larbi; the Amazigh Cultural Association in America; Dr. Heilna du Plooy at the Potchefstroom University for Christian Higher Education; Frances Pritchett, Little Rock; and Catherine B. Rockwell, Marriott Library, University of Utah. Nicole Livar and Petra Fogarty also were of great assistance in correcting proofs.

Needless to say any errors are our own.

INTRODUCTION

The need for a comprehensive bibliographical survey of African literatures has never been more apparent. The successes of Nobel Laureates Naguib Mahfuz of Egypt, Wole Soyinka of Nigeria, and Nadine Gordimer of South Africa ensure that no longer can the rich and varied creative writings of Africa be ignored. The broad Africa-wide and international fame of other writers, such as Chinua Achebe, Nawal al-Saadawi, Ngugi wa Thiong'o, Ama Ata Aïdoo, Mongo Beti, Werewere Liking, or Sembène Ousmane, to name just a few, is testimony to the growing popularity of African writers. However, much of their output is imperfectly documented. Perhaps the most impressive attempt to comprehensively chronicle African literature, that of H. Zell, Carol Bundy and Virginia Coulon, is now 12 years old, and even this work neglected North Africa with its wealth of Arabic literature, Afrikaans, and many other languages.[1]

This work brings together books by major established and new literary writers of the continent and diaspora. The main emphasis of the book is on literatures in English and French, but some in Portuguese, Arabic, and other various major African languages also are included. All countries and literary genres are covered. Themes treated in the bibliography include African women writers, writers with socio-political themes, and post-colonial literature. This work fills a gap in the subject literature occasioned by the explosion of publishing of African writers and provides both a ready-reference to African authors and a detailed, in-depth coverage of the most significant and interesting writers to emerge in recent decades.

The number of books published by African authors has increased at an exponential rate over the last decade. So too has secondary literature, and that alone would make any attempt to produce a comprehensive bibliography impossible. Yet, there is another and arguably bigger obstacle on the road to exhaustivity, that is the contemporary dismissal of universal values and the subjectivity of past criteria allowing the distinction between the "good" writers from the "bad," or the "écrivains" from the "écrivants," the canonic from the mundane, the dilemma of writing in "international"

---

[1] H. Zell, C. Bundy, and V. Coulon, *A New Reader's Guide to African Literature*. London: Heinemann, 1983.

languages or the vernacular. How to frame African literature(s), who to include, how to organise the information? These are some of the questions increasingly difficult to ascertain, at least in terms of a universal consensus. Furthermore, what once came under the single banner of African literature is increasingly perceived in its plurality and referred as African literatures. The issue of who writes what in what language is hotly debated between contemporary African authors. The rich cultural African experience is reflected in its unparalleled linguistic diversity.

The subdivision of this bibliography according to languages spoken in Africa is an acknowledgment of that diversity. The subdivision by countries we have adopted reflects more recent political development in the continent. It is useful as a guide but remains subject to interpretation. Many African authors' mobility would have justified their mention in more than one country. Myriam Warner-Vieyra, born in Guadeloupe, but established in Senegal for most of her life; Werewere Liking born in Cameroon and residing in Côte d'Ivoire, Moroccan Tahar Ben Jelloun or Egyptian Edmond Jabès established in Paris, are only a few examples.

Gender studies are having an increasing impact on the study of African literatures, as well. For example, Margaret Busby's recent anthology *Daughters of Africa* (London: Vintage, 1992) provides a wide cross-section of texts echoing past and present black (but not necessarily African) women's experiences. We have acknowledged the increasing number of African women authors who have published literary texts over the last twenty years by providing a guide to female authors. Given the unfamiliarity of many Western readers with the linguistic complexity and diversity of African names — for example, few would know off-hand that Ken Bugul, Out-el-Kouloub, or Werewere Liking are women authors — we identify women writers of primary literary works (fiction, poetry, drama, etc.) by placing the symbol "F" after their name. This convention does not apply for critics.

Scope

Given the dynamic nature of contemporary African literatures and the tremendous interest raised over the last decade or so by new forms of literary expressions, we have chosen to highlight not only the major established writers but also to give emphasis to more recent writers. Another reason for our emphasis on recent authors is the fact that to date many of the bibliographies published in the early 1980s have not been brought up to date and do not reflect the intense literary activity of the last fifteen years or so. The information and publishing explosion means that it is impossible to include each and every work of relevance, but we hope to provide a guide not only to the major and well-established literary writers and critics of the past but also to the promising authors and scholars of today.

Whilst we concentrate on literatures of the twentieth century, this does not mean that there is not a rich corpus of writings from earlier centuries, from ancient Egyptian literature — not included in our work — to the rich tradition of Arabic literature in Africa. The Arabic heritage includes the poetry of North African-Andalusian writers from the eleventh and twelfth centuries. Arabic-speaking troubadours, such as Ibrahim ibn Sahl (died 1251), a poet of Ceuta, were active across North Africa. Muhammad Ibn Battuta (1304-1377) of Tangier wrote seminal travel prose. Rukn al-Din of Egypt, and Mahmud Kati and Ahmad Baba of Mali chronicled Arabic legends in the thirteenth and sixteenth centuries, respectively. The Somali historian 'Arabfaqih wrote in the mid-sixteenth century on Ethiopian history. Ishak of Ethiopia wrote the *Kebra Nagast* in the thirteenth century. Juan Latino of Guinea and Antonius Amo of Ghana wrote in Latin in the sixteenth and seventeenth centuries, respectively. Ugaas Raage of Somalia composed poetry in Somali in the 1730s. Abdallah Saiyid of Tanzania wrote "Takhmis ya Liyonga" in about 1750. The Senegalese born Phyllis Wheatley wrote poetry in America in the 1770s, and the autobiography of the Nigerian Olaudah Equiano (or Vassa) was published in England in 1789. The Kenyan-based Swahili poet Muyaka and the Sudanese Arabic scholar Muhammad wad Daïf Allah flourished at the end of the eighteenth century. In the nineteenth century, writers such as Umar Saiyid in Kenya and Muhyi Shaikh in Tanzania, Ali Duuh in Somalia, and Ramanato in Malagasy composed oral poetry.[2]

For reasons of space and emphasis, both ancient Egyptian and Ge'ez literatures were excluded from the scope. Ge'ez is a South Semitic language related to Tigrinya and is the classical liturgical language of Ethiopia, in which literature has been written since at least the seventh century A.D. This has

---

[2] Herdeck, Donald E. *African Authors: A Companion to Black African Writing*. Washington: Black Orpheus Press, 1973 gives an excellent overview of these early African writers.

been largely religious in nature, although some religious poetry continues to be written in the language.[3] Also generally excluded are historical chronicles. The important role of oral literature and literatures in African languages in African culture cannot be stressed too much, especially when one considers that some of the finest literature of the continent is written in the vernacular: Ngugi now writes only in Gikuyu. A separate volume would be required to do justice to the volume and quality of vernacular material. Nevertheless, in the African Language Literatures section, we provide readers with an overview, or sample, of some of the best of this literature. Readers wishing to follow-up on African oral literature could do well to consult such major collections as, in English, the "Oxford Library of African Literatures," and, in French, "Classiques Africains" (A. Colin), and "Fleuve et Flamme" (Conseil de la Langue Française) — many titles from which are included in this book.

All countries of continental Africa are included. Excluded are the island-states of the Indian Ocean, except Madagascar. Generally excluded are works by expatriates or colonial writers, such as Rider Haggard or Albert Camus, who are generally considered primarily as English or French writers. This has been qualified to include a few writers, such as Doris Lessing or Leïla Sebbar for example, who continue to identify closely with Africa. The problem of "popular" or "pulp fiction" writers is also complex. In general, we have not given much prominence to this material. However, a selection of this genre, such as anthologies of the Nigerian Onitsha market literature, and works by some writers, such as David Maillu of Kenya or Micheline Coulibaly of Ivory Coast have been included.

The majority of our citations are in English or French. There are also sections devoted to other major languages, such as Arabic, Portuguese, and other literatures of Africa.

Arrangement

The bibliography is arranged primarily by language. The first part consists of a general overview. This lists bibliographies, anthologies, and critical works about African literatures in general. The second part is a selection of authors

---

[3] Thomas Leiper Kane, *Ethiopian Literature in Amharic* (Wiesbaden: Harrasowitz, 1975), pp.1-3, 9.

listed in the following alphabetic order: African languages; Arabic; English; French; and Portuguese and other languages, including Afrikaans. The African language section is necessarily selective, given the large number of languages. To augment the somewhat subjective selection of fifteen languages, a representative sample of works in other African languages is also included. African language literatures are discussed further below.

Within each language section, the arrangement is first by region or country. English and French, the two largest sections, are sub-divided into broad regions, such as Maghreb or Southern Africa, and then further divided into countries. The Arabic and Portuguese sections simply use a country-by-country approach. Within each country, items are arranged in the following sequence: bibliographies; anthologies; general critical works; and, finally, publications by selected literary authors. Critical works about a literary author are indented directly under the primary works by this author. However, bibliographies about a particular author, or anthologies of other people's work edited by this author, or general critical works, are arranged in the relevant initial sections. At times this choice is problematic. Essays by a literary author could equally be regarded as critical works or as primary literary works in their own right. Some bi-lingual authors, such as Breyten Breytenbach and André Brink, translate their own work, which could just as easily be placed in the English as the Afrikaans section. In general, however, we choose to locate a work firstly under the language in which it was written.

Following each entry the genre reflecting the content of the book is added in a note: poetry, drama, novel, short story, autobiography, etc. This gives only a rough indication of the book's contents. From Werewere Liking's "chant-romans" to the "prose-poétique" of Jabès, one can find a wide range of unusual literary expression reflecting the limit of conventional definitions of literary genres.

In keeping with the series format, a simple author index is included. This is modified to include a list of female literary authors (not critics). Finally, a country index helps bring together works in different languages from the same country.

Periodical and Other Sources of Information

This bibliography, like others in the series, concentrates on books or monographs. Periodical articles are generally excluded, though an exception has been made to include a

number of special issues of journals and bibliographical
articles, especially in cases where there is a paucity of
published books. Also generally excluded are audiovisual
material, theses, translations, film scripts, and, with a few
exceptions, children's literature.

Readers wishing to explore the wealth of periodical
literature on African literatures may consult key journals, such
as: *Research in African Literatures*; *Africa. Literatura — Arte e
Cultura*; *African Arts*; *African Literature Today*; *Journal of
Commonwealth Literature*; *Wasafiri*; *Kunapipi*; *Staffrider*;
World Literature Today; *Notre Librairie, Sépia, Diagonales,
Présence Francophone.*[4] A new generation of newsletters
such as the *Bulletin de Liaison de l'Association pour l'Etude
des littératures africaines,* the *Bulletin de Liaison des Etudes
Littéraires Maghrébines,* the *Bulletin of Francophone Africa*
or *the Bulletin of the African Literature Association* give
regular updates of literary publications in and about Africa.
The annual *MLA International Bibliography* (New York:
Modern Language Association of America) has an African
section which lists books and journal articles. Reviews of
African literature are carried in a number of broader
Africanist journals, such as *African Studies Review, Cahier
d'Etudes Africaines* and *Journal of Southern African Studies,*
and also in bibliographical serials such as *African Book
Publishing Record.* Specialist bibliographies, such as Bernth
Lindfors, *A Bibliography of Literary Contributions to
Nigerian Periodicals, 1946-1972* (Ibadan: Ibadan University
Press, 1975) or Julie Strauss (ed.), *A Select Index to South
African Literature in English* (Grahamstown: National English
Literary Museum, 1991-), are further sources of information
about periodical articles. A number of these works are listed
below under the respective literatures and countries.
Unfortunately, many journals on African literature, especially
those published in Africa, have lapsed due to technical
problems.

The arrival on the market of an increasing number of
electronic databases dealing with African literatures provides
access to an ever-increasing range of citations. In the area of
Francophone Literatures, for example, the *banques de
données* LITAF (Francophone African Literatures South of
the Sahara) and LIMAG (Literature of the Maghreb) have

---

[4] A convenient (if now somewhat dated) list of journals relevant to African
litewrature is in Zell, Bundy, and Coulon, *A New Reader's Guide to African
Literature*, pp. 326-341.

been available since late 1994. In English the availability of MLA indexes on CD-ROM and online are exciting developments. Mushrooming Internet discussion groups and listservs include many of relevance to African literature; names such as Afrlit, EthioCulture, Eritrea-Dehai, soc.culture.berber, soc.culture. swahili and za.xhosa are just a few examples of how modern technology is spreading information worldwide about African cultures. In the course of preparing this bibliography, it has been both challenging and rewarding to "surf the net" and communicate electronically with people from countries as diverse as Somalia, Algeria, Egypt, South Africa, Malawi, Rwanda, Namibia, and Sudan. There is as yet no comprehensive guide to African literature-related groups on the Internet. However, Karen Fung of Hoover Institution Library, Stanford University, maintains a guide that is available electronically from this library.5

A Brief Survey of Bibliographical Guides to African Literatures

Readers wishing to orient themselves to an African country with which they are unfamiliar should consult the comprehensive series of volumes in the "African Historical Dictionaries" series published by Scarecrow Press of Metuchen, New Jersey. Although the books in this series are primarily concerned with history, all have detailed bibliographies, most of which include sections on literature and the arts. Thus they can serve as a starting base for exploration of the literature of a country. For example, the titles on Egypt, Cameroon, and the Sudan are particularly useful as sources of literary publications, whilst those on Equatorial Guinea and Western Sahara are important due to the lack of bibliographical coverage in English of these countries.6 Similarly, the World Bibliographical Series of Clio

---

5 Karen Fung, "Africa South of the Sahara: Selected Internet Resources" (Dec. 1994 ed.); World Wide Web address:
http://www—sul.stanford.edu/depts/ssrg/africa/guide.html

6 J. Wucher-King, *Historical Dictionary of Egypt.* 1984, updated by A. Goldschmidt in 1994; M.W. DeLancey and H.B. Mokeba, *Historical Dictionary of the Republic of Cameroon.* 2nd ed. 1990; C. Fluehr-Lobban, R.A. Lobban and J.O. Voll, *Historical Dictionary of the Sudan.* 2nd ed. 1992; M. Liniger-Goumaz, *Historical Dictionary of Equatorial Guinea.* 2nd ed. 1988; T. Hodges, *Historical Dictionary of the Western Sahara.* 1982.

Press in Oxford/Santa Barbara also offer a broad, country-by-country coverage of Africa that includes chapters on literature.

To locate a particular title that is still in print, Hans Zell's massive, two-volume *African Books in Print=Livres Africains Disponibles*. London: H. Zell, 1993 (4th ed.) is invaluable. General guides include: Donald E. Herdeck. *African Authors: A Companion to Black African Writing*. Washington: Black Orpheus Press, 1973; Janheinz Jahn, Ulla Schild, and Almut Nordmann. *Who's Who in African Literature: Biographies, Works, Commentaries*. Tübingen: H. Erdmann, 1972; Janheinz Jahn. *A Bibliography of Neo-African Literature from Africa, America and the Caribbean*. London: A. Deutsch, 1965; and Janheinz Jahn and Claus Peter Dressler. *Bibliography of Creative African Writing*. Nendeln, Lichtenstein; Millwood, NY: Kraus-Thompson, 1971. All are now somewhat dated, but still extremely useful.

For African literatures in English, a good place to start for new readers is Bernth Lindfors. *Black African Literature in English: A Guide to Information Sources*. Detroit: Gale Research, 1979. This is supplemented by the following titles also by the indefatigable Lindfors: *Black African Literature in English, 1977-1981*. New York: Africana, 1986; *Black African Literature in English, 1982-1986*. London: H. Zell, 1989; *Black African Literature in English, 1987-1991*. London: H. Zell, 1994. Also comprehensive, but much broader in scope, is Yvette Scheven. *Bibliographies for African Studies 1970-1986*. London: H. Zell, 1988.

Bernth Lindfors and Reinhard Sander (eds.). *Twentieth-Century Caribbean and Black African Writers*. Detroit: Gale, 1992, provide essays by experts discussing major authors with detailed bibliographies. On individual countries, see the relevant sections of the bibliography. A few examples are given here. On Nigeria, blessed with a vibrant literary output, see Claudia Baldwin. *Nigerian Literature: A Bibliography of Criticism, 1952-1976*. Boston: G. K. Hall, 1980. Peter Hogg and Ilse Sternberg (eds.). *Market Literature from Nigeria: A Checklist*. London: British Library, 1990 detail the often hard-to-locate Onitsha market literature. Gary E. Gorman. *The South African Novel in English Since 1950: An Information and Resource Guide*. Boston: Hall, 1978 remains a most useful survey of English literature of South Africa. More

All published by: Metuchen, NJ: Scarecrow Press in the African Historical Dictionaries series.

recently there is Kevin Goddard. *A Bibliography of South African Literature in English*. Grahamstown: National English Literary Museum, 1994 and C. E. Dubbeld. *Reflecting Apartheid: South African Short Stories in English with Sociopolitical Themes 1960-1987: A Select and Annotated Bibliography*. Johannesburg: South African Institute of International Affairs, 1990. Female African writers are listed, for example, in Brenda F. Berrian. *Bibliography of African Women Writers and Journalists (Ancient Egypt-1984)*. Washington: Three Continents, 1985; Beverley Ormerod and Jean-Marie Volet *Romancières africaines d'expression française: le sud du Sahara*. Paris: L'Harmattan, 1994; and Amelia House. *Black Women Writers from South Africa: A Preliminary Checklist*. Evanston: Northwestern University Program on Women, 1980. Given the large number, and variable quality, of anthologies of African literatures, David L. Ganz and Donald E. Herdeck. *A Critical Guide to Anthologies of African Literature*. Waltham, MA: Brandeis University/African Studies Association, 1973 is a useful companion.

In recent years a number of excellent bibliographies of individual writers have appeared. For example, Carol Sicherman. *Ngugi wa Thiong'o: A Bibliography of Primary and Secondary Sources, 1957-1989*. London: H. Zell, 1989, and Dorothy Driver, Ann Dry, Craig MacKenzie, and John Read. *Nadine Gordimer: A Bibliography of Primary and Secondary Sources, 1937-1992*. London: H. Zell, 1994; and James Gibbs, Ketu H. Katrak, and Henry Louis Gates. *Wole Soyinka: A Bibliography of Primary and Secondary Sources*. Westport: Greenwood, 1986, are some of the best. Works on individual writers in African languages are less extensive. One interesting work is Patricia E. Scott. *Samuel Edward Krune Mqhayi, 1875-1945: A Bibliographic Survey*. Grahamstown: Rhodes University Dept. of African Languages, 1976. Harold Scheub's *African Oral Narratives, Proverbs, Riddles, Poetry and Song* (Boston: GK Hall, 1977) is a detailed listing. Also useful is Véronika Görög-Karady. *Littérature Orale d'Afrique Noire: Bibliographie Annotée*. Paris: Conseil International de la langue française, 1992.

Bibliographic coverage varies for different countries. In Portuguese, the definitive work is Gerald Moser and Manuel Ferreira. *A New Bibliography of the Lusophone Literatures of Africa=Nova Bibliografia das Literaturas Africanas de Expressão Portuguesa*. London: H. Zell, 1993. 2nd rev., expanded ed. For African language literatures, Michael Mann and Valerie Sanders. *A Bibliography of African Language Texts in the Collections of the School of Oriental & African Studies, University of London, to 1963*. London: H. Zell, 1994 is limited to pre-1963 works but includes a number of important literary works in a great many African languages. What promises to be the definitive work on Arabic literature in Africa is J. O. Hunwick and R. S. O'Fahey (eds.). *Arabic Literature in Africa*. Leiden: Brill, 1994. A good introduction at a detailed level is M. M. Badawi. *Modern Arabic Literature*. Cambridge: Cambridge University Press, 1992. Readers interested in Arabic literature of earlier centuries could begin by consulting Ignace Goldziher. *A Short History of Classical Arabic Literature*. Hildesheim: G. Olms, 1966, or Julia Ashtiany et al. (eds.) *'Abbasid Belles-Lettres*. Cambridge: Cambridge University Press 1990 and other volumes in the "Cambridge History of Arabic Literature" series.

Methodology

The question of arriving at just who are the major authors always presents problems such as access to critical literature, publishing and sales figures, and changes over time in the popularity of authors. Bernth Lindfors has proposed a mathematical scheme for approximating the literary stature of African writers in English, based upon measuring the number of citations of works by and about authors out of a sample of 20,734 books and articles covering works published between 1936 and 1991.[7]

Our own selection is based upon a scrutiny of previously published bibliographies and familiarity with published critical literature. One guide ruling our choice of languages is the extent of speakers. The World Almanac (1993) lists the following figures on the number of speakers (in millions): Arabic 208 (not all in Africa); Swahili 46; Hausa 36; Yoruba 19; Amharic 18; Igbo 17; Fula 13; Malagasy 12; Afrikaans 10; Oromo 10; Malinki-Bambara-Dyula 9; Shona 8; Zulu 8; Ruanda 8; Somali 7; Xhosa 7; Efik 6, Lingala 6; Luba-Lulua 6; Rundi 6; Wolof 6; Gikuyu 5; Sotho, Southern 4; Tigrinya 4; Tswana 4; Ewe 3; Kabyle 3; Tamazight 3. Most of these languages are represented in our bibliography.

---

[7] B. Lindfors, "The Famous Authors' Reputation Test," in Lindfors, *Comparative Approaches to African Literatures* (Amsterdam; Atlanta: Rodopi, 1994), pp. 131-40.

African Language Literatures

The immense literary heritage of African languages, including Arabic, Amharic, Yoruba and other languages, and the vexatious question of whether authors should write in European or indigenous languages, makes it imperative that any bibliography seeking to cover the entire continent should include coverage of literatures in these languages. Within the space of a single bibliography of this size, it is not possible to cover comprehensively all literatures of Africa, but it has been possible to give the reader a taste of the richness of this cultural treasure. Firstly, Arabic, with a literary history centuries old in North Africa, has been singled out for treatment in a separate chapter. Secondly, a brief selection of writings in a number of the major indigenous languages has been included. A separate volume just on these language literatures is long overdue. The 15 languages that we have chosen to include are some of the most widely spoken in Africa and their literatures are some of the richest. This in no way infers that other African languages have not produced equally magnificent literary works, and a brief selection of works from some of these other languages are cited in the section entitled "Other Selected African Languages".

The multi-national nature of many African states makes an exhaustive listing of all the literatures of their languages impossible within the framework of this volume. For Ethiopia, for instance, we have only been able to list a few of the many vibrant languages, such as Amharic, Tigrinya, and Oromo. This in no way seeks to diminish the cultural impact of other languages, but reflects limited access to bibliographical sources. In some cases the need for current data is essential to grasp significant changes in literary output. Thus, in the last few years there has seen a flowering of Oromo literature, with dozens of novels, poetry, and plays produced by writers such as Dhaabaa Wayyeessaa. Keeping abreast of recent developments in so many languages is particularly difficult.

Including "major" literatures presumes "minor" literatures, although there is, perhaps, no such thing. If fewer people speak a language, this does not make it any less interesting. The overlap of language-use in some writers further complicates matters. Kateb Yacine, who headed the theatre of Bel-Abbes in Algeria, wrote in Arabic, French, and Tamazight ("Berber").

LIST OF ABBREVIATIONS
AND ACRONYMS

ACCT	Agence de Coopération Culturelle et Technique
ADELF	Association des Ecrivains de Langue Française
AEMO	Associação dos Escritores Moçambicanos
ALAC	África, Literatura, Arte e Cultura
ALT	African Literature Today
APEC	Association Nationale des Poètes et des Ecrivains Camerounais
ARCAM	Agence Régionale de Coordination des Activités Musicales et Chorégraphiques
AWAL	Editions AWAL
AWS	African Writers Series
CCFN	Centre Culturel Franco-Nigérien de Niamey
CEDA	Centre d'Edition et de Diffusion Africaines
C.E.D.S.	Centre d'Etude et de Documentation Scientifiques
CELFAN	Centre d'Etude sur la Littérature Francophone de l'Afrique du Nord (Temple University)
CIDAC	Centro de la Informação e Documentação Amilcar Cabral
CNRS	Centre National de la Recherche Scientifique
Coll.	Collection
Comp.	Compiler
COSAW	Congress of South African Writers
CUP	Cambridge University Press
dir.	Director (of publication)
EACROTANL	Eastern African Centre for Research on Oral Traditions / African National Languages
EALB	East African Literature Bureau
EAPH	East African Publishing House
ECA	Editions et Culture Africaine
Ed.	Editor, Éditions
EDDIF	Edition Diffusion du Livre au Maroc
EDICEF	Editions Classiques d'Expression Française
EDINO	Edition et Diffusion Nouvelles

ENAG	Entreprise Nationale des Arts Graphiques
ENAL	Entreprise Nationale du Livre
ENAP	Entreprise Algérienne de Presse
ENDA	Editions ENDA
ETNA	Editions Techniques Nord-Africaines
(F)	Female literary author [excludes critics]
ICALP	Instituto de Cultura e Lingua Portuguesa
ICL	Instituto Cabo Verdiano de Libro
IFAN	Institut Fondamental d'Afrique Noire
IKO	Verlag für Interkulturelle Kommunikation
ILENA	Institut de Littérature et d'Esthétique Négro-Africaines (Université d'Abidjan)
INADES	Institut Africain pour le Développement Economique et Social
INDRAP	Institut National de Documentation de Recherche et d'Animation Pédagogiques (Niger)
INLD	Instituto Nacional do Livro e do Disco
NEA	Nouvelles Editions Africaines
NECZAM	National Education Company of Zambia
n.d.	No date
OLP	Palestine Liberation Organisation (PLO)
ORTF	Office de Radiodiffusion-Télévision Française
OUP	Oxford University Press
PUF	Presses Universitaires de France
RFI	Radio France Internationale
SELAF/CILF	Société pour l'Etude des Langues Africaines / Conseil International de la Langue Française
SME	Société Malgache d'Edition
SMER	Société Marocaine des Editeurs Réunis
SNED	Société Nationale d'Edition et de Diffusion
Tr.	Translator / Translation
UEA	União de Escritores Angolanos
s.l.	*sine loco*=without place [of publication]
s.n.	*sine nomine*=without name [of publisher]
v.	Volume
ZPH	Zimbabwe Publishing House
=	Parallel title in another language

GENERAL OVERVIEW

Bibliographies

1. Berrian, Brenda F. *Bibliography of African women writers and journalists (ancient Egypt-1984)*. Washington: Three Continents Press, 1985.

2. Ganz, David L., and Donald E. Herdeck (eds.). *A Critical guide to anthologies of African literature*. Waltham: Brandeis University/African Studies Association, 1973.

3. Herdeck, Donald E. *African authors: a companion to black African writing*. Washington: Black Orpheus Press, 1973.

4. Jahn, Janheinz. *A Bibliography of neo-African literature from Africa, America and the Caribbean*. New York; London: Praeger; A. Deutsch, 1965.

5. ———. and Claus Peter Dressler. *Bibliography of creative African writing*. Millwood: Kraus-Thompson, 1971.

6. ———, Ulla Schild, and Almut Nordmann. *Who's who in African literature: biographies, works, commentaries*. Tübingen: H. Erdmann, 1972.

7. Scheven, Yvette. *Bibliographies for African studies 1970-1986*. London: H. Zell, 1988.

8. Westley, David. *Choice of language and African literature: a bibliographic essay*. Boston: African Studies Center, Boston University, 1990. (Working papers in African studies; 145).

9. Zell, Hans. *African books in print=Livres africains disponibles*. London: H. Zell, 1993. 4th ed. 2 v.

10. ———, Carol Bundy, and Virginia Coulon (eds.). *A New reader's guide to African literature*. New York; London: Africana; Heinemann, 1983. 2nd ed. First ed.: A

Reader's guide to African literature. New York: Africana, 1971.

Anthologies

11.   Achebe, Chinua, and C. L. Innes (eds.). *African short stories.* London: Heinemann, 1985.

12.   Bruner, Charlotte H. (ed.). *The Heinemann book of African women's writing.* Oxford: Heinemann, 1993. (AWS). English, French, Portuguese fiction.

13.   ———. *Unwinding threads: writing by women in Africa.* London: Heinemann, 1983. (AWS).

14.   Busby, Margaret (ed.). *Daughters of Africa: an international anthology of words and writings by women of African descent from the ancient Egyptian to the present.* London: J. Cape, 1992.

15.   Cabakulu, Mwamba. *Dictionnaire des proverbes africains.* Paris: L'Harmattan, 1993.

16.   Chinweizu (ed.). *Voices from twentieth-century Africa: griots and towncriers.* Boston: Faber, 1988.

17.   Dathorne, O. R., and Willfried Feuser (eds.). *Africa in prose.* London: Penguin, 1969. (Penguin African library; 24).

18.   Hughes, Langston (ed.). *Poems from black Africa: Ethiopia, South Rhodesia, Sierra Leone. Madagascar, Ivory Coast, Nigeria, Kenya, Gabon, Senegal, Nyasaland, Mozambique, South Africa, Congo, Ghana, Liberia.* Bloomington: Indiana University Press, 1963.

19.   Kgositsile, Keorapetse (ed.). *The Word is here: poetry from modern Africa.* New York: Anchor, 1973.

20.   Moore, Gerald, and Ulli Beier (eds.). *Penguin book of modern African poetry.* London: Penguin, 1984. 3rd ed. First ed.: *Modern poetry from Africa.* London: Penguin, 1963.

21. Mphahlele, Es'kia (ed.). *African writing today.* London: Penguin, 1967.

22. Ngara, Emmanuel, Kimani Gecau, Pauline Dodgson (eds.). *Coming home: poems of Africa.* Harare: ZPH, 1989.

23. Reed, John, and Clive Wake (eds.). *A Book of African verse.* London; Ibadan: Heinemann, 1964.

24. Strathern, Oona. *Traveller's literary companion to Africa.* Brighton: In Print, 1994.

General studies

25. Amuta, Chidi. *The Theory of African literature: implications for practical criticism.* London: Zed, 1989.

26. ————. *Towards the sociology of African literature.* Oguta, Nigeria: Zim Press, 1986.

27. Anozie, Sunday O. *Structural models and African poetics: towards a pragmatic theory of literature.* London: Routledge & Kegan Paul, 1981.

28. Anyidoho, Kofi, et al. (eds.). *Interdisciplinary dimensions of African literature.* Washington: Three Continents Press, 1985.

29. Arnold, Stephen (ed.). *African literature studies: the present state.* Washington: Three Continents Press, 1985.

30. Awoonor, Kofi Nyidevu. *The Breast of the earth: a survey of the history, culture and literature of Africa South of the Sahara.* New York: Nok, 1975.

31. Banham, Martin, and Clive Wake (eds.). *African theatre today.* London: Pitman, 1976. (Theatre today).

32. Beier, Ulli. *An Introduction to African literature: an anthology of critical writing.* London: Longman, 1979. Rev. ed. First ed.: 1967.

33. Bishop, Rand. *African literature, African critics: the form of critical standards, 1947-1966.* New York: Greenwood Press, 1988. (Contributions in Afro-American and African studies).

34. Brown, Lloyd W. *Women writers in black Africa.* Westport: Greenwood Press, 1981.

35. Burness, Don (ed.). *Wanasema: conversations with African writers.* Athens, Ohio: Center for International Studies, Ohio University, Africa Studies Program, 1985. (Monographs in international studies. Africa series; 46).

36. Cartey, Wilfred. *Whispers from a continent: the literature of contemporary black Africa.* New York; London: Vintage; Heinemann, 1969.

37. Chevrier, Jacques. *Littérature africaine: histoire et grands thèmes.* Paris: Hatier, 1990.

38. Chinweizu, Onwuchekwa Jemie, and Ihechukwu Madubuike (eds.). *Towards the decolonization of African literature.* Enugu; Washington: Fourth Dimension; Howard University Press, 1980.

39. Cook, David. *African literature: a critical view.* London: Longman, 1977.

40. Dathorne, O. R. *The Black mind: a history of African literature.* Minneapolis: University of Minnesota Press, 1974. Abridged as: *African literature in the twentieth century.* London: Heinemann,1976.

41. Davies, Carole Boyce, and Elaine Savory Fido (eds.). *Black women's writing: crossing the boundaries.* Frankfurt: Verlag Holger Ehling, 1989. (Matatu; 6, 1989).

42. Davies, Carole Boyce, and Anne Adams Graves (eds.). *Ngambika: studies of women in African literature.* Trenton, NJ: Africa World Press, 1986.

43. Draper, James P. (ed.). *Black literature criticism: excerpts from criticism of the most significant works of black authors over the past 200 years.* Detroit: Gale, 1992. 3 v.

44. Duerden, Dennis, and Cosmo Pieterse (eds.). *African writers talking: a collection of radio interviews.* London: Heinemann, 1972. (Studies in African literature).

45. Egejuru, Phanuel. *Towards African literary independence: a dialogue with contemporary African writers.* Westport: Greenwood Press, 1980. (Contributions in Afro-American and African studies; 53).

46. Gakwandi, S. A. *The Novel and contemporary experience in Africa.* London: Heinemann, 1977.

47. Gates, Henry Louis. *Black literature and literary theory.* New York: Methuen, 1984.

48. Gérard, Albert S. (ed.). *European-language writing in sub-Saharan Africa.* Budapest: Akadémiai Kiadó, 1986. 2 v. (Comparative history of literatures in European languages; v. 6).

49. Gikandi, Simon. *Reading the African novel.* London: Currey, 1987.

50. Graham-White, Anthony. *The Drama of black Africa.* New York: French, 1974.

51. Gugelberger, Georg M. (ed.). *Marxism and African literature.* Trenton, NJ; London: Africa World; Currey, 1986.

52. Gurnah, Abdulrazak (ed.). *Essays on African writing: a re-evaluation.* Oxford: Heinemann, 1993.

53. Harrow, Kenneth W. *Thresholds of change in African literature: the emergence of a tradition.* Portsmouth, NH; London: Heinemann; Currey, 1994. (Studies in African literature).

54. ———, Jonathan Ngate, and Clarisse Zimra (eds.). *Crisscrossing the boundaries in African literature.* Washington: Three Continents Press/African Literature Association, 1991. (Annual selected papers of ALA; 12/1986).

55. Heywood, Christopher (ed.) *Perspectives on African literature: selections from the proceedings of the Conference on African Literature...University of Ife, 1968.* London; New York: Heinemann; Africana, 1971. (Studies in African literature).

56. Ikonne, Chidi, Emeli Oko, and Peter Onwudinjo (eds.). *African literature and African historical experiences.* Ibadan: Heinemann, 1991. (Calabar studies in African literature).

57. Imfeld, A. *Vision und Waffe, Afrikanische Autoren, Themen, Traditionen.* Zurich: Unionsverlag, 1981.

58. Irele, Abiola. *The African experience in literature and ideology.* London: Heinemann, 1981. (Studies in African literature).

59. Jahn, Janheinz. *A History of neo-African literature.* London: Faber, 1969.

60. ————. *Muntu: an outline of the new African culture.* London: Faber, 1961. Orig. pub.: Düsseldorf: Dietrichs, 1958.

61. JanMohammed, Abdul R. *Manichean aesthetics: the politics of literature in colonial Africa.* Amherst, MA: University of Massachusetts Press, 1983.

62. Jones, Eldred, Eustace Palmer, and Marjorie Jones (eds.). *Critical theories and African literature today.* London; Trenton: Currey; Africa World Press, 1993. (ALT).

63. ————. *Women in African literature today.* London; Trenton: Currey; Africa World Press, 1987. (ALT; 15).

64. Julien, Eileen. *African novels and the question of orality.* Bloomington: Indiana University Press, 1992.

65. Kern, Anita. *Women in West African fiction.* Washington: Three Continents Press, 1980.

66. Kerr, David. *African popular theatre: from precolonial times to the present day.* London: Currey, 1994.

67. Killam, G. (ed.). *African writers on African writing.* London: Heinemann, 1973. (Studies in African literature).

68. King, Bruce, and Kolawole Ogungbesan (eds.). *A Celebration of black and African writing.* Zaria; Oxford: Ahmadu Bello University Press; OUP, 1975.

69. Klein, Leonard S. (ed.). *African literatures in the 20th century: a guide.* Harpenden: Oldcastle Books, 1988.

70. Klíma, Vladimir, Frantisek Ruzicka, and Petr Zima. *Black Africa: literature and language.* Prague; Dordrecht: Academia Pub. House; D. Reidel, 1976.

71. Kreimeier, K. *Geborstene Trommeln: Afrikas zweite Zerstörung: Literarisch-politische Expeditionen.* Frankfurt: Verlag Neue Kritik, 1985.

72. Larson, Charles R. *The Emergence of African fiction.* Bloomington; London: Indiana University Press; Macmillan, 1972. 2nd rev. ed.: London: Macmillan, 1978.

73. Lazarus, Neil. *Resistance in postcolonial African fiction.* New Haven: Yale University Press, 1990.

74. Lindfors, Bernth. *Comparative approaches to African literatures.* Amsterdam: Rodopi, 1994. (Cross cultures; 14).

75. ———, et al. *Literature and African identity.* Bayreuth: Bayreuth University, 1986. (Bayreuth African studies series; 6).

76. ———, et al. (eds.). *Palaver: interviews with five African writers in Texas.* Austin: African and Afro-American Research Institute, University of Texas, 1972.

77. ——— and Ulla Schild (eds.). *Neo-African literature and culture: essays in memory of Jahnheinz Jahn.* Wiesbaden: B. Heymann, 1976. (Mainzer Afrika Studien; 1).

78. Liyong, Taban Lo. *Thirteen offensives against our enemies*. Nairobi: EALB, 1973.

79. McEwan, Neil. *Africa and the novel*. London; Atlantic Highlands: Macmillan; Humanities, 1983.

80. Milbury-Steen, Sarah L. *European and African stereotypes in twentieth-century fiction*. London: Macmillan, 1980.

81. Moore, Gerald. *Twelve African writers*. London; Bloomington: Hutchinson; Indiana University Press, 1980. (University library for Africa).

82. Mutiso, Gideon-Cyrus. *Socio-political thought in African literature: weusi?* London: Macmillan, 1974.

83. Nazareth, Peter. *Literature and society in modern Africa: essays on literature*. Nairobi: EALB, 1972. Also pub. as: *An African view of literature*, Evanston: Northwestern University Press, 1974.

84. Nethersole, Reingard (ed.). *Emerging literatures*. Berlin: P. Lang, 1991. (Jo-Fo; 1).

85. Ngara, Emmanuel. *Art and ideology in the African novel: a study of the influence of Marxism on African writing*. London: Heinemann, 1985. (Studies in African literature).

86. ———. *Ideology and form in African poetry: implications for communication*. London: Currey; Heinemann, 1990.

87. ———. *Stylistic criticism and the African novel*. London: Heinemann, 1982.

88. Ngugi wa Thiong'o. *Barrel of a pen*. London: New Beacon, 1983.

89. ———. *Moving the centre: the struggle for cultural freedoms*. London: Currey, 1993.

90. ———. *Writing against neocolonialism*. Wembley: Vita Books, 1986.

91. Nichols, Lee (ed.). *African writers at the microphone*. Washington: Three Continents Press, 1984.

92. ———. (ed.). *Conversations with African writers: interviews with twenty-six African authors*. Washington: Voice of America, 1981.

93. Nkosi, Lewis. *Tasks and masks: themes and styles of African writing*. Harlow: Longman, 1983.

94. Nnolim, Charles. *Approaches to the African novel: essays in analysis*. Epsom: Saros International, 1992.

95. Obiechina, Emmanuel. *Language and theme: essays on African literature*. Washington: Howard University Press, 1990.

96. Olney, James. *Tell me Africa: an approach to African literature*. Princeton: Princeton University Press, 1973.

97. Owomoyela, Oyekan. *African literatures: an introduction*. Waltham, MA : Crossroads Press, 1979.

98. Palmer, Eustace Taiwo. *The Growth of the African novel*. London: Heinemann, 1979.

99. ———. *An Introduction to the African novel*. London; New York: Heinemann; Africana, 1972.

100. Parker, Caroline, and Stephen Arnold (eds.). *When the drumbeat changes*. Washington: Three Continents Press, 1981.

101. Peters, Jonathan (ed.). *Literature of Africa and the African continuum*. Washington: Three Continents Press, 1989.

102. Petersen, Kirsten Holst (ed.). *Criticism and Ideology: Second African Writers' Conference, Stockholm 1986*. Uppsala: Scandinavian Institute of African Studies, 1988.

103. ———— and Anna Rutherford (eds.). *A Double colonization: colonial and post-colonial women's writing.* Aarhus, Denmark: Dangaroo Press, 1986.

104. Pieterse, Cosmo, and Donald Munro (eds.). *Protest and conflict in African literature.* New York: Africana, 1969.

105. Riesz, J., and A. Ricard (eds.). *Semper aliquid novi: littérature comparée et littératures d'Afrique.* Tübingen: Gunter Narr, 1990.

106. Schipper, Mineke. *Beyond the boundaries: African literature and literary theory.* London: Allison & Busby, 1989.

107. ————. *Text and context: methodological explorations in the field of African literature.* Leiden: Afrika-Studiecentrum, 1976. (African perspectives; 1977/1).

108. Senkoro, Fikeni E. M. K. *The Prostitute in African literature.* Dar es Salaam: Dar es Salaam University Press, 1982.

109. Soyinka, Wole. *Art, dialogue and outrage: essays on literature and culture.* Ibadan: New Horn, 1988. 2nd, rev. ed. pub.: London: Methuen, 1990, ed. by B. Jeyifo.

110. ————. *Myth, literature and the African world.* Cambridge: CUP, 1976.

111. Stratton, Florence. *Contemporary African literature and the politics of gender.* London: Routledge, 1994.

112. Taiwo, Oladele. *Female novelists of modern Africa.* London: Macmillan, 1984.

113. Udenta, Udenta O. *Revolutionary aesthetics and the African literary process.* Enugu: Fourth Dimension Publications, 1993.

114. Vivan, Itala. *Interpreti rituali: il romanzo dell'Africa nera.* Bari, Italy: Dedalo, 1978.

115. Wästberg, Peter (ed.). *The Writer in modern Africa.* Stockholm: Almqvist and Wiksell (for Scandinavian Institute of African Studies), 1968. Also pub.: New York: Africana, 1969.

116. Wauthier, Claude. *The Literature and thought of modern Africa.* London: Heinemann, 1978. 2nd ed. Orig. pub.: *Afrique des africains: inventoire de la négritude.* Paris, 1964.

117. Wilentz, Gay Alden. *Binding cultures: black women writers in Africa and the diaspora.* Bloomington: Indiana University Press, 1992. (Blacks in the diaspora).

118. Wilkinson, Jane (ed.). *Talking with African writers: interviews with African poets, playwrights & novelists.* London: Currey, 1992. (Studies in African literature. New series.).

119. Wright, Edgar (ed.). *The Critical evaluation of African literature.* London: Heinemann, 1973.

120. Wylie, Hal, Eileen Julien, and Russell J. Linnemann (eds.). *Contemporary African literature.* Washington: Three Continents Press, 1983.

AFRICAN LANGUAGE LITERATURES

OVERVIEW

Bibliographies

121. Görög-Karady, Véronika. *Littérature orale d'Afrique noire: bibliographie annotée.* Paris: Conseil International de la langue française, 1992. Earlier edition: 1981.

122. Jahn, Janheinz. *A Bibliography of neo-African literature from Africa, America and the Caribbean.* New York; London: Praeger; A. Deutsch, 1965.

123. ———— and Claus Peter Dressler. *Bibliography of creative African writing.* Millwood: Kraus-Thompson, 1971.

124. Lordereau, Paulette. *Littératures africaines à la bibliothèque nationale, 1920-1972: catalogue.* Paris: Bibliothèque Nationale, 1992.

125. Mann, Michael, and Valerie Sanders. *A Bibliography of African language texts in the collections of the School of Oriental & African Studies, University of London, to 1963.* London: H. Zell, 1994. (Documentary research in African literatures; 3).

126. Páricsy, Pal. *A New bibliography of African literature.* Budapest: Center for Afro-Asian Research, Hungarian Academy of Science, 1969. (Studies on developing countries; 24).

127. Scheub, Harold (comp.). *African oral narratives, proverbs, riddles, poetry and song.* Boston: G. K. Hall, 1977. Rev. ed. of: *Bibliography of African oral narratives* (Madison: African Studies Program, University of Wisconsin, 1971; occasional paper; 3).

128. Scheven, Yvette. *Bibliographies for African studies 1970-1986.* London: H. Zell, 1988.

129. Westley, David. *Choice of language and African literature: a bibliographic essay.* Boston: African Studies Center, Boston University, 1990. (Working papers in African studies; 145).

Anthologies

130. Bascom, William (comp.). *African dilemma tales.* The Hague: Mouton, 1975. (World anthropology).

131. Beier, Ulli (ed.). *African poetry: an anthology of traditional African poems.* Cambridge: CUP, 1966.

132. Finnegan, Ruth (ed.). *The Penguin book of oral poetry.* London: Penguin, 1978.

133. Kesteloot, Lilyan (ed.). *L'épopée traditionelle.* Paris: Nathan, 1971. (Littérature africaine; 11). Tales.

134. Knappert, Jan. *Epic poetry in Swahili and other African languages.* Leiden: Brill, 1983. (Nisaba; v.12).

135. Leslau, Charlotte and Wolf Leslau (comps.). *African poems and love songs.* Mount Vernon: P. Pauper Press, 1970.

136. Mapanje, Jack, and Landeg White (eds.). *Oral poetry: an anthology.* Harlow: Longman, 1983.

137. Moody, H. L. B., Elizabeth Gunner, and Edward Finnegan (comps.). *A Teacher's guide to African literature: prose texts.* London: Macmillan, 1984.

138. Okpewho, Isidore (ed.). *The Heritage of African poetry: an anthology of oral and written poetry.* London: Longman, 1985.

139. Whitely, W. H. (ed.). *A Selection of African prose.* Oxford: Clarendon Press, 1964. 2 v.

General studies

140. Andrzejewski, B. W., Stanislaw Pilaszewicz, and W. Tyloch (eds.). *Literatures in African languages: theoretical*

issues and sample surveys. Cambridge; Warswawa: CUP; Wiedza Powszechna, 1985.

141. Barber, Karin, and P. F. de Moraes Farias (eds.). *Discourse and its disguises: the interpretation of African oral texts.* Birmingham: Centre for West African Studies, University of Birmingham, 1989.

142. Eno Belinga, Samuel Martin. *Comprendre la littérature orale africaine.* Issy-les-Moulineaux, France: Ed. Saint Paul, 1978. (Les classiques africains; 80).

143. Finnegan, Ruth. *Oral literature in Africa.* London: OUP, 1970.

144. Gérard, Albert S. *African language literatures: an introduction to the literary history of sub-Saharan literature.* [Washington]; Harlow: Three Continents Press; Longman, 1981.

145. ———. *Comparative literature and African literatures.* Pretoria: Via Afrika, 1983.

146. ———. *Contexts of African literature.* Amsterdam: Rodopi, 1990. (Cross/cultures; 3).

147. ———. *Littératures en langues africaines.* Milan; [Paris?]: Jaca; Mentha, 1992. (Bibliothèque d'orientation).

148. Görög, Véronika. *Noirs et blancs: leur image dans la littérature orale africaine: étude-anthologie.* Paris: SELAF/CILF, 1976. (Langues et civilisations à tradition orale; 23).

149. ——— (ed.). *Genres, forms, meanings: essays in African oral literature.* Oxford; Paris: Journal of Anthropological Society, Oxford; Maison des sciences de l'homme, 1983.

150. Gugler, Josef. *Literary theory and African literature=Théorie littéraire et littérature africaine.* Munster: Lit, 1994. (Beitrage zur Afrikaforschung; 3).

151. Jones, Eldred (ed.). *Oral and written poetry in African literature today: a review.* London; Trenton, NJ: Currey; Africa World Press, 1988. (ALT; 16).

152. ———. *Orature in African literature today: a review.* London; Trenton: Currey; Africa World, 1992. (ALT; 18).

153. ———. *The Question of language in African literature today.* London; Trenton, NJ: Currey; Africa World Press, 1991 (ALT; 17).

154. Kunene, Daniel P., and Randall A. Kirsch. *The Beginning of South African vernacular literature: a historical study.* Los Angeles: University of California, for the Literature Committee of the African Studies Association, 1967.

155. Lindfors, Bernth. *Comparative approaches to African literatures.* Amsterdam: Rodopi, 1994. (Cross/cultures; 14).

156. ——— (ed.). *Research priorities in African literatures.* Munich: H. Zell, 1984.

157. Okpewho, Isidore. *African oral literature: backgrounds, character, and continuity.* Bloomington: Indiana University Press, 1992.

158. ———. *The Oral performance in Africa.* Ibadan: Spectrum, 1990.

159. Olderogge, D. A. (ed.). *Folklor i literatura narodov Afriki.* Moscow: Nauka, 1970.

160. Páricsy, Pál (ed.). *Studies on modern black African literature.* Budapest: Center for Afro-Asian Research, Hungarian Academy Science, 1971. (Studies on developing countries; 43).

161. Parker, Caroline, and Stephen H. Arnold (eds.). *When the drumbeat changes.* Washington: Three Continents Press, 1981.

162. Paulme, Denise. *La Mère dévorante: essai sur la morphologie des contes africains.* Paris: Gallimard, 1976.

163. p'Bitek, Okot. *Africa's cultural revolution.* Nairobi: Macmillan Books for Africa, 1975. Essays.

164. Pius Ngandu Nkashama. *Littératures et écritures en langues africaines.* Paris: L'Harmattan, 1992.

165. Vail, Leroy, and Landeg White. *Power and the praise poem.* Charlottesville; London: University Press of Virginia; Currey, 1991.

AMHARIC (Ethiopia)

Bibliographies

166. Aradoum, Fassil. *Contemporary Amharic creative literature: a guide.* Washington: Library of Congress, 1982.

167. Milkias, Paulos. *Ethiopia: a comprehensive bibliography.* Boston: G. K. Hall, 1989.

Anthologies

168. Bachrach, Shlomo. *Ethiopian folk-tales.* Addis Ababa: OUP, 1972.

169. Courlander, Harold, and Wolf Leslau (comps.). *The Fire on the mountain and other Ethiopian stories.* New York: Henry Holt, 1950. Short stories.

170. Huntsberger, Paul E. *Highland mosaic: a critical anthology of Ethiopian literature in English.* Athens: Ohio University Center for International Studies, 1973. (Papers in international studies. Africa series; 19). Poetry and stories.

171. Summer, Claude. *Poésies éthiopiennes.* Addis Ababa: Artistic Printing Press, 1977. 2 v.

172. Yilma Darasa. *In Praise of independence: hymns of the new era by young Ethiopian writers, 1941-42.* Addis Ababa: Marha Tebab Press, 1942.

General studies

173. Cerulli, Enrico. *La letteratura etiopica con un saggio sull'Oriente Cristiano.* Florence; Milan: Sansoni, 1968. 3rd ed.

174. ———. *Storia della letteratura etiopica.* Milano: Nuova accademica editrice, 1956.

175. Gérard, Albert S. *Four African literatures: Xhosa, Sotho, Zulu, Amharic.* Berkeley: University of California Press, 1971.

176. Guidi, Ignazio. *Storia della letteratura Etiopica.* Roma: Istituto per l'Oriente, 1932.

177. Kane, Thomas Leiper. *Ethiopian literature in Amharic.* Wiesbaden: Harrassowitz, 1975.

178. Molvaer, Reidulf Knut. *Tradition and change in Ethiopia: social and cultural life as reflected in Amharic fictional literature ca. 1930-1974.* Leiden: Brill, 1980.

179. Ricci, Lanfranco. *Letteratura dell'Etiopia.* Milano: Societa Editrice Libraria, 1969.

Authors

180. Abe Gubañna. *And lannatu.* Addis Ababa: Berhanenna Selam Press, 1991. Novel.

181. Afä-Wärq Gäbrä-iyäsus. *Tobiya.* Addis Ababa: Nigid Matemiya Bet, 1961. Orig. pub. as: *Lebb wälläd tarik.* Rome: Casa editrice italiano, 1908. Novel.

182. Rouaud, Alain. *Afä-Wärq: un intellectuel éthiopien témoin de son temps, 1868-1947.* Paris: C.N.R.S., 1991.

183. 'Ali Zagayye. *Qwataroa and naw.* Addis Ababa: Bole Press, 1993. Poetry.

184. Asefa Gebre Mariyam Tesemma. *The Voice: selected poems.* Addis Ababa: Chamber Printing Press, 1980.

185. Ayalnah Mulatu. *Tegat lam: mato fari getmoc.*
Addis Ababa: Artistik Matamiya bét, 1985. Poetry.

186. Berhan Daña. *Sabat 'ena léloc 'acacer tarikoc.*
Addis Ababa: Kuraz, 1983. Short stories.

187. Birhanu Zerihun. *Maebel ye abiyot magist.* Addis
Ababa: Sentral Matemiya Bet, 1973. Novel.

188. Dagu Qumbi. *YaBihon alam.* Addis Ababa:
'Ityopya masaheft dereget, 1990. Science fiction novel.

189. Daniachew Worku. *Embua belu sewoch.* Addis
Ababa: Berhanina Selam, 1974. Poetry.

190. Emuru Haile-Selassie. *Fitawrai belay.* Addis
Ababa: Berhanina Selam Matemiya Bet, 1963. Novel.

191. Eshete Demise. *Hibretina andnet ye abiyot abinet.*
Addis Ababa: Berhanina Selam Matemiya Bet, 1975. Poetry.

192. Eyasu Gorfu. *Poems of thoughts and solitude.*
Addis Ababa: Artistic Printers, 1972.

193. Fikre Tolossa. *The Coffin-dealer and the
gravedigger / A foot of land?: two plays.* Bremen: Ubersee-
Museum, 1982.

194. Heruy Wäldä-Sellasie. *Addis Aläm.* Addis Ababa:
Goha Säbah, 1932. Novel.

195. ———. *Yällebb assab: yäberhanenna yäseyon
mogäsa gabessa.* Addis Ababa: Goha Säbah, 1931.
"Thoughts of the heart: the marriage of Brehane and Tyeson
Mogasa." Novel.

196. Kuraz Asatami Dirijit. *Aba defar ena leloch
achachir tarikoch.* Addis Ababa: Nigd Matemiya Bet, 1985.
Short stories.

197. Mäkkonen Endalkachew. *Three plays: King David
the Third; The Voice of blood; The City of the poor.* Asmara:
Off. Grafica dell' Corriere Eritreo, 1955. Drama.

198. Maqedas Gambaru. *Nebasel.* [Addis Ababa: s.n.], 1991. Poetry.

199. Mengistu Lemma. *The Marriage of unequals: a comedy.* London: Macmillan, 1970. Tr. of: *Yalacca gabca*

200. ———. *Ye Tewnet gubae: serekoloniyalist balekabana baledaba teyaq.* Addis Ababa: Termaed Matemiya Bet, 1982. Three plays.

201. Mulugéta Gasasa. *'Asmal.* Addis Ababa: Kuraz, 1984. Novel.

202. Paulos Gnogno. *Amistegnaw asdenaqi tarikoch.* Addis Ababa: Nigd, 1983. Stories.

203. Qasala Warqu. *Lamen atemotem?* Addis Ababa: 'Itypya masaheft dereget, 1991. Novel.

204. Sahle Selassie. *Wetat yifredewu.* Addis Ababa: Sentral Matemiya Bet, 1966. Novel.

205. Sisay Negusu. *Tensaé.* [Addis Ababa]: 'Artistik Matamiya Bet, 1983. Novel.

206. Tilahun Tasew. *Adabay.* Addis Ababa: 'Artistik Mayemiya Bet, 1982. Novel.

207. Waneyé 'Ali. *Wafé qomac: sena getem.* Addis Ababa: Kuraz, 1984. Poetry.

208. Yusuf Hasan. *'Intalo 'ena leloc acacer leboladoc.* Addis Ababa: Kuraz, 1983. Short stories.

GIKUYU (Kenya)

Bibliography

209. Sicherman, Carol. *Ngugi wa Thiong'o: a bibliography of primary and secondary sources, 1957-1989.* London: H. Zell, 1989.

Anthologies

210. Barra, G. *1,000 Kikuyu proverbs: with translations and English equivalents.* Nairobi: EALB, 1981. 3rd. ed. First pub. 1960.

211. Gecau, R. N. *Kikuyu folk-tales.* Nairobi: Kenya Literature Bureau, 1970. 2nd ed.

General studies

212. Bjorkman, Ingrid. *Mother, sing for me: people's theatre in Kenya.* London: Zed, 1989.

213. Mukabi, W., and K. Muturi. *Gikuyu oral literature.* Nairobi: Heinemann Kenya, 1988.

214. Ngugi wa Thiong'o. *Decolonising the mind.* London: Longman, 1986.

215. Pugliese, Cristiana. *The First company of African writers in Kenya: the African Book Writers Ltd, Karatina 1946-7.* Nairobi: Institut français de recherche en Afrique, 1994.

Authors

216. Gakaara wa Wanjau. *Mau Mau author in detention.* Nairobi: Heinemann Kenya, 1988. Tr. from Gikuyu. Memoirs.

217. Ngugi wa Thiong'o. *Matigari.* London: Heinemann, 1989. (AWS). Tr. by Wangui wa Goro. First pub. in Gikuyu: Nairobi: Heinemann Kenya, 1987. Novel.

218. ———, and Ngugi wa Mirii. *I will marry when I want.* London: Heinemann, 1982. (AWS; 246). First pub. in Gikuyu as: *Ngaahika ndeenda.* Drama.

219. Ruthuku, J. M. *Ni ki kirehage utonga?* London: Macmillan, 1955. Fiction.

HAUSA

(Nigeria, Niger; also Benin, Cameroon, Chad, Ghana, Sudan)

Bibliographies

220. Baldi, Sergio. *Systematic Hausa bibliography*. Roma: Pioda, 1977. (Collana di studi africani; 3).

221. Yahaya, I. Y. *Takaitaccen tarihin rubuce-rubece cikin Hausa*. Kano: CSNL, 1980.

Anthologies

222. Abdulkadir, Dandatti (ed.). *Zababbun wakokin da da na Yanzu*. Lagos: Nelson, 1979. Anthology of poetry.

223. *Antologia wspoczesnej literatury hausa= Zababbun rubuce-rub ucen Hausa na zamani*. Warsaw: Wydawnictwa Universytetu Warszawskiego, 1989.

224. Edgar, Frank. *Hausa tales and traditions: an English translation of Tatsuniyoyi na Hausa*. London: Cass, 1977. 3 v. V. 2-3 pub. by University of Wisconsin Press. Tr. and ed. by Neil Skinner. First pub.: Belfast, 1911-13.

225. Glew, Robert S., and Chaibon Babalé (eds.). *Hausa folk tales from Niger*. Athens: Ohio University Center for International Studies, 1993.

226. Johnston, H. A. S. (ed.). *A Selection of Hausa stories*. London: OUP, 1966 (Oxford library of African literature).

227. Kraft, Charles H. *A Hausa reader: cultural materials with helps for use in teaching intermediate and advanced Hausa*. Berkeley: University of California Press, 1974.

228. Pucheu, Jacques (rec., trad.). *Contes haoussa du Niger*. Paris: Karthala, 1982. (Lettres noires).

229. Robinson, C. H. *Hausa poems*. Cambridge: CUP, 1948.

230. Sa'id, B. (ed.). *Dausayin soyayya*. Lagos: Federal Ministry of Culture, 1982. Poetry.

231. Skinner, Neil. *Anthology of Hausa literature in translation*. Madison: African Studies Program, University of Wisconsin, 1977. (Occasional paper; 7).

232. Wali, Naibi Sulaimanu, et al. *Wakokin Hausa*. Zaria: Northern Nigerian Pub. Co., 1972. Poetry.

General studies

233. Aminu, Mamudu. *Sharhin wakokin Hausa na karni goma sha tara da karni ashirin*. Kano: Aminu Zinariya Recording & Pub. Co., 1977.

234. Beik, Janet. *Hausa theatre in Niger: a contemporary oral art*. New York: Garland, 1987. (Critical studies on black life and culture; 16).

235. Damgambo, A. *Rabe-Raben adabin Hausa da muhimmancinsa ga rayuwar Hausawa*. Nigeria: Triumph, 1984.

236. Furniss, Graham. *De la fantasie à la réalité dans la littérature haoussa en prose; suivre de, Pourquoi étuder la poésie haussa?* Bordeaux: Université de Bordeaux, Centre d'étude d'Afrique noire, 1991. (Travaux et documents; 310).

237. Hiskett, Mervyn. *A History of Hausa Islamic verse*. London: School of Oriental and African Studies, 1975.

238. Lindfors, Bernth (ed.). *Critical perspectives on Nigerian literatures*. Washington: Three Continents Press, 1976. Covers English, Hausa, Yoruba, and Igbo works. Articles originally pub. in: *Research in African Literatures*.

239. Pilaszewicz, Stanislaw. *Historia literatur afrykanskich w jezykach: literatur Hausa*. Warsaw: Wydawnictwa Uniwersytetu Warszawskiego, 1988.

Authors

240. Abubakar, Iman. *Tarihin annabi Muhammadu.*
Zaria: Gaskiya Corp., 1960. Short stories.

241. Aliyu, Akilu. *Fasaha akiliya.* Zaria: Northern
Nigerian Pub. Co., 1977. Poetry.

242. Alkanci, H. A. *Soyayya ta fi Kudi.* Lagos: Federal
Ministry of Culture, 1982. Drama.

243. Balewa, Abubakir Tafawa. *Shaihu Umar: a novel.*
New York: M. Wiener, 1989. Tr. from Hausa by M. Hiskett.
First pub.: London: Longman, 1968.

244. Bello Kagara, Muhammadu. *Gandoki.* Zaria:
Gaskiya Corp., 1952. First pub. in 1934. Fiction.

245. Kwantagora, Salihu. *Kimiyya da Fasaha.* Zaria:
Northern Nigerian Pub. Co., 1972. Poetry.

246. Spikin, Mudi. *Tsofaffin wakoki da Sababbin
wakoki.* Zaria: Northern Nigerian Pub. Co., 1971. Poetry.

247. Umaru, H. *Nuni cikin nisha'di.* Zaria: Northern
Nigerian Pub. Co., 1976. Short stories.

248. Yahaya, I. Y. *Wakokin hikima.* Nigeria: OUP
Nigeria, 1975. Poetry.

249. Zungur, Sa'adu. *Wakokin Sa'adu Zungu.* Zaria:
Northern Nigerian Pub. Co., 1957. Poetry.

250. Abdulkadir, Dandatti. *The Poetry, life and
opinions of Sa'adu Zungur.* Zaria: Northern Nigerian Pub.
Co., 1974. Includes poems in Hausa and English.

IGBO (Nigeria)

Bibliographies

251. Aguolu, Christian C. (comp.). *Nigeria: a
comprehensive bibliography in the humanities and social
sciences, 1900-1971.* Boston: G. K. Hall, 1973.

252. Anafulu, Joseph C. (comp.). *The Ibo-speaking peoples of Southern Nigeria: a selected annotated list of writings 1627-1970.* Munich: Kraus, 1981.

Anthologies

253. Egudu, Romanus N. *The Calabash of wisdom and other Igbo stories.* New York: Nok, 1973.

254. ———. *Igbo traditional verse.* London: Heinemann, 1973. (AWS; 129).

255. Ekechukwu, R. M. *Akpa uche.* Ibadan: OUP, 1975. Poetry anthology.

256. Eligwe, Obioma I. *Beside the fire: two modern Igbo tales.* Washington: Three Continents Press, 1974.

257. Green M. M., and M. O. Onwuamaegbu (eds.). *Akuko ife nke ndi Igbo.* Ibadan: OUP, 1970. Short stories.

258. Ogbalu, F. C. *Omenala Igbo: the book of Igbo custom.* Onitsha: University Pub. Co., 1974. Short stories.

259. ———. (ed.). *Dimkpa taa aku: a hu ichere ya.* Onitsha: University Pub. Co., 1972. Short stories.

260. ———. *Uyoko mbem Igbo: an anthology of Igbo poems.* Onitsha: University Pub. Co., 1984. Poetry.

261. Okele, Uche. *Tales of land of death: Igbo folk tales.* Garden City, NY: Doubleday, 1971.

262. Ugochukwu, Françoise (trad.). *Contes Igbo du Nigeria: de la brousse à la rivière.* Paris: Karthala, 1992.

263. Umeasiegbu, Rems Nna. *Words are sweet: Igbo stories and storytelling.* Leiden: Brill, 1982.

General studies

264. Egudu, Romanus N. *African poetry of the living dead: Igbo masquerade poetry.* Lewiston: Edwin Mellen, 1992.

265. Emenyonu, Ernest. *The Rise of the Igbo novel.* Ibadan: OUP, 1978.

266. Lindfors, Bernth (ed.). *Critical perspectives on Nigerian literatures.* Washington: Three Continents Press, 1976. Covers English, Hausa, Yoruba, and Igbo works.

Authors

267. Gbujie, Chike Osita. *Oguamalam.* Lagos: Macmillan Nigeria, 1979. Drama.

268. Madubuike, Ihechukwu. *Ighota abu Igbo.* Ibadan: University Press, 1981. Poetry.

269. Nwana, Pita. *Omenuko.* Ikeja: Longman, 1933. Novel.

270. Nzeako, J. U. T. *Juochi.* Lagos: Macmillan Nigeria, 1981. Novel.

271. ————. *Okukoagbasaaokpsei.* London: Nelson, 1964. Novel.

272. Onyekaonwu, Goddy O. *Nwate rie awo (O ju anu).* Onitsha: University Pub. Co., 1980. Drama.

273. Osuagwu, Bertram I. N. *Egwuregwu Igbo abuo: akuuwa na Uka a Kpara akpa.* Lagos: Macmillan Nigeria, 1978. Drama.

274. Ubesie, Tony. *Juo obinna.* Ibadan: OUP, 1977. Novel.

275. ————. *Ukpana okpoko buru.* Ibadan: OUP, 1975. Novel.

276. ————. *Ukwa ruo oge ya. O daa.* Ibadan: OUP, 1973. Novel.

277. Ugochukwu, Sam. *Mbem akwamozu.* Onitsha: University Pub. Co., 1985. Poetry.

MALAGASY (Madagascar)

Bibliographies

278. Bradt, Hilary, with Mervyn Brown. *Madagascar.* Oxford; Santa Barbara: Clio Press, 1993 (pp. 83-86).

279. Haring, Lee. *Malagasy tale index.* Helsinki: Suomalainen Tiedeakakatemia Academia Scientarium Fennica, 1982.

280. "Madagascar: 1. La littérature d'expression malgache." *Notre librairie* (Paris: CLEF) no. 109 (1992).

Anthologies

281. Domenichini-Ramiaramanana, Bakola. *Hainteny d'autrefois, poèmes traditionnels malgaches recueillis au début du règne de Ranavalona I (1828-1861)= Haintenin'ny fahiny, voaangona tamin'ny voalohandohan'ny nanjakan-Ranavalona I.* Tananarive: Librairie Mixte, 1968. Poetry.

282. *Fomban-drazana Tsimihety.* Fianarantosa: Editions Ambozontany, 1985. Proverbs and stories.

283. Fox, Leonard (tr. and ed.). *Hainteny: the traditional poetry of Madagascar.* Lewisburg; London: Bucknell University Press; Associated University Presses, 1990. Anthology.

284. Gueunier, N. J. (comp. et trad.). *Contes de la côte ouest de Madagascar.* Antananarivo; Paris: Editions Ambozontany; Karthala, 1990.

285. Haring, Lee (ed.). *Ibonia: epic of Madagascar.* Lewisburg: Bucknell University Press, 1994.

286. Houlder, J. A. *Ohabolana or Malagasy proverbs.* London: Foreign Missionary Association, 1916. New ed.: Antananarivo: Imprimerie Luthérienne, 1960.

287. Longchamps, Jeanne de. *Contes malgaches.* Paris: Ed. Erasme, 1955.

288. Navone, Gabriele. *Ny atao no miverina ou Ethnologie et proverbes malgaches*. Fianarantosa: Editions Ambozontany 1987. Proverbs.

289. Ntaolo, Angonon'ny. *Ny haintenin' ny Ntaolo*. Fianarantosa: Editions Ambozontany, 1990. Poetry.

290. Paes, C., et al. *L'Origine des choses, récits de la côte ouest de Madagascar*. Antananarivo: Foi et Justice, 1991.

291. Paulhan, Jean. *Les Hain-teny merinas: poésies populaires malgaches*. Paris: Gallimard, 1960. First pub.: Paris: Librairie Paul Geuthner, 1913.

292. Rabearivelo, Jean-Joseph (ed.). *Vieilles chansons des pays d'Imerina*. Tananarive: Ed. Madprint, 1980. Poetry.

293. Rajaobelina, P., and Johan Gabriel. *Lahatsoratra voafantina*. Tananarive: Rajaobelina Frères, 1949. Prose/poetry.

294. Rakonoiref, François (ed.). *Le Mythe d'Ibonia*. Antananarivo: Foi et justice, 1993. Malagasy and French. Tales.

295. Rakotonaivo, François (ed.). *Hainteny ankehitriny*. Fianarantosa: Editions Ambozontany, 1989. Poetry.

296. Schrive, P. M. *Contes Antakarana*. Antananarivo: Foi et Justice, 1990. In Antakarana dialect and French.

General studies

297. Andrianarahinjaka, Lucien Michel. *Le Système littéraire betsileo*. Fianarantosa: Editions Ambozontany, 1986.

298. Domenichini-Ramiaramanana, Bakoly. *Du Ohabolana au hainteny: langue, littérature et politique à Madagascar*. Paris: Karthala, 1983.

299. Haring, Lee. *Verbal arts in Madagascar: performance in historical perspective*. Philadelphia: University of Pennsylvania Press, 1992.

300. "Madagascar: 1. La littérature d'expression malgache." *Notre librairie* (Paris: CLEF) no. 109 (1992).

301. Paulhan, Jean. *L'Expérience du proverbe.* Paris: L'Echoppe, 1993. About Malagasy proverbs.

302. Randriamorasata. *Andrianampoinimerina, loharanon' ny literatiora.* Antananarivo: Ny Fikambanan' ny Mpanao Gazety sy ny Mpanoratra Malagasy, 1967. Literary criticism.

303. Razafindramiandra, Moks. *Reichtum und Probleme der madagassischen Literatur: Einfuhrung in die literarischen Gattungen Madagaskars.* Bonn: Jackwerth & Welker, 1983.

Authors

304. Andriamalala, E. D. *Hetraketraka.* Antananarivo: L'Association des professeurs de malgache des écoles publiques, 1965. Novel.

305. ———. *Ilay vohitry ny nofy.* Antananarivo: Office du Livre Malagasy, 1982. Novel.

306. ———. *Maty ve Ratsimandrava.* Tananarive: Office du livre Malagasy, Bibliothèque nationale, 1975. (Aimpirenena; 2). Fiction.

307. ———. *Rabesetra.* Antananarivo: Fiantsorohana ny Boky Malagasy, 1977. (Ny Nosy vaovao; 11). Fiction.

308. Andriamanalina-Rombalahivola. *Rainandriamampandry: an-tononkalo miady rima, misy fizar'ana telo ary fanazavana teny sy tantara.* Antananarivo: Sosaiety Madprint, 1975. Poetry.

309. Andrianjafy, Michel. *Orimbaton'ny fiadanana.* Antananarivo: Ed. Takariva, 1975. Orig. pub.: 1959. Novel.

310. Dahle, Lars, and John Sims. *Anganon'ny ntaolo: tantara mampiseho ny fomban-drazana sy ny finoana sasany nananany.* Antananarivo: Tranto Printy Loterana, 1984. 9th ed. Poetry.

311. Dox [pseud.]. *Hira va.* Tananarive: Edisiona, 1967. (Mpanoratra malagasy). Poetry.

312. ———. *Ny hirako.* Antananarivo: Fofipa, 1977. (Mpanoratra malagasy). Previously pub.: 1968. Poetry.

313. ———. *Rainandriamampandry.* Antananarivo: Ministeran'ny Fanolokoloana sy ny Zavakanto Revolisionera, 1978. Drama.

314. Faralahy. *Mpikarama an 'ady.* Antananarivo: Ed. Takariva, 1980.

315. Nary, R. H. A. *Ny tsarako.* Antananarivo: Rakotoarisoa, 1993. Poetry.

316. Rabearivelo, Jean-Joseph. *Lova.* Tananarivo: Imp. Volamahitsy, 1957. Poetry. See also French section.

317. ———. *Poèmes: Presque-songes.* Tananarive: Les Amis de Rabearivelo, 1960. Trad. par l'autre du malgache (Hova dialecte); texte de: *Saiky-nofy,* et, *Nadika Tamin ny Alina.*

318. ———. *Translations from the night: selected poems.* London: Heinemann, 1975. (AWS). English and French texts. First pub. as: *Traduit de la nuit.* 1935, tr. from Hova dialect.

319. Boudry, Robert. *Jean-Joseph Rabearivelo et la mort.* Paris: Présence africaine, 1958.

320. Valette, P. *J. J. Rabearivelo.* Paris: Nathan, 1967.

321. Rajemisa-Raolison, Régis. *Kilalaon' afo.* Tananarive: Volamahitsy, 1948. Novel.

322. ———. *Mpitantana.* Tananarivo: Librairie Mixte, 1967. Novel.

323. Ramakavelo, Désiré. *Mba saino ange.* Antananarivo: Edisiona Lova, 1993. Poetry.

324. Ramanantoanina, Ny Avana. *Anthologie*. Antananarivo: Ministère de la Culture, 1992. Poetry.

325. ———. *Ny Avana, tononkalo sy lahasoratra.* Antananarivo: Centre d'études et de recherches artistiques de l'Association théatrâle et artistique des Universitaires de Madagascar, 1981. Ed. Andriakotonirina Samoela. Poetry and essays.

326. Randriamiadanarivo. *Ny sikajin i dadabe.* Tananarive: Fiantsorohana ny Boky Malagasy, 1974. (Ny Nosy vavao; 7). Novel.

327. ———. *Vorom-by.* Antananarivo: Imprimerie d'ouvrages educatifs, 1977. (Édisiona saloky). Fiction.

328. Rapatsalahy, P. *Ilay vorona mena.* Antananarivo: Ed. Takariva, 1979.

329. Rasoloarimalala Randriamammonjy, Esther (F). *Ho avy ny maraina.* Antananarivo: Librairie Mixte, 1983. Novel.

330. Raveloharison, B. *Lasitra.* Antananarivo: Office du Livre Malagasy, 1982. (Ny Nosy vaovao; 13).

331. Razakarivony, Arthur. *Sangy mahery.* Antananarivo: Fofipa, 1988. Drama.

332. Soa, I. *Manja.* Antananarivo: Ed. Takariva, 1975.

333. Zanamihoatra, Randja. *Vainafo tononkira.* Fianarantosa: Ambozontany, 1969. Poetry.

NDEBELE (South Africa, Zimbabwe)

Anthologies

334. Mhlanga, C. *Ngakade ngisazi.* Harare: College Press, 1990. Short stories.

335. Mpofu, Pamba (ed.). *Ugqozi lwenzimbongi.* Gweru: Mambo Press, 1973, repr. 1991. Poetry.

336. Mthwakazi, Giya (comp.). *Iqoqo lezinkondlo*. Harare: Longman Zimbabwe, 1990. Poetry.

337. Ndoda, D. N. (ed.). *Isidlodlo sikaMthwakazi*. Gweru: Mambo Press/Literature Bureau, 1984. Poetry.

General studies

338. Krog, E. W. (ed.). *African literature in Rhodesia*. Gwelo: Mambo Press, 1966.

Authors

339. Hleza, Ezekiel S. K. *Uyangisinda lumhlaba*. Gweru: Mambo Press/Literature Bureau, 1991. Novel.

340. Makhalisa, Barbara C. (F). *Impilo Yinkinga*. Salisbury [Harare]: Longman, 1964. Fiction.

341. ———. *Umendo*. Gwelo: Mambo Press/Rhodesia Literature Bureau, 1977. Fiction.

342. ———. *The Underdog and other stories*. Gweru: Mambo Press, 1984. Short stories.

343. Mhlanga, C. *Nansi LeNdoda*. Harare: Longman, 1990. Novel.

344. Moyo, M. D., et. al. *Intandane kaBaba*. Gweru: Mambo Press, 1983. Short stories.

345. Ncube, B. S. *Ukuhlaziya lokucu-bungula izinkonlo*. Gweru: Mambo Press, 1994.

346. Ndlovu, Israel. *Sivela kude*. Gweru: Mambo Press, 1993. (Mambo writers series, Ndebele section; 8). Novel.

347. Ndlovu, Temba Petros. *Izithelo zvokuganga: umdlalo*. Gweru: Mambo Press, 1992. (Mambo writers series, Ndebele section; 8). Drama.

348. ———. *Umkhunjulwa ulkefolwakhe*. Gweru: Mambo Press, 1983. Drama.

349. Ntuli, M. S. *Itsengo 2*. Pretoria: De Jager Haum, 1992. Ndebele poetry.

350. Sigogo, N. S. *Asazi-ke*. Harare: College Press, 1990. Novel.

351. ———. *Yeyeni madoda! Benzani Lababantu*. Harare: College Press, 1982. Novel.

SESOTHO

(Lesotho, South Africa)

Bibliographies

352. Ferragne, M. (comp.). *A Catalogue of 1,000 Sesotho books*. Roma, Lesotho: The Social Centre, 1974.

353. Grobler, G. M. M., and E. Briers. *African literature: pilot bibliography of research in Southern Africa*. Pretoria: University of South Africa, 1993. (Studia composita; 17).

354. Willett, Shelagh M., and David P. Ambrose. *Lesotho*. Oxford; Clio, 1980 (World bibliographical series; 3).

Anthologies

355. Damane, Mosebi. *Marath'a lilepe a puo ea Sesotho, buka ea pele*. Morija: Sesuto Book Depot, 1960.

356. ——— and P. B. Saunders (eds.). *Lithoko: Sotho praise poems*. Oxford: OUP, 1974.

357. Postma, Minnie. *Tales from the Basotho*. Austin: University of Texas Press, 1974. (American Folklore Society Memoir; 59).

General studies

358. Chaphole, Sol. *Dihaeya*. Rondebosch, South Africa: Centre for African Studies, University of Cape Town, 1986. (Communications; 11).

359. Gérard, Albert S. *Four African literatures: Xhosa, Sotho, Zulu, Amharic.* Berkeley: University of California Press, 1971.

360. Guma, Samson Mbizo. *The Form, content and technique of traditional literature in Southern Sotho.* Pretoria; Cape Town: Van Schaik; Balkema, 1967.

361. Kunene, Daniel P. *The Heroic poetry of the Basotho.* London: OUP, 1971. (Oxford library of African literature).

362. Makgamatha, Phaka Moffat. *Characteristics of the Northern Sotho folktales: their form and structure.* Johannesburg: Perskor, 1991.

363. Mda, Zakes. *When people play people: development communication through theatre.* London; Johannesburg: Zed; Witwatersrand University Press, 1993.

Authors

364. Elias, Andreas T. *Phephetso.* Mazenod: Book Centre, 1975. Poetry.

365. Guma, Samson Mbizo. *Likoma.* Pietermaritzburg: Shuter and Shooter, 1966. Poetry.

366. ———. *Tshehlana tseo tsa Basia.* Pietermaritzburg: Shuter and Shooter, 1962. Novel.

367. Khaketla, Bennet Makalo *Meokho ea thabo.* Morija: Morija Sesuto Book Depot, 1984. Novel.

368. Khaketla, Caroline Ntseliseng 'Masechele (F). *'Mantsopa.* Cape Town: OUP, 1963. Poetry.

369. ———. *Mosali eo u 'neileng eena.* Morija: Morija Sesuto Book Depot, 1954. "The Woman you gave me." Drama.

370. Maake, N. P. *Sejamonna ha se mo qete.* Cape Town: Maskew Miller Longman, 1993. Fiction.

371. Mahalefele, Mabasiea Jeannette (F). *Bana ba khomo tsa batho.* Maseru: Macmillan Lesotho, 1990. Drama.

372. Maile, Mallane Libakeng. *Moiketsi.* Cape Town: Via Afrika, 1958. Repr.: Mazenod: Book Centre, 1978. Novel.

373. Mangoaela, Zakea D. *Lithoko tsa Marena a Basotho.* Morija: Sesuto Book Depot, 1921. Praise poems.

374. Mocoancoeng, Jac G. *Tseleng ya Bophelo: le dithothokiso tse Ntjha.* Johannesburg: Witwatersrand University Press, 1979. (Bantu treasury; 10). First pub. in old orthography, 1947. Poetry and drama.

375. Mofokeng, S. M. *Pelong ya ka.* Johannesburg: Witwatersrand University Press, 1975. (Bantu treasury; 15).

376. ———. *Senkatana.* Johannesburg: Witwatersrand University Press, 1952. (Bantu treasury series; 12). Drama.

377. Mofolo, Thomas. *Chaka.* London: Heinemann, 1981. Tr. by D. Kunene. (AWS; 229). First pub. in English: London: International Institute of African Languages & Cultures, 1931. Novel.

378. ———. *Moeti oa bochabela.* Morija: Sesuto Book Depot, 1907. Pub. in English as: *Traveller to the East.* London: Society for Promoting Christian Knowledge, 1934. Novel.

379. ———. *Pitseng.* Morija: Morija Sesuto Book Depot, 1910. Novel.

380. Kunene, Daniel P. *Thomas Mofolo and the emergence of written Sesotho prose.* Johannesburg: Ravan Press, 1989.

381. ———. *The Works of Thomas Mofolo: summaries and critiques.* Los Angeles: African Studies Center, University of California, 1967 (Occasional paper; 2).

382. Mopeli-Paulus, Attwell Sidwell. *Ho tsamaea ke ho bona: lithothokiso.* Morija: Sesuto Book Depot, 1945. Poetry.

383. ———. *Lilahloane oa Batho.* Bloemfontein: Via Afrika, 1950. Novel.

384. Segoete, Everitt Lechesa. *Monono ke moholi mouoane.* Morija: Morija Sesuto Book Depot, 1910. Novel.

385. Sentso, Dyke. *Matlakala.* Morija: Morija Sesuto Book Depot, 1948. Poetry.

386. Senyatsi, Charles P. *Thariyatshepe.* Bloemfontein: Via Afrika, 1962. Northern Sotho/Pedi novel.

SHONA (Zimbabwe)

Bibliography

387. Grobler, G. M. M., and E. Briers. *African literature: pilot bibliography of research in Southern Africa.* Pretoria: University of South Africa, 1993. (Studia composita; 17).

Anthology

388. Hodza, A. C. (comp.), and G. Fortune (ed.). *Shona praise poetry.* Oxford: Clarendon, 1979. (Oxford library of African literature).

General studies

389. Kahari, G. P. *Aspects of the Shona novel.* Gweru: Mambo Press, 1992. 2nd ed. First ed. 1986.

390. ———. *Plots and characters in Shona fiction, 1956-1984: a handbook.* Gweru: Mambo Press, 1990.

391. ———. *The Rise of the Shona novel: a study in development, 1890-1984.* Gweru: Mambo Press, 1990.

392. Kriel, Abraham. *An African horizon: ideals in Shona lore and literature.* Cape Town: School of African Studies, University of Cape Town, 1971. (Communication; 35).

393. Krog, E. W. (ed.). *African literature in Rhodesia.* Gwelo: Mambo Press, 1966.

394. Pongweni, Alec J. C. *Figurative language in Shona discourse: a study of the analogical imagination.* Gweru: Mambo Press, 1989

395. Veit-Wild, Flora. *Survey of Zimbabwean writers: education and literary careers.* Bayreuth: Breitlinger, 1992.

396. Zinyemba, Ranga M. *Zimbabwean drama: a study of Shona and English plays.* Gweru: Mambo Press, 1984. (Mambo writers series; 25).

Authors

397. Banana, Canaan S. *Chido chomwoyo wangu.* Gweru: Mambo Press, 1982. Novel.

398. Bvindi, Francis L. *Kumuzinda hakuna woko.* Salisbury [Harare]: Longman Zimbabwe, 1981. Novel.

399. Chakaipa, Patrick. *Garandichauya.* Salisbury [Harare]: Longman, 1963. Novel.

400. ———. *Karikoga gumiremiseve.* Salisbury: Longman, 1958. Novel.

401. ———. *Pfumo reRopa.* Salisbury: Longman, 1961. Novel.

402. Kahari, G. P. *The Novels of Patrick Chakaipa.* Salisbury [Harare]: Longman, 1972.

403. Chidyausiku, Paul. *Karumekangu.* Salisbury [Harare]: Longman, 1970. Novel.

404. ———. *Nyadzi dzinokunda rufu.* Salisbury [Harare]: OUP, 1962. Novel.

405. ———. *Pfungwa dzaSekuru Mafusire.* Gwelo: Mambo Press, 1960. Novel.

406. Kahari, G. P. *The Imaginative writings of Paul Chidyausiku.* Gwelo: Mambo Press, 1975.

407. Chidzero, Bernard. *Nzvengamutsvairo.* Salisbury [Harare]: Longman, 1957. Novel.

408. Chigidi, Willie L. *Mufaro mwena.* Harare: College Press, 1986. Drama.

409. Chiguvare, David E. *Kutonhodzwa kwaChauruka.* Salisbury [Harare]: College Press, 1976. Novel.

410. Chimhundu, Herbert. *Chakwesha.* Harare: College Press, 1990. (Modern writers series). Novel.

411. Chingono, Julius. *Chipo Changu.* Salisbury [Harare]: Longman, 1979. Novel.

412. Dzoro, Simbarashe T. *Wandigura kunorira.* Salisbury [Harare]: Longman Zimbabwe, 1980. Novel.

413. Hamandishe, Nicholas P. *Sara Ugarike.* Salisbury [Harare]: Longman, 1975. Novel.

414. Hamutyinei, Mordikai A. *Chiparurangoma chaMudyanadzo=A drumming prelude to ancient wisdom.* Gweru: Mambo Press, 1992 (Shona heritage; 6). Epic poem.

415. Hodzongi, Francis D. *Mhosva inoripwa.* Salisbury [Harare]: Longman Zimbabwe, 1981. Novel.

416. Hove, Chenjerai. *Masimba avanhu.* Gweru: Mambo Press, 1986. Novel.

417. Hwendaenda, D. *Mubairo.* Harare: College Press, 1993. Novel.

418. Jaravaza, M. *Shungu hadziurayi.* Harare: Longman Zimbabwe, 1991. Novel.

419. Kaugare, Edward W. *Kukurukura hunge wapotswa.* Salisbury [Harare]: Longman, 1978. Novel.

420. Kawara, James. *Ruchiva*. Salisbury [Harare]: Longman Zimbabwe, 1980. Novel.

421. Khumalo, L. B. *Kambe*. Gweru: Mambo Press, 1992. Novel.

422. Kuimba, Giles. *Gehena harina moto*. Salisbury [Harare]: Longman, 1965. Novel.

423. ———. *Tambaoga mwanangu*. Salisbury [Harare]: Longman, 1963. Novel.

424. Lwanda, Alexious. *Zvichakuwanawo*. Gwelo: Mambo Press, 1981. Novel.

425. Magwa, Wiseman. *Mafaro*. Gweru: Mambo Press, 1990. Drama.

426. ———. *Njuzu: mutambo*. Gweru: Mambo Press, 1991. Drama.

427. Marangwanda, John W. *Kumazivandadzoka*. Salisbury [Harare]: Longman, 1959, repr. 1970. Novel.

428. Mavengere, Eric P. *Akanyangira yaona*. Salisbury [Harare]: Longman, 1979. Novel.

429. Moyo, Aaron C. *Ziva Kwawakabva*. Salisbury [Harare]: Longman, 1977. Novel.

430. Mugugu, Francis C. *Jekanyika*. Salisbury [Harare]: College Press, 1968. Novel.

431. Mungoshi, Charles. *Makunun'unu maodzamwoyo*. Salisbury [Harare]: College Press, 1970. Novel.

432. ———. *Ndiko kupindana kwamazuva*. Gwelo [Gweru]: Mambo Press, 1975. Novel.

433. Munjanja, Amos M. *Rina manyanga hariputirwi*. Gwelo: Mambo Press, 1971. Novel.

434. Musingafi, Maxwell C. C. *Rwizi pakati ko!* Gweru: Mambo Press, 1992. (Mambo writers. Shona section; 32). Novel.

435. Musundire, Edmond. *Mutikitivha dumbuzenene.* Gweru: Mambo Press, 1991. Novel.

436. ———. *Nyanga yenzou.* Gweru: Mambo Press, 1992. Novel.

437. Mutize, Kenneth. *Mary Ponderai.* Gwelo: Mambo Press, 1978. Novel.

438. Mutswairo, Solomon M. *Hamandishe.* Gweru: Mambo Press, 1991. Novel.

439. ———. *Murambiwa goredema.* Cape Town: OUP, 1959. Novel.

440. ———. *Zimbabwe: prose and poetry.* Washington: Three Continents Press, 1974. Tr. of the author's novel *Feso* (1958), with bi-lingual English-Zezuru (Shona) poems of four poets.

441. Nyika, Tambayi O. *Rat on her back: a play.* Gweru: Mambo Press, 1986. (Mambo writers; 24). Tr. from Shona.

442. Ribeiro, Emmanuel. *Muchadura.* Gwelo: Mambo Press, 1967. Novel.

443. Simango, Joyce. (F) *Zviuya zviri mberi.* Salisbury [Harare]: Longman, 1974. Novel.

444. Tsodzo, T. K. *Mudhuri murefurefu.* Ardbennie, Harare: Longman Zimbabwe, 1993. (Zimbabwe writers). Novel.

445. ———. *Pafunge.* Salisbury: Longman, 1972. Novel.

446. Zvarevashe, Ignatius. *Gonawapotera.* Salisbury [Harare]: College Press, 1978. Novel.

447. ———. *Gwararenhamo*. Gweru: Mambo Press, 1991. Novel.

SOMALI

(Djibouti, Ethiopia, Somalia)

Anthologies

448. Andrzejewski, B. W., and I. M. Lewis. *Somali poetry*. Oxford: Clarendon, 1964. (Oxford library of African literature).

449. ———, and Sheila Andrzejewski. *An Anthology of Somali poetry*. Bloomington: Indiana University Press, 1993.

450. Mumin, Hassan Sheikh, Hamad La'Ade, and Ibrahim Ahmed Dini (eds.). *Contes de Djibouti*. Paris: Conseil international de la langue française, 1980. Stories translated from Afar and Somali by Didier Morin.

451. Nakano, Aki'o. *Somali folktales*. Tokyo: Institute for the Study of Languages & Cultures of Asia and Africa, Tokyo University of Foreign Studies, 1982.

452. Sheik-Abdi, Abdi. *Tales of Punt: Somali folktales*. Macomb, IL: Dr. Leisure, 1993.

General studies

453. Andrzejewski, B. W. *The Rise of written Somali literature*. Mogadisho: Academy of Somali Culture, 1975.

454. Antinucci, F., and F. Axmed. *Poesia orale Somala: storia di una nazione*. Roma: Ministero degli affari esteri, 1969.

455. Axmed Cali Abokor. *Suugaanta geela*. Uppsala: Scandinavian Institute of African Studies, 1986. Tr. as: *The Camel in Somali oral traditions*. Mogadisho: Academy of Sciences and Arts, 1987.

456. Johnson, John William. *Heellooy heelleellooy: the development of the genre "heello" in modern Somali poetry*.

Bloomington: Indiana University Press, 1974. (Indiana
University publications, Africa series; 5).

457. Laurence, Margaret. *A Tree for poverty: Somali
poetry and prose.* Hamilton; Shannon: McMaster University
Library; Irish University Press, 1970. First pub.: Nairobi:
Eagle Press, 1954. Also pub.: Toronto: ECW Press, 1993.

458. Maxamed Daahir Afrax. *Fan-masraxeedka
Soomaalida: raad-raac taariikheed iyo faaqihad riwaayado
caan-baxay.* [Kenya]: [s.n.], 1987. Drama criticism.

459. ———. *Somaalida.* Djibouti: Centre National de
Promotion Culturele, 1987.

460. Samatar, Said S. *Oral poetry and Somali
nationalism: the case of Sayyid Mahammad cAbdille Hassan.*
Cambridge: CUP, 1980.

461. Yalhu, 'Ali al-Shaykh 'Abd Allah. *al-Adab al-
sumali al-mu'asir.* al-Ribat: Isisku, 1988. Literary criticism.

Authors

462. Axmed Faarax Cali. *Dabkuu shiday darwiishkii:
(daraama).* Mogadisho: Akademiyah Dhaqanka, 1974.
Drama.

463. Cabdillaahi Suldaan Timacadde. *Maansadi
Timacadde.* Mogadisho: Akademiyada Cilmiga Fanka iyo
Suugaanta, 1983. Poetry.

464. Cabdullaahi Cabdi Xuseen. *Saaxiibteey lilaahi.*
Mogadisho: The Author, [198?]. Novel.

465. Cawl, Faarax Maxamed Jaamac. *Dhibbanaha aan
dhalan.* Mogadisho: [s.n.], 1989. Fiction.

466. ———. *Ignorance is the enemy of love.* London:
Zed, 1982. Tr. and introd. by B.W. Andrzejewski. Orig. pub.
as: *Aqoondarro waa u nacab jacayl.* Wasaaradda Hiddaha iyo
Tacliinta Sare, 1974. Novel.

467. Galaal, Muusa H. I. *Hikmad Soomali.* London: G. Cumberledge, 1956. Ed. by B.W. Andrzejewski (SOAS, Annotated African texts: Somali). Short stories.

468. Hadrawi, Mohamed Warsame. *Hal la qalay ragdeed.* Mogadisho: [s.n.], 1973. Poetry.

469. Jaamac Cumar Ciise, Sheekh (ed.). *Diiwaanka gabayadii sayid Maxamed Cabdulle Xasan.* Xamar, Mogadisho: Akademiyaha Dhaqanka, 1974. Somali poetry.

470. Maxamad Cabdi Maxamad. *Tix: chants et poèmes en somali avec leur traduction.* Besançon: UFR Lettres, 1989. (Recueil de textes choisis; 2). French and Somali. Poetry.

471. Maxamad Cabdulle Xasan, Sayid. *Diiwaanka gabayadii: uruurintii koowaad.* Xamar [Mogadisho]: Akademiyaha Dhaqanka, 1974. Poetry.

472. Mumin, Hassan Sheikh. *Leopard among the women: shabeelnaagood.* London: OUP, 1974. Bi-lingual, Somali-English. Tr. by B.W. Andrzejewski. Drama.

473. Rashid Maxamed Shabeele. *Ma Dhabba Jacayl waa loo Dhintaa.* Mogadisho: Wakaaladda Madbacadda Qaranka, 1975. Poetry.

474. Warsama, S. A. *Hees hawleeddo: hoobaanta afka hooyo.* Djibouti: ISERT (Service Sciences Humaines), 1987. 2nd ed. Somali and French text. Poetry.

SWAHILI

(Tanzania, Kenya, Madagascar, Mozambique, Somalia, Uganda, Zaire)

Bibliographies

475. Bertoncini, Elena Zúbková. *Outline of Swahili literature: prose, fiction and drama.* Leiden: Brill, 1989. (Nisaba; 17), pp. 190-334.

476. Spaandonck, Marcel van. *Practical and systematical Swahili bibliography: linguistics, 1850-1963.* Leiden: Brill, 1965. Includes both linguistics and literature.

Anthologies

477. Allen, J. W. T. (comp.). *Tendi.* London; New York: Heinemann; Africana, 1971. Poems with translations.

478. Blok, H. P. *A Swahili anthology.* Leiden: Sijthoff, 1948.

479. Büttner, Carl Gotthilf. *Anthologie aus der Suaheli-Literatur.* Nendeln: Kraus, 1970. Repr. of: Berlin: Felber, 1894.

480. Gueunier, N. J. *Si mimi mwongo watu wa zamani=ce n'est pas moi qui mens, ce sont les genres d'autrefois: contes en dialecte swahili du village de Marodoka (Nosy Be, Madagascar).* Zanzibar: EACROTANAL, 1980.

481. Harries, Lyndon (ed.). *Swahili prose texts.* London: OUP, 1965. Collected by Carl Velten, 1893-1896.

482. Jahadhmy, Ali A. (ed.). *Anthology of Swahili poetry.* London: Heinemann, 1977. (AWS; 192).

483. Knappert, Jan. *An Anthology of Swahili love poetry.* Berkeley: University of California Press, 1972.

484. ———. *A Choice of flowers: an anthology of Swahili love poetry.* London: Heinemann, 1972. (AWS; 93).

485. ———. *Four centuries of Swahili verse: a literary history and anthology.* London: Heinemann, 1980.

486. ———. *Myths and legends of the Swahili.* London: Heinemann, 1970. (AWS; 75). Legends.

487. ———. *Swahili Islamic poetry.* Leiden: Brill, 1971. 3 v. Collection of liturgical texts in Swahili Arabic.

488. Tourneux, Henry. *Les Nuits de Zanzibar: contes Swahili.* Paris: Karthala, 1983.

489. Zani, Zachariah Mwadebwe Setphen. *Mashairi yangu.* Dar es Salaam: The Eagle Press/EALB, 1953, repr. 1961. Poetry anthology.

General studies

490. Abdulaziz, Mohammed H. *Muyaka: nineteenth century Swahili poetry.* Nairobi: Kenya Literature Bureau, 1979. Parallel Swahili/English texts.

491. Bertoncini, Elena Z. *Outline of Swahili literature: prose, fiction and drama.* Leiden: Brill, 1989. (Nisaba; 17).

492. Blommaert, Jan (ed.). *Swahili studies: essays in honour of Marcel Van Spaandonck.* Ghent: Academia, 1991.

493. Harries, Lyndon. *Swahili poetry.* Oxford: Clarendon, 1962.

494. Knappert, Jan. *Epic poetry in Swahili and other African languages.* Leiden: Brill, 1983. (Nisaba; v.12).

495. ———. *Traditional Swahili poetry: an investigation into the concepts of East African Islam as reflected in the Utenzi literature.* Leiden: Brill, 1967.

496. Ohly, Rajmund. *Aggressive prose: a case study in Kiswahili prose of the seventies.* Dar es Salaam: Institute of Kiswahili Research, 1981.

497. ———. *The Zanzibarian challenge: Swahili prose in the years 1975-1981.* Windhoek: Academy, 1990. (African studies of the Academy; 3).

498. Rollins, Jack D. *A History of Swahili prose.* Leiden: Brill, 1983.

499. Scheven, Albert. *Swahili proverbs: nia zikiwa moja, kilicho mbali huja.* Washington: University Press of America, 1981.

500. Schild, Ulla (ed.). *The East African experience: essays on English & Swahili literature.* Berlin: Reimer, 1980.

501. Sengo, Tigiti S. Y., and S. D. Kiango (eds.). *Ndimi zetu 1 & 2.* Dar es Salaam: Longman Tanzania, 1975.

502. Topan, Farouk (ed.). *Uchambuzi wa maandishi ya Kiswahili, Kitabu cha Pili.* Dar es Salaam: OUP, 1977. Essays.

Authors

503. Abdallah ikn 'Ali ibn Nasir. *al-Inkishafi=The Soul's awakening.* Nairobi: OUP, 1972. Tr. by W. Hichens. Poem.

504. Abdulla, Muhammed Said. *Kosa la bwana msa.* Dar es Salaam: Africana Publishers, 1984. Novel.

505. Adam, Adam Shafi. *Kasri ya Mwinyi Fuad.* Dar es Salaam: Tanzanian Pub. House, 1978. Novel.

506. Ahmed, Said Bakari bin Sultani. *The Swahili chronicle of Ngazija.* Bloomington: African Studies Program, Indiana University, 1977. Ed. and tr. by Lyndon Harries.

507. Balisidya, Ndyanao (F). *Shida.* Nairobi: Foundation Books, 1975. Novel.

508. Chacha, Chacha Nyaigotti. *Hukumu.* Nairobi: Longman Kenya, 1992. (Longman michezo ya kuigiza). Drama.

509. Chachage, C. S. L. *Almasi za bandia.* Dar es Salaam: Dar es Salaam University Press, 1991. Novel.

510. ———. *Kivuli.* Dar es Salaam: BCI Publications, 1981. Novel.

511. Hasani Bin Ismail. *The Medicine man.* London: OUP, 1968. (Oxford library of African literature). Tr. of: *Swifa ya Nguvumali* by P.A. Lienhardt. Poetry.

512. Hichens, William. *Diwani la Muyaka bin Haji al-Ghassaniy.* Johannesburg: Witwatersrand University Press, 1939.

513. Hussein, Ebrahim N. *Arusi.* Nairobi: OUP, 1980. Drama.

514. ———. *Jogoo Kijijini na Ngao ya Jadi.* Dar es Salaam: OUP, 1976. Drama.

515. ———. *Kinjeketile.* Dar es Salaam: OUP, 1974. (New drama from Africa; 4). Drama. English and Swahili versions.

516. ———. *Kwenye ukingo wa dhim.* Nairobi: OUP, 1988. (New drama from Africa; 14). Drama.

517. ———. *Mashetani.* Dar es Salaam: OUP, 1971. (New drama from Africa; 7). Drama.

518. ———. *Michezo ya Kuigiza.* Nairobi: EAPH, 1970. (Mafilisi ya Kisasa; 1). Drama.

519. Kahigi, K. K., and A. A. Ngemera. *Mwanzo wa tufani.* Dar es Salaam: Tanzania Pub. House, 1976. Drama.

520. Kezilahabi, Euphrase. *Gamba la nyoka.* Arusha; Dar es Salaam: Eastern Africa Publications, 1979. Novel.

521. Khamis, Baker Mfaume. *Tufani.* Dar es Salaam: Heko, 1993. Novel.

522. Khatib, Muhammaed Seif. *Fungate ya uhuru.* Dar es Salaam: Education Services Centre, 1988. Poetry.

523. King'ala, Yusuf. *Anasa.* Nairobi: Heinemann, 1984. Novel.

524. Lihamba, Amandina (F). *Hawala ya fedha.* Dar es Salaam: Tanzania Pub. House, 1980. (Michezo ya kuigiza). Adaptation of Semène Ousmane's *Le mandat.* Drama.

525. Macha, Freddy. *Twen'zetu ulaya...na hadithi nyingine*. Dar es Salaam: Grand Arts Promotions, 1984. Stories.

526. Mayoka, J. M. M. *Utenzi wa vita vya uhuru wa Msumbiji*. Arusha: Eastern Africa Publications, 1978. Epic poem on FRELIMO struggle in Mozambique.

527. Mbajo, Nicco Ye. *Sifi mara mbili*. Dar es Salaam: Mcheshi Publications, 1984. Novella.

528. Mnyampala, Mathias E. *Kisa cha mrina asali na wenzake wawili*. Nairobi: EALB, 1968. (Hadithi za Tanganyika; 2). Fiction.

529. Mohamed, Mohamed S. *Nyota ya Rehema*. Nairobi: OUP, 1976. Novel.

530. Mohamed, Said Ahmed. *Dunia mti mkavu*. Nairobi: Longman, 1980. Novel.

531. ———. *Si shetani si wazimu*. Zanzibar: Zanzibar Publications, 1985. Short stories.

532. ———, and Ahmed Mgeni Ali. *Hapa na pale*. Zanzibar: Institute of Kiswahili and Foreign Languages, 1981. Short stories and essays.

533. Mtobwa, Ben R. *Zawadi di ya ushindi*. Dar es Salaam: Heko, 1992. Novel.

534. Muhando, Penina (F). *Haita*. Nairobi: EAPH, 1972. Drama.

535. ———. *Lina ubani*. Dar es Salaam: Dar es Salaam University Press, 1984. Drama.

536. ———. *Pambo*. Nairobi: Foundation Books, 1975. (Jukwaa la Afrika; 1). Drama.

537. Mvungi, Martha (F). *Hana hatia*. Dar es Salaam: Tanzania Pub. House, 1975. Novella.

538. Nassir Bin-Juma Bhalo, Ahmad. *Poems from Kenya: gnomic verses in Swahili.* Madison: University of Wisconsin Press, 1966. Tr. by Lyndon Harries.

539. Robert, Shaaban. *Insha na mashairi: essays and poems.* Tanga: Art and Literature, 1959.

540. ———. *Kufikirika.* Nairobi: OUP, 1967. Also pub.: Dar es Salaam: Mkuki na Nyota, 1991. Fiction.

541. ———. *Maisha yangu na Baada ya miaka hamsini.* London: Nelson, 1949. Autobiography.

542. ———. *Mapenzi bora.* Dar es Salaam: Mkuki na Nyota, 1991. Poetry.

543. ———. *Siku ya watenzi wote.* Nairobi: Nelson, 1968. Novel.

544. Arnold, Rainer. *Afrikanische Literatur und nationale Befreiung: Menschenbild und Gezellschaftskonzeption im Prosawerk Shaaban Robert.* Berlin: Akademie, 1977 (Studien uber Asien, Afrika und Lateinamerika; 28).

545. Sengo, Tigiti S. Y. *Shaaban Robert: uhakiki wa maandishi yake.* Nairobi: Longman, 1975.

546. Topan, Farouk. *Mfalme juha.* Nairobi: OUP, 1971.

547. ———. *A Taste of heaven.* Dar es Salaam: Tanzanian Pub. House, 1980. (Plays in English; 1). Tr. by M. Mkombo. First pub. in 1973 as *Aliyeonja pepo.* Drama.

548. Yahya, A. S., and David Mulwa. *Ukame.* Nairobi: Longman, 1984. Drama.

TAMAZIGHT ("BERBER")

(Maghreb, Sahara)

Bibliography

549. Chaker, Salem. *Une Décennie d'études berbères (1980-1990): bibliographie critique.* Alger: Bouchène, 1993.

Anthologies

550. Albaka, Moussa, and Dominique Casajus [eds.].
*Poésies et chants touaregs de l'Ayr: tandis qu'ils dorment
tous, je dis mon chant d'amour.* Paris: L'Harmattan/AWAL,
1992.

551. Amrouche, Jean. *Chants berbères de Kabylie.*
Paris: L'Harmattan, 1986. Tr. by Tassadit Yacine (Poésie et
théâtre) (Écritures arabes; 20).

552. Amrouche, Marguerite Taos. *Le Grain magique:
contes, poèmes et proverbes berbères de Kabylie.* Paris:
Maspero, 1966.

553. Boulifa, Si Ammar Ben Said. *Recueil de poésies
Kabyles.* Paris; Alger: Éditions AWAL, 1990. Poetry.

554. Bu Ras, Abd al- 'Aziz. *Umiyin n tamazight: Umiy
n: Hamu Umamir.* al-Dar al-Bayda': Manshurat al-Jam'iyah
al-Maghribiyah lil-Bahth wa-al-Tabadul al-Thaqafi, 1991.

555. Casajus, Dominique. *Peau d'ane et autres contes
touaregs.* Paris: L'Harmattan, 1985. In French and Tamashak
(Coll. connaissance des hommes). Niger tales.

556. al-Damsiri, Muhammad. *al-Rayis al-Hajj
Muhammad al-Damsiri: shahadat wa-qasa'id wa-mukhtarah
min aghanih.* al-Ribat: Matba'at al-Ma'arif al-Jadidah, 1993.
2 v. Tamazight songs in Arabic, with commentary.

557. Delheure, Jean. *Contes et legendes berbères de
Ouargla: Tinfusin.* Paris: La Boite et Documents, 1989.
(Collection: bilingues). In French and Tamazight. Tales.

558. Foucauld, Charles, and A. de Calassanti-
Motylinski. *Textes touaregs en prose.* Aix-en-Provence:
Edisud, 1984. (Coll. Monde berbère). Ed. crit. par Salem
Chaker, Helene Claudot, Marceau Gest. Text in French and
Tuareg.

559. Galley, Micheline (ed.). *Badr az-zîn et six contes
algériens.* Paris: Colin, 1971. (Classiques africains).

560. Hanoteau, A. *Poésies populaires de la Kabylie du Djurdjura.* Paris: Imprimerie imperiale, 1867. Poetry.

561. Mammeri, Mouloud. *Machaho!: contes berbères de Kabylie.* Paris: Bordas, 1980. (Aux quatre coins de temps).

562. ———. *Poémes kabyles anciens.* Paris: Maspero, 1980.

563. Moqadem, Hamid. *Contes Adba du Maroc.* Paris: Conseil international de la langue français, 1991. (Fleuve et flamme).

564. Nacib, Youssef. *Contes de Kabylie.* Paris: Publisud, 1986.

565. Ouary, Malek. *Poèmes et chants de Kabylie.* Paris: Librairie Saint-Germain-des-Prés, 1974. (Anthologie de la poésie universelle).

566. Rabia, Boualem. *Recueil de poésies Kabyles des Ait-Ziki, Le viatique du barde.* Paris: L'Harmattan/AWAL, 1993.

567. Savignac, Pierre. *Poésie populaire des Kabyles.* Paris: Maspero, 1964. Poetry.

General studies

568. Aghali-Zakara, Mohamed, and Jeannine Drouin. *Traditions touarègues nigériennes: Amerolqis, héros civilisateur pré-islamique, et Aligurran, archétype social.* Paris: L'Harmattan, 1980.

569. Basset, Henri. *Essai sur la littérature des Berbères.* Alger: J. Carbonel, 1920.

570. Déjeux, Jean. *Djoh'a: heros de la tradition orale arabo-berbère: hier et aujourd'hui.* Sherbrooke, Quebec: Naaman, 1979. (Études; 18).

571. Galand, Lionel. *Langue et littérature berbères: vingt cinq ans d'études.* Paris: CNRS, 1979. (Chroniques de l'Annuaire de l'Afrique du Nord).

572. Lacoste-Dujardin, Camille. *Le Conte kabyle: étude ethnographique*. Paris: Maspero, 1970. (Domaine Maghrébin).

573. Mammeri, Mouloud, et al. (eds.). *Littérature orale: Actes de la Table-Ronde Littérature Orale, juin 1979*. Alger: Centre de recherches anthropologiques, préhistoriques et ethnographiques, 1982.

574. Yacine Titouh, Tassadit. *L'Izli, ou, L'Amour chante en kabyle*. Paris: Maison des Sciences de L'Homme, 1988.

Authors

575. Aliche, R. *Asfel*. Lyon: Federop, 1981. Novel.

576. Hawad. *Chants de la soif et de l'égarement: poèsies et calligraphies tifinar originales de Hawad*. Aix-en-Provence: Edisud, 1987. 2nd ed. pub. as: *Caravane de la soif*, 1988.

577. ———. *Testament nomade: poésies et calligraphies tifinar originales de Hawad*. Paris: Sillages, 1987. (L'Ouverture du champ). Trad. du Touareg et adaptation française, Hawad et Hélène Claudot. 2nd ed.: La Bouilladisse: Amara, 1989.

578. ———. *Yasida*. Paris: N. Blandin, 1991. Poetry.

579. Id Balkassm, Hassan. *Imarayin: majmu'ah qisaasiyah amajighiyah*. al-Ribat: Matba'at al-Ma'arif al-Jadidah, 1992. Fiction.

580. Meki, Arezki. *Le Pain d'orge de l'enfant perdu: poèmes (berbère-français)*. Sherbrooke: Naaman, 1983.

581. Mezdad, Amar. *Tafunast Igujilen, isefra*. Paris: GEB, 1978. Poetry.

582. Mohand-ou-Mohand. *Les Isefra: poèmes de Si Mohand ou Mhand*. Paris: Maspero, 1969. Ed. par Mouloud Mammeri. Texte berbère et traduction.

583. Sadi, Said. *Askuti*. Algiers: Asalu, 1991. Novel.

584. Zenia, Salem. *Les Rêves de Yidir.* Paris: L'Harmattan/AWAL, 1994. Bilingue berbère-français. Poetry.

TSWANA/SETSWANA

(Botswana, Namibia, South Africa)

Bibliography

585. Peters, Marguerite Andrée, and Matthew Mathethe Tabane. *Bibliography of the Tswana language: a bibliography of books, periodicals, pamphlets, and manuscripts to the year 1980.* Pretoria: State Library, 1982 (Bibliographies; 25).

Anthologies

586. Curtis, S. (ed.). *Mainane-Tswana tales.* Gaborone: United Congregational Church of Southern Africa, 1975.

587. Schapera, Isaac. *Praise poems of Tswana chiefs.* Oxford: Clarendon, 1965. (Oxford library of African literature).

Authors

588. Busang, R. R. *Molao wa manong.* Johannesburg: Educum, 1989. Novel.

589. Dipale, Z. S. *Nna ke di bona jalo.* Pretoria: van Schaik, 1988. Poetry.

590. Johnson, M. *Lokwalo lwa morutabana.* Gaborone: Botswana Book Centre, 1986.

591. Kgomotso, Mogapi. *Ka ga ya Setswana.* [Botswana]: Dinaledi, [197?].

592. Kitchin, M. S. *Masalela a puo.* Gaborone: Botswana Book Centre, 1968. (Mackenzie series; 3). Poetry.

593. Matsepe, Oliver Kgadine. *Kgorong ya Mosate.* Pretoria: Van Schaik, 1962. Novel.

594. Mogotsi, M. C. D. *Selelo sa mmoki*. Braamfontein: Sasavona Publications, 1981. Poetry.

595. Mokobi, R. F. *Mothuba lobelo*. Manzini: Macmillan Boleswa, 1986. (Mmaletsatsi). Poetry.

596. Molefe, Ramsey Diane. *Maipelo a puo*. Pretoria: Via Africa, 1991. Poetry.

597. Motlhake, S. F. *Molodi wa puo*. Cape Town: Maskew Miller Longman, 1983. Poetry.

598. Pheto, T. J. *Botlhodi jwa nta ya tlhogo*. Gaborone: Botswana Book Centre, 1985.

599. Plaatje, Solomon T. *Diane tsa Secoana le maele a sekgooa a dumalanang naco=Sechuana proverbs with literal translations and their European equivalents*. London: Kegan Paul, Trench, Trubner, 1916.

600. Raditladi, Lettle Disang. *Dintshontsho tsa loratô*. Johannesburg: Afrikaanse Pers-Boekhandel, 1956, repr. 1962. Drama.

601. ———. *Legae botshabelo*. Johannesburg: Bona Press, 1960. Fiction.

602. ———. *Motswasele II*. Johannesburg: Witwatersrand University Press, 1985 (Black writers; 9). First pub.: 1945. Drama.

603. Seboni, Michael O. M. *Kgosi Isang Pilane*. Johannesburg: Afrikaanse Pers-Boekhandel, 1958. Novel.

604. ———. *Maboko maloba le maabane*. Johannesburg: Nasional Pers, 1949. Poetry.

605. Serote, Mongane Wally. *Tsetlo*. Johannesburg: Ad. Donker, 1974. Poetry.

606. Tamsanqa, W. K. *Botsang rhe*. Cape Town: OUP, 1981. Drama.

XHOSA (South Africa)

Bibliographies

607. Peters, Marguerite Andrée. *Ibhibliyografi yolwimi olusisiXhosa ukuya kutsho kunyaka we-1990=Bibliography of the Xhosa language to the year 1990.* Pretoria: State Library, 1992. (Bibliographies of the State Library; 26).

608. Scott, Patricia E. *James James Ramisi Jolobe: an annotated bibliography.* Grahamstown: Rhodes University Dept. of African Languages, 1973. (Communication; 1).

609. ———. *Samuel Edward Krune Mqhayi, 1875-1945: a bibliographic survey.* Grahamstown: Rhodes University Dept. of African Languages, 1976. (Communication; 5).

Anthologies

610. Jolobe, James J. R. *Indyebo yesihobe.* Johannesburg: Afrikaanse Pers-Boekhandel, 1956. 2 v. Poetry.

611. Jordan, Archibald C. (ed., tr.). *Tales from Southern Africa.* Berkeley: University of California Press, 1973. Anthology.

General studies

612. Gérard, Albert S. *Four African literatures: Xhosa, Sotho, Zulu, Amharic.* Berkeley: University of California Press, 1971.

613. Jordan, Archibald C. *Towards an African literature: the emergence of literary form in Xhosa.* Berkeley: University of California Press, 1973. (Perspectives on Southern Africa; 6).

614. Mahlasela, B. E. N. *A General survey of Xhosa literature from its early beginnings in the 1800s to the present.* Grahamstown: Rhodes University, Dept. of African Languages, 1973. (Working paper; 2).

615. Nkabinde, A. C. (ed.). *Anthology of articles on African linguistics and literature: a Festschrift to C.L.S. Nyembezi.* Johannesburg: Lexicon, 1988.

616. Opland, Jeff. *Xhosa oral poetry: aspects of a black South African tradition.* Cambridge; Johannesburg: CUP; Ravan Press, 1983.

617. Scheub, Harold. *The Xhosa Ntsomi.* Oxford: Clarendon, 1975. (Oxford library of African literature).

Authors

618. Faku, B. S. G. *A! ndluyamandla!* Pietermaritzburg: Shuter and Shooter, 1982. Drama.

619. Futshane, Zora Z. T. (F). *Mhla ngenqaba.* Lovedale: Lovedale Press, 1960. Novel.

620. Jolobe, James J. R. *Amavo: Xhosa essays.* Johannesburg: University of the Witwatersrand Press, 1973. (Bantu treasury; 5). Orig. pub. in 1940.

621. ———. *Elundini loThukela.* Johannesburg: Afrikaanse Pers-Boekhandel, 1958. Novel.

622. ———. *Umyezo = Omyezo.* Johannesburg: University of the Witwatersrand Press, 1961. (Bantu treasury; 2). Orig. pub. 1936. Poetry.

623. ———. *U-Zagula.* Lovedale: Lovedale Press, 1923. Novel.

624. Mahlasela, B. E. N. *Jolobe, Xhosa poet and writer.* Grahamstown: Rhodes University, Dept. of African Languages, 1973. (Working paper; 3).

625. Jordan, Archibald C. *The Wrath of the ancestors.* Lovedale: Lovedale Press, 1940, repr. 1965. Tr. by Phyllis Ntantlana Jordan of: *Ingqumbo yeminyana.* Novel.

626. Kaschula, Russell H. (ed.). *A. C. Jordan: life and work.* Umtata: University of Transkei, 1992. (Occasional

papers, Bureau for African research and documentation; 2).

627. Kakaze, Lota G. (F) *U-Tandive wakwa Gcaleka.* Cape Town: Methodist Book Room, 1940. Novel.

628. Kavanagh, Robert, and Z. S. Quangule (trs.). *The Making of a servant and other poems.* Johannesburg: Ophir/Ravan Press, 1979.

629. Mqhayi, Samuel Edward Krune. *I-nzuzo.* Johannesburg: Witwatersrand University Press, 1974. (Bantu treasury; 7). Orig. pub. 1942. Poetry.

630. ———. *Ityala lamawele.* Lovedale: Lovedale Press, 1970. Novel, short stories, and poetry. Orig. pub.: East London, 1914, as a novel.

631. ———. *U-Mqhayi wase Ntab'ozuko.* Lovedale: Lovedale Press, 1939. Pub. in German: Essen, 1938. Autobiography.

632. Scott, Patricia E. *Mqhayi in translation.* Grahamstown: Rhodes University, Dept. of African Languages, 1976. (Communication; 6).

633. Mtuze, P. T. *Umsinga.* Goodwood, South Africa: Via Afrika, 1978. Fiction.

634. Rubusana, Walter B. *Zemk'iinkomo magwalandini.* Frome; London: Butler & Tanner; Selwood Printing Works, 1906. 2nd. ed. 1911. Abr. ed.: Lovedale Press, 1964. Tales.

635. Sinxo, Guybon Budlwana. *Imfene ka Debeza neminye imidlalwana.* Cape Town: OUP, 1960. Drama.

636. ———. *Thoba sikutyele: amabali emibongo angama-76.* Lovedale: Lovedale Press, 1959. Praise-poems.

637. ———. *Umzali wolahleko = The Lost parent.* Lovedale: Lovedale Press, 1933. Novel.

638. Swaartbooi, Victoria Nombulelo Mermaid (F). *U-Mandisa.* Lovedale: Lovedale Press, 1933. Novella.

639. Tamsanqa, Witness K. *Buzani kubawo*. Cape Town: OUP, 1991. Rev. ed. Prev. pub. 1958. Drama.

640. Zenani, Nongenile Masithathu. *The World and the word: tales and observations from the Xhosa oral tradition*. Madison: University of Wisconsin Press, 1992. Ed. by Harold Scheub.

YORUBA

(Nigeria; also Benin, Togo)

Bibliographies

641. Aguolu, Christian C. (comp.). *Nigeria: a comprehensive bibliography in the humanities and social sciences, 1900-1971*. Boston: G. K. Hall, 1973.

642. Baldwin, David E., and Charlene M. Baldwin. *The Yoruba of Southwestern Nigeria: an indexed bibliography*. Boston: G.K. Hall, 1976.

Anthologies

643. Beier, Ulli. *Yoruba poetry: an anthology of traditional poems*. Cambridge: CUP, 1970.

644. ———— (ed.). *Yoruba myths*. Cambridge: CUP, 1980.

645. Gbadamosi, Bakare, and Ulli Beier (eds.). *Not even God is ripe enough: Yoruba stories*. London: Heinemann, 1968. Tr. from Yoruba. (AWS; 48).

General studies

646. Afolayan, Adebisi (ed.). *Yoruba language and literature*. Ibadan; Ife: University Press; University of Ife Press, 1982.

647. Alston, J. B. *Yoruba drama in English: interpretation and production*. Lewiston, NY: E. Mellen Press, 1989. (Studies in African literature; v. 1).

648. Babalola, S. A. *The Content and form of Yoruba ijala*. London: OUP, 1966. (Oxford library of African literature).

649. Barber, Karin. *Yorùbá popular theatre: three plays by the Oyin Adéjobí Company*. Atlanta: African Studies Association, 1994. Tr. and ed. by Karin Barber and Báyò Ogúndíjo. (African historical sources; 9).

650. Götrick, Kacke. *Apidan theatre and modern drama: a study in a traditional Yoruba theatre and its influence on modern drama by Yoruba playwrights*. Stockholm: Almqvist & Wiksell International, 1984.

651. Jeyifo, Biodun. *The Yoruba popular travelling theatre of Nigeria*. Lagos: Dept. of Culture, 1984.

652. Larsen, Stephan. *A Writer and his gods: a study of the importance of Yoruba myths and religious ideas to the writings of Wole Soyinka*. Stockholm: Dept. of History of Literature, University of Stockholm, 1983.

653. Lindfors, Bernth (ed.). *Critical perspectives on Nigerian literatures*. Washington: Three Continents Press, 1976. Covers English, Hausa, Yoruba, and Igbo works.

654. Ogunsina, Bisi. *The Development of the Yoruba novel, 1930-75*. Ibadan: Gospel Faith Mission Press, 1992.

655. Sekoni, Ropo. *Folk poetics: a sociosemiotic study of Yoruba trickster tales*. Westport: Greenwood, 1994.

Authors

656. Courlander, Harold. *Tales of Yoruba gods and heroes*. New York: Crown Publishers, 1973.

657. Esan, Olanipekun. *Orekelewa*. Ibadan: OUP, 1965. Drama.

658. Fagunwa, D. O. *Adìitu Olódùmarè*. Edinburgh: Nelson, 1961. Novel.

659. ———. *The Forest of a thousand daemons: a hunter's saga.* London: Nelson, 1968. Tr. by Wole Soyinka. Orig. pub. as: *Ogboju ode ninu Igbo irunmale.* Novel.

660. ———. *Igbo Olodumare.* London: Nelson, 1946. Novel.

661. Bamgbose, A. *The Novels of D.O. Fagunwa.* Benin City, Nigeria: Ethiopie, 1974.

662. Gbadamosi, Bakare. *Oriki.* Ibadan: Mbari Press, 1961. Poems.

663. ———. *Oro pelu idire.* Oshogbo: Mbari Mbayo, 1966. Stories.

664. Ijimere, Obotunde. *The imprisonment of Obatala, and other plays.* London: Heinemann, 1966. Tr. and adapted by Ulli Beier. (AWS; 18). Verse plays.

665. Isola, Akinwumi. *Koseegbe.* Ibadan: OUP, 1981. Drama.

666. Ladipo, Duro. *Eda.* Ibadan: Mbari Press, 1965. Drama.

667. ———. *Three Yoruba plays: Oba koso, Oba moro, Oba waja.* Ibadan: Mbari Press, 1964. English adaptation by Ulli Beier.

668. Ogunde, Hubert. *Yorùba Ronú.* Yaba-Lagos: Pacific Printers, 1964. Drama.

669. Olantunji, Babatunde. *Ebbinrin ote.* Ibadan: OUP, 1978. Drama.

ZULU (South Africa)

Bibliography

670. Gérard, Albert S. *Four African literatures: Xhosa, Sotho, Zulu, Amharic.* Berkeley: University of California Press, 1971, pp. 427-30.

Anthologies

671. Cope, Trevor (ed.). *Izibongo: Zulu praise-poems.* London: OUP, 1968. Coll. by James Stuart, tr. by D. Malcolm.

672. Gunner, Liz, and M. Gwala (eds.). *Musho! Zulu popular praises.* East Lansing; Johannesburg: Michigan State University Press; Witwatersrand University Press, 1991, 1994.

673. Msimang, C. T. (ed.). *Izinsungulo: an anthology of Zulu poems.* Pretoria: De Jager Haum, 1980. (African language and literature series).

674. Nyembezi, C. L. Sibusio (ed.). *Imisebe yelanga: imilolozelo nezinkondlo.* Johannesburg: Afrikaanse Pers-Boekhandel, 1961. 3 v. Poetry.

675. ———. *Zulu proverbs.* Johannesburg: Witwatersrand University Press, 1963. 2nd ed.

General studies

676. Burness, Don (ed.). *Shaka, King of the Zulus, in African literature.* Washington: Three Continents Press, 1976.

677. Du Toit, Brian. *Content and context of Zulu folk-narratives.* Gainesville: University Presses of Florida, 1976. (University of Florida monographs. Social sciences; 58).

678. Gérard, Albert S. *Four African literatures: Xhosa, Sotho, Zulu, Amharic.* Berkeley: University of California Press, 1971.

679. Msimang, C. T. *Izimbongi izolo nanamuhla.* [South Africa]: Bard Publishers, 1988. Critical study on Zulu poetry.

680. Ngcongwane, S. D. *The Novel and life [and other essays].* KwaDlangezwa: University of Zululand, 1987. (Publications of the University of Zululand. Series B; 62).

681. Nkabinde, A. C. (ed.). *Anthology of articles on African linguistics and literature: a Festschrift to C.L.S. Nyembezi.* Johannesburg: Lexicon, 1988.

682. Nyembezi, C. L. Sibusio. *A Review of Zulu literature.* Durban: University of Natal Press, 1961. Also pub.: Nendeln: Kraus Reprint, 1973.

683. Vail, Leroy, and Landeg White. *Power and the praise poem.* Charlottesville; London: University Press of Virginia; Currey, 1991.

Authors

684. Dhlomo, Rolf R. R. *R.R.R. Dhlomo: 20 Short Stories.* Ed. by Tim Couzens. Special issue of: *English in Africa* v.2 no.1 1975. Short stories in English and Zulu.

685. ———. *U-Cetshwayo.* Pietermaritzburg: Shuter & Shooter, 1952, 2nd rev. ed. 1966. Novel.

686. ———. *U-Shaka.* Pietermaritzburg: Shuter & Shooter, 1937, repr. 1965. Novel.

687. Dlamini, J. Constance (F). *Amavovo ezinyembezi.* Pietermaritzburg: Shuter & Shooter, 1981. Poetry.

688. ———. *Imfihlo yokunyamalala.* Pretoria: Van Schaik, 1973. Poetry.

689. Dube, John. *Jeqe, the bodyservant of King Tshaka.* Lovedale: Lovedale Press, 1951. Tr. by J. Boxwell. Orig. pub. in 1930 as: *Insila ka Tshaka.* Novel.

690. Dube, Violet (F). *Wozanazo izindaba.* London: OUP, 1935. Novel.

691. Gwayi, Joyce Jessie (F). *Shumpu.* Pretoria: Van Schaik, 1978. 2nd ed. Fiction.

692. ———. *Yekanini!* Johannesburg: Van Schaik, 1976. Novel on the life of Shaka.

693. Kumalo, Alfred A. *Izingoma zika.* Pietermaritzburg: Shuter & Shooter, 1969. Drama.

694. Kunene, Mazisi. *The Ancestors and the sacred mountain.* London: Heinemann, 1982. Poetry.

695. ———. *Anthem of the decades: a Zulu epic.* London: Heinemann, 1981. Tr. by the author (AWS; 234). Poetry.

696. ———. *Emperor Shaka the Great: a Zulu epic.* London: Heinemann, 1979. Tr. by the author (AWS; 211). Poetry.

697. ———. *Zulu poems.* London: A. Deutsch, 1970.

698. Lukhele, Senzenjani. *Nakho phela!* Pietermaritzburg: Indlovu Ubudlelwane Ngezincwadi, 1981. Fiction.

699. Makhaye, N. J. *Isoka Iakwa Zulu.* Johannesburg: Witwatersrand University Press, 1972. (Bantu treasury; 18). Poetry.

700. Matsebula, J. S. M. *Iqoqo lezinkondlo.* Pietermaritzburg: Shuter & Shooter, 1975. Poetry.

701. Mbuli, Mzwhake. *Before Dawn.* Fordsburg, South Africa: COSAW, 1989. 2nd ed. Poetry in English and Zulu.

702. Msimang, C. T. *Iminduze.* Johannesburg: Sasavona Publications, 1986. Poetry.

703. ———. *IZulu eladuma eSandlwana.* Pretoria: Van Schaik, 1976. Drama.

704. Myeni, Phumasilwe. *Hayani maZulu.* Johannesburg: Witwatersrand University Press, 1969. (Bantu treasury; 17). Poetry.

705. Ndebele, Nimrod N. T. *UGubudele namazimuzimu: (umdlalo osenzo-sinye esinemboniso emihlanu).* Johannesburg: Witwatersrand University Press, 1976. (Bantu treasury; 6). Rev. ed. Orig. pub. 1941. Drama.

706. Ngubane, Jordan. *Uvalo lwezinhlonzi.* Johannesburg: Afrikaanse Per-Boekhandel, 1957. Novel.

707. Ntuli, C. S. Z. *Amawisa.* Pietermaritzburg: Indlovu Ubudlelwane Ngezincwadi, 1982. Short stories/essays.

708. Ntuli, D. B. Z. *Ithemba.* Pretoria: Van Schaik, 1974. Drama.

709. ———. *Ugqozi.* Pretoria: Van Schaik, 1975. Poetry.

710. ———, O. E. H. M. Nxumalo, and C. S. Z. Ntuli. *Induku.* Pietermaritzburg: Shuter & Shooter, 1992. Stories and essays.

711. Nxumalo, Natalie Victoria (F). *Ubude abuphangwa.* Pietermaritzburg: Shuter & Shooter, 1936. Novel.

712. Nxumalo, O. E. H. *Ikhwezi.* Cape Town: OUP, 1965. Poetry.

713. Nyembezi, Cyril Lincoln Sibusio. *Inkinsela yaseMgungundlovu.* Pietermaritzburg: Shuter & Shooter, 1961. Novel.

714. ———. *Mntanami! Mntanami!* Johannesburg: Afrikaanse Pers-Boekhandel, 1950. Novel.

715. Qabula, Alfred T. *A Working life, cruel beyond belief.* [Durban]: National Union of Metalworkers of South Africa, 1989. Autobiography, with some poems.

716. Sitas, Ari (ed.). *Black Mamba rising: South African worker poets in struggle: Alfred Temba Qabula, Mi S'dumo Hlatshwayo, Nise Malange.* Durban: Culture and Working Life, for COSATU, 1986. Poetry.

717. Thwala, J. J. *Amaqhabanga.* Pretoria: Van Schaik, 1984. Poetry.

718. Vilakazi, B. Wallet. *Amal'ezulu.* Johannesburg: Witwatersrand University Press, 1960. (Bantu treasury; 8). Reprint, in new orthography, of 1945 ed. Poetry.

719. ———. *Inkondlo kaZulu: Zulu poems.* Johannesburg: Witwatersrand University Press, 1935. (Bantu treasury; 1). Poetry. Repr. in new orthography, 1965.

720. ———. *Izinkondlo zika.* Johannesburg: Witwatersrand University Press, 1993.

721. ———. *UDingiswayo kaJobe.* London: Sheldon Press, 1939. Novel.

722. ———. *Zulu horizons.* Johannesburg: Witwatersrand University Press, 1973. Tr. by Florence Friedman, D. Malcom and J. M. Sikakana. Poetry.

723. Ntuli, D. B. Z. *The Poetry of B.W. Vilakazi.* Pretoria: Van Schaik, 1984.

724. Zondi, Elliot. *Insumansumane.* Johannesburg: Witwatersrand University Press, 1993. (Black writers; 19). Drama.

725. ———. *Ukufa kukaShaka.* Johannesburg: Witwatersrand University Press, 1978. (Black writers; 14). Rev. ed. Orig. pub. 1960. Drama.

OTHER SELECTED AFRICAN LANGUAGES

Bibliographies

726. Amegbleame, Simon. *Le Livre ewe: essai de bibliographie.* Bordeaux: Centre d'étude d'Afrique noire, 1975.

727. Chimombo, Steve. *A Bibliography of oral literature in Malawi, 1860-1986.* Zomba: Chancellor College, 1987.

728. d'Hertefelt, Marcel, and Danielle de Lame. *Société, culture et histoire du Rwanda: encyclopédie bibliographique*

1863-1980/87. Tervuren, Belgium: Musée royal de l'Afrique centrale, 1987. 2 v.

729. Görög-Karady, Véronika. *Littérature orale d'Afrique noire: bibliographie annotée*. Paris: Conseil International de la langue française, 1992.

Anthologies

730. Amadu, Malum. *Amadu's bundle*. London: Heinemann, 1972. (AWS; 118). Collected by Gulla Kell. Fulani stories from Cameroon and Nigeria.

731. Awoonor, Kofi Nyidevu (ed.). *Guardians of the sacred word: Ewe poetry*. New York: Nok, 1974. Oral poetry.

732. Bâ, Amadou Hampâté, and Lilyan Kesteloot. *Kaïdara: récit initiatique peul*. Paris: A. Colin, 1968. (Classiques africains; 7). Peul tales from Senegal.

733. Baumbach, E. J. M., and C. T. D. Marivate (eds.). *Xironga folk-tales*. Pretoria: University of South Africa, 1973. (Documenta; 12). Tsonga tales from Mozambique.

734. Bird, Charles S. (ed.). *The Songs of Seydou Camara*. Bloomington: African Studies Centre, Indiana University, 1974. Manding epic tale.

735. Bouc, Hadji (ed.). *Demb ak Tey (Cahiers du mythe)*. Dakar: Centre d'études des civilisations, 1975. Tale in Wolof, Peule and French versions.

736. Cissoko, S. M., and K. Sambou. *Recueil des traditions orales des mandingues de Gambie et da Casamance*. Yaoundé: Centre d'études linguistiques et historiques par tradition orale, 1974.

737. Coupez, André, and Thomas Kamanzi (eds.). *Littérature courtoise du Rwanda*. London: Clarendon, 1969. Kinyarwanda and French. (Oxford library of African literature). Poetry.

738. Creus, Jacint (ed.). *Cuentos de los ndowe de Guinea Ecuatorial*. Malabo: Centro Cultural Hispano-

Guineano Ediciones, 1991. (Coleccion ensayos; 6). In Spanish and Kombe. Kombe tales from Equatorial Guinea.

739. Davis, Jennifer. *The Stolen water and other stories: traditional tales from Namibia*. Windhoek: New Namibia, 1993.

740. Deng, Francis Mading. *Dinka folktales: African stories from the Sudan*. New York: Africana, 1974. Dinka tales.

741. Diabaté, Massa M. *Janjon, et autres chants populaires du Mali*. Paris: Présence africaine, 1970. Anthology.

742. Evans-Pritchard, E. E. (ed.). *The Zande trickster*. London: OUP, 1967. (Oxford library of African literature). Azande tales of the Central African Republic.

743. Finnegan, Ruth. *Limba stories and storytelling*. Oxford: Clarendon, 1970. Stories from Sierra Leone.

744. Hasheela, P. *Omishe di dule eyovi=More than a thousand proverbs*. Windhoek: Gamsberg Macmillan, 1986. Namibian proverbs in Oshikwanyama and English.

745. Hourdeau, S. *Panorama de la littérature Rwandaise: bilan-bibliographie, choix de textes en français*. Butare, Rwanda: The Author, 1979. Kinyarwanda poetry.

746. Innes, Gordon. *Sunjata: three Mandika versions*. London: School of Oriental and African Studies, 1974.

747. Kagame, Alexis. *Introduction aux grands genres lyriques de l'ancien Rwanda*. Butare: Éditions universitaires du Rwanda, 1969. (Collection Muntu; 1). Anthology.

748. Kaschula, Russell H. (ed.). *Foundations in Southern African oral literature*. Johannesburg: Witwatersrand University Press, 1993. (African studies reprint; 2).

749. Kesteloot, Lilyan (ed.). *L'épopée traditionelle*. Paris: Nathan, 1971. (Littérature africaine; 11). Tales.

750. ———. *Da Monzon de Ségou: épopée bambara.* Paris: Nathan, 1978. 2 v. Bambara epic of Mali.

751. ———. *La poésie traditionelle.* Paris: Nathan, 1971. (Littérature africaine; 12). Poetry from West and Central Africa.

752. Kilson, Marion (comp.). *Royal antelope and spider: West African Mende tales.* Cambridge, MA: Press of the Langdon Associates, 1976.

753. Knappert, Jan. *Myths and legends of the Congo.* London: Heinemann, 1971. (AWS; 83).

754. ———. *Myths and legends of Botswana, Lesotho and Swaziland.* Leiden: Brill, 1985. (Nisaba; 14).

755. ———. *Namibia: land and peoples, myths and fables.* Leiden: Brill, 1981. (Nisaba; 11).

756. Lange, Werner. *Domination and resistance: narrative songs of the Kafa Highlands.* East Lansing: African Studies Center Michigan State University, 1979. (Ethiopian series. monograph; 8). Oral poetry in Kafa, Seka, and Oromo languages.

757. Magel, Emil (tr.) *Folktales from The Gambia: Wolof fictional narratives.* Washington: Three Continents Press, 1981. 2 v.

758. Markowitz, Arthur. *The Rebirth of the ostrich and other stories of the Kalahari Bushmen, told in their manner.* Gaborone: National Museum and Art Gallery, 1971. San tales.

759. Mbiti, John. *Akamba stories.* Oxford: Clarendon Press, 1966. (Oxford library of African literature).

760. Mombeya, Tierno Mouhammadou. *Le Filon du bonheur éternel.* Paris: A. Colin, 1971 (Classiques africains; 10). Tr. by Alfa Ibrahim Sow. Fulani Islamic poetry.

761. Morris, Henry F. *The Heroic recitations of the Bahima of Ankole.* Oxford: Clarendon Press, 1964. (Oxford

library of African literature). Nyankole epic poetry of Uganda.

762. Onyango-Ogutu, Benedict, and Adrian Roscoe (ed.) *Keep my words: Luo oral literature.* Nairobi: EALH, 1974.

763. Rikitu, Mengesha. *Oromo folk-tales for a new generation.* London: [s.n.], 1992.

764. Rodegem, F. M. (ed.). *Anthologie rundi.* Paris: A. Colin, 1973. (Classiques africains; 12). Literature from Burundi.

765. Ruelland, Suzanne, and Jean-Pierre Caprille (eds.). *Contes et récits du Tchad: la femme dans la littérature orale tchadienne.* Paris: Edicef, 1978.

766. Saro-Wiwa, Ken. *The Singing anthill: Ogoni folktales.* Port Harcourt: Saros, 1991. (Saros star; 11).

767. Seydou, Christiabe (ed. et trad.). *Contes et fables des veillées.* Paris: Nubia, 1976. (Kocc-Barma Faal; 1). Peul tales from the Fula people of Mali and Niger.

768. Shack, William A., and Habte-Mariam Marcos (eds.). *Gods and heroes: oral traditions of the Gurage of Ethiopia.* Oxford: Clarendon, 1974. (Oxford library of African literature). Texts in Gurage with English parallel translations.

769. Sidahome, Joseph E. *Stories of the Benin Empire.* London: OUP, 1964. Edo tales from Nigeria.

770. Sissoko, Kabine. *La Prise de Dionkoloni: un épisode de l'épopée bambara* Paris: A. Colin, 1975. (Classiques africains; 16). Coll. by Gérard Dumstre and Lilyan Kesteloot.

771. Smith, P. (ed.). *Le récit populaire au Rwanda.* Paris: A. Colin, 1976. (Classiques africains; 17). Anthology of tales.

772. Stone, Ruth M. *Dried millet breaking: time, words, and song in the Woi epic of the Kpelle.* Bloomington: Indiana University Press, 1988. Epic poetry of Sierra Leone.

773. Svoboda, Terese. *Cleaned the crocodile's teeth: Nuer song.* Greenfield Center, NY: Greenfield Review Press, 1985.

774. Sy, Amadou Abel (ed.). *Seul contre tous.* Dakar: Nouvelles éditions africaines, 1978. Epic Fulbe tales.

General studies

775. Barber, Karin, and P. F. de Moraes Farias (eds.). *Discourse and its disguises: the interpretation of African oral texts.* Birmingham: Centre for West African Studies, University of Birmingham, 1989.

776. Belvaude, Catherine. *Ouverture sur la littérature en Mauritanie: tradition orale, écriture, témoignages.* Paris: L'Harmattan, 1989. (Critiques littéraires).

777. Biebuyck, Daniel P. *Hero and chief: epic literature from the Banyanga, Zaire Republic.* Berkeley: University of California Press, 1978.

778. ———, and C. Kahombo (eds.). *The Mwindo epic from the Banyanga (Congo Republic).* Berkeley: University of California Press, 1969.

779. Camara, Sory. *Gens de la parole: essai sur la condition et le rôle des griots dans la société malinké.* Paris: Mouton, 1976.

780. Chimombo, Steve. *Malawian oral literature: the aesthetics of indigenous arts.* Zomba: University of Malawi, Centre for Social Research, 1988.

781. Cooper, Brenda. *To lay these secrets open: evaluating African writing.* Cape Town: D. Philip, 1992.

782. Crépeau, P. *Parole et sagesse: valeurs sociales dans les proverbes du Rwanda.* Tervuren, Belgium: Musée royal de l'Afrique centrale, 1985.

783. Hale, Thomas A. *Scribe, griot and novelist: narrative interpreters of the Songhay Empire; followed by The Epic of Askia Mohammad recounted by Nouhou Malio.* Gainesville: University of Florida Press, 1990.

784. Johnson, John William. *The Epic of Son-Jara: a West African tradition: analytical study and translation.* Bloomington: Indiana University Press, 1986. Text by Fa-Digi Sisòkò.

785. Julien, Eileen. *African novels and the question of orality.* Bloomington: Indiana University Press, 1992.

786. Krampah, D. E. K. *Mfantse kodzisem ho adzesua.* Accra: Bureau of Ghana Languages, 1993. On Fante literature.

787. Liyong, Taban Lo. *Popular culture of East Africa: oral literature.* Nairobi: Longman Kenya, 1972.

788. Mwiyeriwa, S. *Vernacular literature of Malawi, 1854-1975.* Zomba, Malawi: National Archives, 1978.

789. Nethersole, Reingard (ed.). *Emerging literatures.* Berlin: Lang, 1991 (Jo-Fo; 1). Literatures in South Africa.

790. Ohly, Rajmund. *The Poetics of Herero song: an outline.* Windhoek: University of Namibia, 1991. (Discourse; 1).

791. Okafor, Clement Abiaziem. *The Banished child: a study in Tonga oral literature.* London: Folklore Society, University College, 1983. Tonga folklore of Zambia.

792. Rosário, Lourenço. *A narrativa africana de expressão oral.* Lisbon: ICALP & Angolé, 1989.

Authors

793. Amakali, P. *Kotokeni.* Windhoek: Gamsberg Macmillan, 1990. Novella in oshiNdonga.

794. Amunyela, P. P. *Momasilu guupika.* Ondangwa, Namibia: Elcin Press, 1991. Poetry in Oshiwambo.

795. Apedo-Ameh, Moorhouse. *Le Mariage d'Isaac et de Rebecca: pièce de Kantata.* Lomé: Haho, 1990. (Trad. en français d'une pièce écrite en éwé, 1943). Théâtre.

796. Asras Tasama. *Dahay bahli.* Asmara: Bét mahtam dogala, 1992. Poetry in Tigrinya.

797. Brukh Habtemicael. *Abon tegadalayen/Makhiefu.* Geneva: [s.n.], 1994. Eritrean short stories in Tigrinya.

798. Clark, J. P. (John Pepper), and Okabou Ojobolo (eds.). *The Ozidi saga.* Ibadan: Ibadan University Press; OUP, 1977. Tr. of epic drama of the Ijo people of Nigeria.

799. David, Raúl. *Ekaluko lyakwafeka: brado patriótico.* Luanda: UEA, 1988. (Cadernos Lavra & Oficina; 78). Umbundu poetry of Angola with Portuguese tr.

800. Defa Jemo. *Hursa.* Addis Ababa: Mene Metensa Birhanina Salamit, 1976. Oromo novel.

801. Dhaabaa Wayyeessaa. *Godaannisa.* Addis Ababa: Berhanena Selam Print. Press, 1992. "The Scar." Oromo novel.

802. Dlamini, J. Constance (F). *IMali yimphandze yesono.* Manzini: Macmillan Boleswa, 1987. (Babhali besiSwati). Swazi drama.

803. Eyob Beemnat. *Baga harnat.* Addis Ababa: [s.n.], 1992. (Berhanena Salam Matamiya Bet). Novel.

804. Feqadu Gabraselasé. *Bhil waladena.* Asmara: Ethiopia Studies Centre, 1990. Tigrinya tales.

805. Hampande, Abel H. *Hena wakabetekwa kale munkuta?* Lusaka: Kenneth Kaunda Foundation, 1991. Novel in Tsonga.

806. Hamutenya, Petrina N. *Kombwana okoluvanda.* Windhoek: Gamsberg Macmillan, 1992. OshiKwanyama poetry of Namibia.

807. Hayalom Adhana. *Rahwa dehri seqay.* Addis Ababa: Commercial Press, 1990. Novel in Tigrinya.

808. Kagame, Alexis. *Isokó y' ámäjyambere.* Kabgayi, Rwanda: Ed. morales, 1949-51. 3 v. Poetry in Rwanda.

809. Kapirika, S. (ed.). *Mbeli: dimutango daRugciriku.* Windhoek: Gamsberg Macmillan, 1993. Poetry in Gciriku.

810. Kawere, Edward K. N. *Omuzimu gwa Kasooba.* Kampala: Crane Publishers, 1991. Novel in Ganda.

811. Kumsa Buraayyuu. *Suuraa Abdii.* Addis Ababa: Bole Enterprise, 1993. "Charm of hope." Novel in Oromo.

812. Launshi, Mwila L. *Ukutangila tekufika.* Lusaka: Kenneth Kaunda Foundation, 1991. Bemba novel.

813. Maaramee Harqaa. *Gundoo booree.* Addis Ababa: Bole P. Enterprise, 1993. "Challenges." Novel in Oromo.

814. Maaza Hayla. *Taamerat.* Stockholm: Dogali madabar darasyan, 1991. Poetry in Tigrinya.

815. Maumela, T. N. *Mafangambiti: the story of a bull.* Johannesburg: Ravan Press, 1975. (Staffrider; 28). First pub. in Tshivenda: Pretoria: Schaik, 1975. Novel.

816. Mgabhi, Thoko E. *Nalu lubhamo lwami.* Manzini: Macmillan Boleswa, 1990. Swazi fiction.

817. Mkhonta, Elias A. B. *Ubolibamba lingashoni.* Manzini: Macmillan Boleswa, 1990. Novel in Swazi.

818. Nketia, Joseph Hanson Kwabena. *Ananwoma.* London: OUP, 1951. Drama in Twi.

819. Ntaba, Jolly Max. *Ikakuona litsiro sikata.* Blantyre, Malawi: Dzuka, 1986. (Dzuka writers). Orig. pub.: Lusaka: NECZAM, 1983. Novel in Chewa.

820. ———. *Mwana wa mnzako.* Limbe; Lilongwe: Popular Publications; Likuni Press, 1985. (Malawian writers series; 8). Novel in Chewa.

821. Ntiwane, N. D. *Takitsi.* Manzini: Macmillan Boleswa, 1986. Swazi poetry.

822. Obianim, Sam. *Amegbetoa ou les aventures d'Agbezuge.* Paris: Silex, 1990. Traduit de l'éwé en français par Yawovi Ahiavee Agbéko. (Coll. Lettres du Sud). Contes.

823. Ogot, Grace (F). *The Strange bride.* Nairobi: East African Publishing House, 1989. Tr. from Dholuo. Novel.

824. Sahle Selassie. *Shinega's village: scenes of Ethiopian life.* Berkeley: University of California Press, 1964. Tr. from Chaha by Wolf Leslau. Novel.

825. Sitoe, Bento. *Musongi.* Maputo: AEMO, 1985. Shangaan novel.

826. ———. *Zabela.* Maputo: Cadernos Tempo, 1983. (Collecção "Gostar de Ler"; 7). Shangaan novella.

827. Taha A. Abdi. *Billiqa.* Berlin: [s.n.], 1993. ["The Spark"]. Orig. pub.: Bara, 1982. Poetry in Oromo.

828. Taklay Za-Waldi. *Wag'i qadamot.* Asmara: Adulu, 1992. First pub.: Asmara: Govt. Press, 1956. Tigrinya stories.

829. Tamasgan Tekue. *Dahan kuni enda afras.* Asmara: Bét mahtam Dogala, 1992. Novel in Tigrinya.

830. Tavares, Eugénio. *Mornas: cantigas crioulas.* Lisbon: J. Rodrigues Ca., 1932. Poetry in Creole from Cape Verde.

831. yaAngula, A. D. *Namusheshe.* Ondangwa, Namibia: Elcin Press, 1990. Poetry in Oshidonga.

832. Yeshaq Yoséf. *Henzám feqri Hedat.* Addis Ababa: Negd matamiya bét, 1993. Novel in Tigrinya.

833. Zingani, Willie T. *Njala bwana.* Limbe: Popular Publications, 1984. (Malawian writers series). In Chewa.

ARABIC LITERATURES

OVERVIEW

Bibliographies

834. Altoma, Salih J. *Modern Arabic literature: a bibliography of articles, books, dissertations and translations in English.* Bloomington: Indiana University, 1975.

835. ————. *Modern Arabic poetry in English: a bibliography.* Tangier: Abdelmalek Essadi University, King Fahd School of Translation, 1993.

836. Anderson, Margaret. *Arabic materials in English translation: a bibliography of works from the pre-Islamic period to 1977.* Boston: G.K. Hall, 1980.

837. *Annotated bibliography of old Arabic manuscripts collected in Zanzibar Island.* Zanzibar: Eastern African Centre for Research on Oral Traditions/African National Languages, 1989. 4 v.

838. Hunwick, J. O., and R. S. O'Fahey (eds.). *Arabic literature in Africa.* Leiden: Brill, 1994. (Handbuch der Orientalistik. Erste Abteilung, Nahe und Mittlere Osten; 13).

Anthologies

839. al-Hamdani, Salah. *Mémoire de braise.* Paris: L'Harmattan, 1993. Trad. par E. Brunet. (Collection Poète des cinq continents; 34). Poetry.

840. Norris, H. T. *Saharan myth and saga.* Oxford: Clarendon, 1972. (Oxford library of African literature).

General studies

841. Accad, Evelyne. *Veil of shame: the role of women in the contemporary fiction of North Africa and the Arab world.* Sherbrooke: Naaman, 1978.

842. Allen, Roger. *The Arabic novel: an historical and critical introduction*. Manchester: University of Manchester, 1982. (Journal of semitic studies. Monograph; 4).

843. Badawi, M. M. *A Critical introduction to modern Arabic poetry*. Cambridge: CUP, 1975.

844. ———. *Early Arabic drama*. Cambridge: CUP, 1988.

845. ———. (ed.). *Modern Arabic literature*. Cambridge: CUP, 1992.

846. Harrow, Kenneth W. (ed.). *Islam in African literature*. London: Heinemann, 1991. (Studies in African literature).

847. Hunwick, J. O., and R. S. O'Fahey (eds.). *Arabic literature in Africa*. Leiden: Brill, 1994. (Handbuch der Orientalistik. Erste Abteilung, Nahe und Mittlere Osten; 13).

848. Jayyusi, Salma Khadra. *Trends and movements in modern Arabic poetry*. Leiden: Brill, 1977. 2 v.

849. al-Khozai, Mohamed A. *The Development of early Arabic drama, 1847-1900*. London; New York: Longman, 1983.

850. Moosa, Matti. *The Origins of modern Arabic fiction*. Washington: Three Continents Press, 1983.

851. Moreh, Shmuel. *Live theatre and dramatic literature in the medieval Arab world*. Edinburgh: Edinburgh University Press, 1991.

852. al-Mubarak, K. *Arabic drama: a critical introduction*. Khartoum: Khartoum University Press, 1986.

853. al-Zayyat, Latifah. *Min suwar al-marah fi al-qisas wa-al-riwayat al-Arabiyah*. Cairo: Dar al-Thaqafah al-Jadidah, 1989. On women in Arabic literature.

ALGERIA

Bibliography

854. Bouayed, M. Khammar A. *Dix ans de production intellectuelle en Algérie, 1962-1972: 1.: les écrits en langue arabe.* Alger: Société nationale d'édition et de diffusion, 1974.

Anthologies

855. Belamri, Rabah. *Proverbes et dictons algériens.* Paris: L'Harmattan, 1986. (Histoire et perspectives mediterranéenes). French and Arabic on facing pages.

856. Déjeux, Jean. *Jeunes poètes algériens.* Paris: Saint-Germain-des-Prés, 1981. (Anthologie de la poésie universelle).

857. Galley, Micheline (ed.). *Badr az-zîn et six contes algériens.* Paris: A. Colin, 1971. French and Arabic on facing pages (Classiques africains). Short stories.

858. Lanasri, Ahmed. *Anthologie de la poésie algérienne de langue arabe.* Paris: Publisud, 1992. (Collection littérature).

859. Saadallah, Aboul-Kassem (ed.). *Ashar Jazairiyah.* al-Jazair: al-Muassasah al-Wataniyah lil-Kitab, 1988. Includes poetry chiefly by Muhammad ibn Muhammad ibn Ali (1090-1169) and Ahmad ibn Ammar al-Jazairi (d. 1758).

860. Yalas, Jallul (ed.). *al-Muwashshahat wa-al-azjal.* al-Jazair: al-Sharikah al-Wataniyah, 1975-1982. 3 v. Poetry.

General studies

861. Allalou. *L'Aurore du théâtre algérien (1926-1932).* Oran: Université d'Oran Centre de recherche et d'information documentaire en sciences sociales/humaines, 1982. (Cahiers; 9).

862. Araj, Wasini. *al-Usul al-tarikhiyah lil-waqi'iyah al-ishtirakiyah fi al-adab al-riwai al-Jaziri.* Bayrut: Mu'assasat Dar al-Kitab al-Hadith, 1986.

863. Déjeux, Jean. *Djoh'a: heros de la tradition orale arabo-berbere: hier et aujourd'hui.* Sherbrooke, Quebec: Naaman, 1979. (Études; 18).

864. Muhammad, Ahmad Sayyid. *Dirasat fi al-adab al-Arabi.* Cairo: Dar al-Fikr al-Arabi, 1986. On the poetry of Abd al-Qadir ibn Muhyi al-Din (1807-1883) and Mufdi Zakariya. (Silsilat al-dirasat al-adabiyah wa-al-lughawiyah; 1-2).

865. Nasir, Muhammad. *al-Shir al-Jazairi al-hadith: ittijahatuhu wa-khasaisuhu al-fanniyah, 1925-1975.* Beirut: Dar al-Gharb al-Islami, 1985. On Algerian Arabic poetry.

866. Pantucek, Svetozar. *La Littérature algérienne moderne.* Prague: Oriental Institute in Academia, 1969.

867. Roth, Arlette. *Le théâtre algérien de langue dialectale, 1926-1954.* Paris: F. Maspero, 1967. (Domain maghrebin).

868. Tahar, Ahmed. *La Poésie populaire algérienne (melhun): rythme, mètres et formes.* Alger: Société nationale d'édition et de diffusion, 1975. (Littérature populaire; 1).

869. *Trente ans après: Nouvelles de la guerre d'Algérie.* Paris: Le Monde-Editions et Nouvelles-Nouvelles, 1992. Chiefly on literature in French, but also discusses Arabic writers.

Authors

870. Benhadouga, Abdelhamid. *al-Ashiah al-sabah: qisas.* al-Jazair: al-Sharikah al-Wataniyah, 1981.

871. ———. *al-Jaziyah wa-al-darawish: riwayah.* al-Jazair: al-Muassasah al-Wataniyah lil-Kitab, 1983.

872. ———. *La Fin d'hier.* Alger: SNED, 1980. Tr. de l'arabe par Marcel Bois. Pub. in Arabic in 1974. Novel.

873. ———. *La Mise à nu.* Alger: SNED, 1981. Tr. de l'arabe par Marcel Bois. Pub. in Arabic in 1978. Novel.

874. ———. *Rih al-janub.* al-Jazir: al-Sharikah al-Wataniyah lil-Nashr wa-al-Tawzi, 1976. Novel.

875. ———. *Le Vent du Sud.* Alger: SNED, 1975. Tr. de l'arabe par Marcel Bois. Pub. in Arabic in 1970. Novel.

876. Bin Zayid, Ammar. *al-Naqd al-adabi al-Jazairi al-hadith.* al-Jazair: al-Muassasah al-Wataniyah lil-Kitab, 1990.

877. Boudjedra, Rachid. *Le Demantelement: roman.* Paris: Denoël, 1982. Tr. of *al-Tafakkuk* by the author. Novel.

878. ———. *Le Desordre des choses: roman.* Paris: Denoël, 1991. Orig. pub. as: *Faoudha al-achia.* Alger: Bouchene, 1990.

879. ———. *Greffe: poèmes.* Paris: Denoël, 1984. Orig. pub. as: *Likah.* Alger: Amal, 1983. Tr. de l'arabe par A. Moussali.

880. ———. *La Pluie: roman.* Paris: Denoël, 1987. Tr. of: *Leiliyat imraatin arik.* Novel.

881. ———. *Timimoun: roman.* Paris: Denoël, 1994. Texte français de l'auteur. Tr. de l'arabe.

882. Gafaiti, Hafid. *Boudjedra, ou, La passion de la modernité.* Paris: Denoël, 1987. Interviews.

883. Ouettar, Tahar. *L'As.* Paris: Temps Actuels, 1983. Tr. de l'arabe par Bouzid Kouza. Novel.

884. ———. *Les Martyrs reviennent cette semaine.* Alger: ENAP, 1981. Tr. de l'arabe par Marcel Bois. Short stories.

885. Zakariya, Mufdi. *al-Lahab al-muqadas.* al-Jazair: al-Muassasah al-Wataniyah lil-Kitab, 1991. Poetry.

EGYPT

Bibliographies

886. Abu Haybah, 'Izat Yasin. *al-Makhtutat al-'Aribiyah: faharishua wa-fahrasatuha wa-mawtinuha fi Jumhuriyat Misr al-'Arabiyah.* Cairo: al-Hay'ah al-Misriyah al-'Ammah lil-Kitab, 1989.

887. 'Awad, Ramsis. *Mawsu'at al-masrah al-Misri al-bibliyujrafiyah, 1900-1930.* Cairo: al-Hay'ah al-Misriyah al-'Ammah lil-Kitab, 1983.

888. Goldschmidt, A. *Historical Dictionary of Egypt.* Metuchen, NJ: Scarecrow Press, 1994. 2nd ed. First ed. by Joan Wucher-King, 1984. (African historical dictionaries; 56).

889. Hajrasi, Sa'd Muhammad. *Hafiz wa-Shawqi fi khamsin 'aman (1932-1982).* Cairo: al-Hay'ah al-Misriyah al-'Ammah lil-Kitab, 1982.

890. Kotsarev, N. K. *Pisateli Egipta, XX vek: materialy k biobibliografii.* Moscow: Nauka, 1975.

891. Makar, Ragai N. *Egypt.* Oxford: Clio, 1988. (World bibliographical series; 86).

892. Shalash, 'Ali. *Dalil al-majallat al-adabiyah fi Misr: bibliyujrafiya 'ammah, 1939-1952.* Cairo: al-Hay'ah al-Misriyah al-'Ammah lil-Kitab, 1989.

Anthologies

893. Abdel Wahab, Farouk (ed.). *Modern Egyptian drama: an anthology.* Minneapolis; Chicago: Bibliotheca Islamica, 1974.

894. Booth, Marilyn. *My Grandmother's cactus: stories by Egyptian women.* London: Quartet, 1991. Pub. as: *Stories by Egyptian women.* Austin: University of Texas Press, 1993.

895. el-Gabalawi, Saad. *Modern Egyptian short stories.* Fredericton, New Brunswick: York Press, 1977.

896. ———. (ed.). *Three pioneering Egyptian novels.*
Fredericton: York Press, 1986. Contents: *The Maiden of
Dinshway, and, Eve without Adam* by Mahmud Tahir Haggi;
Ulysses's hallucinations or the like by Saad El-Khadem.

897. Johnson-Davies, Denys (tr.). *Egyptian one-act
plays.* Washington: Three Continents Press, 1981.

898. ———. *Egyptian short stories.* London;
Washington: Heinemann; Three Continents Press, 1978.

899. Manzalaoui, Mahmoud (ed.). *Arabic writing
today: drama.* Cairo: American Research Center in Egypt,
1977.

900. ———. *Arabic writing today: the short story.*
Cairo: American Research Center in Egypt, 1968.

901. Misri, Husayn Shafiq. *Adventures and opinions of
Hadji Darwis and Umm Isma'il: dictations taken by Hisen
Safiq il-Masri.* Copenhagen: Akademisk Forlag, 1980. Ed. by
'Abd is-Salam 'Ali Nur. Folk Arabic tales.

902. Mitchnick, Helen. *Egyptian and Sudanese folk
tales.* Oxford: OUP, 1978.

903. Nakano, Aki'o. *Folktales of lower Egypt.* Tokyo:
Institute for the Study of Languages & Cultures of Asia and
Africa, Tokyo University of Foreign Studies, 1982. (Studia
culturae Islamicae; 18).

904. al-Zayyat, Latifah (ed.). *Kull hadha al-sawt al-
jamil: muktarat qasasiyah li-katibat Arabiyat.* Cairo: Dar Far
al-Marah al-Arabiyah lil-Nashr, 1994. Short stories.

General studies

905. 'Abd al-Qadir, Faruq. *Awraq ukra min al-ramad
wa-al-jamr: mutaba'at Misriyah wa-'Arabiyah 1986-1989.*
Cairo: Mu'assasat al-'Urubah, 1990.

906. Al-Ali, N. S. *Gender writing/writing gender: the
representation of women in a selection of modern Egyptian
literature.* Cairo: American University in Cairo Press, 1994.

907. Allen, Roger. *A Study of Hadith Isa ibn Hisham: Muhammad al-Muwaylihi's view of Egyptian society during the British occupation.* Albany, NY: State University of New York Press, 1974.

908. 'Aqqad, 'Abbas Mahmu, et al. *Fi al-Siyasah wa-al-Adab wa-al-Fann.* Cairo: Muda Grafik lil-Nashr, 1991.

909. 'Awad, Luwis. *Dirasat adabiyah.* Cairo: Dar al-Mustaqbal al'Arabi, 1989.

910. Badawi, M. M. *Modern Arabic drama in Egypt.* Cambridge: CUP, 1988.

911. Barakat, Halim. *Visions of social reality in the contemporary Arab novel.* Washington: Center for Contemporary Arab Studies, Georgetown University, 1977.

912. Booth, Marilyn. *Bayram al-Tunisi's Egypt: social criticism and narrative strategies.* Exeter: Ithaca Press for St. Antony's College, Oxford, 1990.

913. Brugman, J. *An Introduction to the history of modern Arabic literature in Egypt.* Leiden: Brill, 1984. (Studies in Arabic literature; v. 10).

914. Cachia, Pierre. *An Overview of modern Arabic literature.* Edinburgh: Edinburgh University Press, 1990.

915. ———. *Popular narrative ballads of modern Egypt.* Oxford: Clarendon, 1989.

916. Dayf, Shawqi. *'Asr al-duwal wa-al-imarat: Misr.* Cairo: Dar al-Ma'arif, 1990. (Tarikh al-adab al-Arabi; 7).

917. El Beheiry, Kawsar Abdel Salam. *L'influence de la littérature française sur le roman arabe.* Sherbrooke: Namaan, 1980. (Collection études; 23).

918. El-Khadem, Saad. *History of the Egyptian novel: its rise and early beginning.* Fredericton: York Press, 1985.

919. Fu'ad, Ni'mat Ahmad. *al-Nil fi aladab al-sha'bi.* Cairo: al-Hay'ah al-Misriyah al'Ammah lil-Kitab, 1973. (al-Maktabah al-thaqafiyah; 292). The River Nile in literature.

920. Hegazy, Samir. *Littérature et société en Egypte: de la guerre de 1967 à celle de 1973.* Alger: Entreprise nationale du livre, 1986. On Arabic fiction.

921. Jad, Ali B. *Form and technique in the Egyptian novel, 1912-1971.* London: Ithaca Press, 1983.

922. Khouri, Mounah. *Poetry and the making of modern Egypt.* Leiden: Brill, 1971. (Studies in Arabic literature; v. 1).

923. al-Khozai, Mohamed A. *The Development of early Arabic drama, 1847-1900.* London; New York: Longman, 1983.

924. Kilpatrick, Hilary. *The Modern Egyptian novel: a study in social criticism.* London: Ithaca Press, 1974. (St. Anthony's Middle East monographs; 1).

925. Mehrez, Samia. *Egyptian writers between history and fiction: essays on Naguib Mahfouz, Sonallah Ibrahim, and Gamal al-Ghitani.* Cairo: American University in Cairo Press, 1994.

926. Mikhail, Mona N. *Studies in the short fiction of Mahfouz and Idris.* New York: New York University Press, 1992. (New York University studies in Near Eastern civilization; 16).

927. Moussa-Mahmoud, Fatma. *The Arabic novel in Egypt, 1914-1970.* Cairo: Egyptian General Book Organ., 1973.

928. *Qira'at al-nass bayn al-nazariyya wa'l-tatbiq.* Tunis: Institut National des Sciences de l'Education, 1990. Articles on Egyptian and Sudanese literature.

929. Sakkut, Hamdi. *Abbas Mahmud al-Aqqad.* Cairo: American University in Cairo Press, 1983. 2 v. (Leaders in contemporary Egyptian literature series; 5).

930. ———. *Dirasat fi al-adab wa-al-naqd.* Cairo: Maktabat al-Anjilu al-Misriyah, 1990. Arabic-Western literature compared.

931. ———. *The Egyptian novel and its main trends from 1913 to 1952.* Cairo: American University in Cairo Press, 1971.

932. Samaan, Angele B. *The Egyptian novel.* New York; London: Longman, 1984.

933. Semah, David. *Four Egyptian literary critics.* Leiden: Brill, 1974.

934. Slyomovics, Susan. *The Merchant of art: an Egyptian Hilali oral epic poet in performance.* Berkeley: University of California Press, 1987. (University of California publications in modern philology; 120).

935. Stagh, Marina. *The Limits of freedom of speech: prose literature and prose writers in Egypt under Nasser and Sadat.* Stockholm: Almqvist & Wiksell, 1993. (Acta universitatis Stockholmiensis. Stockholm oriental studies; 14).

936. Tomiche, Nada. *Histoire de la littérature romanesque de l'Egypte moderne.* Paris: G.-P. Maisoneuve et Larose, 1981.

937. Vial, Charles. *Le Personnage de la femme dans le roman et la nouvelle en Egypte de 1914 à 1960.* Damas: Institut français, 1979.

938. Ya'qub, Lusi. *al-Usrah al-Taymuriyah wa-al-adab al'Arabi.* Cairo: Maktabat al-Adab, 1993.

Authors

939. 'Abd al-Majid, Ahmad. *Hamasat.* [Cairo]: Dar al-marifat, 1961. Poetry.

940. 'Abd al-Rahman, 'A'ishah (F). *'Ala' l-jisr.* Cairo: 1967. "On the bridge." Autobiography.

941. 'Abd al-Sabur, Salah. *Murder in Baghdad*. Leiden: Brill, 1972. Tr. by K. I. Samaan. Orig. pub. as: *Ma'sat al-Hallaj*. Cairo, 1965. Drama.

942. ———. *The Princess waits*. Cairo: American University in Cairo, 1975. Tr. by S. Megally. Orig. pub. as: *al-Amirah tantazir*. Cairo, 1971. Drama.

943. Bakr, Salwa (F). *Ajin al-fallahah*. Cairo: Sina li-l-Nashr, 1992. "Monkey business." Short stories.

944. ———. *'An al-ruh allati suriqat tadrijiyyan*. Cairo: Masriyyah li-l-Nashr wa-l-Tawzi, 1989. "About the soul that was spirited away." Short stories.

945. ———. *The Golden chariot does not ascend to heaven*. Reading: Garnet, 1994. Orig. pub.: *Al-'arabah al-dhahabiyyah la tas'ad ila al-sama* (Cairo: Sina li-l-Nashr, 1991). Novel.

946. ———. *Such a beautiful voice*. Cairo: General Egyptian Book Organization, 1992. (Contemporary Arabic literature; 35). Orig. pub. as: *Wasf al-bulbul*. Novel.

947. ———. *The Wiles of men and other stories*. London; Austin: Quartet; University of Texas Press, 1992. Tr. by D. Johnson-Davies.

948. ———. *Zinat fi janazat al-Ra'is*. Cairo: [Privately printed], 1986. "Zinat at the President's funeral." Short stories.

949. Bindari, Sami. *The House of power*. Boston: Houghton Miflin, 1980. Tr. by S. Bindari and Mona St. Leger. Orig. pub. as: *al-Sarayah*. Novel.

950. El-Khadem, Saad. *Avante-garde Egyptian fiction: the Ulysees trilogy*. Fredericton: York, 1988. Tr. by Saad El-Gabalawy.

951. ———. *Wings of lead: a modern Egyptian novella*. Fredericton: York, 1994. Tr. by the author.

952. Faraj, Alfrid. *The Caravan or Ali Janah al-Tabrizi and his servant Quffa.* Cairo: General Egyptian Book Organization, 1989. Tr. by Rasheed El-Enany. Fiction.

953. Ghanem, Fathy. *The Man who lost his shadow: a novel in four books.* Boston; London: Houghton Miflin; Chapman Hall, 1966. Tr. by D. Stewart. (Repr.: London; Washington: Heinemann, Three Continents Press, 1980). Novel.

954. al-Gitani, Gamâl. *Ithâf al-zamân bi-hikaâyat galbay al-sultân.* Cairo: Dâr al-Mustaqbal al-Arabî, 1984. Short stories.

955. ———. *Zayni barakat.* London: Penguin, 1990. Tr. by Farouk Abdel Wahab. Novel.

956. al-Hakim, Tawfiq. *The Fate of a cockroach and other plays.* London: Heinemann, 1973. Tr. by D. Johnson-Davies. (AWS; 117).

957. ———. *Isis.* [Cairo]: Organisation égyptienne générale du livre, 1975. Tr. d'Edouard Gemayel. Drama.

958. ———. *Maze of justice.* London: Harvill Press, 1947. Tr. by A. S. Eban. Orig. pub. as: *Yawmiyyât nâ'ib fi al-aryâf.* Cairo, 1937. Also pub.: London: Saqi, 1989, and Austin: University of Texas Press, 1989. Novel.

959. ———. *Planet Earth.* [Cairo]: General Egyptian Book Organization, 1985. Tr. of: *Hadith ma'a al-kawkab, and, al-Dunya riwayah hazliyah.* Drama.

960. ———. *Plays, prefaces and postscripts of Tawfiq al-Hakim.* Washington: Three Continents Press, 1984. 2 v. Tr. by W. M. Hutchins. (UNESCO collection of representative works. Contemporary Arabic authors series). Drama.

961. ———. *The Prison of life: an autobiographical essay.* [Cairo]: American University in Cairo Press, 1992. Tr. of: *Sijn al-umr.*

962. ———. *Return of the spirit: Tawfiq al-Hakim's classic novel of the 1919 revolution.* Washington: Three Continents Press, 1990. Tr. by W. M. Hutchins.

963. ———. *The Tree climber.* London: OUP, 1966. Tr. by D. Johnson-Davies. Orig. pub. as: *Yatali' al-shajarah.* Cairo, 1962. Drama.

964. Fontaine, Jean. *Mort-resurrection: une lecture de Tawfiq al-Hakim.* Tunis: Éditions Bouslama, 1973.

965. Long, Richard. *Tawfiq al-Hakim, playwright of Egypt.* London: Ithaca Press, 1979.

966. Starkey, Paul. *From the ivory tower: a critical study of Tawfiq al-Hakim.* London: Ithaca Press, 1987. (St. Anthony's Middle East monographs; 19).

967. Haqqi, Yahya, *Good morning! and other stories.* Washington: Three Continents Press, 1987.

968. Cooke, Miriam. *The Anatomy of an Egyptian intellectual: Yahya Haqqi.* Washington: Three Continents Press, 1984.

969. Hatatah, Sarif. *The Eye with an iron lid.* London: Onyx Press, 1982. 2 v. Orig. pub.: *yn dhat al-jafn al-madiniyah* (v. 1, 1974) and *Janahan lil-rih* (v. 2, 1976). Novel.

970. ———. *The Net.* London: Zed Press, 1986. Orig. pub. as: *Al-Shabaka.* 1982. Novel.

971. Ibrahim, Sun' Allah. *The Smell of it, and other stories.* London: Heinemann, 1971. Tr. by D. Johnson-Davies.

972. Idris, Yusuf. *The Cheapest night and other stories.* London; Washington: Heinemann; Three Continents Press, 1978. Tr. by W. Wassef. (UNESCO collection of representative works. Contemporary Arab authors series).

973. ———. *In the eye of the beholder: tales of Egyptian life from the writings of Yusuf Idris.* Minneapolis;

Chicago: Bibliotheca Islamica, 1978. Ed. by Roger Allen. (Studies in Middle Eastern literatures; 10). Short stories.

974. ———. *Rings of burnished brass.* London; Washington: Heinemann; Three Continents Press, 1984. Tr. by Catherine Cobham. (Arab authors; 21). Short stories.

975. Kurpershoek, P. M. *The Short stories of Yusuf Idris, a modern Egyptian author.* Leiden: Brill, 1981. (Studies in Arabic literatures; 7).

976. Mahfuz, Naguib. *'Abath al-aqdâr.* Cairo: Maktabat Misr, 1939. Novel.

977. ———. *Adrift on the Nile.* New York: Doubleday, 1994. Tr. by Frances Liadet. First pub. as: *Tharthara fawq al-Nil.* Cairo: Misr, 1966. Novel.

978. ———. *Autumn quail.* New York; London: Doubleday; Saqi, 1990. First pub. as: *al-Summan wa-al-kharif.* Tr. by Roger Allen. Also pub.: Cairo: American University of Cairo Press, 1985. Novel.

979. ———. *The Beggar.* Cairo; New York: American University in Cairo Press; Doubleday, 1986. First pub. as: *Shahhadh.* Tr. by K. Henry and N. Khales Naili al-Warraki.

980. ———. *The Beginning and the end.* Cairo: American University in Cairo Press, 1985. Tr. by R. Hanna Awad. Orig. pub. as: *Bidaya wa-nihaya.* Cairo, 1945. Novel.

981. ———. *Children of Gebalawi.* London; Washington: Heinemann; Three Continents Press, 1981. Tr. by Philip Steward. (Arab authors; 15). Orig. pub. as: *Awlad haratina.* Beirut: Dar al-Adab, 1967. Novel.

982. ———. *The Day the leader was killed.* Cairo: General Egyptian Book Organization, 1989. Orig. pub. as: *Yawm qutila al-za'im.* Cairo: Misr, 1985. Novel.

983. ———. *God's world: an anthology of short stories.* Minneapolis: Bibliotheca Islamica, 1973. Tr. by Akef Abadir and Roger Allen. (Studies in Middle Eastern literatures; 2).

984. ———. *The Harafish*. Cairo; New York: American University in Cairo Press; Doubleday, 1994. Tr. by Catherine Cobham. Orig. pub. as: *Malhamat al-harafish*. Cairo: Misr, 1977. Novel.

985. ———. *The Journey of ibn Fattouma*. Cairo; London: American University in Cairo; Doubleday, 1992. Tr. of: *Rihlat ibn Fattuma*. Novel.

986. ———. *Midaq alley*. London; Washington: Heinemann; Three Continents Press, 1975. Tr. by T. Le Gassick. (Arab authors; 2). Orig. pub. as: *Zuqaq al-Midaqq*. Cairo: Misr, 1947. Novel.

987. ———. *Miramar*. London; Cairo: Heinemann; American University in Cairo Press, 1978. Tr. by F. Mousa-Mahmoud; ed. by Maged el Kommos and J. Rodenbeck. (Arab authors; 9; AWS; 197). Orig. pub.: *Miramar*. Cairo: Misr, 1967. Novel.

988. ———. *Mirrors*. Minneapolis: Bibliotheca Islamica, 1977. Tr. by Roger Allen. (Studies in Middle Eastern literatures; 8). Orig. pub. as: *Al-maraya*. Cairo: Misr, 1972. Novel.

989. ———. *One-act plays*. Cairo: General Egyptian Book Organization, 1989. Tr. by Nehad Seleiha.

990. ———. *Palace of desire*. New York; London: Doubleday, 1991. Tr. by W. M. Hutchins. (Part 2 of the Cairo Trilogy, *Al-thulathiya*). Orig. pub. as: *Qasr al-shawq*. Cairo: Misr, 1957. Novel.

991. ———. *Palace walk*. New York; London: Doubleday, 1990. Tr. by W. M. Hutchins. (Part 1 of the Cairo Trilogy, *Al-thulathiya*). Orig. pub. as: *Bayn al-Qasrayn*. Cairo: Misr, 1956. Novel.

992. ———. *Sugar street*. New York; London: Doubleday, 1992. Tr. by W. M. Hutchins. (Part 3 of the Cairo Trilogy, *Al-thulathiya*). Orig. pub. as: *Al-sukkariya*. Cairo: Misr, 1957. Novel.

993. ———. *The Thief and the dogs*. New York: Doubleday, 1989. Tr. by M. M. Badawi and Trevor Le Gassick. Orig. pub. as: *al-Liss wa al kilab*. Novel.

994. ———. *Wedding song*. Cairo; New York: American University in Cairo Press; Doubleday, 1984. Tr. by O. E. Kenny; ed. by M. Saad el Din and J. Rodenbeck. (Arab authors; 15). Orig. pub. as: *Afrah al-Qubbah*. Cairo: Misr, 1981. Novel.

995. Badr, ʿAbd al-Mushin Taha. *Najib Mahfuz: al-ruʾya wa-al-adat*. Cairo: Dar al-Thaqafa li-al-tibaʿa, 1978.

996. Beard, Michael, and Adnan Haydar (eds.). *Naguib Mahfouz: from regional fame to global recognition*. Syracuse, NY: Syracuse University Press, 1993.

997. el-Enany, Rasheed. *Naguib Mahfouz: the pursuit of meaning*. New York: Routledge, 1993.

998. Gordon, H. *Naguib Mahfouz's Egypt: existential themes in his writings*. New York: Greenwood, 1990.

999. Herdeck, Donald E. (ed.). *Three dynamite authors: Derek Walcott (Nobel 1992), Naguib Mahfouz (Nobel 1988), Wole Soyinka (Nobel 1986)*. Colorado Springs: Three Continents Press, 1994.

1000. Najmi, Kamal. *Najib Mahfuz wa-asda' mu'asirih*. Cairo: Dar al-Hilal, 1990.

1001. Peled, Mattiyahu. *Religion, my own: the literary works of Najib Mahfuz*. New Brunswick; London: Transaction Books, 1983.

1002. Somekh, Sasson. *The Changing rhythm: a study of Najib Mahfuz's novels*. Leiden: Brill, 1973.

1003. al-Zayyat, Latifah. *Najib Mahfuz, al-surah wa-al-mithal: maqalat naqdiyah*. Cairo: Jaridat al-Ahali, 1989. (Kitab al-Ahali; 22).

1004. al-Mazini, Ibrahim 'Abd al-Qadir. *Al-Mazini's Egypt*. Washington: Three Continents Press, 1983. Tr. by W.

M. Hutchins. (UNESCO collection of representative works, Arabic series). Short stories and novel.

1005.   Rifaat, Alifah. *Distant view of a minaret and other stories*. London: Quartet, 1983. Tr. by D. Johnson-Davies. Also pub.: London: Heinemann, 1985. Short stories.

1006.   al-Sadawi, Nawal (F). *The Circling song*. London: Zed, 1989. Orig. pub. as: *Ughniyat al-atfal al-da'iriyah*. Novel.

1007.   ———. *Death of an ex-minister*. London: Methuen, 1987. Orig. pub. as: *Mawt mali al-wazir sabiqan*. Short stories.

1008.   ———. *The Fall of the Imam*. London: Methuen, 1988. Orig. pub. as: *Suqut al-imam*. Cairo, 1988. Novel.

1009.   ———. *God dies by the Nile*. London: Zed, 1985. Orig. pub. as: *Mawt al-rajul al-wahid ala' l-ard*. Cairo, 1974. Novel.

1010.   ———. *The Innocence of the Devil*. Berkeley; London: University of California Press; Methuen, 1994. First pub. as: *Jannat wa-Iblis*. Tr. by Sherif Hetata. Novel.

1011.   ———. *Memoirs from the women's prison*. London: Zed, 1986. Orig. pub. as: *Mudhakkirati fi sijn al-nisa*. Cairo: Dar al-Mustaqbal al-Arabi, 1982. Autobiography.

1012.   ———. *Memoirs of a woman doctor: a novel*. London: Saqi Books, 1988. First pub. as: *Mudhakkirat tabibah*.

1013.   ———. *She has no place in paradise*. London: Methuen, 1987. Tr. by Shirley Eber. Novel.

1014.   ———. *Two women in one*. London: Al Saqi, 1985. Orig. pub. as: *Imra' atan fi imra'a*. Beirut, 1975). Tr. by O. Nusairi and J. Gough. Novel.

1015.   ———. *The Well of life; and, The Thread: two short novels*. London: Lime Tree, 1993.

1016. ————. *Woman at point zero.* London: Zed, 1983. Orig. pub. as: *Imra'ah 'ind nuqtat al-sifr.* Cairo, 1975. Tr. into French as: *Ferdaous: une voix à l'enfer.* Paris, 1981. Novel.

1017. Tarabishi, Georges. *Woman against her sex: a critique of Nawal el-Saadawi, with a reply by Nawal el-Saadawi.* London: Saqi, 1988.

1018. Taha Hussein. *The Call of the curlew.* Leiden: Brill, 1980. Tr. by A. B. As-Safi. (Arabic translations series of the Journal of Arabic literature; v. 5). Novel.

1019. ————. *The Dreams of Scheherazade.* Cairo: General Egyptian Book Organization, 1974. Tr. by M. Wahba. Novel.

1020. ————. *An Egyptian childhood.* Washington: Three Continents Press, 1981. Tr. by E. H. Paxton. First pub.: London, 1932. (Arab authors; 16). Autobiography (v. 1).

1021. ————. *A Passage to France.* Leiden: Brill, 1976. Tr. by K. Cragg. (Arabic translations series of the Journal of Arabic literature; v. 4). Autobiography (v. 3).

1022. ————. *The Stream of days: a student at the Azhar.* Cairo: Al-Maaref, 1943. Tr. by Hilary Wayment. Rev. ed. pub.: London, 1948. Autobiography (v. 2).

1023. ————. *The Sufferers: stories and polemics.* Cairo: American University in Cairo Press, 1993. (Modern Arabic writing). Tr. by Mona El-Zayyat.

1024. Cachia, Pierre. *Taha Husayn: his place in the Egyptian literary renaissance.* London: Luzac, 1956.

1025. Jones, Marsden, and Hamdi Sakkut. *Taha Hussein.* Cairo: American University in Cairo Press, 1975. (Leaders in contemporary Egyptian literature; 1).

1026. Malti-Douglas, Fedwa. *Blindness and autobiography: "Al-Ayyam" of Taha Husayn.* Princeton: Princeton University Press, 1988.

1027. Taymur, Mahmud. *al-Amal al-kamilah*. Cairo: Dar Alif, 1990. 2 v. Collected works.

1028. ———. *The Call of the unknown*. Beirut: Khayats, 1964. (Khayats Oriental translations; 1). Tr. by Hume Horan. Fiction.

1029. ———. *Tales from Egyptian life*. Cairo: Resistance Bookshop, 1960. Short stories.

1030. De Moor, Ed C. M. *Un Oiseau en cage: le discours littéraire de Muhammad Taymûr (1892-1921)*. Amsterdam; Atlanta: Rodopi, 1991.

1031. Zayyat, Anayat. *al-Hubbu wa al-Samt: rawayat misriyah*. Cairo: Wizarat al-thaqafah, 1967. Novel.

1032. al-Zayyat, Latifah (F). *Al-Bab al-maftuh*. Cairo: Maktabat al-Anjlu-al-Misriyya, 1960. "The Open door." Novel.

LIBYA

Anthologies

1033. Abdelkafi, Mohamed. *One hundred Arabic proverbs from Libya*. London: Vernon & Yate, 1968.

1034. Hashimi, Bashir (ed.). *Ara fi kitabat jadidah*. Tripoli: al-Munshaah al-Ammah, 1984. (Kitabat jadidah; 14).

1035. Misrati, Ali Mustafa. *Juha fi Libiya: dirasah fi al-adab al-shabi*. Tripoli: al-Munsha'ah al-Ammah, 1985. Folklore.

1036. Shalabi, Salim Salim. *Uyun al-nas wa-mi'at al-tabir*. Tripoli: al-Munsha'ah al-Ammah, 1984. Proverbs.

General studies

1037. Afifi, Muhammad al-Sadiq. *al-Itti jahat al-wataniyah fi al-shir al-Libi*. Beirut: Dar al-Kashshaf, 1969. On poetry.

1038. Faysal, Samar Ruhi. *Dirasat fi al-riwayah al-Libiyah*. Tripoli: al-Munsha'ah al-Ammah, 1983. On Libyan fiction.

1039. ———. *Nuhud al-riwayah al-Arabiyah al-Libiyah: dirsah*. Damascus: Ittihad al-Kuttab al-Arab, 1990. On Libyan fiction.

1040. Hajiri, Taha. *al-Hayat al-adabiyah fi Libiya: al-shir*. [Cairo]: High Institute of Arab Studies, 1962. On Libyan poetry.

1041. Wurayyith, Muhammad Ahmad. *A-indakum naba'?* Tripoli: al-Munsha'ah al-Ammah, 1984. Essays.

Authors

1042. 'Abbar, Salim. *Tajalliyat al-murrah: qisas qasirah*. Tripoli: al-Munsha'ah al-Ammah, 1984. Short stories.

1043. Abu Ruqaybah, 'Abd al-Sâlim. *al-Thaman*. Tripoli: al-Munsha'ah al-Ammah, 1984. Short stories.

1044. Bashti, Fawzi al-Tahir. *Fajar fi 'uyun al-shuhada': qisas qasirah*. Tripoli: al-Munsha'ah al-Ammah, 1983. Stories.

1045. Dallal, 'Abd al-Basit. *Taqasim 'ala watar al-ghurbah: shi'r*. Tripoli: al-Munsha'ah al-Ammah, 1984. Poetry.

1046. Faqih, Ahmad Ibrahim. *al-Ghazalat: masrahiyah*. Tripoli: al-Munsha'ah al-Ammah, 1984. Drama.

1047. ———. *al-Sahra' wa-ashjar al-naft*. Libya & Tunis: al-Dar al-'Arabiyah lil-Kitab, 1979. Essays.

1048. ———. *Ikhtafat al-nujum fa-ayna inti?* Tripoli: al-Munsha'ah al-Ammah, 1984. Short stories.

1049. Haji, Muhammad Salim. *Mushahadat fi bahr al-dam: qisas qasirah*. Tripoli: al-Munsha'ah al-Ammah, 1984. Stories.

1050. Hindawi, Salim. *al-Afwah: qisas qasirah.* Tripoli: al-Munsha'ah al-Ammah, 1984. Short stories.

1051. Kashlaf, Sulayman. *al-'Ashiq wa-al-ma'shuq.* Tripoli: al-Munsha'ah al-Ammah, 1983. Novel.

1052. ———. *al-Hubb, al-mawt, rajul wa-imra'ah.* Tripoli: al-Munsha'ah al-Ammah, 1984. Novel.

1053. Khafaji, Muhammad Abd al-Munim. *Qissat al-adab fi Libiya al-Arabiyah min al-fath al-Islami ila al-yawm.* Benghazi: Dar al-Kitab al-Libi, 1968. 3 v.

1054. Kharm, 'Ali. *al-Ju' fi mawasim al-hasad: shi'r.* Tripoli: al-Munsha'ah al-Ammah, 1984. Poetry.

1055. Misallati, Muhammad. *al-Dawa'ir: qisas qasirah.* Tripoli: al-Munsha'ah al-Ammah, 1983. Short stories.

1056. ———. *Dajij.* Tripoli: al-Dar al-'Arabiyah lil-Kitab, 1977. Short stories.

1057. Mustafa, Khalifah. *al-Qadiyah: qisas qasirah.* Tripoli: al-Munsha'ah al-Ammah, 1985. Short stories.

1058. Nasr, Ahmad. *Wamid fi jidar al-layl: riwayah Libiyah.* Tripoli: al-Munsha'ah al-Ammah, 1984. Novel.

1059. Qadhdhafi, 'Abd al-Basit 'Abd al-Samad. *al-Akhras: masra.hiyah.* Tripoli: al-Munsha'ah al-Ammah, 1984. Drama.

1060. ———. *Thawrat al-fallahin: masrahiyah.* Tripoli: al-Munsha'ah al-Ammah, 1983. Drama.

1061. Qiyadi, Sharifah. *Hadir al-shifah al-raqiqah.* Tripoli: al-Munsha'ah al-Ammah, 1983. Novel.

1062. 'Uwayti, Nadirah. *al-Mar'ah allati istan taqat al-tabiah.* Tripoli: al-Munsha'ah al-Ammah, 1983. Novel.

MAURITANIA

Anthologies

1063. Martin-Granel, Nicolas, Idoumou Ould Mohammed Lemine, and Georges Voisset. *Guide de littérature mauritanienne: une anthologie methodique*. Paris: L'Harmattan, 1992. (Collection critiques littératures).

1064. Norris, H. T. *Shinqiti folk literature and song*. Oxford: Clarendon, 1968. (Oxford library of African literature).

1065. Tauzin, Aline (ed.). *Contes arabes de Mauritanie*. Paris: Karthala, 1993. (Coll. Hommes et sociétés).

General studies

1066. Baduel, P. R. (ed.). *Mauritanie: entre arabite et africanite*. Aix-en-Provence: Edisud, 1990. (Revue du monde musulman et de la Mediterranée; 54).

1067. Belvaude, Catherine. *Ouverture sur la littérature en Mauritanie: tradition orale, écriture, témoignages*. Paris: L'Harmattan, 1989. (Critiques littéraires).

1068. Bin Hamid, al-Mukhtar. *Hayat Muritaniya*. Tunis: al-Dar al-'Arabiyah lil-Kitab, 1990. 2 v.

MOROCCO

Bibliographies

1069. Tankul, Abd al-Rahman. *al-Adab al-Maghribi al-hadith: bibliyughrafiya shamilah*. al-Dar al-Bayda: Manshurat "al-Jamiah," 1984. (al-Silsilah al-bibliyughrafiya; 2).

1070. Tazi, Abd al-Salam. *al-Udaba al-Magharibah al-mu'asirun: dirasah bibliyughrafiyah ihsaiyah*. al-Dar al-Bayda: Manshurat "al-Jamiah," 1983. (al-Silsilah al-bibliyughrafiya; 1).

Anthologies

1071. Ben Jelloun, Tahar. *La Memoire future: anthologie de la nouvelle poésie du Maroc*. Paris: F. Maspero, 1976.

1072. al-Damsiri, Muhammad. *al-Rayis al-Hajj Muhammad al-Damsiri: shahadat wa-qasa'id wa-mukhtarah min aghanih*. al-Ribat: Matba'at al-Ma'arif al-Jadidah, 1993. 2 v. Tamazight songs in Arabic with commentary.

1073. Lakhdar, Mohammed. *La vie littéraire au Maroc sous la dynastie alawide (1075-1311=1664-1894)*. Rabat: Editions techniques nord-africaines, 1971.

1074. Moqadem, Hamid. *Contes Adba du Maroc*. Paris: Conseil International de la Langue Français, 1991. Tales.

1075. Touimi, Mohammad Benjelloun, Adbelkebir Khatibi, and Mohammed Kably (eds.) *Écrivains marocains du protectorat à 1965: anthologie*. Paris: Sinbad, 1974 (Bibliothèque arabe).

General studies

1076. Binjallun, al-Arabi. *Tayyar al-way fi al-adab al-Maghribi al-mu asir*. Dimashq: Ittihad al-Kuttab, 1983.

1077. Ghallab, 'Abd al-Karim. *Alam Shair al-Hamra*. al-Dar al-Bayda: Dar al-Thaqafah, 1982. Biography.

1078. Hamid, Lahmidani. *Fi' l-tanzir wa' l-mumarasah: dirasat fi' l-riwayah al-Maghribiyyah*. Al-Dar al-Bayda: Uyun al-Maqalat, 1986.

1079. Nur al-Din, Saduq. *Hudud al-nass al-adabi: dirasah fi al-tanzir wa-al-ibda*. al-Dar al-Bayda: Dar al-Thaqafah, 1984. (Silsilat al-dirasat al-naqdiyah; 2).

Authors

1080. Abu Zayd, Layla (F). *'Am al-fil*. Rabat: Matbaat al-Maarif al-Jadidah, 1983. Fiction.

1081. Amran Al-Maleh, E. *Al Majra attabit.* Casablanca: Ed. le Fennec, 1993.

1082. Benjelloun, Ahmed. *Kheïra.* Rabat: Okad, 1992. Trad. de Jean-Pierre Koffel. Novel.

1083. Berrada, M. *Addawè al-harib.* Casablanca: Ed. le Fennec, 1993.

1084. Choukri, Mohammed. *For Bread alone.* London: P. Owen, 1973. Tr. by P. Bowles. Autobiographical novel.

1085. Ghallab, 'Abd al-Karim. *Le Passé enterré: roman.* Morocco: Okad, 1988. Tr. of: *Dafanna al-madi* (1966).

1086. ———. *Wa-akhrajaha min al-jannah.* Tunis: al-Dar al-Arabiyah lil-kitab, 1977. Short stories.

1087. Id Balkassm, Hassan. *Imarayin: majmu'ah qisaasiyah amajighiyah.* al-Ribat: Matba'at al-Ma'arif al-Jadidah, 1992. Fiction.

1088. Mrabet, Mohammed. *The Lemon.* London: Peter Owen, 1969. Tr. by Paul Bowles. Novel.

1089. ———. *Look and move on.* London: Peter Owen, 1989. Tr. by Paul Bowles. Novel.

1090. ———. *Love with a few hairs.* London: Peter Owen, 1967. Tr. by Paul Bowles. Novel.

1091. Zifzaf, Muhammad. *al-Aqwa: qisas.* Dimashq: Ittihad al-Kuttab al-Arab, 1978. Short stories.

1092. ———. *al-Hayy al-khalfi.* Rabat: Alam al-Sihafah, 1992.

SUDAN

Bibliography

1093. Daghir, Yusuf As'ad. *al-Usul al'Arabiyah lil-dirasat al-Sudaniyah.* Beirut: Librairie orientale, 1968. Sudanese bibliography, Arabic sources, 1875-1967.

Anthologies

1094. Ahmed, Osman Hassan (ed.). *Sixteen Sudanese short stories*. Washington: Office of the Cultural Counsellor, Embassy of Sudan, 1981. (Sudanese publications; 6).

1095. ———, and Constance E. Berkley (eds.). *Anthology of modern Sudanese poetry*. Washington: Office of the Cultural Counsellor, Embassy of Sudan, 1983. (Sudan publications; 10).

1096. Hillelson, Samuel. *Sudan Arabic texts, with translation and glossary*. Cambridge: CUP, 1935.

1097. Mitchnick, Helen. *Egyptian and Sudanese folk tales*. Oxford: OUP, 1978.

1098. Tinay, Fath al-Rahman Hasan (ed.). *Mukhtarat min al-shir al-Sudani al muasir*. Dubai: F. Tinay, 1990. Poetry.

General studies

1099. Abdul-Hai, Muhammad. *Conflict and identity: the cultural poetics of contemporary Sudanese poetry*. Khartoum: Khartoum University Press, 1976.

1100. Abu Sad, Ahmad. *al-Shir wa-l-shuara fi al-Sudan, 1900-1958*. Beirut: Dar Al-Maarif, 1959. On poetry.

1101. Ahmad, Abd al-Hamid Muhammad (ed.). *al-Shir wa-al-mujtama fi al-Sudan: qiraat fi al-shir al-Sudani al-hadith wa-al-muasir*. al-Khartum: Dar al-Way, 1987. On poetry.

1102. Hassangeltenay, F. *River Nile in Sudanese poetry*. Khartoum: Al Dar Al Soudania, 1986.

1103. Hurriez, Sayyid H. *Ja'aliyyin folktales: an interplay of African, Arabian and Islamic elements*. Bloomington: Indiana University Press, 1977. (Indiana University publics. African series; 8).

1104. Ibrahim, 'Abd Allah 'Ali. *Min adab al-Rubatab al-sha'bi.* Khartoum: Jami'at al-Khartoum, 1968. (Silsilat dirasat fi al-turath al-Sudani; 4). Arabic folk literature.

1105. Jamma', Fudayli. *Qira'ah fi al-adab al-Sudani al-hadith.* Amman: F. Jamma', 1991.

1106. *Qira'at al-nass bayn al-nazariyya wa'l-tatbiq.* Tunis: Institut National des Sciences de l'Education, 1990. Articles on Egyptian and Sudanese literature.

1107. Shush, Muhammad Ibrahim. *Some background notes on modern Sudanese poetry.* Khartoum: National Council for Letters & Arts, 1973.

1108. Subhi, Hasan Abbas. *al-Surah fi al-shir al-Sudani.* [Cairo]: al-Hayah al-Misriyah al-Ammah lil-Kitab, 1982. (al-Maktabah al-thaqafiyah; 368). On poetry.

1109. Yaziji, Halim. *al-Sudan wa-al-harakah al-adabiyah.* Beirut: al-Tawzi' al-Maktabah al-Sharqiyah, 1985. 2 v.

Authors

1110. Al-Mak, Ali. *A City of dust.* Washington: Office of the Cultural Counsellor, Sudan Embassy, 1982. (Sudanese publications series; 11).

1111. Fituri, Muhammad. *Diwan Muhammad al-Fituri.* Bayrut: Dar al-Awdah, 1979. Poetry.

1112. ———. *Yati al-ashiqun ilayki.* Cairo: Dar al-Shuruq, 1992. Poetry.

1113. Salih, al-Tayyib (Tayeb). *al-Amah al-kamilah.* Beirut: Dar al-Awdah, 1988. Selected fictional works.

1114. ———. *Bandar Shah, daw al-bayt.* Beirut: Dar al-Awdah, 1988. "The House's light." Fiction.

1115. ———. *Season of migration to the north.* London: Heinemann, 1969. Orig. pub. as: *Mawsim al-hijrah ila 'l-shamal,* 1966. Tr. by D. Johnson-Davies. (AWS; 66). Novel.

1116. ———. *The Wedding of Zein, and other stories.* London: Heinemann, 1968. Tr. of *Urs az-Zain wa sab'qisas* (1964) by D. Johnson-Davies. (AWS; 47). Short stories.

1117. Amyuni, Mona Takieddine (ed.). *Tayeb Salih's Season of migration to the north: a casebook.* Beirut: American University of Beirut, 1985.

1118. Berkeley, Constance E., and O. H. Ahmed. *Tayeb Salih speaks: four interviews with the Sudanese novelist.* Washington: Sudan Embassy, 1982.

1119. al-Tayyib, Abdallah. *Al-Qasida al-madiha: wa-maqalat ukhra.* Khartoum: Khartoum University Press, 1973. Poetry.

1120. ———. *Kalimat min Fas.* al-Khartum: Dar Jamiat al-Khartum lil-Nashr, 1991. Poetry.

1121. ———. *Min haqibat al-dhikrayat.* Khartoum: Khartoum University Press, 1983. Poetry.

TUNISIA

Bibliography

1122. Fontaine, Jean. *Fihris tarikhi lil-mullafat al-Tunisayah.* Tunis: al-Muassasah, 1986.

Anthologies

1123. Baccar, Taoufik, and Salah Garmadi (eds.). *Écrivains de Tunisie: anthologie de textes et poèmes traduits de l'arabe.* Paris: Sindbad, 1981. (Bibliotheque arabe).

1124. Guiga, Abderrahman. *La Geste hilalienne.* Tunis: Maison Tunisienne de l'Edition, 1969. Tr. par Tahar Guiga.

General studies

1125. Driss, Mohamed Messaoud. *Dirassât fi tarikh al-masrah at-tûnûsî (1881-1956).* Tunis: Sahar-ISAD, 1993.

1126. Fontaine, Jean. *Études de littérature tunisienne.* Tunis: Dar Annawras, 1989. (Collections "Les Essais"; 2).

1127. ———. *Histoire de la littérature tunisienne par les textes.* Le Bardo [Tunis]: Éditions Turki, 1988.

1128. ———. *La Littérature tunisienne contemporaine.* Paris: CNRS, 1990. (Société arabes et musulmanes; 2).

1129. ———. *Vingt ans de littérature tunisienne, 1956-1975.* Tunis: Maison tunisienne de l'édition, 1977.

1130. Galley, Micheline, and Abderrahman Ayoub. *Histoire des Beni Hilal et de ce qui leur advint dans leur marche vers l'ouest: versions tunisiennes de la geste hilalienne.* Paris: A. Colin, 1983. (Classiques africains).

1131. Halima, H. B. *Un Demi siècle de théâtre arabe en Tunisie (1907-1957).* Tunis: Université de Tunis, 1973.

1132. Majed, Jaafar. *La Presse littérature en Tunisie de 1904 à 1955.* Tunis: Imprimerie officielle, 1979.

1133. Naser, Abdelkader Belhaj. *Quelques aspects du roman tunisien.* Tunis: Maison Tunisienne d'édition, 1981.

Authors

1134. al-Mas'adi, Mahmud. *al-Sudd.* Tunis: Maison Tunisienne d'édition, 1974. Novel.

1135. al-Mitwi, Arussi. *Halima.* Tunis: STD, 1973. Novel.

1136. Shabbi, Abu al-Qasim. *al-Khayal al-Shiri inda al-Arab.* Tunis: al-Dar al-Tunisiyah, 1983. Poetry.

1137. ———. *Mudhakkirat.* Tunis: al-Dar al-Tunisiyah, 1983.

1138. Karo, Abu al-Qasim Muhammad. *Durasat an al-Shabbi: maktab al-Shabbi.* Tunis: Dar al-maghrib al-arabi, 1966.

OTHER COUNTRIES: NIGERIA, SENEGAL

1139. Ghaladant, Shaykhu Ahmad Said. *Harakat al-lughah al-Arabiyah wa-adabiha fi Nayjiriya min sant 1804 ila sanat 1966.* al-Qahirah: Dar al-Ma'arif, 1982. Nigeria.

1140. Samb, A. *Essai sur la contribution du Sénégal à la littérature d'expression arabe.* Dakar: IFAN, 1972.

ENGLISH LITERATURES

OVERVIEW

Bibliographies

1141. Jahn, Janheinz, and Claus Peter Dressler. *Bibliography of creative African writing.* Millwood, NY: Kraus-Thompson, 1971.

1142. Lindfors, Bernth. *Black African literature in English: a guide to information sources.* Detroit: Gale, 1979. (American literature, English literature and world literatures in English information guide series; 23). Supplements: *Black African literature in English, 1977-1981.* New York: Africana, 1986; *Black African literature in English, 1982-1986.* London: H. Zell, 1989; *Black African literature in English, 1987-1991.* London: H. Zell, 1994. (Bibliographical research in African literatures; 3).

1143. Scheven, Yvette. *Bibliographies for African studies 1970-1986.* London: H. Zell, 1988.

1144. Zell, Hans, Carol Bundy, and Virginia Coulon (eds.). *A New reader's guide to African literature.* New York; London: Africana; Heinemann, 1983. 2nd ed.

Anthologies

1145. Achebe, Chinua, and C. L. Innes (eds.). *African short stories.* London: Heinemann, 1985.

1146. Bruner, Charlotte H. (ed.). *The Heinemann book of African women's writing.* Oxford: Heinemann, 1993. (AWS).

1147. ———. *Unwinding threads: writing by women in Africa.* London: Heinemann, 1983. (AWS).

1148. Dathorne, O. R., and Willfried Feuser (eds.). *Africa in prose.* London: Penguin, 1969. (Penguin African library; 24).

1149. Moore, Gerald, and Ulli Beier (eds.). *Penguin book of modern African poetry*. London: Penguin, 1984. 3rd ed. First ed. pub. as: *Modern poetry from Africa*, Penguin, 1963.

1150. Mphahlele, Es'kia (ed.). *African writing today*. London: Penguin, 1967.

General studies

1151. Achebe, Chinua. *Literature and society: an African view*. Enugu, Nigeria: Fourth Dimension, 1980.

1152. Balogun, F. Odun. *Tradition and modernity in the African short story: an introduction to a literature in search of critics*. New York: Greenwood, 1991. (Contributions in Afro-American and African studies; 141).

1153. Cartey, Wilfred. *Whispers from a continent: the literature of contemporary black Africa*. New York; London: Vintage; Heinemann, 1969.

1154. Clark, J. P. (John Pepper). *The Example of Shakespeare*. Harlow: Longmans, 1970.

1155. Cook, David. *African literature: a critical view*. London: Longman, 1977.

1156. Dathorne, O. R. *The Black mind: a history of African literature*. Minneapolis: University of Minnesota Press, 1974. Abridged as: *African literature in the twentieth century*. London: Heinemann, 1976.

1157. Davis, Geoffrey V., and Hena Maes-Jelinek (eds.). *Crisis and creativity in the new literatures in English*. Amsterdam; Atlanta: Rodopi, 1990.

1158. Draper, James P. (ed.). *Black literature criticism: excerpts from criticism of the most significant works of black authors over the past 200 years*. Detroit: Gale, 1992. 3 v.

1159. Duerden, Dennis, and Cosmo Pieterse (eds.). *African writers talking: a collection of radio interviews*. London: Heinemann, 1972. (Studies in African literature).

1160. Etherton, Michael. *The Development of African drama.* London: Hutchinson, 1982.

1161. Gakwandi, S. A. *The Novel and contemporary experience in Africa.* London: Heinemann, 1977.

1162. Gates, Henry Louis. *Black literature and literary theory.* New York: Methuen, 1984.

1163. Gordimer, Nadine. *The Black interpreters: notes on African writing.* Johannesburg: Spro-Cas/Ravan, 1973.

1164. Gugelberger, Georg M. (ed.). *Marxism and African literature.* Trenton, NJ; London: Africa World; Currey, 1986.

1165. Gurnah, Abdulrazak (ed.). *Essays on African writing: a re-evaluation.* Oxford: Heinemann, 1993.

1166. Harrow, Kenneth W. *Thresholds of change in African literature: the emergence of a tradition.* London: Currey, 1994. (Studies in African literature).

1167. Haynes, John. *African poetry and the English language.* Basingstoke, England: Macmillan Education, 1987.

1168. James, Adeola (ed.). *In their own voices: African women writers talk.* London: Currey, 1990.

1169. Jeyifo, Biodun. *The Truthful lie: essays in a sociology of African drama.* London: New Beacon, 1985.

1170. Jones, Eldred. *Othello's countrymen: the African in English Renaissance drama.* Oxford: OUP, 1965.

1171. Kerr, David. *African popular theatre: from precolonial times to the present day.* London: Currey, 1994.

1172. Larson, Charles R. *The Emergence of African fiction.* Bloomington; London: Indiana University Press; Macmillan, 1972. 2nd ed.: London: Macmillan, 1978.

1173. Lindfors, Bernth, et al. (eds.). *Palaver: interviews with five African writers in Texas.* Austin: African and Afro-American Research Institute, University of Texas, 1972.

1174. ———. and Reinhard Sander (eds.). *Twentieth-Century Caribbean and Black African writers*. Detroit: Gale, 1992.

1175. McLeod, A. L. (ed.). *African literature in English: development and identity*. Philadelphia: African Studies Association, Literature in English Group, 1981.

1176. Nkosi, Lewis. *Tasks and masks: themes and styles of African writing*. Harlow: Longman, 1983.

1177. Obiechina, Emmanuel. *Language and theme: essays on African literature*. Washington: Howard University Press, 1990.

1178. Ogude, S. E. *Genius in bondage: a study of the origins of African literature in English*. Ile-Ife, Nigeria: University of Ife Press, 1983.

1179. Ogunba, Oyin, and Abiola Irele (eds.). *Theatre in Africa*. Ibadan: Ibadan University Press, 1978.

1180. Olney, James. *Tell me Africa: an approach to African literature*. Princeton: Princeton University Press, 1973.

1181. Omotoso, Kole. *The Form of the African novel*. Akure: Fagbamigbe Publishers, 1985.

1182. Palmer, Eustace Taiwo. *An Introduction to the African novel*. London: Heinemann, 1972.

1183. Peters, Jonathan (ed.). *Literature of Africa and the African continuum*. Washington: Three Continents Press, 1989.

1184. Soyinka, Wole. *Art, dialogue and outrage: essays on literature and culture*. Ibadan: New Horn, 1988.

1185. ———. *Myth, literature and the African world*. Cambridge: CUP, 1976. 2nd ed.: London: Methuen, 1990.

1186. Stewart, Danièle. *Le Roman africain anglophone depuis 1965: d'Achebe à Soyinka*. Paris: L'Harmattan, 1988.

1187. Taiwo, Oladele. *Female novelists of modern Africa.* London: Macmillan, 1984.

1188. Wilkinson, Jane. *Orpheus in Africa: fragmentation and renewal in the work of four African writers.* Roma: Bulzoni, 1990 (Studi e richerche; 30). Soyinka, Serote, and Ngugi.

EAST AFRICA

OVERVIEW

Anthologies

1189. Amateshe, A. D. (ed.). *An Anthology of East African poetry*. London: Longman, 1988. Poetry.

1190. Cook, David, and David Rubadiri (eds.). *Poems from East Africa*. London: Heinemann, 1971. (AWS; 96).

1191. Zettersten, Arne (ed.). *East African literature: an anthology*. London: Longman, 1983.

General studies

1192. Killam, G. D. (ed.). *The Writing of East and Central Africa*. Nairobi: Heinemann, 1984.

1193. Lindfors, Bernth (ed.) *Mazungumzo: interviews with East African writers, publishers, editors and scholars*. Athens, Ohio: Ohio University Center for International Studies, Africa Program, 1980. (Papers in international studies: Africa; 41).

1194. Liyong, Taban Lo. *Another last word*. Nairobi: Heinemann Kenya, 1990.

1195. ———. *The Last word, cultural synthesism*. Nairobi: East African Publishing House, 1969. Literary criticism.

1196. Mayamba, N. *The East African narrative fiction: towards an aesthetic and a socio-political Uhuru*. Lagos: Cross Continent, 1988. (Literary criticism series; 4).

1197. Roscoe, Adrian. *Uhuru's fire: African literature east to south*. Cambridge: CUP, 1977.

1198. Schild, Ulla (ed.). *Modern East-African literature and its audience*. Wiesbaden: B. Heymann, 1978. (Mainzer Afrika Studien; 4).

1199. Wanjala, Chris L. *The Season of harvest: a literary harvest: a literary discussion.* Nairobi: Kenya Literature Bureau, 1978.

1200. ———. (ed.). *Standpoints on African literature: a critical anthology.* Nairobi: EALB, 1973.

ETHIOPIA

Authors

1201. Daniachew Worku. *The Thirteenth sun.* London: Heinemann, 1973. (AWS; 125). Novel.

1202. Sahle Selassie. *The Afersata: an Ethiopian novel.* London: Heinemann, 1969. (AWS; 52). Novel.

1203. ———. *Firebrands.* London; Washington: Longman; Three Continents Press, 1979. Novel.

1204. ———. *Warrior king.* London: Heinemann, 1974. (AWS; 163). Novel.

1205. Tsegaye Gabre-Medhin. *Collision of altars.* London: Rex Collings, 1977. Drama.

1206. Tuma, Hama. *The Case of the socialist witchdoctor and other stories.* Oxford: Heinemann, 1993. (AWS).

KENYA

Bibliographies

1207. Sicherman, Carol. *Ngugi wa Thiong'o: a bibliography of primary and secondary sources, 1957-1989.* London: H. Zell, 1989. (Bibliographical research in African written literatures; 1).

1208. Zell, Hans, Carol Bundy, and Virginia Coulon (eds.). *A New reader's guide to African literature.* New York; London: Africana; Heinemann, 1983. 2nd ed. pp. 181-195.

Anthology

1209. Luvai, Arthur I. (ed.). *Boundless voices: poems from Kenya.* Nairobi: Heinemann Kenya, 1988.

General studies

1210. Maughan-Brown, David. *Land, freedom and fiction: history and ideology in Kenya.* London: Zed, 1985.

1211. Ngugi wa Thiong'o. *Decolonising the mind.* London: Longman, 1986.

1212. ———. *Homecoming: essays on African and Caribbean literature, culture and politics.* London: Heinemann, 1972. (Studies in African literature). Essays.

Authors

1213. Angira, Jared. *Cascades.* London; Washington: Longman; Three Continents Press, 1979. Poetry.

1214. ———. *Silent voices.* London: Heinemann, 1972. (AWS; 111). Poetry.

1215. Gicheru, Mwangi. *The Mixers.* Nairobi: Longman Kenya, 1991. (Masterpiece series). Novel.

1216. Imbuga, Francis S. *The Married bachelor.* Nairobi: EAPH, 1973. (African theatre; 3). Drama.

1217. ———. *Shrine of tears.* Nairobi: Longman Kenya, 1993. (Masterpiece series). Novel.

1218. Ruganda, John. *Telling the truth laughingly: the politics of Francis Imbuga's drama.* Nairobi: East African Educational Publishers, 1992.

1219. Kahiga, Sam. *The Girl from abroad.* London: Heinemann, 1974. (AWS; 158). Novel.

1220. ———. *Paradise farm.* Nairobi: Longman Kenya, 1993. (Masterpiece series). Novel.

1221. Kulet, Ole H. R. *Moran no more.* Nairobi: Longman Kenya, 1990. Novel.

1222. Likimani, Muthoni. *They shall be chastised.* Nairobi: EAPH, 1974. Novel.

1223. ———. *What does a man want?* Nairobi: Kenya Literature Bureau, 1974. Novel.

1224. Maillu, David. *The Equatorial assignment.* London: Macmillan, 1980. Novel.

1225. Mazrui, Alamin. *Shadows of the moon: a play.* Nairobi: East African Educational Publishers, 1991. (E.A.E.P. drama series). Drama.

1226. Mugo, Micere Githae (F). *Daughter of my people, sing!* Nairobi: EALB, 1976. Poetry.

1227. ———. *The Long illness of ex-chief Kiti.* Nairobi: EALB, 1976. Drama.

1228. ———. *My mother's poem and other songs: songs and poems.* Nairobi: East African Educational Publishers, 1994.

1229. Mwangi, Meja. *Carcass for hounds.* London: Heinemann, 1974. (AWS; 145). Novel.

1230. ———. *Going down river road.* London: Heinemann, 1976. (AWS; 176). Novel.

1231. ———. *Kill me quick.* London: Heinemann, 1973. (AWS; 143). Novel.

1232. ———. *Taste of death.* Nairobi: EAPH, 1975.

1233. ———. *Weapon of hunger.* Nairobi: Longman Kenya, 1989. Novel.

1234. Johansson, Lars. *In the shadow of neocolonialism: a study of Meja Mwangi's novels 1973-1990.* Umeå, Sweden: Acta Universatis Umensis, 1992.

1235. Ngugi wa Thiong'o. *The Black hermit*. London: Heinemann, 1968. (AWS; 51). Drama. See also Gikuyu section.

1236. ———. *Detained: a writer's prison diary*. London: Heinemann, 1981. (AWS; 240).

1237. ———. *Devil on the cross*. London: Heinemann, 1982. (AWS; 200). First pub. in Gikuyu: Nairobi, 1980. Novel.

1238. ———. *A Grain of wheat*. London: Heinemann, 1967. (AWS; 36). Novel.

1239. ———. *Matigari*. London: Heinemann, 1989. (AWS). Tr. by Wangui wa Goro. First pub. in Gikuyu: Nairobi: Heinemann Kenya, 1987. Novel.

1240. ———. *Petals of blood*. London: Heinemann, 1977. (AWS; 188). Also pub.: Harare: ZPH, 1982. Novel.

1241. ———. *The River between*. London: Heinemann, 1965. (AWS; 17). Also pub.: Harare: ZPH, 1984. Novel.

1242. ———. *Secret lives*. London; Westport: Heinemann; Lawrence Hill, 1975. (AWS; 150). Short stories.

1243. ———. *This time tomorrow*. Nairobi; London: EALB; Heinemann, 1970. (AWS; 78). Drama.

1244. ———. *Weep not, child*. London: Heinemann, 1964. (AWS; 7). Novel.

1245. ———. *Writers in politics: essays*. London: Heinemann, 1981.

1246. ——— and Micere Githae Mugo. *The Trial of Dedan Kimathi*. London: Heinemann, 1976. (AWS; 191). Drama.

1247. ——— and Ngugi wa Mirii. *I will marry when I want*. London: Heinemann, 1982. (AWS; 246). First pub. in Gikuyu as: *Ngaahika ndeenda*. Drama.

1248. Bardolph, Jacqueline. *Ngugi wa Thiong'o: l'homme et l'oeuvre.* Paris: Présence africaine, 1991.

1249. Killam. G. D. (ed.). *Critical perspectives on Ngugi wa Thiong'o.* Washington: Three Continents Press, 1984. (Critical perspectives; 13).

1250. ———. *An Introduction to the writings of Ngugi.* London: Heinemann, 1980.

1251. Meyer, Herta. *"Justice for the oppressed": the political dimension in the language use of Ngugi wa Thiong'o.* Essen: Die Blaue Eule, 1991. (African literatures in English; 4).

1252. Mugo, Micere Githae. *Visions of Africa: the fiction of Chinua Achebe, Margaret Laurence, Elspeth Huxley and Ngugi wa Thiong'o.* Nairobi: Kenya Literature Bureau, 1978.

1253. Nwanko, C. *The Works of Ngugi wa Thiong'o.* Ibadan: Longman Nigeria, 1992.

1254. Robson, Clifford B. *Ngugi wa Thiong'o.* London: Macmillan, 1979. (Macmillan Commonwealth writers).

1255. Sicherman, Carol. *Ngugi wa Thiong'o: the making of a rebel: a source book in Kenyan literature and resistance.* London: H. Zell, 1990.

1256. Tsabedze, Clara. *African independence from fancophone and anglophone voices: a comparative study of the post-independence novels of Ngugi and Sembene Ousmane.* New York: Peter Lang, 1994. (Comparative culture and literatures; 3).

1257. Ngurukie, Pat Wambui. *Tough choices.* Nairobi: Macmillan Education, 1991. Novel.

1258. Nguya, Lydiah Mumbi (F). *The First seed.* Nairobi: EALB, 1975. Novel.

1259. Njau, Rebeka (F). *The Hypocrite.* Nairobi: Uzima Press, 1977. Short stories.

1260. ———. *Ripples in the pool.* Nairobi; London: Transafrica Pub.; Heinemann, 1975. (AWS; 203). Novel.

1261. ———. *The Scar: a tragedy in one act.* Moshi, Tanzania: Kibo Art Gallery, 1965. Drama.

1262. Ogot, Grace (F). *The Graduate.* Nairobi: Uzima Press, 1980. Novel.

1263. ———. *The Island of tears.* Nairobi: Uzima Press, 1980. Short stories.

1264. ———. *Land without thunder.* Nairobi: EAPH, 1968. Short stories.

1265. ———. *The Other woman.* Nairobi: East African Educational Publishers, 1992. Short stories.

1266. ———. *The Promised land.* Nairobi: EAPH, 1966. (Modern African library). New ed.: Nairobi: Heinemann Kenya, 1990. Novel.

1267. Ruheni, Mwangi. *The Minister's daughters.* London: Heinemann, 1975. (AWS; 156). Novel.

1268. Watene, Kenneth. *Dedan Kimathi.* Nairobi: Transafrica Publications, 1974. Novel.

1269. Were, Miriam (F). *Your heart is my altar.* Nairobi: EAPH, 1980. Novel.

SOMALIA

Anthology

1270. Eby, Omar. *The Sons of Adam: stories of Somalia.* Scottdale, PA: Herald Press, 1970. Author is an American.

Authors

1271. Farah, Nuruddin. *Close sesame.* London: Allison and Busby, 1983. Novel.

1272. ———. *From a crooked rib.* London: Heinemann, 1970. (AWS; 80). Novel.

1273. ———. *Gifts.* London: Serrif, 1993. Novel.

1274. ———. *Maps.* New York: Pantheon, 1986. Fiction.

1275. ———. *A Naked needle.* London: Heinemann, 1976. (AWS; 184). Novel.

1276. ———. *Sardines.* London: Allison and Busby, 1981. Also pub.: London: Heinemann, 1982 (AWS; 252). Novel.

1277. ———. *Sweet and sour milk.* London: Allison & Busby, 1979; London: Heinemann, 1980. (AWS; 226). Novel.

1278. Wright, Derek. *The Novels of Nuruddin Farah.* Bayreuth: Eckhard Breitlinger, 1994. (Bayreuth African studies series; 32).

SUDAN

Anthology

1279. Liyong, Taban Lo. *Eating chiefs: Lwo culture from Lolwe to Malkal.* London: Heinemann, 1970. (AWS; 74). Poetry and short stories based on folk literature.

General studies

1280. Liyong, Taban Lo. *Culture is rutan.* Nairobi: Longman Kenya, 1991. Essays.

Authors

1281. Ahmed, Z. *Stories of Serra East.* Khartoum: Khartoum University Press, 1985.

1282. Deng, Francis Mading. *Cry of the owl.* New York: L. Barber, 1989. Novel.

1283. ————. *Seed of redemption: a political novel*. New York: L. Barber, 1986.

1284. Fadl, El Sir Hassan. *Their finest days*. London; Washington: Collings; Three Continents Press, 1969. Stories.

1285. Kelueljang, Anai. *The Myth of freedom*. London: New Beacon Books, 1975. Poetry.

1286. Liyong, Taban Lo. *Another nigger dead*. London: Heinemann, 1972. (AWS; 116). Poetry.

1287. ————. *Ballads of underdevelopment*. Nairobi: EALB, 1976. Poems and short stories.

1288. ————. *The Cows of Sambat: Sudanese poems*. Harare: ZPH, 1992. (ZPH writers series; 44). Poetry.

1289. ————. *Fixions and other stories*. London: Heinemann, 1969. (AWS; 69). Short stories.

1290. ————. *Frantz Fanon's uneven ribs: poems more and more*. London: Heinemann, 1971. (AWS; 90). Poetry.

1291. ————. *The Uniformed man*. Nairobi: EALB, 1971. Short stories.

1292. Mahjoub, Jamal. *Navigation of a rainmaker*. Oxford: Heinemann International, 1989. (AWS). Novel.

1293. ————. *Wings of dust*. Oxford: Heinemann, 1994 (AWS). Fiction.

TANZANIA

Anthology

1294. Mabala, Richard S. (ed.). *Summons: poems from Tanzania*. Dar es Salaam: Tanzania Pub. House, 1980 Poetry.

Authors

1295. Bukenya, Austin Lwanga. *The Bride: a play in four*

movements. Nairobi: Heinemann Kenya, 1987. (Plays for schools series; 19).

1296. Gurnah, Abdulrazak. *Dottie.* London: J. Cape, 1990. Novel.

1297. ————. *Memory of departure.* London: J. Cape, 1987. Novel.

1298. ————. *Pilgrim's way.* London: J. Cape, 1988. Novel.

1299. Kagwema, Prince. *Chausiku's dozen: a novel.* Dar es Salaam: Three Stars Publications, 1983.

1300. ————. *Society in the dock: a novel.* Dar es Salaam: Three Stars Publications, 1984.

1301. Kaigarula, Wilson. *Poisoned love.* Dar es Salaam: Heko, 1987. Novel.

1302. Mabala, Richard S. *The Sinza gang.* Arusha: Eastern Africa Pubs., 1991. Novella.

1303. Makaidi, Emmanuel J. E. *The Serpent-hearted politician.* Dar es Salaam: Sunrise Publishers, 1982. Novel.

1304. Malyi, Ebenezer. *Revolution in South Africa: a Christian response: a play.* Arusha: Logos, 1986.

1305. Marti, Tolowa. *Waters of the vultures.* Dar es Salaam: Dar es Salaam University Press, 1991.

1306. Mbise, Ismael R. *Blood on our land.* Dar es Salaam: Tanzania Pub. House, 1974. Novel.

1307. Mkufa, W. E. *The Wicked walk.* Dar es Salaam: Tanzania Pub. House, 1977. Novel.

1308. Mloka, Cesar. *The Cocktail.* Stockholm: Forttares Bokmaskin, 1989. Poetry and short stories.

1309. Mwanga, Abel K. *Nyangeta: the name from the calabash.* Nairobi: EALB, 1976. Novel.

1310. Ngalo, D. S. *The Gray years*. Dar es Salaam: General Publishers, 1984. Novel.

1311. Palangyo, Peter K. *Dying in the sun*. London: Heinemann, 1969. (AWS; 53). Novel.

1312. Pwegoshora, Prosper. *The Plight of succession*. Dar es Salaam: Dar es Salaam University Press, 1993. Novel.

1313. Sokko, Hamza. *The Gathering storm: a novel*. Dar es Salaam: Tanzania Pub. House, 1977.

1314. Urrio, Tengio. *The Girl from Uganda*. Nairobi: East African Educational Publishers, 1993. Novel.

1315. Vassanji, M. G. *The Gunny sack*. Oxford: Heinemann, 1989. (AWS). Novel.

1316. ———. *No new land*. Toronto: McClelland & Stewart, 1991. Novel.

1317. ———. *Uhuru Street*. Oxford: Heinemann, 1991. (AWS). Short stories.

UGANDA

Anthologies

1318. p'Bitek, Okot. *Acholi proverbs*. Nairobi: East African Educational Publishers, 1985.

1319. ———. *Hare and hornbill*. London: Heinemann, 1978. (AWS; 193). Acoli tales.

1320. ———. *Horn of my love*. London: Heinemann, 1974. (AWS; 147). Acoli poetry from Sudan and Uganda.

1321. Wanjala, Chris. *Faces at crossroads: a "Currents" anthology*. Nairobi: EALB, 1971.

Authors

1322. Akello, Grace (F). *My barren song*. Arusha: Dar es Salaam: EAPH, 1979. Poetry.

1323. Buruga, Joseph. *The Abandoned hut.* [Nairobi]: EAPH, 1969. Poem.

1324. Kabumba, Ijuka. *The Wedding ring and other stories.* Kampala: Nyonyi Pub. Co., 1992.

1325. Kalimugogo, Godfrey. *Trials and tribulations in Sandu's house.* Nairobi: EALB, 1976. Novel.

1326. Kimenye, Barbara (F). *Kalasanda.* Oxford: OUP, 1965. Short stories.

1327. Lubega, Bonnie. *The Outcasts.* London: Heinemann, 1971. (AWS; 105). Novel.

1328. Magala-Nyago. *The Rape of the pearl.* London: Macmillan, 1985. Novel.

1329. Mazrui, Ali. *The Trial of Christopher Okigbo.* London: Heinemann, 1971. (AWS; 97). Novel.

1330. Nagenda, John. *The Seasons of Thomas Tebo.* London: Heinemann, 1986. (AWS; 262). Novel.

1331. Nazareth, Peter. *In a brown mantle.* Kampala: EALB, 1972. Novel.

1332. Ntiru, Richard. *Tensions.* Nairobi: EAPH, 1971. Poetry.

1333. Nyabongo, Akiki. *Africa answers back.* London: Routledge, 1936. Novel.

1334. Oculi, Okello. *Malak.* Nairobi: EAPH, 1977. Poem.

1335. Osinya, Alumidi. *The Amazing saga of Field Marshal Abdulla Salim Fisi, or, How the hyena got his tail.* Nairobi: Joe Magazine/Transafrica Publications, 1976. Short stories.

1336. p'Bitek, Okot. *Song of Lawino: a lament.* [Nairobi]: EAPH, 1966. Tr. from *Wer pa Lawino.* Poetry.

1337. ———. *Song of Lawino, and, Song of Ocol.* London: Heinemann, 1972. (AWS; 266). Poetry.

1338. ———. *Song of Ocol.* Nairobi: EAPH, 1970. Poetry.

1339. ———. *Song of a prisoner.* New York: Third Press, 1971. Poetry.

1340. ———. *Two songs.* Nairobi: EAPH, 1971. Poetry.

1341. Heron, G. A. *Notes on Okot p'Bitek's Song of Lawino and Song of Ocol.* Nairobi: Heinemann, 1975.

1342. ———. *The Poetry of Okot p'Bitek.* London; New York: Heinemann; Africana, 1976.

1343. Ruganda, John. *The Burdens.* Nairobi: OUP, 1972. Drama.

1344. ———. *The Floods.* Nairobi: EAPH, 1980. (African theatre; 7). Drama.

1345. Rugyendo, Mukotani. *The Barbed wire and other plays.* London: Heinemann, 1977. (AWS; 187).

1346. Seruma, Eneriko. *The Heart seller: short stories.* Nairobi: EAPH, 1971. (Modern African library; 21).

1347. Serumaga, Robert. *Majangwa, and, A Play.* Nairobi: EAPH, 1974. Orig. pub. as: *A Play.* Uganda Pub. House, 1967.

1348. ———. *Return to the shadows.* London: Heinemann, 1969. (AWS; 54). Novel.

1349. Wangusa, Timothy. *Upon this mountain.* London: Heinemann, 1989. (AWS). Novel.

1350. Zirimu, Elvania. *Kamasiira and other stories.* Nairobi: EAPH, 1980. Short stories.

1351. ———. *When the hunchback made rain.* Nairobi: EAPH, 1975. Drama.

SOUTHERN AFRICA

OVERVIEW

Bibliography

1352. Richter, Barbara, and Sandra Kotze. *A Bibliography of criticism of Southern African literature in English*. Bloemfontein: University of Orange Free State, 1983. (Series C; 7).

Anthologies

1353. Chapman, Michael, and A. Dangor (eds.). *Voices from within: black poetry from Southern Africa.* Johannesburg: Ad. Donker, 1982. Poetry.

1354. Chipasula, Frank (ed.). *When my brothers come home: poems from Central and Southern Africa.* Middletown, CT: Wesleyan University Press, 1985.

1355. Malan, Robin (ed.). *Being here: modern shoﾗt stories from Southern Africa.* Cape Town: D. Philip, 1994.

1356. Plumpp, Sterling (ed.). *Somehow we survive: an anthology of Southern African writing.* New York: Thunder's Mouth Press, 1982.

1357. Scanlon, Paul A. (ed.). *Stories from Central and Southern Africa.* London: Heinemann, 1983. (AWS; 254).

1358. Zimunya, Musaemura (ed.). *Birthright: a selection of poems from Southern Africa.* Harlow: Longman, 1989.

General studies

1359. Davis, Geoffrey V. (ed.). *Southern African writing: voyages and explorations.* Amsterdam; Atlanta: Rodopi, 1994. (Matatu; 11).

1360. Gray, Stephen (ed.). *Southern African literature: an introduction.* Cape Town; London: D. Philip; Collins, 1979.

1361. Gunner, Liz (ed.). *Politics and performance: theatre, poetry and song in Southern Africa.* Johannesburg: Witwatersrand University Press, 1994. Articles prev. pub. in: *Journal of Southern African Studies,* June 1990.

1362. Kaarsholm, Preben. *Cultural struggle and development in Southern Africa.* Harare: Baobab, 1991.

ANGOLA

Authors

1363. Jamba, José Sousa. *A Lonely devil.* London: Fourth Estate, 1993. Novel.

1364. ———. *Patriots.* London: Viking, 1990. Portuguese ed.: Lisbon: Cotovia, 1991. Novel.

BOTSWANA

Bibliographies

1365. Gardner, Susan, and Patricia E. Scott. *Bessie Head: a bibliography.* Grahamstown: National English Literary Museum, 1986. (NELM bibliographic series; 1).

1366. Giffuni, Cathy. *Bessie Head: a bibliography.* Gaborone: Botswana National Library Service, 1987.

1367. Mackenzie, Craig, and Catherine Woeber (eds.). *Bessie Head: a bibliography.* Grahamstown: National English Literary Museum, 1992. (NELM bibliographic series; 1).

Anthology

1368. Head, Bessie. *The Collector of treasures, and other Botswana village tales.* London: Heinemann, 1977.

Authors

1369. Baruti, G. R. E. *Mr Heart breaker.* Gaborone: The Author, 1993. Novel.

1370. Ehrmann, Rita M. (F). *African footprints.* [s.l.]: Villanova University Press, 1986.

1371. Head, Bessie (F). *The Cardinals, with meditations and short stories.* Cape Town: D. Philip, 1993. Ed. by M. J. Daymond. (Africasouth new writing series). Novella and stories.

1372. ———. *A Gesture of belonging: letters from Bessie Head, 1965-1979.* London; Johannesburg: SA Writers; Witwatersrand University Press, 1991. Ed. by Randolph Vigne.

1373. ———. *Maru.* London; New York: Gollancz; McCall, 1971, and London: Heinemann, 1972. (AWS; 101). Novel.

1374. ———. *A Question of power.* London: Heinemann; Davis-Poynter, 1973. (AWS; 149). Novel.

1375. ———. *Tales of tenderness and power.* Johannesburg; London: Ad. Donker; Heinemann, 1989. Short stories.

1376. ———. *When rain clouds gather.* London: Gollancz, 1968. Novel.

1377. ———. *A Woman alone: autobiographical writings.* London: Heinemann, 1990. Ed. by Craig Mackenzie. (AWS).

1378. Abrahams, Cecil A. (ed.). *The Tragic life: Bessie Head and literature in Southern Africa.* Trenton, NJ: Africa World Press, 1990.

1379. Eilersen, Gillian. *Bessie Head: a biography.* London: J. Currey, 1995.

1380. Mackenzie, Craig. *Bessie Head: an introduction.* Grahamstown: National English Literary Museum, 1989.

1381. Rush, Norman. *Whites: stories.* London; New York: Heinemann; Knopf, 1986.

1382. Sesinyi, Andrew. *Love on the rocks*. London: Macmillan, 1981. Novel.

LESOTHO

Bibliography

1383. Willett, Shelagh M., and David P. Ambrose. *Lesotho*. Oxford; Clio, 1980. (World bibliographical series; 3).

Authors

1384. Leshoai, Bob. *Wrath of the ancestors and other plays*. Nairobi: EAPH, 1972.

1385. Mopeli-Paulus, Attwell Sidwell, and Peter Lanham. *Blanket boy's moon*. Cape Town: D. Philip, 1984. First pub.: London: Collins, 1953. Novel.

1386. ———. *Turn to the dark*. London: Cape, 1956. Novel.

MALAWI

Anthologies

1387. Gibbs, James (ed.). *Nine Malawian plays*. Limbe: Popular Publications, 1977. (Malawian writers series; 3).

1388. Nazombe, Anthony (ed.). *The Haunting wind: new poetry from Malawi*. Blantyre: Dzuka, 1990. Poetry.

General studies

1389. Kamlongera, Christopher F. *Dance and theatre in Malawi*. Zomba: Research & Pub. Committee, University of Malawi, 1992.

1390. Lindfors, Bernth (ed.). *Kulankula: interviews with writers from Malawi and Lesotho*. Bayreuth: University of Bayreuth, 1989. (Bayreuth African studies series; 14).

1391. Roscoe, Adrian, and Mpalive-Hangson Msiska. *The Quiet chameleon: modern poetry from Central Africa.* London: H. Zell, 1992. (New perspectives on African literature; 2).

Authors

1392. Banda, Joseph A. K. *Best left unsaid.* Limbe, Malawi: Popular Publications, 1991. (Malawian writers series). Novel.

1393. ———. *The Startling revelation.* Limbe, Malawi: Popular Publications, 1991. (Malawian writers series). Fiction.

1394. Banda, Tito. *Sekani's solution.* Limbe, Malawi: Popular Publications, 1979. (Malawian writers series; 5). Novel.

1395. Chimombo, Steve. *The Basket girl.* Limbe, Malawi: Popular Publications, 1990. (Malawian writers series). Fiction.

1396. ———. *The Elections of the forest creatures: a long poem.* Zomba: WASI Publications, 1994.

1397. ———. *Napolo poems.* Zomba, Malawi: Manchici Publishers, 1987.

1398. ———. *Napolo and the python: selected poetry.* Oxford: Heinemann, 1994. (AWS).

1399. ———. *Python! Python!* Domasi, Malawi: WASI Publications, 1992. Epic poem.

1400. ———. *The Rainmaker.* Limbe, Malawi: Popular Publications, 1978. (Malawian writers series; 4). Drama.

1401. ———. *Tell me a story.* Blantyre: Dzuka, 1992. (Dzuka writers series). Short stories.

1402. Chipasula, Frank. *Nightwatcher, nightsong.* Peterborough, Eng.: P. Green, 1986. Poetry.

1403. ———. *O Earth, wait for me.* Johannesburg: Ravan Press, 1984. (Staffrider series; 22). Poetry.

1404. ———. *Visions and reflections.* Lusaka: NECZAM, 1972. Poetry.

1405. ———. *Whispers in the wings: poems.* Oxford: Heinemann, 1991. (Heinemann African poets). Poetry.

1406. Kachingwe, Aubrey. *No easy task.* London: Heinemann, 1966. (AWS; 24). Novel.

1407. Kalitera, Aubrey. *Why, father, why?* Blantyre: Power Pen Books, 1982. Novel.

1408. ———. *Why, son, why?* Blantyre: Power Pen Books, 1983. Novel.

1409. Kamkondo, Dede. *For the living.* Blantyre: Dzuka, 1989. Novel

1410. Kayira, Legson. *The Civil servant.* London: Longman, 1971. Novel.

1411. ———. *The Detainee.* London: Heinemann, 1974. (AWS; 162). Novel.

1412. ———. *Jingala.* London; Washington: Longman; Three Continents Press, 1969. Novel.

1413. ———. *The Looming shadow.* London: Longman, 1968. Novel.

1414. Lipenga, Ken. *Waiting for a turn: short stories.* Limbe, Malawi: Popular Publications, 1981. (Malawian writers series; 6).

1415. Mapanje, Jack. *The Chattering wagtails of Mikuyu Prison.* Oxford: Heinemann, 1993. Poetry.

1416. ———. *Of Chameleons and gods.* London: Heinemann, 1981. (AWS; 236). Poetry.

1417. M'Passou, Denis. *A Pig in the coffin.* Limbe, Malawi: Popular Publications, 1991. (Malawian writers series). Fiction.

1418. Mpina, Edison. *Freedom Avenue*. Limbe, Malawi: Popular Publications, 1991. (Malawian writers series). Novel.

1419. ———. *The Low road to death*. Limbe, Malawi: Popular Publications, 1991. (Malawian writers series). Novel.

1420. Ng'ombe, James. *The King's pillow and other plays*. London: Evans, 1986.

1421. ———. *Sugarcane with salt*. Harlow: Longman, 1989. Novel.

1422. Ntaba, Jolly Max. *Avenger's fury*. Chichiri, Blantyre, Malawi: Malawi Book Service, 1987. Novel.

1423. Phiri, Desmond. *The Chief's bride*. London: Evans, 1968. Drama.

1424. Rubadiri, David. *No bride price*. Nairobi: EAPH, 1967. Novel.

1425. Zeleza, Tiyambe Paul. *The Joys of exile: stories*. Concord, Ontario: Anansi, 1994. Short stories.

1426. ———. *Night of darkness, and other stories*. Limbe, Malawi: Popular Publications, 1976. (Malawian writers series; 2). Short stories.

1427. ———. *Smouldering charcoal*. Oxford: Heinemann, 1992. (AWS). Novel.

NAMIBIA

Anthologies

1428. Mbako, Simon Z. (ed.). *Tell them of Namibia: poems from the national liberation struggle*. London: Karia, 1989.

1429. Melber, Henning (ed.). *It is no more a cry: Namibian poetry in exile*. Basel: Basler Afrika Bibliographien, 1982. (Basler Afrika Bibliographien. Beitrage zur Afrikakunde).

1430. Namibia Young Writers' Club. *The Innermost explosion: poems from Augustineum Secondary School.* Windhoek: New Namibian Books, 1993.

1431. Patemann, Helgard, and Nangola Mbumba (eds.). *Through the flames: poems from the Namibian liberation struggle.* Bremen: Centre for African Studies, [199?].

1432. *Young Namibian poetry.* Lusaka: UNIN/Creative Writing Club, 1979. Poetry of exiles.

General studies

1433. Haarhoff, Dorian. *The Wild South-West: frontier myths and metaphors in literature set in Namibia, 1760-1988.* Johannesburg: Witwatersrand University Press, 1991.

Authors

1434. Angula, Helmut Pau Kangulohi. *The Two thousand days of Haimbodi ya Haufiku.* Windhoek: Gamsberg Macmillan, 1990. First pub. in German as: *Die Zweitausend Tage des Haimbooi ya Haufika.* Bremen: University of Bremen, 1986. Autobiographical fiction.

1435. Davis, Jennifer (F). *Song of the Namib.* Windhoek: New Namibia Books, 1991. Poetry.

1436. ———. *The Stolen water and other stories: traditional tales from Namibia.* Windhoek: New Namibia Books, 1993.

1437. Diescho, Joseph. *Born of the sun: a Namibian novel.* New York: Friendship Press, 1988.

1438. ———. *Troubled waters: a novel.* Windhoek: Gamsberg Macmillan, 1993.

1439. Hishongwa, Ndeutala (F). *Marrying apartheid.* Abbotsford, Vic.: Imprenta, 1986. Novel.

1440. McLain, Liz (F). *Desert detritus.* Windhoek: New Namibia Books, 1992. Poetry.

1441. Mvula ya Nangalo. *Thoughts from exile.*
Windhoek: Longman Namibia/Namibia Project, 1991. Poetry.

1442. Philander, Frederick Brian. *The Curse: a four-act
play on the Namibian struggle.* Braamfontein: Skotaville,
1990.

1443. Shityuwete, H. *Never follow the wolf: the
autobiography of a Namibian freedom fighter.* London:
Kliptown, 1990.

1444. Strander, Siegfried. *Flight from the hunter: a
novel.* London: Gollancz, 1977.

1445. Victor, Kapache. *On the run.* Windhoek: New
Namibia Books, 1994. Novel.

SOUTH AFRICA

Bibliographies

1446. Adey, D., et al. *Companion to South African
English literature.* Johannesburg: Ad. Donker, 1985.

1447. Driver, Dorothy, Ann Dry, Craig MacKenzie, and
John Read (eds.). *Nadine Gordimer: a bibliography of
primary and secondary sources, 1937-1992.* London: H. Zell,
1994. (Bibliographical research in African literatures; 4).
Orig. pub.: Grahamstown: National English Literary Museum,
1993 (NELM bibliographic series; 6).

1448. Dubbeld, C. E. *Reflecting apartheid: South African
short stories in English with socio-political themes 1960-
1987: a select and annotated bibliography.* Johannesburg:
South African Institute of International Affairs, 1990.
(Bibliographical series; 21)

1449. Goddard, Kevin, and John Read (comp.). *J. M.
Coetzee: a bibliography.* Grahamstown: National English
Literary Museum, 1990. (NELM bibliographic series; 3).

1450. Goldstein, Gillian (comp.). *Oswald Mbuyiseni Mtshali, South African poet: an annotated bibliography.* Johannesburg: University of the Witwatersrand, 1974.

1451. Gorman, Gary E. *The South African novel in English since 1950: an information and resource guide.* Boston: Hall, 1978. (Bibliographies and guides in African studies).

1452. Hauptfleisch, Temple, et al. (eds.). *Athol Fugard: a source guide.* Johannesburg: Ad. Donker, 1982. (Centre for South African Theatre Research; 7).

1453. House, Amelia. *Black women writers from South Africa: a preliminary checklist.* Evanston: Northwestern University Program on Women, 1980.

1454. Parson, David S. J. *Roy Campbell: a descriptive and annotated bibliography, with notes on unpublished sources.* New York: Garland, 1980. (Garland reference library of the humanities; 197).

1455. Raju, Jayarani, and Catherine Dubbeld (eds.). *Richard Rive: a select bibliography.* Durban: University of Natal, E.G. Malherbe Library, 1990.

1456. Read, John (comp.). *Athol Fugard: a bibliography.* Grahamstown: National English Literary Museum, 1991. (NELM bibliographic series; 4).

1457. ———. *Guy Butler: a bibliography.* Grahamstown: National English Literary Museum, 1992. (NELM bibliographic series; 5).

1458. Richter, Barbara and Sandra Kotze. *A Bibliography of criticism of Southern African literature in English.* Bloemfontein: University of Orange Free State. (Series C; 7).

1459. Strauss, Julie (ed.). *A Select index to South African literature in English 1992.* (Grahamstown: National English Literary Museum, 1993. (NELM index series; 3).

1460. Woeber, Catherine, and John Read. *Es'kia Mphahlele: a bibliography*. Grahamstown: National English Literary Museum, 1989. (NELM bibliographic series; 2).

Anthologies

1461. Brink, André, and J. M. Coetzee (eds.). *A Land apart: a contemporary South African reader*. London: Faber, 1986.

1462. Chapman, Michael, and A. Dangor (eds.). *Voices from within: black poetry from Southern Africa*. Johannesburg: Ad. Donker, 1982.

1463. Clayton, Cherry (ed.). *Women and writing in South Africa: a critical anthology*. London: Heinemann, 1989.

1464. Coetzee, Ampie, and Hein Willemse (eds.). *I Qabane Labantu: poetry in the emergency=poesie in die Noodtoestand*. Johannesburg: Taurus, 1989. In English and Afrikaans.

1465. Couzens, Tim, and Essop Patel (eds.). *The Return of the Amasi bird: black South African poetry 1891-1981*. Johannesburg: Ravan Press, 1982.

1466. Feinberg, Barry (ed.). *Poets to the people: South African freedom poems*. London: Heinemann, 1980. Enlarged ed. (AWS; 230). First pub.: G. Allen & Unwin, 1974.

1467. Gibbons, Reginald (ed.). *Writers from South Africa: fourteen writers on culture, politics and literary theory and activity in South Africa today*. Illinois: TriQuarterly Books, 1989. (TriQuarterly series on criticism and culture; 2).

1468. Gordimer, Nadine, and Lionel Abrahams (eds.). *South African writing today*. London: Penguin, 1967. Anthology of fiction, poetry, drama and prose.

1469. Gray, Stephen (ed.). *The Penguin book of contemporary South African short stories*. Johannesburg: Longman Penguin, 1992.

1470. ——— (ed.). *South African plays.* London: Heinemann, 1993.

1471. Kavanagh, Robert (ed.). *South African people's plays: ons phola hi.* London: Heinemann, 1981. (AWS; 224). Plays by Gibson Kente, Credo V. Mutwa, Mthuli Shezi.

1472. Kerfoot, Caroline (ed.). *We came to town.* Johannesburg: Ravan Press, 1985. (Staffrider series; 18). Worker stories.

1473. Krige, Uys, and Jack Cope (eds.). *The Penguin book of South African verse.* Harmondsworth: Penguin, 1968. English, Afrikaans, and African language poems.

1474. Lindfors, Bernth (ed.). *South African voices.* Austin: University of Texas Press, 1975. (Occasional publications in African literature; 11). Poetry.

1475. Lockett, Cecily (ed.). *Breaking the silence: a century of South African women's poetry.* Johannesburg: Ad. Donker, 1990.

1476. Loyson, Madeleine (ed.). *The Open door omnibus: selections from new writers.* Cape Town: Buchu Books, 1993. Poetry and prose.

1477. Mabuza, Lindiwe (comp.). *One never knows: an anthology of black South African women in exile.* Johannesburg: Skotaville, 1989. Short stories.

1478. Marquard, Jean (ed.). *A Century of South African short stories.* Johannesburg: Ad. Donker, 1978. Anthology.

1479. Molefe, Sono (ed.). *Malibongwe: ANC women: poetry is also their weapon.* Sweden: ANC, 1982.

1480. Mutloatse, Mothobi (ed.). *Forced landing: writings from the Staffrider generation.* Johannesburg: Ravan Press, 1980. (Staffrider series; 3). Also pub. as: *Africa South: contemporary writings.* London: Heinemann, 1981 (AWS; 243).

1481. Mzamane, Mbulelo V. (ed.). *Hungry flames and other black South African short stories.* Harlow: Longman, 1986. (Longman African classics).

1482. Ndlovu, Duma (ed.). *Woza Afrika! an anthology of South African plays.* New York: G. Braziller, 1986.

1483. Oliphant, Andries (ed.). *Essential things: an anthology of new South African poetry.* Johannesburg: COSAW, 1992.

1484. ———. *The Finishing touch: stories from the 1991 Nadine Gordimer Short Story Award.* Johannesburg: COSAW, 1992.

1485. ———, and Ivan Vladislavic (eds.). *Ten years of Staffrider: 1978-1988.* Johannesburg: Ravan Press, 1988. (Staffrider; v. 7 no. 3/4).

1486. Oosthuizen, Ann (ed.). *Sometimes when it rains: writings by South African women.* London: Pandora/Routledge & Kegan Paul, 1987.

1487. Orkin, Mark (ed.). *At the junction. Four plays by the Junction Avenue Theatre Company.* Johannesburg: Witwatersrand University Press, 1994.

1488. Plumpp, Sterling (ed.). *Somehow we survive: an anthology of Southern African writing.* New York: Thunder's Mouth Press, 1982.

1489. Rive, Richard (ed.). *Quartet: new voices from South Africa: Alex La Guma, James Matthews, Richard Rive, Alf Wannenburgh.* New York; London: Crown; Heinemann, 1963. Short stories.

1490. Royston, Robert (ed.). *Black poets in South Africa.* London: Heinemann, 1974. (AWS; 164). First pub. as: *To whom it may concern.* Johannesburg: Ad. Donker, 1973. Poetry.

1491. Sévry, Jean. *Afrique du Sud: ségregation et littérature: anthologie critique.* Paris: L'Harmattan, 1989.

1492. Shore, L., and M. Shore-Bos (eds.). *Come back, Africa!: short stories from South Africa.* New York: International Publishers, 1968. Short stories.

1493. Sitas, Ari (ed.). *Black Mamba rising: South African worker poets in struggle: Alfred Temba Qabula, Mi S'dumo Hlatshwayo, Nise Malange.* Durban: Culture and Working Life, for COSATU, 1986. Poetry.

1494. Tsikang, Seageng, and Dinah Lefakane (eds.). *Women in South Africa: from the heart: an anthology of stories written by a new generation of writers.* Johannesburg: Seriti sa Sechaba, 1988.

1495. Van Niekerk, Annmarie (ed.). *Raising the blinds: a century of South African women's stories.* Parklands, South Africa: Ad. Donker, 1990. Short stories.

General studies

1496. Alvarez-Péreyre, Jacques. *The poetry of commitment in South Africa.* London: Heinemann, 1979. Tr. by Clive Wake. Orig. pub. as: *Les Guetteurs de l'aube: poésie et apartheid.* Grenoble: Presses universitaires de Grenoble, 1979.

1497. Barnett, Ursula A. *A Vision of order: a study of black South African literature in English (1914-1980).* London; Amherst: Sinclair Browne; University of Massachusetts Press, 1983.

1498. Boehmer, Elleke (ed.). *Altered state?: writing and South Africa.* Sydney: Dangaroo Press, 1994.

1499. Brown, Duncan, and Bruno Van Dyk (eds.). *Exchanges: South African writing in transition.* Pietermaritzburg: University of Natal Press, 1991.

1500. Campschreur, W., and J. Divendal (eds.). *Culture in another South Africa.* London: Zed, 1989.

1501. Chandramohan, Balasubramanyam. *A Study in trans-ethnicity in modern South Africa.* Lewiston: Mellen Research University Press, 1992.

1502. Chapman, Michael, Colin Gardner, and Es'kia Mphahlele (eds.). *Perspectives on South African English literature.* Johannesburg: Ad. Donker, 1992.

1503. ———. *South African English poetry: a modern perspective.* Johannesburg: Ad. Donker, 1984.

1504. Coetzee, J. M. *White writing: on the culture of letters in South Africa.* New Haven: Yale University Press, 1988.

1505. Derrida, Jacques, et al. (eds.). *For Nelson Mandela.* New York: Seaver, 1987. Essays and literary tributes.

1506. DeShazer, Mary K. *A Poetics of resistance: women writing in El Salvador, South Africa, and the United States.* Ann Arbor: University of Michigan Press, 1994.

1507. February, V. A. *Mind your colour: the "coloured" stereotype in South African literature.* London: Kegan Paul, 1981. (Afrika-Studiecentrum; monographs).

1508. Fletcher, Pauline (ed.). *Black/white writing: essays on South African literature.* Lewisburg: Bucknell University Press, 1993. (Bucknell review; v. 37, no. 1).

1509. Fuchs, Anne, and Geoffrey V. Davis. *Theatre and change in South Africa.* Reading: Harwood, 1995.

1510. Gordimer, Nadine. *The Essential gesture: writing, politics and places.* London: J. Cape, 1988.

1511. ———. *Writing and being: the Charles Eliot Norton Lectures.* Cambridge, MA: Harvard University Press, 1995.

1512. Heywood, Christopher. *Aspects of South African literature.* London; New York: Heinemann; Africana, 1976.

1513. Hunter, Eva, and Craig Mackenzie (eds.). *Between the lines II: interviews with Nadine Gordimer, Menán du Plessis, Zoë Wicomb, Lauretta Ngcobo.* Grahamstown: National English Literary Museum, 1993. (Interviews series; 6).

1514. Kavanagh, Robert. *Theatre and cultural struggle in South Africa.* London: Zed, 1985.

1515. Klíma, Vladimir. *South African prose writing in English.* Prague: Oriental Institute Academia, 1969.

1516. Leveson, M. *The Image of the Jew in South African English fiction.* Johannesburg: Witwatersrand University Press, 1994.

1517. Mackenzie, Craig, and Cherry Clayton (eds.). *Between the lines: interviews with Bessie Head, Sheila Roberts, Ellen Kuzwayo, Miriam Tlali.* Grahamstown: National English Literary Museum, 1989. (Interview series; 4).

1518. Mphahlele, Es'kia, Colin Gardner, and Michael Chapman (eds.). *Perspectives on South African English literature.* Johannesburg: Ad. Donker, 1992.

1519. Ndebele, Najabulo S. *South African literature and culture: rediscovery of the ordinary.* Manchester: Manchester University Press, 1994.

1520. Orkin, Mark. *Drama and the South African state.* Manchester; Johannesburg: Manchester University Press; Witwatersrand University Press, 1991.

1521. Parker, Kenneth (ed.). *The South African novel in English: essays in criticism and society.* New York; London: Africana Press; Macmillan, 1978.

1522. Petersen, Kirsten Holst (ed.). *On Shifting sands: new art and literature from South Africa.* Sydney: Dangaroo Press, 1991.

1523. Sachs, Albie, et al. *Spring is rebellious: arguments about cultural freedom.* Cape Town: Buchu Books, 1990. Ed. by Ingrid de Kok and Karen Press.

1524. Shava, Piniel Viriri. *A People's voice: Black South African writing in the twentieth century.* London; Athens; Harare: Zed; Ohio University Press; Baobab Books, 1989.

1525. Trump, Martin (ed.). *Rendering things visible: essays on South African literary culture.* Johannesburg; Athens, Ohio: Ravan Press; Ohio University Press, 1990.

1526. Wade, Michael. *White on black in South Africa: a study of English-language inscriptions of skin colour.* London; New York: Macmillan; St. Martin's, 1993.

1527. Ward, David. *Chronicles of darkness.* London; New York: Routledge, 1989.

1528. Watts, Jane. *Black writers from South Africa: towards a discourse of liberation.* London: Macmillan, in association with St. Antony's College, 1989.

1529. Welz, Dieter. *Mayibuye wiederkehr des verdrangten: berichte aus sudafrika.* Essen: Verlag Die Blaue Eule, 1992.

1530. ———. *Writing against apartheid: interviews with South African authors.* Grahamstown: National English Literary Museum, 1987. (NELM interview series; 2).

1531. White, Landeg, and Tim Couzens (eds.). *Literature and society in South Africa.* Cape Town; London: Maskew Miller Longman; Longman, 1984.

Authors

1532. Abrahams, Peter. *A Blackman speaks of freedom!* Durban: Universal, 1941. Poetry.

1533. ———. *Dark testament.* London: Allen & Unwin, 1942. Repr.: Nendeln: Kraus Reprint, 1970. Short stories.

1534. ———. *Mine boy.* London: Heinemann, 1963. (AWS; 6). First pub.: London: Crisp, 1946. Novel.

1535. ———. *The Path of thunder.* Cape Town: D. Philip, 1984. First pub.: New York: Harper, 1948. Novel.

1536. ———. *Return to Goli.* London: Faber, 1953. Autobiography.

1537. ———. *Tell freedom*. London: Faber, 1954. Autobiography.

1538. ———. *Wild conquest*. New York: Harper, 1950. Novel.

1539. ———. *A Wreath for Udomo*. London: Faber, 1956. Novel.

1540. Ensor, Robert. *The Novels of Peter Abrahams and the rise of nationalism in Africa*. Essen: Die Bleue Eule, 1992. (Englischsprachige literaturen Afrikas; 7).

1541. Ogungbesan, Kolawole. *The Writing of Peter Abrahams*. London; New York: Hodder; Africana, 1979.

1542. Wade, Michael. *Peter Abrahams*. London; Ibadan: Evans, 1972.

1543. Afrika, Tatamkulu. *Dark rider*. Plumstead, South Africa: Snailpress/Mayibuye Books, 1992. (Mayibuye history and literature series; 44). Poetry.

1544. Altman, Phyllis (F). *The Law of the vultures*. Johannesburg: Ad. Donker, 1987. (Paper books). Novel.

1545. Asvat, Farouk. *A Celebration of flames*. Craighall: Ad. Donker, 1987. (Donker poetry). Poetry.

1546. Blackburn, Douglas. *A Burgher quixote*. Cape Town: D. Philip, 1984. Repr. of 1903 ed., with new introd. by S. Gray (Africasouth paperbacks). Novel.

1547. Gray, Stephen. *Douglas Blackburn*. Boston: Twayne, 1984. (Twayne's world authors. African literature; 719).

1548. Bloom, Harry. *Transvaal episode*. Sagaponack, NY; London: Second Chance Press; Jay Landesman, 1981. Orig. pub.: London: Collins, 1956. Novel.

1549. Boehmer, Elleke (F). *An Immaculate figure*. London: Bloomsbury, 1993. Novel.

1550. ———. *Screens against the sky.* London: Bloomsbury/Penguin, 1990. Novel.

1551. Bosman, Herman Charles. *A Bosman treasury.* Cape Town: Human & Rousseau, 1991. Ed. by Lionel Abrahams. Short stories.

1552. ———. *The Collected works of Herman Charles Bosman.* Johannesburg: J. Ball, 1981. Ed. by Lionel Abrahams.

1553. Breytenbach, Breyten. *Memory of snow and dust.* London: Faber, 1990. Novel. See also Afrikaans section.

1554. ———. *Return to paradise.* Cape Town: D. Philip, 1993. Prose.

1555. ———. *The True confessions of an albino terrorist.* London: Faber, 1984. Prose.

1556. Brink, André. *An Act of terror: a novel.* London: Minerva, 1992. See also Afrikaans section.

1557. ———. *States of emergency.* London: Faber, 1988. Novel.

1558. Brutus, Dennis. *Airs and tributes.* Camden, NJ: Whirlwind, 1989. Ed. by Gil Ott. Poetry.

1559. ———. *Letters to Martha, and other poems from a South African prison.* London: Heinemann, 1969. (AWS; 46). Poetry.

1560. ———. *Salutes and censures.* Enugu: Fourth Dimension, 1984. Poetry.

1561. ———. *A Simple lust: selected poems including Sirens knuckles boots, Letters to Martha, Poems from Algiers, Thoughts abroad.* London: Heinemann, 1973. (AWS; 115).

1562. ———. *Sirens, knuckles, boots.* Ibadan: Mbari Press, 1963. Poetry.

1563. ———. *Strains.* Austin, TX: Troubadour, 1975. Poetry.

1564. ———. *Stubborn hope: new poems and selections from China poems and Strains.* London; Washington: Heinemann; Three Continents Press, 1978. (AWS; 208).

1565. ———. *Thoughts abroad.* De Valle, TX: Troubadour, 1975. Pub. under the name: "John Bruin." Poetry.

1566. Butler, Guy. *Essays and lectures, 1949-1991.* Cape Town: D. Philip, 1994. Ed. by Stephen Watson.

1567. ———. *Pilgrimage to Dias Cross: a narrative poem.* Cape Town: D. Philip, 1987.

1568. Campbell, Roy. *Adamastor.* London: Faber, 1930. Poetry.

1569. ———. *The Collected poems.* London: Bodley Head, 1960.

1570. ———. *Light on a dark horse.* London: Hollis and Carter, 1951. Autobiography.

1571. Povey, John. *Roy Campbell.* New York: Twayne, 1977. (Twayne's world authors series).

1572. Smith, Rowland. *Lyric and polemic: the literary personality of Roy Campbell.* Montreal: McGill-Queen's University Press, 1972.

1573. Clayton, Cherry (F). *Leaving home.* Cape Town: Snailpress, 1994. Poetry.

1574. Cloete, Stuart. *The Turning wheels.* Boston: Houghton Mifflin, 1937. Novel.

1575. Coetzee, J. M. *Age of iron.* London; New York: Secker & Warburg; Random House, 1990. Novel.

1576. ———. *Doubling the point: essays and interviews.* Cambridge, MA: Harvard University Press, 1992. Ed. by David Atwell.

1577. ———. *Dusklands.* Johannesburg: Ravan Press, 1974. Also pub.: London: Secker & Warburg, 1982. Novel.

1578. ———. *Foe.* London: Secker & Warburg, 1987. Novel.

1579. ———. *In the heart of the country.* London: Secker & Warburg, 1977. Novel.

1580. ———. *Life & times of Michael K.* London: Secker & Warburg, 1983. Novel.

1581. ———. *The Master of Petersburg.* London: Secker & Warburg, 1994. Novel.

1582. ———. *Waiting for the barbarians.* London; Johannesburg: Secker & Warburg; Ravan Press, 1980. Novel.

1583. Atwell, David. *J. M. Coetzee: South Africa and the politics of writing.* Cape Town; Berkeley: D. Philip; University of California Press, 1993.

1584. Dovey, Teresa. *The Novels of J. M. Coetzee: Lacanian allegories.* Johannesburg: Ad. Donker, 1988.

1585. Gallagher, Susan V. *A Story of South Africa: J. M. Coetzee's fiction in context.* Cambridge, MA: Harvard University Press, 1991.

1586. Penner, A. R. *Countries of the mind: the fiction of J. M. Coetzee.* New York: Greenwood, 1989. (Contributions to the study of world literature; 32).

1587. Cope, Jack. *The Fair house.* Berlin: Seven Seas Publishers, 1960. Novel.

1588. Cronin, Jeremy. *Inside.* Johannesburg: Ravan Press, 1983. New ed.: London: Cape, 1987. Poetry.

1589. Dangor, Achmat. *Private voices*. Johannesburg: COSAW, 1992. Poetry.

1590. ———. *Waiting for Leila*. Johannesburg: Ravan Press, 1981. Short stories.

1591. ———. *The Z town trilogy*. Johannesburg: Ravan Press, 1990. Short stories.

1592. De Kok, Ingrid (F). *Familiar ground: poems*. Johannesburg: Ravan Press, 1988.

1593. Dhlomo, H. I. E. *Collected works*. Johannesburg: Ravan Press, 1985. Ed. by Nick Visser and Tim Couzens. Drama, poetry, and short stories.

1594. ———. *The Girl who killed to save: Nongqause the liberator: a play*. Lovedale: Lovedale Press, 1936.

1595. ———. *Valley of a thousand hills*. Durban: Knox, 1941. Poem.

1596. Couzens, Tim. *The New African: a study of the life and work of H. I. E. Dhlomo*. Johannesburg: Ravan Press, 1985.

1597. Visser, N. W. (ed.). *Literary theory and criticism of H. I. E. Dhlomo*. (*English in Africa* v.4 no.2 1977).

1598. Dhlomo, Rolf R. R. *An African tragedy*. Lovedale: Lovedale Press, 1928. Short story.

1599. ———. *R. R. R. Dhlomo: 20 short stories*. Ed. by Tim Couzens. (*English in Africa* v.2 no.1 1975).

1600. Dike, Fatima (F). *The First South African*. Johannesburg: Ravan Press, 1979. (Ravan playscripts; 4). Drama.

1601. Dikeni, Sandile. *Guava juice*. Bellville: Mayibuye Books, 1992. (Mayibuye history and literature; 43). Poetry.

1602. Dikobe, Modikwe. *The Marabi dance*. London: Heinemann, 1973. (AWS; 124). Novel.

1603. Driver, C. J. *Elegy for a revolutionary*. Cape Town: Philip, 1984. (Africasouth paperbacks). Novel.

1604. ———. *In the water-margins*. Cape Town: Snailpress, 1994. Poetry.

1605. Du Plessis, Menán (F). *Longlive!* Cape Town: D. Philip, 1989. Novel.

1606. ———. *A State of fear*. Claremont, South Africa: D. Philip, 1983. Also pub.: London: Pandora, 1987. Novel.

1607. Essop, Ahmed. *The Hajji and other stories*. Johannesburg: Ravan Press, 1978. Short stories.

1608. ———. *Noorjehan and other stories*. Johannesburg: Ravan Press, 1990. Short stories.

1609. ———. *The Visitation*. Johannesburg: Ravan Press, 1980. Novel.

1610. Feinberg, Barry. *Gardens of struggle*. Bellville, South Africa: Mayibuye Books, 1992. (Mayibuye history and literature series; 42). Poetry.

1611. Fugard, Athol. *My children! My Africa! and selected shorter plays*. Johannesburg; London: Witwatersrand University Press; Faber, 1990. Ed. by Stephen Gray.

1612. ———. *Playland . . . and other words*. Johannesburg: Witwatersrand University Press, 1992. Drama.

1613. ———. *The Road to Mecca: a play in two acts*. London: Faber, 1985.

1614. ———. *Selected plays*. Oxford: OUP, 1987.

1615. ———. *The Township plays*. Oxford: OUP, 1994.

1616. ———. *Tsotsi*. London: Rex Collings, 1980. Drama.

1617. ———. John Kani, and Winston Ntshona. *Sizwe Bansi is dead*. London: OUP, 1974. Drama.

1618. Walder, Dennis. *Athol Fugard.* Basingstoke, Eng.: Macmillan, 1984. (Macmillan modern dramatists).

1619. Fugard, Sheila (F). *A Revolutionary woman: a novel.* Johannesburg: Ad. Donker, 1983.

1620. Galgut, Damon. *The Quarry.* Johannesburg: Viking Penguin, 1995. Novel.

1621. Gordimer, Nadine (F). *Burger's daughter.* New York; London: Viking; Cape, 1980. Novel.

1622. ———. *The Conservationist.* London: Cape, 1974. Novel.

1623. ———. *Crimes of conscience.* Oxford: Heinemann, 1991. Short stories.

1624. ———. *Face to face.* Johannesburg: Silver Leaf, 1949. Short stories.

1625. ———. *Friday's footprint.* London; Toronto: Gollancz; Macmillan, 1960. Short stories.

1626. ———. *A Guest of honour.* New York: Viking, 1970. Novel.

1627. ———. *July's people.* Johannesburg; New York; London: Ravan/Taurus; Viking; Cape, 1982. Short stories.

1628. ———. *Jump and other stories.* Cape Town; London: D. Philip; Bloomsbury, 1991.

1629. ———. *The Late bourgeois world.* New York; London: Viking; Gollancz, 1966. Novel.

1630. ———. *Livingstone's companions.* New York: Viking, 1972. Short stories.

1631. ———. *The Lying days.* London; New York: Gollancz; Simon, 1953. Novel.

1632. ———. *My son's story.* New York; London; Johannesburg: Knopf; Cape; Taurus, 1990. Novel.

1633. ———. *None to accompany me.* London; New York: Bloomsbury; Farrar, Strauss & Giroux, 1994. Novel.

1634. ———. *Not for publication.* London; New York: Gollancz; Viking, 1965. Short stories.

1635. ———. *Occasion for loving.* New York; London: Viking; Gollancz, 1963. Novel.

1636. ———. *Selected stories.* London: Cape, 1975.

1637. ———. *Six feet of the country: fifteen short stories.* New York; Harmondsworth: Simon; Penguin, 1982.

1638. ———. *The Soft voice of the serpent and other stories.* New York; Toronto: Simon; Musson, 1952. Short stories.

1639. ———. *A Soldier's embrace: stories.* New York; London: Viking; Cape, 1980.

1640. ———. *Some Sunday for sure.* London: Heinemann, 1976. (AWS; 177). Short stories.

1641. ———. *Something out there.* Johannesburg; London; New York: Ravan Press; Cape; Viking, 1984. Short stories.

1642. ———. *A Sport of nature.* New York; London; Cape Town: Knopf; Cape; D. Philip, 1987. Novel.

1643. ———. *Why haven't you written: selected stories 1950-1972.* London: Penguin, 1992.

1644. ———. *A World of strangers.* London: Gollancz, 1958. Novel.

1645. Clingman, Stephen. *The Novels of Nadine Gordimer.* Amherst: University of Massachusetts Press, 1992. First pub.: Johannesburg; London: Ravan Press; Allen, 1986.

1646. Cooke, John. *The Novels of Nadine Gordimer: private lives/public landscapes.* Baton Rouge: Louisiana State University Press, 1985.

1647. Ettin, Andrew Vogel. *Betrayals of the body politic: the literary commitments of Nadine Gordimer.* Charlottesville: University Press of Virginia, 1993.

1648. Head, Dominic. *Nadine Gordimer.* Cambridge: CUP, 1994.

1649. Heywood, Christopher. *Nadine Gordimer.* Windsor: Profile, 1983. (Writers and their work; 281).

1650. King, Bruce (ed.). *The Later fiction of Nadine Gordimer.* New York; London: St. Martin's; Macmillan, 1993.

1651. Newman, Julie. *Nadine Gordimer.* London: Routledge, 1988.

1652. Smith, Rowland (ed.). *Critical essays on Nadine Gordimer.* Boston: G.K. Hall, 1990.

1653. Wade, Michael. *Nadine Gordimer.* London: Evans, 1978. (Modern African writers series).

1654. Wagner, Kathrin. *Rereading Nadine Gordimer.* Johannesburg; Bloomington: Witwatersrand University Press; Indiana University Press, 1994.

1655. Gottschalk, Keith. *Emergency poems.* Bellville: Mayibuye, 1992. (Mayibuye history & literature series; 41).

1656. Gray, Stephen. *Selected poems, 1960-92.* Cape Town: D. Philip, 1994.

1657. ———. *War child.* Rivonia: Ashanti, 1992. Novel.

1658. Gwala, Mafika. *Jol'iinkomo.* Johannesburg: Ad. Donker, 1976. Poetry.

1659. ———. *No more lullabies.* Johannesburg: Ravan Press, 1982. (Staffrider series; 15). Poetry.

1660. Hirson, Denis. *The House next door to Africa.* Cape Town; Manchester: D. Philip; Carcanet, 1986. Novel.

1661. Hope, Christopher. *The Love songs of Nathan J. Swirsky.* London: Macmillan, 1993. Novel.

1662. Horn, Peter. *An Axe in the ice.* Johannesburg: COSAW, 1992. Poetry.

1663. ———. *Poems, 1964-89.* Johannesburg: Ravan Press, 1991.

1664. Hutchinson, Alfred. *The Rain-killers.* London: University of London Press, 1964. Drama.

1665. ———. *Road to Ghana.* London: Gollancz, 1960. Autobiography.

1666. Jabavu, Noni (F). *The Ochre people: scenes from a South African life.* London: Murray, 1963. Autobiographical novel.

1667. Karodia, Farida (F). *Against an African sky and other stories.* Cape Town: D. Philip, 1995.

1668. ———. *Coming home and other stories.* London: Heinemann, 1988. (AWS).

1669. ———. *A Shattering of silence.* Portsmouth, NH; London: Heinemann, 1993. (AWS). Novel set in Mozambique.

1670. Kgositsile, Keorapetse. *My name is Afrika.* New York: Doubleday. Poetry.

1671. ———. *Spirits unchained.* Detroit: Broadside Press, 1969. Poetry.

1672. ———. *When the clouds clear.* Johannesburg: COSAW, 1990. Introd. by Ari Sitas. Poetry.

1673. Kriel, Maja (F). *Original sin and other stories.* Cape Town: Carrefour Press, 1993.

1674. Kunene, Daniel P. *From the pit of hell to the spring of life.* Johannesburg: Ravan Press, 1986. Short stories.

1675. ———. *A Seed must seem to die.* Johannesburg: Ravan Press, 1981. Poetry.

1676. Kuzwayo, Ellen (F). *Call me woman.* London; Cape Town: Women's Press; D. Philip, 1985. Autobiography.

1677. La Guma, Alex. *And a Threefold cord.* Berlin: Seven Seas, 1964. Repr.: London: Kliptown, 1988. Novel.

1678. ———. *In the fog of the season's end.* London: Heinemann, 1972. (AWS; 110). Novel.

1679. ———. *Liberation chabalaza: the world of Alex La Guma.* Bellville: Mayibuye Books, 1993. Ed. by A. Odendaal and R. Field.

1680. ———. *Memories of home: the writings of Alex La Guma.* Trenton, NJ: Africa World Press, 1991. Ed. by Cecil A. Abrahams. Articles, interviews, and tributes.

1681. ———. *The Stone country.* London: Heinemann, 1974. (AWS; 152). First pub.: Berlin: Seven Seas, 1967. Novel.

1682. ———. *Time of the butcherbird.* London: Heinemann, 1979. (AWS; 212). Novel.

1683. ———. *A Walk in the night.* Ibadan: Mbari Press, 1961. Novella.

1684. ———. *A Walk in the night, and other stories.* London: Heinemann, 1967. (AWS; 35). Repr.: Cape Town: D. Philip, 1991.

1685. Abrahams, Cecil A. *Alex La Guma.* Boston: Twayne, 1985.

1686. Asein, Samuel O. *Alex La Guma: the man and his work*. Ibadan: New Horn/Heinemann, 1987.

1687. Chandramohan, Balasubramanyam. *A Study of trans-ethnicity in modern South Africa: the writings of Alex La Guma*. Lewiston: Mellen Research, 1992.

1688. JanMohammed, Abdul R. *Alex La Guma: the literary and political functions of marginality in the colonial situation*. Boston: African Studies Center, Boston University, 1982.

1689. Langa, Mandla. *A Rainbow on a paper sky*. London: Kliptown Books, 1989. Novel.

1690. ———. *Tenderness of blood*. Harare: ZPH, 1987. (ZPH writers series; 31). Novel.

1691. Lewis, Ethelreda (F). *Wild Deer*. Cape Town: D. Philip, 1933. Ed. by Tim Couzens. Historical novel.

1692. Mabuza, Lindiwe (F). *Letter to Letta*. Johannesburg: Skotaville, 1991. Poems dedicated to Oliver Tambo.

1693. Madingoane, Ingoapele. *Africa my beginning*. Johannesburg; London: Ravan Press; Rex Collings, 1979. Poetry.

1694. Maemola, Thabo Nkosinathi. *Mixed signals*. Johannesburg: Skotaville, 1994. Novel.

1695. Magona, Sindiwe (F). *Living, loving and lying awake at night*. Cape Town: D. Philip, 1991. (Africasouth new writing). Short stories.

1696. ———. *To my children's children* and *Forced to grow*. Cape Town: D. Philip, 1990-1992. 2 v. Autobiography.

1697. Maimane, Arthur. *Victims*. London: Allison and Busby, 1976. Novel.

1698. Makhoba, B. *On the eve*. Johannesburg: Skotaville, 1986. (Skotaville series; 3). Fiction.

1699. Manaka, Matsemela. *Egoli: city of gold.* Johannesburg: Ravan Press, 1980. Drama.

1700. Mandela, Zindziswa (F). *Black as I am.* Los Angeles: Guild of Tutors Press, 1978. Poetry.

1701. Maseko, Bheki. *Mamlambo and other stories.* Johannesburg: COSAW, 1991.

1702. Matshikiza, Todd. *Chocolates for my wife: slices of my life.* London: Hodder, 1961. Autobiography.

1703. Matshoba, Mtutuzeli. *Call me not a man: and other stories.* Johannesburg; London: Ravan Press; Rex Collings, 1979. Also pub.: Harlow: Longman, 1981.

1704. ———. *Seeds of war.* Johannesburg: Ravan Press, 1981. Drama.

1705. Matthews, James. *Cry rage!* Johannesburg: Spro-Cas/Ravan, 1972. Poetry.

1706. ———. *Pass me a meatball, Jones.* New York: Simon and Schuster, 1977. Poetry.

1707. Mchunu, Vusi D. *Stronger souls.* Cape Town: Buchu Books, 1990. Poetry.

1708. Mda, Zakes. *And the girls in their Sunday dresses: four works.* Johannesburg: Witwatersrand University Press, 1993. Drama.

1709. ———. *The Plays of Zakes Mda.* Johannesburg: Ravan Press, 1990.

1710. ———. *We shall sing for the fatherland.* Johannesburg: Ravan Press, 1980. (Ravan playscripts; 3). Drama.

1711. Melamu, Moteane. *Children of the twilight.* Johannesburg: Skotaville, 1987. Short stories.

1712. Mfeketo, Nomathemba (F). *Why, can't a man.* Uppsala: Reprocentralen, Uppsala University, 1992.

1713. Millin, Sarah Gertude (F). *The Dark river.* London: Collins, 1919. Novel.

1714. Mogotsi, Isaac. *The Alexandra tales.* Johannesburg: Ravan Press, 1993. Novel.

1715. Mphahlele, Es'kia. *Afrika my music: an autobiography 1957-1983.* Johannesburg: Ravan Press, 1984.

1716. ———. *Bury me at the marketplace: selected letters of Es'kia Mphahlele 1943-1980.* Johannesburg: Skotaville, 1984. Ed. by N. Chabani Manganyi.

1717. ———. *Chirundu.* Johannesburg; Westport: Ravan Press; Lawrence Hill, 1979. 2nd ed.: Ravan Press, 1994. Novel.

1718. ———. *Down Second Avenue.* London: Faber, 1959. Autobiography.

1719. ———. *In Corner B.* Nairobi: EAPH, 1967. Short stories.

1720. ———. *Man must live, and other stories.* Cape Town: African Bookman, 1947.

1721. ———. *Renewal time.* Columbia, LA: Readers International, 1988. Short stories.

1722. ———. *The Unbroken song: selected writings of Es'kia Mphahlele.* Johannesburg: Ravan Press, 1981. (Staffrider series; 9).

1723. ———. *Voices in the whirlwind and other essays.* London; New York: Macmillan; Hill and Wang, 1972.

1724. ———. *The Wanderers.* New York: Macmillan, 1971. Novel.

1725. Barnett, Ursula A. *Ezekiel Mphahlele.* Boston: Twayne, 1976. (Twayne's world author series; 417).

1726. Manganyi, N. Chabani. *Exiles and homecomings: a biography of Es'kia Mphahlele.* Johannesburg: Ravan Press, 1983.

1727. Thuynsma, Peter N. (ed.). *Footsteps along the way: a tribute to Es'kia Mphahlele.* Johannesburg: Justified Press and Skotaville, 1989.

1728. Mqayisa, Khayalethu. *Confused Mhlaba.* Johannesburg: Ravan Press, 1974. Drama.

1729. Mtshali, Oswald Mbuyiseni. *Fireflames.* Pietermaritzburg: Shuter and Shooter, 1980. Poetry.

1730. ———. *Sounds of a cowhide drum.* Johannesburg; London: Renoster; OUP, 1971. Poetry.

1731. Mtwa, Percy, Mbongeni Ngema, and Barney Simon. *Woza Albert!* London: Methuen, 1983. Drama.

1732. Mzamane, Mbulelo V. *The Children of Soweto: a trilogy.* London: Longman, 1982. (Drumbeat novel). Novel.

1733. ———. *Mzala.* Johannesburg: Ravan Press, 1980. Short stories.

1734. Nakasa, Nathaniel N. *The World of Nat Nakasa.* Johannesburg: Ravan Press, 1975. Ed. by Essop Patel. Essays.

1735. Ndebele, Najabulo S. *Fools and other stories.* Johannesburg: Ravan Press, 1983. (Staffrider series; 19).

1736. Ngcobo, Lauretta (F). *Cross of gold.* London: Longman, 1981. Novel.

1737. ———. *And They didn't die.* London: Virago, 1990. Novel.

1738. Ngubane, Jordan. *Ushaba, the hurtle to Blood River.* Washington: Three Continents Press, 1979. Novel.

1739. Nicol, Mike. *This day and age.* Cape Town: D. Philip, 1992. Novel.

1740. Nkondo, Sankie (F). *Flames of fury and other poems*. Johannesburg: COSAW, 1990.

1741. Nkosi, Lewis. *Home and exile, and other selections*. London: Longmans, Green, 1965. Essays.

1742. ———. *Mating birds*. London: Constable; Flamingo, 1986. Short stories.

1743. ———. *The Rhythm of violence*. London: OUP, 1964. (Three crowns book). Drama.

1744. ———. *The Transplanted heart: essays on South Africa*. Benin City, Nigeria: Ethiope, 1975.

1745. Nortje, Arthur. *Dead roots*. London: Heinemann, 1973. (AWS; 141). Poetry.

1746. Nyatsumba, Kaizer Mabhilidi. *A Vision of paradise*. Fordsburg, South Africa: COSAW, 1991. Short stories.

1747. Paton, Alan. *Cry the beloved country*. London: J. Cape, 1948. Novel.

1748. ———. *Journey continued*. Oxford: OUP, 1989. Autobiography.

1749. ———. *Too late the phalarope*. London: J. Cape, 1953. Novel.

1750. ———, and Krishna Shah. *Sponono: a play in three acts*. Cape Town; New York: D. Philip; Scribner, 1965.

1751. Alexander, Peter F. *Alan Paton*. Oxford: OUP 1994.

1752. Callan, Edward. *Alan Paton*. Boston: Twayne, 1968. Rev. ed. 1982. (Twayne's world authors series; 40).

1753. Peteni, R. L. *Hill of fools*. London: Heinemann, 1976. (AWS; 178). Novel.

1754. Plaatje, Solomon Thekiso. *Mhudi: an epic of South African native life a hundred years ago.* London; Washington: Heinemann; Three Continents Press, 1978. (AWS; 201). Ed. by Stephen Gray. First pub.: Lovedale Press, 1930. Novel.

1755. Plomer, William. *The autobiography of William Plomer.* London: Cape, 1975. Orig. pub.: *Double lives: an autobiography.* (London: Cape, 1943).

1756. ———. *Selected poems.* London: Hogarth, 1940.

1757. ———. *Turbot Wolfe.* Oxford: OUP, 1985. Orig. pub.: London: Hogarth, 1928. Novel.

1758. Alexander, Peter F. *William Plomer: a biography.* Oxford; New York: OUP, 1989.

1759. Pringle, Thomas. *Africa poems of Thomas Pringle.* Pietermaritzburg: University of Natal Press, 1989. Ed. by E. Pereira and M. Chapman.

1760. ———. *Narrative of a residence in South Africa.* Cape Town: Struik, 1966. Repr. of 1834 ed. entitled *African sketches*; contains: *Poems illustrative of South Africa.*

1761. Doyle, John R. Jr. *Thomas Pringle.* New York: Twayne, 1972. (Twayne's world authors series).

1762. Qabula, Alfred T. *A Working life, cruel beyond belief.* [Durban]: National Union of Metalworkers, South Africa, 1989. Autobiography, with poems.

1763. Rive, Richard. *Advance, retreat: selected short stories.* Cape Town: D. Philip, 1983. Short stories.

1764. ———. *"Buckingham Palace," District Six.* Cape Town: D. Philip, 1986. Novel.

1765. ———. *Emergency.* Cape Town: D. Philip, 1988. First pub.: London: Faber, 1964. Novel.

1766. ———. *Emergency continued.* Cape Town: D. Philip, 1990. Novel.

1767. ———. *Writing black.* Cape Town: D. Philip, 1981. Autobiography.

1768. Roberts, Sheila (F). *Coming in and other stories.* Johannesburg: Justified Press, 1993. Short stories.

1769. Rosenthal, Jane (F). *Uncertain consolations.* Cape Town: Snailpress, 1994. Novel.

1770. Schreiner, Olive (F). *The Story of an African farm.* Oxford: OUP, 1992. Orig. pub.: London: Hutchinson, 1883. Novel.

1771. ———. *Trooper Peter Halket of Mashonaland.* Johannesburg: Ad. Donker, 1992. (Africana library). Orig. pub.: London: Unwin, 1897. Novel.

1772. Berkman, J. A. *The Healing imagination of Olive Schreiner: beyond South African colonialism.* Amherst: University of Massachussetts Press, 1989.

1773. First, Ruth, and Ann Scott. *Olive Schreiner.* London: Deutsch, 1980.

1774. Vivan, I. (ed.). *The Flawed diamond: essays on Olive Schreiner.* Sydney: Dangaroo Press, 1991.

1775. Sepamla, Sipho. *Hurry up to it!* Johannesburg: Ad. Donker, 1975. Poetry.

1776. ———. *A Ride on the whirlwind.* London: Heinemann, 1981. Novel.

1777. ———. *The Root is one.* London: Rex Collings, 1979. Novel.

1778. Serote, Mongane Wally. *Behold mama, flowers.* Johannesburg: Ad. Donker, 1978. Poetry.

1779. ———. *Come and hope with me.* Cape Town: D. Philip, 1994. Poetry.

1780. ———. *The Night keeps winking.* Gaborone, Botswana: Medu Arts Ensemble, 1982. Poetry.

1781. ———. *No baby must weep*. Johannesburg: Ad. Donker, 1975. Poetry.

1782. ———. *On the horizon*. Johannesburg: COSAW, 1990. Essays.

1783. ———. *Selected poems*. Johannesburg: Ad. Donker, 1982. Ed. by M.V. Mzamane.

1784. ———. *Third world express*. Cape Town: D. Philip, 1992. Poetry.

1785. ———. *To every birth its blood*. Johannesburg; London: Ravan Press; Heinemann, 1981. (AWS; 263). Novel.

1786. ———. *A Tough tale*. London: Kliptown Books, 1987. Epic poem.

1787. ———. *Yakhal 'nkomo*. Johannesburg; Washington: Renoster Books; Three Continents Press, 1972. Poetry.

1788. Sharpe, Tom. *Riotous assembly*. London: Pan, 1973. Novel.

1789. Sitas, Ari. *Etopia: a week in the life of a worker in the year 2020 (an instruction manual)*. Durban: Madiba, 1993. Novel.

1790. ———. *Tropical scars*. Fordsburg, South Africa: Congress of South African Writers, 1990. 2nd ed. Poetry.

1791. ———. *William Zungu: a Xmas story*. Cape Town: Buchu Books, 1991. Novella.

1792. Slabolepszy, Paul. *Mooi Street and other moves: six plays*. Johannesburg: Witwatersrand University Press, 1994.

1793. Slovo, Gillian (F). *The Betrayal*. London: M. Joseph, 1991. Novel.

1794. ———. *Ties of blood*. London: M. Joseph, 1989. Novel.

1795. Slovo, Shawn (F). *A World apart.* London: Faber, 1988. Drama.

1796. Small, Adam. *Black bronze beautiful.* Johannesburg: Ad. Donker, 1975. Poetry. See also Afrikaans section.

1797. Smith, Pauline (F). *The Little Karoo.* Cape Town: D. Philip, 1990. Ed. by D. Driver. First pub.: London: J. Cape, 1925. Short stories.

1798. ———. *The Unknown Pauline Smith: unpublished and of print stories, diaries and other prose writings.* Pietermaritzburg: University of Natal Press, 1993. Ed. by E. Pereira.

1799. Haresnape, Geoffrey. *Pauline Smith.* New York: Twayne, 1969. (Twayne's world author series).

1800. Sole, Kelwyn. *The Blood of our silence.* Johannesburg: Ravan Press, 1988. Poetry.

1801. ———. *Projections in the past tense.* Johannesburg: Ravan Press, 1992. Poetry.

1802. Stein, Sylvester. *Second-class taxi.* London: Faber & Faber, 1958. Also pub.: Cape Town: D. Philip, 1983. Novel.

1803. Themba, Can. *The Will to die.* London: Heinemann, 1972. (AWS; 104). Short stories.

1804. ———. *The World of Can Themba: selected writings of the late Can Themba.* Braamfontein: Ravan Press, 1985. Ed. by Essop Patel. (Staffrider series; 18). Poetry, stories, essays.

1805. Tlali, Miriam (F). *Amandla.* Johannesburg: Ravan Press, 1980. Novel.

1806. ———. *Footprints in the Quag: stories and dialogues from Soweto.* Cape Town: D. Philip, 1989. Also pub. as: *Soweto stories.* London: Pandora, 1989.

1807. ———. *Muriel at Metropolitan.* Johannesburg; London: Ravan Press; Longman, 1979. Novel.

1808. Van der Post, Laurens. *In a province.* London: Penguin, 1988. Novel. First pub. 1934.

1809. Vladislavic, Ivan. *The Folly.* Cape Town: D. Philip, 1993. Novel.

1810. ———. *Missing persons.* Cape Town: D. Philip, 1989. Short stories.

1811. Wicomb, Zoë (F). *You can't get lost in Cape Town.* London: Virago, 1987. Fiction.

1812. Woodward, Wendy (F). *Seance for the body.* Cape Town: Snailpress, 1994. Poetry.

1813. Xhegwana, Sithembele Isaac. *The faint-hearted man.* Cape Town: Buchu Books, 1991. Fiction.

1814. Zwelonke, D. M. *Robben Island.* London: Heinemann, 1973. (AWS; 128). Novel.

SWAZILAND

Authors

1815. Kuper, Hilda (F). *Bite of hunger: a novel of Africa.* New York: Harcourt Brace, 1965. Novel.

1816. ———. *A Witch in my heart: a play set in Swaziland in the late 1930's.* London: OUP for the International African Institute, 1970.

1817. Lukhele, Senzenjani. *Tell me no more.* Mbabane: Macmillan Boleswa, 1980. Novel.

1818. Miller, Allister M. *Mamisa, the Swazi warrior.* Pietermaritzburg: Shuter & Shooter, 1955. Novel.

ZAMBIA

Anthologies

1819. Chipasula, Frank (comp.). *A Decade in poetry.* Lusaka: K. Kaunda Foundation, 1991. (Voices in poetry).

1820. Chirwa, C. H. (ed.). *Five plays from Zambia.* Lusaka: NECZAM, 1975.

1821. Liswaniso, Mufalo (ed.). *Voices of Zambia: short stories.* Lusaka: NECZAM, 1971.

1822. Vyas, Chiman L. *A Collection of Zambian verse.* Lusaka: Zambia Cultural Services, 1971. 2 v.

General studies

1823. Kamlongera, Christopher F. *Theatre for development in Africa, with case studies from Malawi and Zambia.* Bonn: Education, Science and Documentation Centre, 1987.

1824. Roscoe, Adrian, and Mpalive-Hangson Msiska. *The Quiet chameleon: modern poetry from Central Africa.* London: H. Zell, 1992. (New perspectives on African literature; 2).

Authors

1825. Chima, Richard. *The Loneliness of a drunkard.* Lusaka: NECZAM, 1973. Poetry.

1826. Chipeta, Dominic. *The Pregnant clouds.* Lusaka: Kenneth Kaunda Foundation, 1986. (Foundation library series; E7). Novel.

1827. Himunyanga-Phiri, Tsitsi V. (F). *The Legacy.* Harare: ZPH, 1992. Novel.

1828. Kasoma, Kabwe. *The Fools marry.* Lusaka: NECZAM, 1976. Drama.

1829. Lu, Georzef. *Woman of my uncle.* Lusaka: NECZAM, 1985. (Neczam library series; E6). Novel.

1830. Mambwe, L. C. *Africa mine and yours.* Lusaka: Kenneth Kaunda Fund, 1989. Poetry.

1831. Masiye, Anddreya S. *Before dawn.* Lusaka: NECZAM, 1971. Drama.

1832. ———. *The Lands of Kazembe.* Lusaka: NECZAM, 1973. Historical drama.

1833. Moono, Muchimba Simuwana. *The Ring.* Lusaka: NECZAM, 1985. Novel.

1834. Mulaisho, Dominic. *The Smoke that thunders.* London: Heinemann, 1979. (AWS; 204). Novel.

1835. ———. *The Tongue of the dumb.* London: Heinemann, 1971. (AWS; 98). Novel.

1836. Mulikita, Fwanyanga M. *Shaka Zulu.* London: Longman, 1967. Drama.

1837. Munatamba, P. M. *My battle cry.* Lusaka: NECZAM, 1982. Poetry.

1838. Musenge, H. M. *Changing shadows.* Lusaka: NECZAM, 1985. Novel.

1839. Ngalande, E. *I Cannot see.* Ndola, Zambia: Mission Press, 1987. Poetry.

1840. Phiri, Matsautso. *Soweto: flowers will grow.* Lusaka: NECZAM, 1979. Drama.

1841. Sibale, G. *Between two worlds.* Lusaka: NECZAM, 1979. (Library series; E2). Novel.

1842. Simoko, Patu. *Africa is made of clay.* Lusaka: NECZAM, 1975. Poetry.

1843. Sinyangwe, Binwell. *Quills of desire.* Harare: Baobab Books, 1993. Novel.

1844. Vyas, Chiman L. *The Falls, and other poems.* Lusaka: Teresianum Press, 1969.

1845. Zgambo, Derrick. *Passages.* Lusaka: NECZAM, 1978. Novel.

1846. Zulu, Patrick C. *A Sheaf of gold.* Lusaka: Unity Press, 1971. Poetry.

ZIMBABWE

Bibliographies

1847. Pichanick, J., A. J. Chennells, and L. B. Rix (comps.). *Rhodesian literature in English: a bibliography (1890-1974/5).* Gwelo: Mambo Press, 1977. (Zambeziana; 2).

1848. Seligman, Dee. *Doris Lessing: an annotated bibliography of criticism.* Westport: Greenwood Press, 1981.

Anthologies

1849. Kadhani, Mudereri, and Musaemura Zimunya (eds.). *And Now the poets speak.* Gwelo: Mambo Press, 1981.

1850. Kitson, Norma (ed.). *Zimbabwe women writers anthology.* Harare: Zimbabwe Women Writers, 1994. Stories and poems.

1851. Muchemwa, K. Z. (ed.). *Zimbabwean poetry in English: an anthology.* Gwelo: Mambo Press, 1978. (Mambo writers series; 4). Poetry.

1852. Nyamfukudza, Stanley (ed.). *New accents one: an anthology of new poetry.* Harare: College Press, 1993.

1853. Style, Colin, and O-lan Style (eds.). *The Mambo book of Zimbabwean verse in English.* Gweru: Mambo Press, 1986. (Mambo writers series. English section; 23).

General studies

1854. Gaidzanwa, Rudo B. *Images of women in Zimbabwean literature.* Harare: College Press, 1985.

1855. Kahari, G. P. *The Search for Zimbabwean identity: an introduction to the black Zimbabwean novel.* Gwelo: Mambo Press, 1980. (Mambo writers series. English section; 5).

1856. Krog, E. W. (ed.). *African literature in Rhodesia.* Gwelo: Mambo Press, 1966.

1857. McLoughlin, T. O., and F. R. Mhonyera. *Insights, an introduction to the criticism of Zimbabwean and other poetry.* Gweru: Mambo Press, 1984.

1858. Roscoe, Adrian, and Mpalive-Hangson Msiska. *The Quiet chameleon: modern poetry from Central Africa.* London: H. Zell, 1992. (New perspectives on African literature; 2).

1859. Veit-Wild, Flora. *Patterns of poetry in Zimbabwe.* Gweru: Mambo Press, 1988.

1860. ———. *Survey of Zimbabwean writers: education and literary careers.* Bayreuth: Breitlinger, 1992.

1861. ———. *Teachers, preachers, non-believers: a social history of Zimbabwean literature.* London; Harare: H. Zell; Baobab, 1992. (New perspectives on African literatures; 6).

1862. Zimunya, Musaemura. *Those years of drought and hunger: the birth of African fiction in English in Zimbabwe.* Gweru: Mambo Press, 1982. (Mambo writers series. English section; 9).

1863. Zinyemba, Ranga M. *Zimbabwean drama: a study of Shona and English plays.* Gweru: Mambo Press, 1984. (Mambo writers series; 25).

Authors

1864. Banana, Canaan S. *The Woman of my imagination.* Gweru: Mambo Press, 1980.

1865. Chidyausiku, Paul. *Broken roots: a biographical narrative on the culture of the Shona people in Zimbabwe.* Gweru: Mambo Press, 1984. Novel. See also Shona section.

1866. Chifunyise, Stephen. *Medicine for love and other plays*. Gweru: Mambo Press, 1984. (Mambo writers series. English section;14).

1867. Chimsoro, Samuel. *Nothing is impossible*. Harlow: Longman, 1983. Novel.

1868. ———. *Smoke and flames*. Gwelo [Gweru]: Mambo Press, 1978. (Mambo writers series; 3). Poetry.

1869. Chinodya, Shimmer. *Dew in the morning*. Gweru: Mambo Press, 1982. (Mambo writers series. English section; 8). Novel.

1870. ———. *Farai's girls*. Harare: College Press, 1984. (African literature in English). Novel.

1871. ———. *Harvest of thorns*. Harare: Baobab Books, 1989. Novel.

1872. Abrahams, Beverley, and Lesley Humphrey. *Study guide to Harvest of thorns [by Shimmer Chinodya]*. Harare: Academic Books, 1993.

1873. Chipamaunga, Edmund. *A Fighter for freedom*. Gweru: Mambo Press, 1983. (Mambo writers; 10). Novel.

1874. Chipunza, A. *Svikiro*. Harare: Longman, 1981. (Zimbabwe writers series). Drama.

1875. Dangaremba, Tsitsi (F). *Nervous conditions*. Harare; London: ZPH; Women's Press, 1988. (ZPH writers). Novel.

1876. Dorras, Joanne (F). *She never knew, and, Like any other lovers*. Harare: College Press, 1992. (On stage). Drama.

1877. Hove, Chenjerai. *Bones*. Harare: Baobab Books, 1988. Novel.

1878. ———. *Red hills of home*. Harare: Mambo Press, 1990. 2nd ed. First ed. 1985 (Mambo writers series. English section; 21). Poetry.

1879. ———. *Shadows.* Harare: Baobab Books, 1991. Novel/prose poem.

1880. ———. *Up in arms.* Harare: ZPH, 1982. (ZPH writers series; 3). Poetry.

1881. Kadhani, Mudereri. *Quarantine rhythms.* Aberdeen: Palladio Press, 1976. Poetry.

1882. Kanengoni, Alexander. *Effortless tears.* Harare: Baobab Books, 1993. Novel.

1883. ———. *When the rainbird cries.* Ardbennie, Harare: Longman Zimbabwe, 1987. (Zimbabwe writers). Novel.

1884. Katiyo, Wilson. *Going to heaven.* London: Rex Collings, 1979. Novel.

1885. ———. *A Son of the soil.* London; Washington: Rex Collings; Three Continents Press, 1976. Novel.

1886. Lessing, Doris (F). *African laughter: four visits to Zimbabwe.* London: HarperCollins, 1992.

1887. ———. *The Children of violence.* London: Mac-Gibbon & Kee, 1965-69. 5 v.: Martha Quest; A Proper marriage; A Ripple from the storm; Landlocked; The Four-gated city. Novel.

1888. ———. *Collected African stories.* London: Paladin, 1990-92. 2 v.

1889. ———. *The Grass in singing.* London: Heinemann, 1973 (AWS; 131). Orig. pub.: London: Joseph, 1950. Novel.

1890. ———. *Under my skin: volume one of my autobiography, to 1949.* New York: HarperCollins, 1994.

1891. Brewster, Dorothy. *Doris Lessing.* New York: Twayne Publishers, 1965. (Twayne's English authors; 21).

1892. Dembo, L. S., and Annis Pratt (ed.). *Doris Lessing: critical studies.* Madison: University of Wisconsin Press, 1974.

1893. Ingersoll, Earl G. (ed.). *Doris Lessing: conversations.* Princeton: Ontario Review Press, 1994.

1894. Schlueter, Paul. *The Novels of Doris Lessing.* Carbondale: Southern Illinois University Press, 1973.

1895. Sprague, Claire, and Virginia Tiger. *Critical essays on Doris Lessing.* Boston: G.K. Hall, 1986.

1896. Thorpe, Michael. *Doris Lessing.* Harlow: Longman, 1973.

1897. ———. *Doris Lessing's Africa.* London: Evans, 1978.

1898. Whittaker, Ruth. *Doris Lessing.* Basingstoke, Eng.: Macmillan Education, 1988. (Modern novelists).

1899. Marechera, Dambudzo. *The Black insider.* Harare; London: Baobab; Lawrence & Wishart, 1990. Ed. by F. Veit-Wild. Novel.

1900. ———. *Black sunlight.* London: Heinemann, 1980. (AWS; 237). Novel.

1901. ———. *Cemetery of mind: collected poems of Dambudzo Marechera.* Harare: Baobab, 1992. Ed. by F. Veit-Wild.

1902. ———. *The House of hunger: short stories.* London: Heinemann, 1978. Also: Harare: ZPH, 1982. (ZPH writers; 4).

1903. ———. *Mindblast, or, The Definitive buddy.* Harare: College Press, 1984. (African literature in English). Drama, prose, poetry.

1904. Petersen, Kirsten Holst. *An Articulate anger: Dambudzo Marechera: 1952-87.* Mundelstrup, Denmark: Dangaroo Press, 1988. 1987 interview.

1905. Veit-Wild, Flora. *Dambudzo Marechera: a source book of his life and work.* London: H. Zell, 1992. (Documentary research in African literatures; 2).

1906. Veit-Wild, Flora, and E. Schade (eds.). *Dambudzo Marechera: 4 June 1952–18 August 1987: pictures, poems, prose, tributes.* Harare: Baobab Books, 1988.

1907. Mathema, Cain. *I love you, Joy Hwami.* Marlborough, Harare: Mathema Publications, 1992. Poetry.

1908. Mazorodze, Isheunesu Valentine. *Silent journey from the East.* Harare: ZPH, 1989. (ZPH writers series; 36). Novel.

1909. McLoughlin, T. O. *Karima.* Gweru: Mambo Press, 1985. Novel.

1910. Mhlanga, Cont Mdladla. *Workshop negative.* Harare: College Press, 1992. Drama.

1911. Moetsabi, Titus. *Fruits and other poems.* Harare: ZPH, 1992. (ZPH writers series; 42).

1912. Mpofu, Stephen. *Shadows on the horizon.* Harare: ZPH, 1984. (ZPH writers series; 21). Novel.

1913. Mujajati, George. *The Rain of my blood: a play.* Gweru: Mambo Press, 1991.

1914. ———. *Victory.* Harare: College Press, 1993.

1915. Mungoshi, Charles L. *The Coming of the dry season.* Nairobi: OUP, 1972. Also pub.: Harare: ZPH, 1981. (ZPH writers series; 2). Novel.

1916. ———. *The Setting sun and the rolling world: selected short stories.* London: Heinemann, 1989. (AWS). Short stories.

1917. ———. *Some kinds of wounds and other short stories.* Gwelo: Mambo Press, 1980. (Mambo writers series. English section ; v. 7).

1918. ———. *Waiting for the rain*. London: Heinemann, 1975. (AWS; 170). Also pub.: Harare: ZPH, 1981. (ZPH writers series; 1). Novel.

1919. Musengezi, Gonzo H. *The Honourable M.P.* Gweru: Mambo Press, 1984. (Mambo writers series. English section; 16). Drama.

1920. Mutasa, Garikai. *The Contact*. Gweru: Mambo Press, 1985. Novel.

1921. Mutswairo, Solomon M. *Chaminuka: prophet of Zimbabwe*. Washington: Three Continents Press, 1983. Novel.

1922. ———. *Mapondera, soldier of Zimbabwe*. Washington: Three Continents Press, 1974. Novel.

1923. Ndhlala, Geoffrey C. T. *Jikinya*. Harare: College Press, 1984. First pub.: Salisbury: Macmillan, 1979. Novel.

1924. ———. *The Southern circle*. Harlow: Longman, 1984. (Drumbeat). Novel.

1925. Ngara, Emmanuel. *Songs from the temple: poems*. Gweru: Mambo Press, 1992. Intro. by Micere Githae Mugo. (Mambo writers series. English section; v. 31).

1926. Nyamfukudza, Stanley. *Aftermaths*. Harare: College Press, 1983. (African literature in English). Novel.

1927. ———. *If God was a woman: a collection of short stories*. Harare: College Press, 1991.

1928. ———. *The Non-believer's journey*. London: Heinemann, 1980. (AWS; 233). Also pub.: Harare: ZPH, 1983. (ZPH writers series; 15). Novel.

1929. Nyamubaya, Freedom T. V. (F). *On the road again: poems during and after the national liberation of Zimbabwe*. Harare: ZPH, 1986. (ZPH writers series; 29).

1930. Nyika, Tambayi O. *Old Mapicha, and other stories*. Gweru: Mambo Press, 1983. (Mambo writers series. English section;13).

1931. Nzenza, Sekai (F). *Zimbabwean woman: my own story*. London: Karia Press, 1988. Autobiography.

1932. Rungano, Kristina (F). *A Storm is brewing*. Harare: ZPH, 1984. (ZPH writers series; 23). Poetry.

1933. Saidi, William. *The Brothers of Chatima Road*. Harare: College Press, 1992. (Modern writers). Novel.

1934. ———. *Gwebede's wars*. Harare: College Press, 1989. (Modern writers). Novel.

1935. ———. *The Old bricks lives*. Gweru: Mambo Press, 1988. (Mambo writers series. English section; vol. 28). Novel.

1936. Samkange, Stanlake. *The Mourned one*. London: Heinemann, 1975. (AWS; 169). Novel.

1937. ———. *On Trial for my country*. London: Heinemann, 1967. (AWS; 33). Novel.

1938. ———. *The Year of the uprising*. London: Heinemann, 1978. (AWS; 190). Novel.

1939. Samupindi, Charles. *Death throes: the trial of Mbuya Nehanda*. Gweru: Mambo Press, 1990. (Mambo writers series. English section; 30). Novella.

1940. ———. *Pawns*. Harare: Baobab, 1992. Novel.

1941. Sithole, Ndabaningi. *The Polygamist*. New York: The Third Press, 1972. Novel.

1942. Tizora, Spencer. *Crossroads*. Gweru: Mambo Press, 1985. Novel.

1943. Vera, Yvonne (F). *Nehanda*. Harare: Baobab Books, 1993. Novel.

1944. Zimunya, Musaemura. *Country dawns and city lights*. Harare: Longman Zimbabwe, 1985. (Zimbabwe writers). Poetry.

1945. ———. *Kingfisher, Jikinya and other poems.* Harare: Longman, 1982. (Zimbabwe writers series).

1946. ———. *Nightshift and other stories.* Harare: Longman Zimbabwe, 1993.

1947. ———. *Perfect poise and other poems.* Harare: College Press, 1993.

WEST AFRICA

OVERVIEW

Bibliography

1948. Zell, Hans, Carol Bundy, and Virginia Coulon (eds.). *A New reader's guide to African literature*. New York; London: Africana; Heinemann, 1983. 2nd ed., pp. 126-177.

Anthologies

1949. Bassir, Olumbe (ed.). *An Anthology of West African verse*. Ibadan: Ibadan University Press, 1967.

1950. Djoleto, Amu, and Thomas Kwami (eds.). *West African prose*. London: Heinemann, 1972.

1951. Nwoga, Donatus Ibe (ed.). *West African verse: an annotated anthology*. London: Longman, 1965.

General studies

1952. Egudu, Romanus N. *Four modern West African poets*. New York: Nok, 1977.

1953. ———. *Modern African poetry and the African predicament*. London: Macmillan, 1978.

1954. Fraser, Robert. *West African poetry: a critical history*. Cambridge: CUP, 1986.

1955. Goodwin, Ken. *Understanding African poetry: a study of ten poets*. London: Heinemann, 1982.

1956. Griffiths, Gareth. *A Double exile: African and West Indian writing between two cultures*. London: Boyars, 1978. (Critical appraisals series).

1957. Kern, Anita. *Women in West African fiction*. Washington: Three Continents Press, 1980.

1958. Little, Kenneth. *The Sociology of urban African women's image in African literature.* London: Macmillan, 1980.

1959. Morell, Karen L. (ed.). *In person: Achebe, Awoonor, and Soyinka at the University of Washington.* Seattle: University of Washington, Institute for Comparative and Area Studies, African Studies Program, 1975.

1960. Nyamdi, George. *The West African village novel, with particular reference to Elechi Amadi's "The Concubine."* Berne: Lang, 1982.

1961. Obiechina, Emmanuel. *Culture, tradition and society in the West African novel.* Cambridge: CUP, 1975. (African studies series; 14).

1962. Ogungbesan, Kolawole (ed.). *New West African literature.* London: Heinemann, 1979.

1963. Oko-Aseme, E. *The West African novel and social evolution.* [Nigeria: s.n.], 1989.

1964. Priebe, Richard K. *Myth, realism and the West African writer.* Trenton, NJ: Africa World Press, 1988. (Comparative studies in African/Caribbean literature).

1965. Roscoe, Adrian A. *Mother is gold: a study of West African literature.* Cambridge: CUP, 1971.

1966. Zabus, Chantal. *The African palimpsest: indigenization of language in the West African Europhone novel.* Amsterdam: Rodopi, 1991. (Cross/cultures; 4).

CAMEROON

Anthologies

1967. Butake, Bole (ed.). *Thunder on the mountain: an anthology of modern Cameroon poetry.* Yaoundé: The Author, 1979.

1968. Taille, Geneviève de la, and Kristine Werner (eds.). *Balaton: an anthology of Cameroon literature in English.* Harlow: Longman, 1986.

General studies

1969. Ndachi Tagne, David. *Roman et réalités camerounaises, 1960-1985.* Paris: L'Harmattan, 1986.

1970. Lyonga, Nalova (ed.). *Anglophone Cameroon writing.* Bayreuth: Bayreuth University, 1993. (Weka; 1).

Authors

1971. Asong, L. T. *The Last man to die.* Yaoundé: Buma Kor, 1980. Novel.

1972. Dipoko, Mbella Sonne. *Because of women.* London: Heinemann, 1969. (AWS; 57). Novel.

1973. ———. *Black and white in love: poems.* London: Heinemann, 1972. (AWS; 107). Poetry.

1974. ———. *A Few nights and days: a novel.* London: Heinemann, 1970. (AWS; 82). First pub.: Longman, 1966.

1975. Eba, Nsanda. *The Good foot.* Ibadan: OUP, 1977.

1976. Kenjo wan Jumbam. *The White man of god.* London: Heinemann, 1980. (AWS; 231). Novel.

1977. Maimo, Sankie. *The Mask: a one-act play.* Yaoundé: Cowrie Publications, 1980.

1978. ———. *Sasse symphony: a golden jubilee play.* Limbe, Cameroon: Nooremac Press, 1989.

1979. Mokoso, Ndeley. *Man pass man and other stories.* Harlow: Longman, 1987.

1980. Nchami, T. A. *Footprints of destiny.* Yaoundé: Alfresco Books, 1985. Fiction.

GAMBIA

General studies

1981. Fraser, Robert. *West African poetry: a critical history.* Cambridge: CUP, 1986 (chapter 8 on Lenrie Peters).

Authors

1982. Conton, William. *The African.* London: Heinemann, 1964. (AWS; 12). First pub.: London: W. Heinemann, 1960. Novel. Author was born in Gambia but lived in Sierra Leone.

1983. Conateh, Swaebou J. *The Poems of Swaebou Conateh.* Banjul: Baro-Ueli, 1981. 2 v.

1984. Dibba, Ebou. *Alhaji.* London: Macmillan, 1992. Novel.

1985. ———. *Chaff on the wind.* London: Macmillan, 1986. Novel

1986. ———. *Fafa: an idyll on the banks of a river: a novel.* London: Macmillan, 1989. (Macmillan modern writers).

1987. Kinteh, Ramatoulie (F). *Rebellion.* New York: Philosophical Library, 1968. Drama.

1988. Peters, Lenrie. *Katchikali.* London: Heinemann, 1971. (AWS; 103). Poetry.

1989. ———. *Poems.* Ibadan: Mbari Press, 1964.

1990. ———. *Satellites.* London: Heinemann, 1967. (AWS; 37). Poetry.

1991. ———. *The Second round.* London: Heinemann, 1965. (AWS; 22). Novel.

1992. ———. *Selected poetry.* London: Heinemann, 1981. (AWS; 238). Poetry.

1993. Sallah, Tijan M. *Before the new earth.* Calcutta: Writers' Workshop, 1988. Short stories.

1994. ———. *Kora land: poems.* Washington: Three Continents Press, 1989.

GHANA

Bibliography

1995. Patten, Margaret D. *Ghanaian imaginative writing in English, 1950-1969: an annotated bibliography.* Legon: University of Ghana, Dept. of Library Studies, 1971. (Occasional papers; 4).

Anthology

1996. Awoonor, Kofi, and G. Adali-Mortty (eds.). *Messages: poems from Ghana.* London: Heinemann, 1971. (AWS; 42).

General studies

1997. Fraser, Robert. *West African poetry: a critical history.* Cambridge: CUP, 1986.

1998. Kayper-Mensah, Albert W., and Horst Wolff (eds.). *Ghanaian writing: Ghana as seen by her own writers as well as by German authors.* Tübingen: Horst Erdmann Verlag, 1972.

1999. Sutherland, Efua. *Anansegoro: story-telling drama in Ghana.* Accra: Afram, 1975.

Authors

2000. Abdallah, Mohammed ben. *The fall of Kumbi, and other plays.* Accra: Woeli, 1989.

2001. ———. *Land of a million magicians: an abibigoro.* Accra: Woeli, 1993. Drama.

2002. ———. *The Trial of Mallam Ilya and other plays.* Accra: Woeli, 1987.

2003. Aidoo, Ama Ata (F). *An Angry letter in January.* Sydney: Dangaroo Press, 1992. Poetry.

2004. ———. *Anowa.* Harlow: Longmans, 1970. New ed. 1980. Drama.

2005. ———. *Changes: a love story.* London: Women's Press, 1991. Novel.

2006. ———. *The Dilemma of a ghost.* London; Accra: Longmans, 1965. New ed. 1980. Drama.

2007. ———. *No sweetness here.* Harlow: Longmans, 1970. Short stories.

2008. ———. *Our sister Killjoy, or, Reflections from a black-eyed squint.* London: Longman, 1977. (African creative writing series). Novel.

2009. ———. *Someone talking to sometime.* Harare: College Press, 1985. Poetry.

2010. Grant, Jane W. *Ama Ata Aidoo: the dilemma of a ghost.* London: Longman, 1980. (Longman guide to literature).

2011. Odamtten, Vincent O. *The Art of Ama Ata Aidoo: polytechnics and reading against neocolonialism.* Gainesville: University Press of Florida, 1994.

2012. Aidoo, John. *This turning face.* Accra: Ghana University Press, 1991. Poetry.

2013. Armah, Ayi Kwei. *The Beautyful ones are not yet born.* Boston; London: Houghton Mifflin; Heinemann, 1968. (AWS; 43). Novel.

2014. ———. *Fragments.* Boston; London: Houghton Mifflin; Heinemann, 1970. (AWS; 154). Novel.

2015. ————. *The Healers*. Nairobi; London: EAPH; Heinemann, 1978. (AWS; 194). Novel.

2016. ————. *Two thousand seasons*. London: Heinemann, 1979. (AWS; 218). First pub.: EAPH, 1973. Novel.

2017. ————. *Why are we so blest?* New York; London: Doubleday; Heinemann, 1972. (AWS; 155). Novel.

2018. Fraser, Robert. *The Novels of Ayi Kwei Armah: a study in polemical fiction*. London: Heinemann, 1980.

2019. Lazarus, Neil. *Resistance in postcolonial African fiction*. New Haven: Yale University Press, 1990.

2020. Wright, Derek. *Ayi Kwei Armah's Africa: the sources of his fiction*. London: H. Zell, 1989. (New perspectives on African literature; 1).

2021. ————. (ed.). *Critical perspectives on Ayi Kwei Armah*. Washington: Three Continents Press, 1992.

2022. Awoonor, Kofi. *The House by the sea*. Greenfield Center, NY: Greenfield Review, 1978. Poetry.

2023. ————. *The Latin American and Caribbean notebook*. Trenton, NJ: Africa World, 1992. Poetry.

2024. ————. *Night of my blood*. Garden City, NY: Doubleday, 1971. Poetry.

2025. ————. *Rediscovery, and other poems*. Ibadan: Mbari Press, 1964.

2026. ————. *Ride me, memory*. Greenfield Center, NY: Greenfield Review, 1973. Poetry.

2027. ————. *This earth, my brother . . . an allegorical tale of Africa*. Garden City, NY: Doubleday, 1971. Novel.

2028. ————. *Until the morning after: collected poems*. London: Heinemann, 1987.

2029. Brew, Kwesi. *The Shadows of laughter*. London: Longmans Green, 1968. Poetry.

2030. Casely-Hayford, Joseph E. *Ethiopia unbound: studies in race emancipation*. London: Cass, 1969. 2nd ed. (Cass library of African studies; 8). Orig. pub.: London: C.M. Philips, 1911.

2031. De Graft, Joe. *Beneath the jazz and brass*. London: Heinemann, 1975. (AWS; 166). Poetry.

2032. ———. *Muntu: a play*. London; Nairobi: Heinemann, 1975. Drama.

2033. ———. *Sons and daughters*. London: OUP, 1964. Drama.

2034. ———. *Through a film darkly*. London: OUP, 1970. Drama.

2035. Djoleto, Amu. *Hurricane of dust*. London: Longman, 1987. Novel.

2036. ———. *Money galore*. London: Heinemann, 1975. (AWS; 161). Novel.

2037. ———. *The Strange man*. London: Heinemann, 1967. (AWS; 41). Novel.

2038. Dove-Danquah, Mabel (F), and Phebean Itayemi-Ogundipe. *The Torn veil and other stories*. London: Evans Brothers, 1976. Short stories.

2039. Kayper-Mensah, Albert W. *The Drummer in our time*. London: Heinemann, 1975. (AWS; 157). Poetry.

2040. Konadu, Asare. *Ordained by the miracle*. London: Heinemann, 1969. (AWS; 55). First pub. as: *Come back Dora*. Accra: Anowuo, 1966. Novel.

2041. ———. *A Woman in her prime*. London: Heinemann, 1967. (AWS; 40). Novel.

2042. Laing, Kojo. *Godhorse*. Oxford: Heinemann International, 1989. Poetry.

2043. ———. *Major Gentl and the Achimota Wars*. London: Heinemann, 1992. Novel.

2044. ———. *Search sweet country*. London; Boston: Heinemann; Faber, 1986. Novel.

2045. ———. *Woman of the aeroplanes*. London: Heinemann, 1988. Novel.

2046. Okai, Atukwei. *Lorgorligi logarithms and other poems*. Accra: Ghana Publishing Corporation, 1974.

2047. Owusu, Martin. *The Sudden return and other plays*. London: Heinemann, 1973. (AWS; 138). Drama.

2048. Safo, Lucy (F). *Cry a whisper*. London: Bogle-L'Ouverture, 1993. Fiction.

2049. Sekyi, Kobina. *The Blinkards*. London; Washington: Rex Collings/Heinemann; Three Continents Press, 1974. (AWS; 136). Written in 1915. Drama.

2050. Selormey, Francis. *The Narrow path*. London: Heinemann, 1966. (AWS; 27). Novel.

2051. Sutherland, Efua (F). *Edufa*. London; Washington: Longmans Green; Three Continents Press, 1969. Drama.

2052. ———. *The Marriage of Anansewa, and Edufa*. Harlow: Longman, 1987. Drama.

2053. ———. *Odasani*. Accra: Anowuo, 1967. Drama.

2054. Dibba, Ebou. *Efua T. Sutherland, "The Marriage of Anansewa."* London: Longman, 1978. (Longman guides to literature).

2055. Yirenkyi, Asiedu. *Kivuli and other plays*. London: Heinemann, 1980. (AWS; 216).

LIBERIA

Bibliography

2056. Cordor, S. Henry. *Bibliography of Liberian literature: a bibliographical review of literary works by Liberians.* Monrovia: Liberian Literature Studies Programme, 1971.

Anthologies

2057. Banks-Henries, A. Doris (ed.). *Poems of Liberia (1836-1961).* London: Macmillan, 1963.

2058. Cordor, S. Henry (ed.). *An Anthology of short stories by writers from the West African Republic of Liberia.* Monrovia: Liberian Literature Studies Programme, 1974.

2059. ——— (ed.). *New voices from West Africa: the first major anthology of contemporary Liberian short stories.* Monrovia: Liberian Literary and Educational Publishers, 1979.

2060. ——— (ed.). *The Writings of Roland T. Dempster and Edwin J. Barclay: a prose and poetry collection of two leading Liberian poets.* Monrovia: Liberian Literature Studies Programme, 1975.

General studies

2061. Cordor, S. Henry (ed.). *Towards the study of Liberian literature: an anthology of critical essays on the literature of Liberia.* Monrovia: Liberian Literature Studies Programme, 1972.

Authors

2062. Dempster, Ronald Tomekai. *To Monrovia old and new.* London: Dragon Press, 1958. Poetry.

2063. ———, Bai Moore, and H. C. Thomas. *Echoes from a valley.* Cape Mount: Douglas Muir Press, 1947. Poetry.

2064. Moore, Bai. *The Money doubler.* Lagos: Unicom, 1976. Novel.

2065. Sankawulo, Wilton. *The Marriage of wisdom and other tales from Liberia.* London: Heinemann, 1974.

NIGERIA

Bibliographies

2066. Aguolu, Christian C. (comp.). *Nigeria: a comprehensive bibliography in the humanities and social sciences, 1900-1971.* Boston: G. K. Hall, 1973.

2067. Anafulu, Joseph C. (comp.). *Chinua Achebe: a preliminary checklist.* Nsukka, Nigeria: University of Nigeria Library, 1978. (Nsukka library notes; special issue 3).

2068. Baldwin, Claudia. *Nigerian literature: a bibliography of criticism, 1952-1976.* Boston: G. K. Hall, 1980.

2069. *Chinua Achebe: a bio-bibliography.* Nsukka, Nigeria: Nnamdi Azikiwe Library, University of Nigeria, 1990.

2070. Gibbs, James, Ketu H. Katrak, and Henry Louis Gates. *Wole Soyinka: a bibliography of primary and secondary sources.* Westport: Greenwood, 1986. (Bibliographies and indexes in Afro-American and African studies; 7).

2071. Hogg, Peter, and Ilse Sternberg (eds.). *Market literature from Nigeria: a checklist.* London: British Library, 1990.

2072. Lindfors, Bernth. *A Bibliography of literary contributions to Nigerian periodicals, 1946-1972.* Ibadan: Ibadan University Press, 1975. (Ibadan University Library. Bibliographical series; 3).

2073. Okpu, Bole. *Chinua Achebe: a bibliography.* Lagos: Libriservice, 1984.

Anthologies

2074. Achebe, Chinua, and Dubem Okafor (eds.). *Don't let him die: an anthology of memorial poems for Christopher Okigbo 1932-67.* Enugu: Fourth Dimension, 1978. Poetry.

2075. Ademola, Frances (ed.). *Reflections: Nigerian prose and verse.* Lagos, Nigeria: African Universities Press, 1965.

2076. Azuonye, Chukwuma (ed.). *Nsukka harvest: poetry from Nsukka, 1966-72.* Nsukka, Nigeria: Odunke, 1972. (Odunke publications; 1).

2077. Coussy, Denise, et al. (eds.). *Anthologie critique de la littérature africaine anglophone.* Paris: Union générale d'éditions, 1983.

2078. Garuba, Harry (ed.). *Voices from the fringe: an ANA anthology of new Nigerian poetry.* Lagos: Malthouse Press, 1988.

2079. Ngangah, C. (ed.). *Through laughter and tears: modern Nigerian short stories.* Kaduna: Klamidas, 1993.

2080. Obiechina, Emmanuel (ed.). *Onitsha market literature.* London; New York: Heinemann; Africana, 1972. (AWS; 109).

General studies

2081. Alston, J. B. *Yoruba drama in English: interpretation and production.* Lewiston, NY: E. Mellen Press, 1989. (Studies in African literature; v. 1).

2082. Booth, James. *Writers and politics in Nigeria.* New York: Africana, 1981.

2083. Coussy, Denise. *Le Roman nigérien anglophone.* Paris: Silex, 1988.

2084. Darah, G. C. *Radical themes in Nigerian literatures.* Lagos: Malthouse Press, 1989.

2085. Dunton, Chris. *Make man talk true: Nigerian drama in English since 1970.* London: H. Zell, 1992. (New perspectives on African literature; 5).

2086. Klíma, Vladimir. *Modern Nigerian novels.* Prague: Oriental Institute, 1969. (Dissertationes orientales; 18).

2087. Laurence, Margaret. *Long drums and cannons: Nigerian dramatists and novelists.* London: Macmillan, 1968.

2088. Lindfors, Bernth (ed.). *Critical perspectives on Nigerian literatures.* Washington: Three Continents Press, 1976. Covers English, Hausa, Yoruba, and Igbo works. Articles originally pub. in: *Research in African Literatures.*

2089. ———. (ed.). *Dem-say: interviews with eight Nigerian writers.* Austin: African and Afro-American Studies Research Center, University of Texas, 1974.

2090. ———. *Early Nigerian literature.* New York: Africana, 1982.

2091. ———. *Folklore in Nigerian literature.* New York: Africana, 1973.

2092. Maja-Pearce, Adewale. *A Mask dancing: Nigerian novelists of the 1980's.* London: H. Zell, 1992. (New perspectives on African literature; 4).

2093. Obiechina, Emmanuel. *An African popular literature: a study of Onitsha pamphlets.* Cambridge: CUP, 1973. Includes three pamphlets in facsimile.

2094. ———. *Literature for the masses: an analytical study of popular pamphleteering in Nigeria.* Enugu, Nigeria: Nwamife, 1971. Discusses Onitsha market literature.

2095. Ogunbiyi, Yemi (ed.). *Drama and theatre in Nigeria: a critical source book.* Lagos: Nigerian Magazine and Federal Ministry of Social Development, Youth, Sport & Culture, 1981.

2096. ———. *Perspectives on Nigerian literature, 1700 to the present.* Lagos: Guardian Books (Nigeria), 1988. 2 v.

2097. Otokunefor, H. C. and O. C. Nwodo (eds.) *Nigerian female writers: a critical perspective.* Lagos: Malthouse, 1989.

2098. Taiwo, Oladele. *Culture and the Nigerian novel.* London; New York: Macmillan; St. Martin's, 1976.

2099. Udoeyop, N. J. *Three Nigerian poets: a critical study of the poetry of Soyinka, Clark and Okigbo.* Ibaban: Ibadan University Press, 1973.

Authors

2100. Achebe, Chinua. *The African trilogy: Things fall apart; No longer at ease; Arrow of God.* London: Picador, 1988. Collection of novels.

2101. ———. *Anthills of the savannah.* London: Heinemann, 1987. Novel.

2102. ———. *Arrow of God.* London: Heinemann, 1964. (AWS; 16). Novel.

2103. ———. *Beware, soul brother, and other poems.* London: Heinemann, 1972. (AWS; 120). First pub.: Enugu: Nwankwo-Ifejika, 1973. Also pub. as: *Christmas in Biafra and other poems.* New York: Doubleday, 1973. Poetry.

2104. ———. *The Flute.* Enugu: Fourth Dimension, 1977. Short story.

2105. ———. *Girls at war and other stories.* London: Heinemann, 1972. (AWS; 100). Short stories.

2106. ———. *Hopes and impediments: selected essays, 1965-1987.* London: Heinemann, 1988. Essays.

2107. ———. *A Man of the people.* London: Heinemann, 1966. (AWS; 31). Novel.

2108. ———. *Morning yet on creation day: essays.* London: Heinemann, 1975. Essays.

2109. ————. *No longer at ease.* London: Heinemann, 1960. (AWS; 3). Novel.

2110. ————. *The Sacrificial egg, and other stories.* Onitsha, Nigeria: Etudo, 1962.

2111. ————. *Things fall apart.* London: Heinemann, 1958. Pub. in 1962 in: (AWS; 1). Novel.

2112. ————, et al. *The Insider: stories of war and peace from Nigeria.* Enugu: Nwamife, 1971. Contributors include: Flora Nwapa, Samuel Ifejika, Arthur Nwanko.

2113. Carroll, David. *Chinua Achebe.* New York: Twayne, 1970. (Twayne's world authors).

2114. ————. *Chinua Achebe, novelist, poet, critic.* Basingstoke, Eng.: Macmillan, 1990. 2nd ed. First pub. 1980.

2115. Coussy, Denise. *L'Oeuvre de Chinua Achebe.* Paris: Présence africaine, 1985.

2116. Ehling, Holger G. (ed.). *Critical approaches to "Anthills of the Savannah."* Amsterdam: Rodopi, 1991.

2117. Gikandi, Simon. *Reading Achebe.* London: Currey, 1991.

2118. Heywood, Christopher. *Chinua Achebe, Things fall apart.* London: Collins, 1985. Ed. by Y. Cantu.

2119. Innes, C. L. *Chinua Achebe.* Cambridge: CUP, 1990. (Cambridge studies in African and Caribbean literature; 1).

2120. ————. *Chinua Achebe, Arrow of God: a critical view.* London: Collins, 1985. Ed. Y. Cantu.

2121. ————. and Bernth Lindfors (eds.). *Critical perspectives on Chinua Achebe.* Washington: Three Continents Press, 1978. Also pub.: London: Heinemann, 1979.

2122. Killam, G. D. *The Writings of Chinua Achebe: a commentary.* London: Heinemann, 1977. Rev. ed. Pub. in 1969 as: *The Novels of Chinua Achebe.*

2123. Lindfors, Bernth (ed.). *Approaches to teaching "Things fall apart."* New York: Modern Language Association, 1991.

2124. Melone, Thomas. *Chinua Achebe et la tragédie de l'histoire.* Paris: Présence africaine, 1973.

2125. Njoku, Benedict Chiaka. *The Four novels of Chinua Achebe.* New York: P. Lang, 1984. (American university studies. Series XVIII African literature; 1).

2126. Ogbaa, Kalu. *Gods, oracles, and divination: folkways in Chinua Achebe's novels.* Trenton, NJ: Africa World Press, 1992.

2127. Ojinmah, Umelo. *Chinua Achebe: new perspectives.* Ibadan: Spectrum Books, 1991.

2128. Okoye, Emmanuel M. *The Traditional religion and its encounter with Christianity in Achebe's novels.* New York: P. Lang, 1987.

2129. Peters, Jonathan. *A Dance of masks: Senghor, Achebe, Soyinka.* Washington: Three Continents Press, 1978.

2130. Petersen, Kirsten Holst, and Anna Rutherford (eds.). *Chinua Achebe: a celebration.* Oxford; Sydney: Heinemann; Dangaroo Press, 1991.

2131. Ravenscroft, Arthur. *Chinua Achebe.* Harlow: Longmans, Green, 1969.

2132. Wren, Robert M. *Achebe's world: the historical and cultural context of the novels of Chinua Achebe.* Washington; Harlow: Three Continents Press; Longman, 1981. (Longman studies in African literature).

2133. Adebeyo, Augustus. *My village captured Hitler.* Ibadan: Spectrum Books, 1993. Novel.

2134. Alkali, Zaynab (F). *The Stillborn*. Harlow: Longman, 1984. Novel.

2135. ———. *The Virtuous woman*. Harlow: Longman, 1987. Novel.

2136. Aluko, T. M. *Chief the honourable minister*. London: Heinemann, 1970. (AWS; 70). Novel.

2137. ———. *Conduct unbecoming*. Ibadan: Heinemann (Nigeria), 1993. Novel.

2138. ———. *His worshipful majesty*. London: Heinemann, 1973. (AWS; 130). Novel.

2139. ———. *One man, one matchet*. London: Heinemann, 1964. (AWS; 11). Novel.

2140. ———. *One man, one wife*. Lagos: Nigerian Printing & Pub. Co., 1959. Rev. ed.: London: Heinemann, 1967 (AWS; 30). Novel.

2141. ———. *A State of our own*. London: Macmillan, 1986. Novel.

2142. ———. *Wrong ones in the dock*. London: Heinemann, 1982. (AWS; 242). Novel.

2143. Amadi, Elechi. *The Concubine*. London: Heinemann, 1966. (AWS; 25). Novel.

2144. ———. *Estrangement*. London: Heinemann, 1986. (AWS; 272). Novel.

2145. ———. *The Great ponds*. London: Heinemann, 1969. (AWS; 44). Novel.

2146. ———. *The Slave*. London: Heinemann, 1978. (AWS; 210). Novel.

2147. Eko, Ebele. *Elechi Amadi: the man and his work*. Lagos: Kraft, 1991.

2148. Niven, Alastair. *Elechi Amadi's "The Concubine":
a critical view.* London: Rex Collings, 1981.

2149. Nyamdi, George. *The West African village novel,
with particular reference to Elechi Amadi's "The
Concubine."* Berne: Lang, 1982.

2150. Amadiume, Ifi (F). *Passion waves.* London:
Karnak House, 1985. Poetry.

2151. Aniebo, I. N. C. *The Journey within.* London:
Heinemann, 1978. (AWS; 206). Novel.

2152. Bandele-Thomas, 'Biyi. *The Man who came in
from the back of beyond.* Oxford: Heinemann, 1992. (AWS).
Novel.

2153. ———. *Marching for Fausa.* London: Amber
Lane Press, 1993. Drama.

2154. ———. *The Sympathetic undertaker and other
dreams.* Oxford: Heinemann, 1993. (AWS). First pub.: Bellew,
1991. Short stories.

2155. Clark, J. P. (John Pepper). *America, their America.*
London: Heinemann, 1969. (AWS; 50). First pub.: London:
Deutsch, 1964.

2156. ———. *The Bikoroa plays.* Oxford: OUP, 1985.

2157. ———. *Casualties: poems 1966-68.* Harlow; New
York: Longmans; Africana, 1970.

2158. ———. *Collected plays and poems, 1958-1988.*
Washington: Howard University Press, 1991.

2159. ———. *A Decade of tongues: selected poems,
1958-1968.* London: Longman, 1981.

2160. ———. *Mandela and other poems.* Ikeja:
Longman Nigeria, 1988.

2161. ———. *Ozidi.* London: OUP, 1966. Drama.

2162. ———. *Poems*. Ibadan: Mbari Press, 1962.

2163. ———. *A Reed in the tide*. London: Longmans, 1965. Poetry.

2164. ———. *Song of a goat*. Ibadan: Mbari Press, 1961. Drama.

2165. ———. *State of the union*. London: Longman, 1985. (Drumbeat). Poetry.

2166. ———. *Three plays*. London; Ibadan: OUP, 1964.

2167. O'Malley, P. *Problems of second-language drama: a study of J.P. Clark*. Yaba, Nigeria: Cross Continents Press, 1988. (Literary criticism series; 6).

2168. Petersen, Kirsten Holst. *John Pepper Clark, selected poems: a critical view*. London: Rex Collings, 1981.

2169. Wren, Robert M. *J.P. Clark*. Boston: Hall, 1984.

2170. Echewa, T. Obinkaram. *The Crippled dancer*. London: Heinemann, 1986. (AWS). Fiction.

2171. Egbuna, Obi B. *The Anthill*. London: OUP, 1965. Drama.

2172. ———. *Daughters of the sun and other stories*. London; New York: OUP, 1970.

2173. ———. *Emperor of the sea and other stories*. Glasgow: Collins, 1974. Short stories.

2174. ———. *The Minister's daughter*. Glasgow: Collins, 1975.

2175. ———. *Wind versus polygamy: where "wind" is the "wind of change" and polygamy the "change of eves."* London: Faber, 1964. Pub. as: *Elina*. Glasgow: Fontana, 1980. Novel.

2176. Egejuru, Phanuel (F). *The Seed yams have been eaten.* Ibadan: Heinemann Educational Books (Nigeria), 1993. Novel.

2177. Ekwensi, Cyprian. *Beautiful feathers.* London: Heinemann, 1971. (AWS; 84). First pub.: London: Hutchinson, 1963. Novel.

2178. ———. *Burning grass.* London: Heinemann, 1962. (AWS; 2). Novel.

2179. ———. *Divided we stand.* Enugu, Nigeria: Fourth Dimension, 1980. Novel.

2180. ———. *For a roll of parchment.* Ibadan: Heinemann, 1986. Novel.

2181. ———. *Ikolo the wrestler, and other Igbo tales.* London: Nelson, 1947. Short stories.

2182. ———. *Iska.* London: Hutchinson, 1966. Novel.

2183. ———. *Jagua Nana.* London: Heinemann, 1975. (AWS; 14). First pub.: London: Hutchinson, 1961. Novel.

2184. ———. *Jagua Nana's daughter.* Ibadan: Spectrum, 1986. Novel.

2185. ———. *Lokotown and other stories.* London: Heinemann, 1966. (AWS; 19). Short stories.

2186. ———. *People of the city.* London: Andrew Dakers, 1954. Rev. ed.: London: Heinemann, 1963 (AWS; 5). Novel.

2187. ———. *Restless city and Christmas gold: with other stories.* London: Heinemann, 1975. (AWS; 172). Short stories.

2188. ———. *Survive the peace.* London: Heinemann, 1976. (AWS; 185). Novel.

2189. ———. *When love whispers.* Onitsha, Nigeria: Tabansi, 1947. Novel.

2190. Emenyonu, Ernest. *Cyprian Ekwensi.* London: Evans, 1974.

2191. ———. *The Essential Ekwensi.* Ibadan: Heinemann, 1987.

2192. Emecheta, Buchi (F). *The Bride price.* London; New York: Allison and Busby; Brazillier, 1976. Novel.

2193. ———. *Destination Biafra.* London: Allison & Busby, 1982. Novel.

2194. ———. *Double yoke.* London; Ibuza, Nigeria: Ogwugwu Afor, 1983. Novel.

2195. ———. *Gwendolen.* London: Collins, 1989. Also pub. as: *The family.* New York: G. Braziller, 1990. Novel.

2196. ———. *The Joys of motherhood.* London: Heinemann, 1980. (AWS; 227). First pub.: London: Allison & Busby, 1979. Novel.

2197. ———. *Kehinde.* Portsmouth, NH; Oxford: Heinemann, 1994. (AWS). Novel.

2198. ———. *The Rape of Shavi.* London; Ibuza, Nigeria: Ogwugwu Afor, 1983. Novel.

2199. ———. *The Slave girl.* London: Alison & Busby, 1977. Novel.

2200. Equiano, Olaudah. *Equiano's travels: his autobiography.* London: Heinemann, 1967. Abridged and edited by Paul Harrison. (AWS; 10). Originally pub.: London, 1789 as *The Interesting narrative of the life of Olaudah Equiano, or Gustavus Vassa the African, written by himself.*

2201. Acholonu, Catherine Obianuju. *The Igbo roots of Olaudah Equiano.* Owerri, Nigeria: AFA, 1989.

2202. Costanzo, Angelo. *Surprising narrative: Olaudah Equiano and the beginning of black autobiography.* New York: Greenwood, 1987.

2203. Fatunde, Tunde. *No food, no country*. Benin: Adena, 1985. Drama.

2204. ———. *No more oil boom, and Blood and sweat*. Benin: Adena, 1984. Drama.

2205. Garuba, Harry. *Shadow and dream, and other poems*. Ibadan: New Horn, 1982. (Opon Ifa series; 1).

2206. Gbadamosi, Rasheed. *Sunset over Nairobi*. Ibadan: Heinemann (Nigeria), 1992. (Frontline series). Short stories.

2207. Genga-Idowu, F. M. (F). *Lady in chains*. Nairobi: East African Educational Publishers, 1993. Novel.

2208. Ike, Chukwuemeka. *The Bottled leopard*. Ibadan: University Press, 1985. Novel.

2209. ———. *The Potter's wheel*. London: Fontana/Collins, 1974. Novel.

2210. ———. *The Search*. Ibadan: Heinemann Educ. Books Nigeria, 1991. (Heinemann frontline series). Novel.

2211. Iroh, Eddie. *Forty-eight guns for the general*. London: Heinemann, 1976. (AWS; 189). Novel.

2212. ———. *The Siren in the night*. London: Heinemann, 1982. Novel.

2213. ———. *Toads of war*. London: Heinemann, 1979. (AWS; 213). Novel.

2214. Iyayi, Festus. *The Contract*. London: Longman, 1982. Novel.

2215. ———. *Heroes*. London: Longman, 1986. (Longman African writers). Novel.

2216. ———. *Violence*. London: Longman, 1979. (Drumbeat; 1). Novel.

2217. King-Aribisala, Karen (F). *Our wife and other stories*. Lagos: Malthouse Press, 1990.

2218. Maja-Pearce, Adewale. *In my father's country.* London: Heinemann, 1987. Essays.

2219. ———. *Loyalties and other stories.* Harlow: Longman, 1987. (Longman African writers).

2220. Mezu, S. Okechukwu. *Behind the rising sun.* London: Heinemann, 1972. (AWS; 113). First pub. 1970. Novel.

2221. Munonye, John. *Bridge to a wedding.* London: Heinemann, 1978. (AWS; 195). Novel.

2222. ———. *A Dancer of fortune.* London: Heinemann, 1974. (AWS; 153). Novel.

2223. ———. *Obi.* London: Heinemann, 1969. (AWS; 45). Novel.

2224. ———. *Oil man of Obange.* London: Heinemann, 1971. (AWS; 94). Novel.

2225. ———. *The Only son.* London: Heinemann, 1966. (AWS; 21). Novel.

2226. ———. *A Wreath for the maidens.* London: Heinemann, 1973. (AWS; 121). Novel.

2227. Nwagboso, Maxwell. *A Message from the madhouse.* London: Saros International, 1991. Novellas.

2228. Nwankwo, Agwuncha Arthur. *Incarnation of hope.* Enugu, Nigeria: Fourth Dimension Publishers, 1993. Poetry.

2229. ———. *Season of hurricane.* Enugu, Nigeria: Fourth Dimension Publishers, 1993. Novel.

2230. ———. *Shadow over breaking waves.* Enugu, Nigeria: Fourth Dimension Publishers, 1993. Novel.

2231. Nwankwo, Nkem. *Danda.* London: Heinemann, 1969. (AWS; 67). First pub.: London: Deutsch, 1964. Novel.

2232. ———. *My Mercedes is bigger than yours.* London: Heinemann, 1975. (AWS; 173). First pub.: London: A. Deutsch, 1975. Novel.

2233. Nwapa, Flora (F). *Cassava song and rice song.* Enugu, Nigeria: Tana Press, 1986. Poetry.

2234. ———. *Efuru.* London: Heinemann, 1966. (AWS; 26). Novel.

2235. ———. *Idu.* London: Heinemann, 1969. (AWS; 56). Novel.

2236. ———. *Never again.* Enugu, Nigeria: Tana Press, 1975. Also pub.: Trenton, NJ: Africa World Press, 1992. (African women writers series). Novel.

2237. ———. *One is enough.* Enugu, Nigeria: Flora Nwapa Co., 1981. Also pub.: Trenton, NJ: Africa World Press, 1992. (African women writers series). Novel.

2238. ———. *This is Lagos and other stories.* Enugu, Nigeria: Nwamife, 1971. Also pub.: Trenton, NJ: Africa World Press, 1992. (African women writers series). Short stories.

2239. ———. *Wives at war and other stories.* Enugu, Nigeria: Nwamife, 1980. Also pub.: Trenton, NJ: Africa World Press, 1992. (African women writers series). Short stories.

2240. ———. *Women are different.* Enugu, Nigeria: Tana Press, 1986. Also pub.: Trenton, NJ: Africa World Press, 1992. (African women writers series). Novel.

2241. Githaiga, Anna. *Notes on Flora Nwapa's "Efuru."* Nairobi: Heinemann, 1979.

2242. Nzekwu, Onuora. *Blade among the boys.* London: Heinemann, 1972. (AWS; 91). First pub.: London: Hutchinson, 1962. Novel

2243. Ogali, Agu Ogali. *Veronica my daughter and other Onitsha plays and stories.* Washington: Three Continents Press, 1980.

2244. Oguibe, Olu. *A Gathering fear.* Lagos: Kraft Books, 1992. Poetry.

2245. Ogundipe-Leslie, Molara (F). *Sew the old days and other poems.* Ibadan: Evans Bros., 1986.

2246. Ojaide, Tanure. *The Blood of peace and other poems.* London: Heinemann, 1991.

2247. ———. *Children of Iroko.* New York: Greenfield Review Press, 1973. Poetry.

2248. ———. *Eagle's vision.* Detroit: Lotus Press, 1987. Poetry.

2249. Okara, Gabriel. *The Fisherman's invocation.* London: Heinemann, 1978. (AWS; 183). Poetry.

2250. ———. *The Voice.* London: Heinemann, 1970. (AWS; 68). First pub.: London: Deutsch, 1964. Novel.

2251. Okigbo, Christopher. *Collected poems.* London: Heinemann, 1986. Pref. by Paul Theroux; intro. by Adewale Maja-Pearce.

2252. ———. *Heavensgate.* Ibadan: Mbari Press, 1962. Poetry.

2253. ———. *Labyrinths: with Path of thunder: poems.* London; New York: Heinemann; Africana, 1971. (AWS; 62).

2254. ———. *Limits.* Ibadan: Mbari Press, 1964. Poetry.

2255. Anozie, Sunday O. *Christopher Okigbo: creative rhetoric.* London; New York: Evans; Africana, 1972.

2256. Okri, Ben. *An African elegy.* London: Cape, 1992. Poetry.

2257. ———. *The Famished road*. London: J. Cape, 1991. Novel.

2258. ———. *Flowers and shadows*. Harlow: Longman, 1988. Novel.

2259. ———. *Incidents at the shrine*. London: Heinemann; Flamingo, 1986. Short stories.

2260. ———. *The Landscapes within*. Harlow: Longman, 1981. (Drumbeat; 38). Novel.

2261. ———. *Songs of enchantment*. London: J. Cape, 1993. Novel.

2262. ———. *Stars of the new curfew*. London: Penguin, 1989. Short stories.

2263. Omotoso, Kole. *The Edifice*. London: Heinemann, 1971. (AWS; 102). Novel.

2264. ———. *Memories of our recent boom*. Harlow: Longman, 1982. (Drumbeat; 74). Novel.

2265. ———. *Miracles and other stories*. Ibadan: Onibonoje Publications, 1973.

2266. Onwueme, Tess. *The Broken calabash*. Ibadan: Heinemann Nigeria, 1988. Drama.

2267. ———. *The Reign of Wazobia*. Ibadan: Heinemann Nigeria, 1988. Drama.

2268. Osofisan, Femi. *Esu and the vagabond minstrels: a fertility rite for the modern state*. Ibadan: New Horn Press, 1991. Drama.

2269. ———. *Farewell to cannibal rage*. Ibadan: Evans Bros., 1986. Drama.

2270. ———. *Kolera kolej: a novel*. Ibadan: New Horn Press, 1975.

2271. ———. *Minted coins.* Ibadan: Heinemann, 1987. Poetry.

2272. ———. *Morountodun and other plays.* Ikeja; Ibadan: Longman Nigeria; Heinemann, 1982.

2273. ———. *Once upon four robbers.* Ibadan: BIO Education Service, 1980. Drama.

2274. ———. *Who's afraid of Solarin?* Ibadan: Scholars Press, 1978. Drama.

2275. ———. *Yungba-yungba and the dance contest: parable for our time.* Ibadan: Heinemann (Nigeria), 1993. Drama.

2276. Awodiya, M. P. (ed.). *Excursions in drama and literature: interviews with Femi Osofisan.* Nigeria: Kraft, 1993.

2277. Osofisan, Sola. *The Living and the dead.* Ibadan: Heinemann, 1991. (Heinemann frontline). Short stories.

2278. Osundare, Niyi. *The Eye of the Earth.* Ibadan: Heinemann, 1986. Poetry.

2279. ———. *Midlife.* Ibadan: Heinemann, 1993. (Heinemann frontline). Poems.

2280. ———. *Selected poems.* Portsmouth: Heinemann, 1992.

2281. ———. *Songs of the marketplace.* Ibadan: New Horn Press, 1983. Poetry.

2282. ———. *Village voices.* Ibadan: Evans Bros., 1984. Poetry.

2283. ———. *Waiting laughters.* Nigeria: Malthouse Press, 1991. Poetry.

2284. Rotimi, Ola. *The Gods are not to blame.* London: OUP, 1971. Drama.

2285. ———. *Hopes of the living dead: a drama of struggle*. Ibadan: Spectrum: 1988,

2286. Saro-Wiwa, Ken. *Pita Dumbrok's prison*. Lagos: Saros International, 1991. (Saros stars series). Novel.

2287. ———. *Songs in a time of war*. Port Harcourt: Saros, 1985. Poetry.

2288. ———. *Sozaboy*. Port Harcourt: Saros, 1985. "A novel in rotten English."

2289. Nnolim, C. (ed.). *Critical essays on Ken Saro-Wiwa's "Sozaboy: a novel in rotten English."* Port Harcourt: Saros, 1992.

2290. Segun, Mabel (F). *Conflict and other poems*. Ibadan: New Horn Press, 1987.

2291. Sofola, Zulu (F). *The Deer hunter, and The Hunter's pearl*. London: Evans Bros., 1969. Drama.

2292. ———. *The Disturbed peace of Christmas*. Ibadan: Daystar, 1971. Drama.

2293. ———. *King Emene: tragedy of a rebellion*. London: Heinemann, 1974. Drama.

2294. ———. *Old wines are tasty*. Ibadan: OUP, 1981. Drama.

2295. Sowande, Bode. *Farewell to Babylon and other plays*. London; Washington: Longman; Three Continents Press, 1979.

2296. ———. *Flamingo and other plays*. London: Longman, 1986. (Longman African writers).

2297. Soyinka, Wole. *Aké: the years of childhood*. London: Rex Collings, 1981. Autobiography.

2298. ———. *The Bacchae of Euripides: a communion rite*. London: Methuen, 1973. Drama.

2299. ———. *The Blackman and the veil, and Beyond the Berlin Wall*. Accra: Sedco, 1993. Essays.

2300. ———. *Camwood on the leaves*. London: Eyre Methuen, 1973. Drama.

2301. ———. *Collected plays*. London: OUP, 1974. 2 v.

2302. ———. *A Dance of the forests*. London: OUP, 1963. Drama.

2303. ———. *Death and the king's horseman*. London: Eyre Methuen, 1975. Drama.

2304. ———. *Idanre and other poems*. London: Methuen, 1967.

2305. ———. *The Interpreters*. London: Heinemann, 1970. (AWS; 76). First pub.: London: A. Deutsch, 1965. Novel.

2306. ———. *Isarà: a voyage around essay*. New York; London: Random House; Methuen, 1989. Autobiography.

2307. ———. *The Jero plays*. London: Methuen, 1973.

2308. ———. *Kongi's harvest*. London: OUP, 1967. Drama.

2309. ———. *The Lion and the jewel*. London: OUP, 1963. Drama.

2310. ———. *Madmen and specialists*. London: Methuen, 1971. Drama.

2311. ———. *The Man died: prison notes*. London: Rex Collings, 1972. Autobiography.

2312. ———. *Mandela's earth and other poems*. London; New York: A. Deutsch; Random House, 1988.

2313. ———. *Ogun Abibiman*. Johannesburg; London: Ravan Press; Rex Collings, 1980. "Epic poem dedicated to the fallen of Soweto."

2314. ———. *Opera wonyosi.* London; Bloomington: Rex Collings; Indiana University Press, 1981. Drama.

2315. ———. *A Play of giants.* London: Methuen, 1984.

2316. ———. *Poems from prison.* London: Rex Collings, 1969.

2317. ———. *Requiem for a futurologist.* London: Rex Collings, 1985. Drama.

2318. ———. *Season of anomy.* London: Rex Collings, 1973. Novel.

2319. ———. *A Shuttle in the crypt.* London: Rex Collings, 1972. Poetry.

2320. Adejare, Olowole. *Language and style in Soyinka: a systemic textlinguistic study of a literary idiolect.* Ibadan: Heinemann (Nigeria), 1994.

2321. Adelugba, Dapo (ed.). *Before our eyes: tributes to Wole Soyinka.* Ibadan: Spectrum, 1987.

2322. Baminkunle, A. *Introduction to Soyinka's poetry: analysis of "A Shuttle in the crypt."* Zaria: Ahmadu Bello University Press, 1991.

2323. Böttcher-Wöbcke, Rita. *Komik: Ironie und Satire im dramatischen Werk von Wole Soyinka.* Hamburg: Buske, 1976.

2324. Gibbs, James. *Critical perspectives on Wole Soyinka.* Washington; London: Three Continents Press; Heinemann, 1980. (Critical perspectives series).

2325. ———. *Wole Soyinka.* London: Macmillan, 1986. (Modern dramatists series).

2326. ——— and Bernth Lindfors (eds.) *Researches on Wole Soyinka.* Trenton: Africa World Press, 1993.

2327. Gikandi, Simon. *Wole Soyinka's "The Road."* Nairobi: Heinemann, 1985.

2328. Herdeck, Donald E. (ed.). *Three dynamite authors: Derek Walcott (Nobel 1992), Naguib Mahfouz (Nobel 1988), Wole Soyinka (Nobel 1986)*. Colorado Springs: Three Continents Press, 1994.

2329. Kacou, Denise. *Shakespeare et Soyinka: le théâtre du monde*. Abidjan: Nouvelles éditions africaines, 1988.

2330. Katrak, Ketu H. *Wole Soyinka and modern tragedy: a study of dramatic theory and practice*. Westport: Greenwood, 1986.

2331. Larsen, Stephan. *A Writer and his gods: a study of the importance of Yoruba myths and religious ideas to the writings of Wole Soyinka*. Stockholm: Dept. of History of Literature University of Stockholm, 1983.

2332. Maduakor, Obi. *Wole Soyinka: an introduction to his writing*. New York: Garland, 1986. (Critical studies on black life and culture; 15).

2333. Moore, Gerald. *Wole Soyinka*. London: Evans 1978. (Modern African writers) rev. ed. First pub. 1971.

2334. Ogunba, Oyin. *The Movement of transition: a study of the plays of Wole Soyinka*. Ibadan: Ibadan University Press, 1975.

2335. Ojaide, Tanure. *The Poetry of Wole Soyinka*. Lagos: Malthouse Press, 1994.

2336. Omotoso, Kole. *Achebe or Soyinka?: a re-interpretation and a study in contrasts*. London: H. Zell, 1994. (New perspectives on African literature; 3).

2337. Peters, Jonathan. *A Dance of masks: Senghor, Achebe, Soyinka*. Washington: Three Continents Press, 1978.

2338. Ricard, Alain. *Théâtre et nationalisme: Wole Soyinka et LeRoi Jones*. Paris: Présence africaine, 1972.

2339. ———. *Wole Soyinka: l'ambition démocratique*. Paris; Lomé: Silex; Nouvelles éditions africaines, 1988.

2340. Sotto, Wiveca. *The Rounded rite: a study of Wole Soyinka's play "The Bacchae of Euripides."* Malmö, Sweden: CWK Gleerup, 1985.

2341. Wright, Derek. *Wole Soyinka revisited.* New York: Twayne, 1993. (Twayne's world authors; 833).

2342. Tutuola, Amos. *Ajayi and his inherited poverty.* London: Faber & Faber, 1967. Novel.

2343. ———. *My life in the bush of ghosts.* London: Faber & Faber, 1954. Novel.

2344. ———. *The Palm-wine drinkard and his dead palm-wine tapster in the Deads' Town.* London: Faber, 1952. Novel.

2345. ———. *Pauper, brawler, and slanderer.* London: Faber, 1987. Novel.

2346. Lindfors, Bernth (ed.). *Critical perspectives on Amos Tutuola.* Washington: Three Continents Press, 1975.

2347. Ukala, Sam. *Break a boil.* Agbor [Nigeria]: Oris Press, 1992. Drama.

2348. Ulasi, Adaora Lily (F). *The Man from Sagamu.* London; New York: Collins; Collier Macmillan, 1978. Novel.

2349. ———. *Many thing you no understand.* London: M. Joseph, 1970. Novel.

2350. ———. *Who is Jonah?* Ibadan: Onibonoje, 1978. Novel.

SIERRA LEONE

Bibliography

2351. Binns, Margaret, and Tony Binns. *Sierra Leone.* London; Santa Barbara: Clio Press, 1992 (World bibliographical series; 148), pp. 173-180.

Anthology

2352. Hughes, Langston (ed.). *Poems from black Africa: Ethiopia, South Rhodesia, Sierra Leone, Madagascar, Ivory Coast, Nigeria, Kenya, Gabon, Senegal, Nyasaland, Mozambique, South Africa. Congo, Ghana, Liberia.* Bloomington: Indiana University Press, 1963. (UNESCO collection of contemporary works).

Authors

2353. Casely-Hayford, Adelaide (F), and Gladys May Casely-Hayford (F). *Memoirs and poems.* Freetown: Sierra Leone University Press, 1983. Ed. by Lucilda Hunter.

2354. Casely-Hayford, Gladys May. *Take 'um So.* Freetown: New Era Press, 1948. Poetry in English and Krio.

2355. Cheney-Coker, Syl. *The Blood in the desert's eyes.* London: Heinemann, 1990. (AWS). Poetry.

2356. ———. *Concerto for an exile.* London: Heinemann, 1973. (AWS; 126). Poetry.

2357. ———. *The Graveyard also has teeth.* London: Heinemann, 1980. (AWS; 221). Poetry.

2358. ———. *The Last harmattan of Alusine Dunbar.* Oxford: Heinemann, 1990. (AWS). Novel.

2359. Cole, Robert Wellesley. *Kossoh town boy.* Cambridge: CUP, 1960. Autobiographical novel.

2360. Conton, William. *The African.* London: Heinemann, 1964. (AWS; 12). First pub.: London: W. Heinemann, 1960. Novel. Author was born in Gambia but lived in Sierra Leone.

2361. Easmon, R. Sarif. *The Burnt-out marriage.* London: Nelson, 1967. Novel.

2362. ———. *The Feud.* London: Longman, 1981. Stories.

2363. James, Frederick Bobor. *The Weaver birds.* Freetown: People's Educational Association of Sierra Leone, 1986. (Stories and songs from Sierra Leone; 15). Drama.

2364. Maddy, Yulisa Amadu. *No past, no present, no future.* London: Heinemann, 1973. Novel.

2365. ———. *Obasai and other plays.* London: Heinemann, 1971. (AWS; 89).

2366. Nicol, Davidson [Abioseh]. *The Truly married woman and other stories.* Oxford: OUP, 1965.

2367. Swaray, Nabie Yayah. *Worl' do for fraid: a play in three acts, with music.* Washington: Three Continents Press, 1986.

FRENCH LITERATURES

NORTH OF THE SAHARA
AND
MAGHREB

OVERVIEW

Bibliographies

2368. Déjeux, Jean. *Dictionnaire des auteurs maghrébins de langue française*. Paris: Karthala, 1984.

2369. ———. *Maghreb: littératures de la langue française*. Paris: Arcanthère, 1993.

Anthologies

2370. Amrani, F., G. Manceron et B. Wallon (éds). *Cents poèmes sur l'exil*. Paris: Le Cherche-Midi, 1993.

2371. Arnaud, Jacqueline, et al. *Anthologie des écrivains maghrébins d'expression française*. Paris: Présence africaine, 1964.

2372. Brahimi, Denise (éd.). *Un Siècle de nouvelles franco-maghrébines*. Paris: Minerve, 1992.

2373. Memmi, Albert (dir.). *Ecrivains francophones du Maghreb*. Paris: Seghers, 1985.

General studies

2374. Allami, Noria. *Voilées, dévoilées. Etre femme dans le monde arabe*. Paris: L'Harmattan, 1988.

2375. Arnaud, Jacqueline et F. Anacker. *Répertoire mondial des travaux universitaires sur la littérature maghrébine de langue française*. Paris: L'Harmattan, 1984.

Publié en collaboration avec le Centre d'études francophones, Université Paris-XIII.

2376. Bekri, Tahar. *Littératures du Maghreb: Algérie, Maroc, Tunisie.* Paris: Club des lecteurs d'expression française, 1989.

2377. Daoud, Takya. *Féminisme et politique au Maghreb: soixante ans de lutte.* Paris: Maisonneux et Larose, 1993.

2378. ———. *La Littérature maghrébine d'expression française.* Paris: PUF, 1992. (Coll. Que sais-je? 2675).

2379. "Dialogue Maghreb-Afrique noire: 1. Au delà du désert." *Notre Librairie,* no. 95 (1988).

2380. "Dialogue Maghreb-Afrique noire: 2. L'Indépendance...et après." *Notre Librairie,* no. 96 (1989).

2381. Dugas, Guy. *La Littérature judéo-maghrébine d'expression française.* Paris: L'Harmattan, 1990.

2382. El Khayat, Ghita. *Le Monde arabe au féminin.* Paris: L'Harmattan, 1985.

2383. ———. *Le Maghreb des femmes: les femmes dans l'UMA.* Casablanca: Eddif, 1992.

2384. *Femmes du Maghreb au présent.* Paris: Editions du CNRS, 1990.

2385. Grenaud, Pierre. *La Littérature au soleil du Maghreb: de l'Antiquité à nos jours.* Paris: L'Harmattan, 1993.

2386. Khatibi, Abdelkébir. *Penser le Maghreb.* Rabat: Socété marocaine des éditeurs réunis, 1993. Essai.

2387. Madelain, Jacques. *L'Errance et l'itinéraire: lectures du roman maghrébin de langue française.* Paris: Sindbad, 1983.

2388. "Maghreb et modernité." *Cahiers d'études maghrébines*, no. 1 (1989). Université de Cologne.

2389. Mernissi, Fatima. *Le Harem politique: le Prophète et les femmes.* Paris: Albin Michel, 1987.

2390. ———. *Sultanes oubliées: femmes chefs d'Etat en Islam.* Paris: Albin Michel, 1990.

2391. Nisbet, Anne-Marie. *Le Personnage féminin dans le roman maghrébin de langue française, des indépendances à 1980: représentation et fonction.* Sherbrooke: Naaman, 1982.

2392. Obenga, Théophile. *Origine commune de l'Egyptien ancien, du copte et des langues négro-africaines modernes. Introduction à la linguistique historique africaine.* Paris: L'Harmattan, 1993.

2393. *Visions du Maghreb.* La Calade-Aix: Edisud, 1987. Actes des Rencontres de Montpellier de novembre 1985.

EGYPT/EGYPTE

Bibliography

2394. Luthi, Jean-Jacques. *Introduction à la littérature d'expression française en Egypte (1798-1945).* Paris: L'Ecole, 1974. Bibliographie couvrant une période allant du début du XIXe siècle à l'année 1972. Pp. 307-342.

Anthology

2395. Luthi, Jean-Jacques. *Le Français en Egypte. Essai d'anthologie.* Journieh: Naaman, 1981.

General studies

2396. Fontaine, Jean. "Le Nouveau roman égyptien, 1975-1985." *IBLA* 49, no. 158 (1986): 215-252.

2397. Tomiche, Nada. *Histoire de la littérature romanesque de l'Egypte moderne.* Paris: Maisonneuve et Larose, 1981.

2398. Vial, Charles. *Le Personnage de la femme dans le roman et la nouvelle en Egypte de 1914 à 1960.* Damas: Institut français, 1979.

Authors

2399. Ackad, Tewfick. *Une Nuit au pied des pyramides.* Harissa: Imprimerie Saint-Paul, 1937. Théâtre.

2400. Adès, Albert. *Un Roi tout nu.* Paris: Calmann-Lévy, 1922. Roman.

2401. ———— et Albert Josipovici. *Le Livre de Goha le simple.* Paris: Calmann-Lévy, 1919. Nombreuses rééditions au cours des ans. Roman.

2402. Agoub, Joseph. *Discours historique sur l'Egypte.* Paris: Imprimerie Rignoux, 1823. Ecrit.

2403. ————. *Mélange de littérature orientale et française avec notice sur l'auteur par M. de Pongerville.* Paris: Werdet, 1837. Publié à titre posthume. Ecrits.

2404. Arcache, Jeanne (F). *L'Egypte dans mon miroir.* Paris: Editions des Cahiers libres, 1931.

2405. ————. *L'Emir à la Croix.* Paris: Plon, 1938.

2406. Assaad, Fawzia (F). *L'Egyptienne.* Paris: Mercure de France, 1975. Roman.

2407. ————. *Des Enfants et des chats.* Paris: Favre, 1987.

2408. ————. *La Gande maison de Louxor.* Paris: L'Harmattan, 1992. Roman.

2409. Axelos, Céline (F). *Les Deux chapelles.* Alexandrie: Cosmopolis, 1943. Poésie.

2410. ———. *Les Marches d'Ivoire*. Monte-Carlo: Regain, 1952. Poésie.

2411. Blum, Robert. *Ah! Misère.* . . Le Caire: Parme, 1930. Contes.

2412. ———. *Chosettes*. Le Caire: Imprimerie Molco, 1925. Poésie.

2413. ———. *Cinq Actes*. Le Caire: Imprimerie Lancioni, 1932. Comédies.

2414. ———. *Insolitude*. Paris: L'Atelier, 1965. Aphorismes.

2415. ———. *Notes d'un mobilisé*. Le Caire: Imprimerie la Patrie, 1940. Témoignage autobiographique.

2416. ———. *Tumulte*. Besançon: L'Atelier, 1969. Poésie.

2417. Boutros Ghali, Wacyf. *Les Perles éparpillées*. Paris: Plon, 1923. Contes.

2418. Chedid, Andrée (F). *A la mort, à la vie*. Paris: Flammarion, 1992. Nouvelles.

2419. ———. *L'Autre*. Paris: Flammarion, 1981. (Nouvelle édition en 1990 dans la coll. J'ai lu, 2730). Roman.

2420. ———. *Cavernes et soleils*. Paris: Flammarion, 1979. Poésie.

2421. ———. *La Cité fertile*. Paris: Flammarion, 1972. (Nouvelle édition en 1992 dans la coll. J'ai lu). Roman.

2422. ———. *Echec à la reine, partie en 9 jeux*. Paris: Flammarion, 1984. Théâtre.

2423. ———. *L'Enfant multiple*. Paris: Flammarion, 1989. Roman.

2424. ———. *L'Etroite peau*. Paris: Julliard, 1965. (Nouvelle édtion en 1978 chez Flammarion, Paris). Nouvelles.

2425. ———. *La Femme de Job.* Paris: Calmann-Lévy, 1993. Récit.

2426. ———. *Jonathan.* Paris: Seuil, 1955. Roman.

2427. ———. *La Maison sans racines.* Paris: Flammarion, 1985. (Nouvelle édition en 1986 dans la coll. J'ai lu, 2065). Roman.

2428. ———. *Les Manèges de la vie.* Paris: Flammarion, 1989. Nouvelles.

2429. ———. *Les Marches de sable.* Paris: Flammarion, 1981. (Nouvelle édition en 1990 dans la coll. J'ai lu, 2286). Roman.

2430. ———. *Mondes, miroirs, magies.* Paris: Flammarion, 1988. Nouvelles.

2431. ———. *Nefertiti et le rêve d'Akhnaton: les mémoires d'un scribe.* Paris: Flammarion, 1974. Roman.

2432. ———. *On the Trails of my Fancy.* Le Caire: Horus, 1943. (Poèmes de jeunesse écrits en anglais). Poésie.

2433. ———. *Le Sixième jour.* Paris: Julliard, 1960. (Nouvelle édition en 1989 dans la coll. J'ai lu, 2529). Roman.

2434. ———. *Le Sommeil délivré.* Paris: Stock, 1952. Roman.

2435. ———. *Le Survivant.* Paris: Julliard, 1963. (Nouvelle édition en 1992 dans la coll. J'ai lu, 3171). Roman.

2436. ———. *Théâtre I. Bérénice d'Egypte. Les Nombres. Le Montreur.* Paris: Flammarion, 1981. Théâtre.

2437. Cossery, Albert. *Les Fainéants de la vallée fertile.* Paris: Dormat, 1948. (Nouvelle édition en 1977 chez Gallimard, Paris). Roman.

2438. ———. *Les Hommes oubliés de Dieu.* Le Caire: La Semaine égyptienne, 1941. (Nouvelle édition en 1946 chez Charlot, Paris). Contes.

2439. ———. *La Maison de la mort incertaine.* Le Caire: Masses, 1944. (Nouvelle édition en 1990 chez Terrain vague, Paris). Roman.

2440. ———. *Mendiants et orgueilleux.* Paris: Julliard, 1955. (Nouvelle édition en 1993 chez J. Losfeld, Paris). Roman.

2441. ———. *Les Morsures.* Le Caire: Imprimerie Karouth, 1931. Poésie.

2442. ———. *La Violence et la dérision.* Paris: Julliard, 1964. (Nouvelle édition en 1993 chez J. Losfeld, Paris). Roman.

2443. Cyril des Baux. *Les Bacchantes.* Alexandrie: Edition du Scarabée, 1944. Théâtre.

2444. Finbert, Elian-Juda. *Le Batelier du Nil.* Paris: Grasset, 1928. Roman.

2445. ———. *Le Destin difficile.* Paris: Albin Michel, 1937. Roman.

2446. ———. *Le Fou de Dieu.* Paris: Fasquelles, 1933. Roman.

2447. ———. *Un Homme vient de l'Orient.* Paris: Grasset, 1930. Roman.

2448. ———. *Hussein.* Paris: Grasset, 1930. (Nouvelle édition en 1947 sous le titre *Tempête sur l'orient,* chez Hier et Aujourd'hui, Paris). Roman.

2449. ———. *Le Livre de la sagesse arabe.* Paris: Laffont, 1948.

2450. ———. *Sous le signe de la licorne et du lion.* Paris: Edition du Monde moderne, 1925. Roman.

2451. ———. *La Vie du chameau.* Paris: Albin Michel, 1938. Roman.

2452. Henein, Georges. *L'Incompatible*. Le Caire: La Part du sable, 1952.

2453. ———. *Notes sur un pays inutile*. Paris: Le Tout sur le tout, 1982. Nouvelles.

2454. ———. *Un Temps de petite fille*. Paris: Editions de Minuit, 1947. Contes.

2455. Ivray, Jehan d' (F). *Le Moulin des Djinns*. Paris: A. Méricant, 1911. Roman.

2456. ———. *Le Prince Mourad*. Paris: Lemerre, 1898. De son vrai nom Mme Jeanne Puech d'Allisac-Fahmy. Roman.

2457. Jabès, Edmond. *Aely*. Paris: Gallimard, 1972. (Le Livre des questions VI). Texte-poésie.

2458. ———. *Je bâtis ma demeure*. Paris: Gallimard, 1959. (Nouvelle édition augmentée en 1975). Poésie.

2459. ———. *El ou le dernier livre*. Paris: Gallimard, 1973. (Le Livre des questions VII). Texte-poésie.

2460. ———. *Elya*. Paris: Gallimard, 1969. (Le Livre des questions V).

2461. ———. *Un Etranger avec, sous le bras, un livre de petit format*. Paris: Gallimard, 1989.

2462. ———. *Illusions sentimentales*. Paris: Figuière, 1930. Poésie.

2463. ———. *L'Ineffaçable, l'inaperçu*. Paris: Gallimard, 1980. (Le Livre des ressemblances III. Nouvelle édition en 1991 dans la coll. L'Imaginaire, 252). Texte-poésie.

2464. ———. *Le Livre de l'hospitalité*. Paris: Gallimard, 1991. Texte-poésie.

2465. ———. *Le Livre des marges*. Paris: Librairie générale française, 1987. (Livre de poche, 4043). Texte-poésie.

2466. ———. *Le Livre des questions*. Paris: Gallimard, 1963. (Premier volume. Nouvelle édition en 1990). Texte-poésie.

2467. ———. *Le Livre des ressemblances*. Paris: Gallimard, 1976. (Premier volume). Texte-poésie.

2468. ———. *Le Livre du dialogue*. Paris: Gallimard, 1984. Texte-poésie.

2469. ———. *Le Livre du partage*. Paris: Gallimard, 1987. Texte-poésie.

2470. ———. *La Mémoire et la main*. Fontfroide-le-Haut: Fanta Morgana, 1987. Poésie.

2471. ———. *Le Parcours*. Paris: Gallimard, 1985. Texte-poésie.

2472. ———. *Le Petit livre de la subversion hors de soupçon*. Paris: Gallimard, 1982. Texte-poésie.

2473. ———. *Petites poésies pour les jours de pluie et de soleil*. Paris: Gallimard, 1991. Poésie.

2474. ———. *Les Pieds en l'air*. Le Caire: Revue du Caire, 1936. Poésie.

2475. ———. *Récit*. Fontfroide-le-Haut: Fanta Morgana, 1987.

2476. ———. *Le Seuil, le sable: poésie complète 1943-1988*. Paris: Gallimard, 1990. Poésie.

2477. ———. *Le Soupçon, le désert*. Paris: Gallimard, 1978. (Le Livre des ressemblances II. Nouvelle édition en 1991 dans la coll. L'Imaginaire, 252). Texte-poésie.

2478. ———. *Yaël*. Paris: Gallimard, 1967. (Le Livre des questions IV. Nouvelle édition en 1989 dans la coll. L'Imaginaire, 214). Texte-poèsie.

2479. Leprette, Fernand. *Les Fauconnières ou le domaine des quatre ezbehs.* Paris: Mercure de France, 1960. Roman.

2480. Mansour, Joyce (F). *Le Bleu des fonds.* Paris: Soleil noir, 1968. Poésie.

2481. ———. *Ça.* Paris: Soleil noir, 1970. Poésie.

2482. ———. *Carré blanc.* Paris: Soleil noir, 1970. Poésie.

2483. ———. *Cris.* Paris: Seghers, 1953. Poésie.

2484. ———. *Déchirures.* Paris: Editions de Minuit, 1955. Poésie.

2485. ———. *Faire signe au machiniste.* Paris: Soleil noir, 1977.

2486. ———. *Histoires nocives.* Paris: Gallimard, 1973. Réuni deux nouvelles intitulées Jules César et Iles flottantes. Nouvelles.

2487. ———. *Jules César.* Paris: Seghers, 1956. Récit.

2488. ———. *Prose et poésie: œuvre complète.* Arles: Actes sud, 1991. Poésie.

2489. Moscatelli, Jean. *Neurasthénie.* Paris: La Caravelle, 1926. Poésie.

2490. ———. *Roubaïyat pour l'aimée.* Le Caire: Aldéraban, 1952. Poésie.

2491. Niya Salima (F). *Les Répudiées.* Paris: Juvens, 1908. (De son vrai nom Eugénie Rouchdi). Roman.

2492. Out-el-Kouloub (F). *Au Hasard de la pensée.* Le Caire: El-Maaref, 1937. (Il s'agit de la seconde édition de l'ouvrage).

2493. ———. *Le Coffret hindou.* Paris: Gallimard, 1951. Roman.

2494. ———. *Harem*. Paris: Gallimard, 1937. Roman.

2495. ———. *Hefnaoui le magnifique*. Paris: Gallimard, 1961. Roman.

2496. ———. *La Nuit de la destinée*. Paris: Gallimard, 1954. Roman.

2497. ———. *Ramza*. Paris: Gallimard, 1958. Roman.

2498. ———. *Trois Contes de l'amour et de la mort*. Paris: Corréa, 1940. Nouvelles.

2499. ———. *Zanouba*. Paris: Gallimard, 1950. Roman.

2500. Parme, Raoul. *Poèmes d'Angleterre*. Le Caire: La Salamandre, 1942. Poésie.

2501. ———. *Première cueillette*. Le Caire: Imprimerie Parladi, 1926. Poésie.

2502. ———. *La Prière dansée*. Genève: Imprimerie Avenir, 1969. Poésie.

2503. ———. *Le Rameau d'or*. Milan: Milici, 1971. Poésie.

2504. Rassim Bey, Ahmed. *Et Grand-mère dit encore...* Le Caire: La Semaine égyptienne, 1932. Poésie.

2505. Schemeil, Marius. *Le Grand fléau*. Le Caire: Imprimerie Parladi, 1918. Théâtre.

2506. Scouffi, Alec. *Navire à l'encre*. Paris: L. Querelle, 1932. Roman.

2507. ———. *Premiers poèmes*. Paris: Sansot, 1909. Poésie.

2508. Sinadino, Agostino John. *Poésies (1902-1925)*. Paris: A la Jeune Parque, 1929. Poésie.

2509. Thuile, Henri. *La Lampe de terre*. Paris: Grasset, 1912. Poésie.

2510. Vaucher-Zananiri, Nelly (F). *Le Jardin matinal.* Paris: A. Messein, 1920. Poésie.

2511. ————. *Soleil absent.* Paris: Saint-Germain-des-Prés, 1974. Poésie.

2512. ————. *Vierges d'Orient.* Paris: Jouve, 1922. Roman.

2513. Vincendon, Mireille (F). *Les Cahiers d'Annabelle.* Paris: Mercure de France, 1957. Roman.

2514. ————. *Faux-usages.* Paris: Julliard, 1960. Nouvelles.

2515. Yacoub Artin, Pacha. *Contes populaires inédits de la vallée du Nil, traduits de l'arabe parlé par Yacoub Artin.* Paris: Maisonneuve, 1895. (Nouvelle édition en 1968). Contes.

2516. ————. *Contes populaires du Soudan, recueillis en 1908 sur le Nil Blanc et le Nil Bleu.* Paris: Leroux, 1909. Contes.

2517. Yergath, Arsène. *Les Yeux limpides.* Paris: La Bouteille à la mer, 1932. Poésie.

2518. Zénié-Ziegler, Wedad (F). *La Face voilée des femmes d'Egypte.* Paris: Mercure de France, 1986. Document.

ALGERIA/ALGÉRIE

Bibliographies

2519. Achour, Christiane. *Dictionnaire des œuvres algériennes de langue française.* Paris: L'Harmattan, 1990.

2520. Déjeux, Jean. *Dictionnaire des auteurs maghrébins de langue française.* Paris: Karthala, 1984. Algérie 1880-1982: pp. 14-214.

2521. ————. *Maghreb: littératures de langue française.* Paris: Arcantère, 1993. Algérie 1945-1989: pp. 337-457.

Anthologies

2522. Achour, Christiane et Zineb Ali-Benali. *Contes algériens*. Paris: L'Harmattan, 1989.

2523. *L'Enfance au cœur*. Reghaïa: ENAD, 1988. 86 p. en français et 24 en arabe.

2524. *Poèmes pour la paix*. Alger: Hiwar, 1985.

General studies

2525. Allouache, Merzak et Vincent Colonna (dir.). *Algérie, trente ans: les enfants de l'indépendance*. Paris: Autrement, 1992. Recueil d'articles.

2526. Bonn, Charles. *Le Roman algérien de langue française. Vers un espace de communication décolonisée*. Paris: L'Harmattan, 1985.

2527. Déjeux, Jean. *Femmes d'Algérie. Légendes, traditions, histoire et littérature*. Paris: La Boîte à Documents, 1987.

2528. Khodja, Souad. *A comme Algériennes*. Alger: ENAL, 1991.

2529. Laoust-Chantréaux, Germaine. *Kabylie côté femmes*. Aix en Provence: Edisud, 1990.

2530. Laronde, Michel. *Autour du roman beur: immigration et identité*. Paris: L'Harmattan, 1993.

2531. Mosteghanemi, Ahlem. *Algérie: Femmes et écritures*. Paris: L'Harmattan, 1985.

Authors

2532. Aba, Noureddine. *L'Annonce faite à Marco ou à l'aube sans couronne*. Paris: L'Harmattan, 1983. Théâtre.

2533. ———. *L'Arbre qui cachait la mer*. Paris: L'Harmattan, 1992. Théâtre.

2534. ———. sous le pseudonyme d'Abaoub. *L'Aube de l'amour*. Paris: Editions Intellectuels réunis, 1941. Recueil de poèmes.

2535. ———. *Le Dernier jour d'un nazi*. Paris: Stock, 1982. Théâtre.

2536. ———. *Deux étoiles filantes dans le ciel d'Alger*. Paris: Nathan, 1979. Contes pour les enfants.

2537. ———. *Et l'Algérie des Rois, Sire?* Paris: L'Harmattan, 1992. Poésie.

2538. ———. *Gazelle après minuit*. Paris: L'Harmattan, 1978. (Nouvelle édition en 1979 aux Editions de Minuit, Paris). Poésie.

2539. ———. *Montjoie Palestine! ou l'an dernier à Jérusalem*. Honfleur: P. J. Oswald, 1970. (Nouvelle édition bilingue français-anglais chez l'Harmattan). Poésie.

2540. ———. *La Récréation des clowns*. Paris: Galilée, 1980. Théâtre.

2541. ———. *Tell El Zaatar s'est tu à la tombée du soir*. Paris: L'Harmattan, 1981. Théâtre.

2542. ———. *La Toussaint des énigmes*. Paris: Présence Africaine, 1963. Poésie.

2543. Abbas, Ferhat. *Autopsie d'une guerre. L'Aurore*. Paris: Garnier, 1980. Roman.

2544. ———. *Guerre et révolution d'Algérie: la Nuit coloniale*. Paris: Julliard, 1962. Roman.

2545. ———. *L'Indépendance confisquée*. Paris: Flammarion, 1984. Roman.

2546. Abdessemed, Rabia. *La Voyante du Hodna*. Paris: L'Harmattan, 1993. (Coll. Ecriture arabe). Roman.

2547. Aïsha (F). *Décharge publique: les emmurés de l'assistance*. Paris: Maspero, 1980. Autobiographie.

2548. Aïssa, Salim. *Mimouna.* Alger: Laphomic, 1987. Roman policier.

2549. Ait Djafer, Ismaël. *Complainte des mendiants arabes de la Casbah et de la petite Yasmina tuée par son père.* Alger: Editions de Judma, 1953. (Nouvelle édition en 1987 chez Bouchène, Alger). Poésie.

2550. Aktouf, Omar. *Algérie: entre l'exil et la curée.* Paris: L'Harmattan, 1989. Mémoires.

2551. Alloula, Malek. *Le Harem colonial: images d'un sous-érotisme.* Paris; Genève: Garance; Slatkine, 1981. Album de photographies avec textes de commentaires.

2552. ———. *Mesures du vent.* Paris: Sindbad, 1984. Poésie.

2553. Amrani, Djamal. *L'Eté de ta peau.* Alger: SNED, 1982. Poésie.

2554. ———. *Le Témoin.* Paris: Editions de Minuit, 1960. Récit-témoignage.

2555. ———. *Vers l'amont.* Alger: ENAL, 1989. Poésie.

2556. Amrouche, Fadhma Aït Mansour (F). *Histoire de ma vie.* Paris: Maspero, 1968. Autobiographie.

2557. Amrouche, Jean. *Cendres.* Tunis: Mirages, 1934. (Nouvelle édition en 1983 chez l'Harmattan). Poésie.

2558. ———. *Etoile secrète.* Tunis: Mirages, 1937. (Nouvelle édition en 1983 chez l'Harmattan). Poésie.

2559. *Jean Amrouche. L'éternel Jugurtha (1906-1962).* Marseille: Archives de la Ville, 1985.

2560. Amrouche, Marie-Louise (F). *L'Amant imaginaire.* Paris: Nouvelle Société Morel, 1975. Roman.

2561. ———. *Le Grain magique.* Paris: Maspero, 1966. Contes, poèmes et proverbes.

2562. ———. *Jacinthe noire*. Paris: Charlot, 1947. Publie aussi sous le pseudonyme de Amrouche Marguerite Taos. Roman.

2563. ———. *Rue des tambourins*. Paris: La Table Ronde, 1960. Roman.

2564. Aouchal, Leïla (F). *Une Autre vie*. Alger: SNED, 1970. Autobiographie.

2565. Arriz Tamza, Maya (F). *Ombres*. Paris: L'Harmattan, 1989. Roman.

2566. ———. *Quelque part en Barbarie*. Paris: L'Harmattan, 1993. (Coll. Ecritures arabes). Roman.

2567. ———. *Zaïd le mendiant*. Paris: Publisud, 1989. Contes.

2568. Azeggagh, Ahmed. *République des ombres*. Paris: Les Quatre Vents, 1976. Théâtre.

2569. Azzedine. *Et Alger ne brûla pas*. Paris: Stock, 1980. Mémoires.

2570. ———. *On nous appelait fellaghas*. Paris: Stock, 1976. Autobiographie.

2571. Bachir, Bediya (F). *L'Oued en crue*. Paris: Edition du Centenaire, 1979. Roman.

2572. Bakhaï, Fatima (F). *La Scalera*. Paris: L'Harmattan, 1993. (Coll. Ecritures arabes, 86). Roman.

2573. Begag, Azouz. *Béni ou le Paradis privé*. Paris: Seuil, 1989. (Coll. Points, série Point virgule, 114). Roman.

2574. ———. *L'Ilet-aux-Vents*. Paris: Seuil, 1992. Roman.

2575. Belaïdi, Malika (F). *Vie couleur black*. Paris: Radio Beur, Grenel, 1986. Poésie.

2576. Belamri, Rabah. *L'Asile de pierre*. Paris: Gallimard, 1989. Roman.

2577. ———. *Femmes sans visage*. Paris: Gallimard, 1992. Roman.

2578. ———. *Les Graines de la douleur*. Paris: Publisud, 1982. (Contes populaires traduits de l'arabe en français). Contes.

2579. ———. *L'Oiseau du grenadier*. Paris: Flammarion, 1986. Roman.

2580. ———. *L'Olivier boit son ombre*. Aix-en-Provence: Edisud, 1989. Poésie.

2581. ———. *Pierres d'équilibre*. Noroît et Montréal: Le Dé bleu et Chaillé, 1993. Poésie.

2582. ———. *Proverbes et dictons sahariens*. Paris: L'Harmattan, 1986. Proverbes.

2583. ———. *Regard blessé*. Paris: Gallimard, 1987. Roman.

2584. ———. *Le Soleil sous le tamis*. Paris: Publisud, 1982. Récit autobiographique.

2585. Belghanem. *El Gabal ou la nuit de l'erreur*. Paris: P. J. Oswald, 1974. (Coll. Théâtre injouable). Théâtre.

2586. ———. *La Troisième nuit d'Ugnalé*. Paris: Caractères, 1956. Poésie.

2587. Belghoul, Farida (F). *Georgette*. Paris: Barrault, 1986. Roman.

2588. Belkacemi, Mohammed. *Belka*. Paris: Fayard, 1974. Autobiographie.

2589. Ben Ali, Fazia (F). *La Goutte d'Or ou le mal des racines*. Paris: Stock, 1979. En collaboration avec Catherine Von Bülow. Récit-témoignage.

2590. Ben Cherif, Mohammed Ben Si Ahmed. *Ahmed Ben Mostapha, goumier.* Paris: Payot, 1920. Roman.

2591. Ben Mansour, Latifa (F). *Le Chant du lys et du basilic.* Paris: Lattès, 1990. Roman.

2592. Ben, Myriam (F). *Ainsi naquit un homme.* Paris: L'Harmattan, 1982. Nouvelles.

2593. ———. *Au Carrefour des sacrifices.* Paris: L'Harmattan, 1992. Poésie.

2594. ———. *Sabrina, ils t'ont volé ta vie.* Paris: L'Harmattan, 1986. Roman.

2595. ———. *Sur le chemin de nos pas.* Paris: L'Harmattan, 1984. Poésie.

2596. Achour, Christiane. *Myriam Ben.* Paris: L'Harmattan, 1989. (Coll. Classiques pour demain).

2597. Ben Slimane, Jacqueline (F). *Poèmes.* Alger: Imprimerie officielle, 1963. Poésie.

2598. Benaïssa, Aïcha (F). *Née en France.* Paris: Payot, 1990. Roman.

2599. Benmaleck, Anouar. *Ludmila ou le violon à la mort lente.* Alger: ENAL, 1986. Roman.

2600. Benmansour, Leïla (F). *Poèmes.* Paris: L'Arthanor, 1977. Poésie.

2601. Bennabi, Maleck. *Lebbeik, pélerinage du pauvre.* Alger: En-Nadha, 1948. Roman.

2602. Benslimane, Jacqueline (F). *Poèmes.* Alger: Imprimerie officielle, 1963. Poésie.

2603. Bensoussan, Albert. *Au Nadir.* Paris: Flammarion, 1978. Roman.

2604. ———. *Les Bagnoulis.* Paris: Mercure de France, 1965. Roman.

2605. ———. *La Bréhaigne.* Paris: Denoël, 1974. Roman.

2606. ———. *Le Dernier devoir.* Paris: L'Harmattan, 1988. Roman.

2607. ———. *L'Echelle de Mesrod.* Paris: L'Harmattan, 1984. Roman.

2608. ———. *Frimaldjézar.* Paris: Calmann-Lévy, 1976. Roman.

2609. ———. *Isbilia.* Honfleur: P. J. Oswald, 1970. Roman.

2610. ———. *Le Marrane ou la confession d'un traître.* Paris: L'Harmattan, 1991. (Coll. Ecritures arabes, 64). Roman.

2611. ———. *Mirage à trois.* Paris: L'Harmattan, 1989. Roman.

2612. ———. *Visage de ton absence.* Paris: L'Harmattan, 1990. Roman.

2613. Schousboë, Elisabeth. *Albert Bensoussan.* Paris: L'Harmattan, 1991. (Coll. Classiques pour demain).

2614. Benyahia, Mohammed. *La Conjuration au pouvoir.* Paris: Arcantère, 1989. Mémoires.

2615. Berezak, Fatiha (F). *Homsik.* Paris: L'Harmattan, 1993. (Coll. Ecritures arabes, 90). Récit.

2616. ———. *Le Regard aquarelle: spectacle poétique.* Paris: L'Harmattan, 1985. Poésie.

2617. ———. *Le Regard aquarelle 2: quotidien pluriel,* suivi de *L'Envers des corps.* Paris: L'Harmattan, 1988. Poésie.

2618. ———. *Le Regard aquarelle 3.* Paris: L'Harmattan, 1992. Poésie.

2619. Bittari, Zoubida (F). *Ô mes sœurs musulmanes, pleurez!* Paris: Gallimard, 1964. Roman.

2620. Bouabaci, Aïcha (F). *L'Aube est née sur nos lèvres*. Alger: ENAL, 1985. Poésie.

2621. ———. *Peau d'exil*. Alger: ENAL, 1991. Nouvelles.

2622. Boudjedra, Mohamed. *Barbès-Palace*. Paris: Edition le Rocher, 1993. Roman.

2623. Boudjedra, Rachid. *Le Démantèlement*. Paris: Denoël, 1982. Roman.

2624. ———. *Le Désordre des choses*. Paris: Denoël, 1991. Tr. de l'arabe par Antoine Moussali. Roman.

2625. ———. *FIS de la haine*. Paris: Denoël, 1992. Roman.

2626. ———. *L'Insolation*. Paris: Denoël, 1972. Roman.

2627. ———. *La Répudiation*. Paris: Denoël, 1969. Roman.

2628. ———. *Timimoun*. Paris: Denoël, 1994. Tr. de l'arabe par l'auteur. Roman.

2629. ———. *Le Vainqueur de coupe*. Paris: Denoël, 1981. Roman.

2630. Gafaiti, Hafid. *Rachid Boudjedra ou la passion de la modernité*. Paris: Denoël, 1987. Entretien avec Rachid Boudjedra.

2631. Bouguerra, M. K. *Fenêtres barbares*. Paris: L'Harmattan, 1993. Roman.

2632. Boukhanoufa, Abdelkrim. *Yugurtha*. Paris: La Pensée Universelle, 1988. Théâtre.

2633. Boukhedenna, Sakinna (F). *Journal: nationalité: immigrée*. Paris: L'Harmattan, 1987. Autobiographie.

2634. Boukortt, Zoulika (F). *Le Corps en pièces*. Montpellier: Coprah, 1977. Nouvelle.

2635. Boumédiene, Anissa (F). *La Fin d'un monde.* Alger: Bouchêne, 1991. Roman. L'auteur avait déjà publié quelques poèmes sous le titre *Le Jour et la nuit.* Paris: Saint-Germain-des-Prés, 1980.

2636. Bounemeur, Azzedine. *Cette guerre qui ne dit pas son nom.* Paris: L'Harmattan, 1993. (Coll. Ecritures arabes, 86). Roman.

2637. Bouraoui, Nina (F). *Poing mort.* Paris: Gallimard, 1992. Roman.

2638. ———. *La Voyeuse interdite.* Paris: Gallimard, 1991. (Nouvelle édition en 1993 chez Gallimard, Folio 2479). Roman.

2639. Boutarene, Kadda. *Kaddour, un enfant algérien témoin des débuts du vingtième siècle.* Alger: SNED, 1982. Autobiographie.

2640. Bouzaher, Hocine. *Des Voix dans la casbah.* Paris: Maspero, 1960. (Nouvelle édition en 1986 chez ENAL, Alger). Théâtre.

2641. ———. *L'Honneur réconcilié.* Alger: ENAL, 1988. Recueil contenant quatres pièces écrites avant 1962. Théâtre.

2642. Bouzar, Wadi. *Les Fleuves ont toujours deux rives.* Alger: ENAL, 1986. Roman.

2643. Bouzid. *La Marche: traversée de la France profonde.* Paris: Sindbad, 1984. Carnet de route.

2644. Brouri, Malik. *Les Orangers de Sidi Bou Saïd.* Paris: La Pensée Universelle, 1992. Roman.

2645. Chergou, Abderrahmane. *Demain reste toujours à faire.* Alger: ENAL, 1984. Témoignage.

2646. Cherifi, Louisette (F). *Entre terre et brume.* Alger: ENAL, 1985. Poésie.

2647. Commissaire Llob (F). *Le Dingue au bistouri.* Alger: Laphomic, 1990. Roman policier.

2648. ———. *La Foire des enfoirés.* Alger: Laphomic, 1993. Roman policier.

2649. Daïf, Mohammed. *Ulysse.* Alger: ENAL, 1989. Théâtre.

2650. Debèche, Djamila (F). *Aziza.* Alger: Imprimerie Imbert, 1955. Roman.

2651. ———. *Leila, la jeune fille d'Algérie.* Alger: Imprimerie Charras, 1947. Roman.

2652. Dib, Djamel. *La Saga des djinns.* Alger: ENAL, 1986. Roman policier.

2653. Dib, Mohammed. *Au Café.* Paris: Gallimard, 1956. Nouvelles.

2654. ———. *Cours sur la rive sauvage.* Paris: Seuil, 1964. Roman.

2655. ———. *La Danse du roi.* Paris: Seuil, 1968. Roman.

2656. ———. *Le Désert sans retour.* Paris: Sindbad, 1992. Roman.

2657. ———. *Dieu en Barbarie.* Paris: Seuil, 1970. Roman.

2658. ———. *Un Eté africain.* Paris: Seuil, 1959. Roman.

2659. ———. *Formulaires.* Paris: Seuil, 1970. Poésie.

2660. ———. *La Grande maison.* Paris: Seuil, 1952. Roman.

2661. ———. *Habel.* Paris: Seuil, 1977. Roman.

2662. ———. *L'Incendie.* Paris: Seuil, 1954. (Nouvelle édition revue et corrigée en 1967). Roman.

2663. ———. *L'Infante maure*. Paris: Albin Michel, 1994. Roman.

2664. ———. *Le Maître de chasse*. Paris: Seuil, 1973. Roman.

2665. ———. *Le Métier à tisser*. Paris: Seuil, 1957. Roman.

2666. ———. *Mille houras pour une gueuse*. Paris: Seuil, 1980. Théâtre.

2667. ———. *Neiges de marbre*. Paris: Seuil, 1990. Roman.

2668. ———. *O Vive*. Paris: Sindbad, 1987. Poésie.

2669. ———. *Ombre gardienne*. Paris: Sindbad, 1984. Poésie.

2670. ———. *Omneros*. Paris: Seuil, 1975. Poésie.

2671. ———. *Qui se souvient de la mer?* Paris: Seuil, 1962. Roman.

2672. ———. *Le Sommeil d'Eve*. Paris: Seuil, 1989. Roman.

2673. ———. *Le Talisman*. Paris: Seuil, 1966. Nouvelles.

2674. ———. *Les Terrasses d'Orsol*. Paris: Seuil, 1985. Roman.

2675. Daninos, Guy. *Dieu en barbarie de Mohammed Dib ou la recherche d'un nouvel humanisme*. Sherbrooke: Naaman, 1985.

2676. Déjeux, Jean. *Mohammed Dib, écrivain algérien*. Sherbrooke: Naaman, 1977.

2677. Khadda, Naget. *L'Œuvre romanesque de Mohammed Dib: propositions d'analyse de deux romans*. Alger: Office des publications universitaires, 1983.

2678. Djabali, Hawa (F). *Agave.* Paris: Publisud, 1983. Roman.

2679. Djaout, Tahar. *Les Chercheurs d'os.* Paris: Seuil, 1984. Roman.

2680. ———. *L'Exproprié.* Alger: SNED, 1981. (Nouvelle édition en 1991). Roman.

2681. ———. *L'Invention du désert.* Paris: Seuil, 1987. Roman.

2682. ———. *Les Vigiles.* Paris: Seuil, 1991. Roman.

2683. Djebar, Assia (F). *Les Alouettes naïves.* Paris: Julliard, 1967. (Nouvelle édition dans la coll. 10/18). Roman.

2684. ———. *L'Amour, la fantasia.* Paris: J. C. Lattès, 1985. (Nouvelle édition en 1992 chez Eddif, Casablanca). Roman.

2685. ———. *Chronique d'un été algérien: ici et là bas.* Paris: Plumes, 1993. Texte de Djebar: 25p. et photos de différents photographes environ 125 pages. Album.

2686. ———. *Les Enfants du nouveau monde.* Paris: Julliard, 1962. (Nouvelle édition dans la coll. 10/18). Roman.

2687. ———. *Femmes d'Alger dans leur appartement.* Paris: Des Femmes, 1980. Nouvelles.

2688. ———. *Les Impatients.* Paris: Julliard, 1958. Roman.

2689. ———. *Loin de Médine.* Paris: Albin Michel, 1991. Roman.

2690. ———. *La Soif.* Paris: Julliard, 1957. Roman.

2691. Déjeux, Jean. *Assia Djebar, romancière algérienne, cinéaste arabe.* Sherbrooke: Naaman, 1984.

2692. Mortimer, Milfred. *Assia Djebar.* Philadelphie: CELFAN. Editions monographs, 1989.

2693. Djebar, Assia (F) et Walid Garn. *Rouge l'aube.* Alger: SNED, 1969. Théâtre.

2694. Djelloul, Ahmed. *Al Kahena.* Paris: Debresse, 1957. Théâtre.

2695. Djura (F). *La Saison des narcisses.* Paris: Laffont, 1993. Roman.

2696. ———. *Le Voile du silence.* Paris: Laffont, 1990. Autobiographie.

2697. Drif, Zohra (F). *La Mort de mes frères.* Paris: Maspero, 1960. Roman.

2698. El Hammami, Ali. *Idris.* Le Caire: Imprimerie sociale, 1948. (Nouvelle édition en 1976 chez SNED, Alger). Roman.

2699. El Koubi, Salem. *Rosées d'Orient.* Paris: Editions françaises les Gémeaux, 1920. Poésie.

2700. Farès, Nabile. *Le Champ des oliviers.* Paris: Seuil, 1972. Roman.

2701. ———. *L'Exil et le désarroi.* Paris: Maspero, 1976. Poésie et prose.

2702. ———. *La Mort de Salah Baye ou la vie obscure d'un Maghrébin.* Paris: L'Harmattan, 1980. Roman.

2703. ———. *Yahia, pas de chance.* Paris: Seuil, 1970. Autobiographie.

2704. Feraoun, Mouloud. *L'Anniversaire.* Paris: Seuil, 1972. Roman.

2705. ———. *Les Chemins qui montent.* Paris: Seuil, 1957. Roman.

2706. ———. *Le Fils du pauvre.* Le Puy: Cahiers du Nouvel Humanisme, 1951. Roman.

2707. ———. *Journal (1955-1962)*. Paris: Seuil, 1962. Autobiographie.

2708. ———. *Jours de Kabylie*. Alger: Baconnier, 1954. (Nouvelle édition en 1968 chez Seuil). Récits.

2709. ———. *Lettres à ses amis*. Paris: Seuil, 1969. Correspondance.

2710. ———. *Les Poèmes de Si Mohand*. Paris: Editions de Minuit, 1960. Poésie.

2711. ———. *La Terre et le sang*. Paris: Seuil, 1953. Roman.

2712. Achour, Christiane. *Mouloud Feraoun: une voix en contrepoint*. Paris: Silex, 1986.

2713. Chèze, Marie-Hélène. *Mouloud Feraoun: la voix du silence*. Paris: Seuil, 1982.

2714. Gleize, Jack. *Mouloud Feraoun*. Paris: L'Harmattan, 1990. (Coll. Classiques pour demain).

2715. Nacib, Youssef. *Mouloud Feraoun*. Paris; Alger: Nathan; SNED, 1982. (Coll. Classiques du monde).

2716. Ferdi, Saïd. *Un Enfant dans la guerre: Algérie 1954-1962*. Paris: Seuil, 1981. Autobiographie.

2717. Flici, Laadi. *Les Feux de la rampe*. Alger: SNED, 1982. Nouvelles.

2718. ———. *La Passion humaine*. Paris: Millas-Martin, 1959. Poésie.

2719. Gallaire, Fatima (F). *Ah! vous êtes venus... là où il y a quelques tombes*. Paris: Les Quatre Vents, 1988. Théâtre.

2720. ———. *Au loin, les caroubiers,* suivi de *Rim, la gazelle*. Paris: Les Quatre Vents, 1993. Théâtre.

2721. ———. *Les Co-épouses*. Paris: Les Quatre Vents, 1990. Théâtre.

2722. ———. *La Fête virile*. Paris: Les Quatre Vents, 1992. Théâtre.

2723. ———. *Princesses*. Paris: Les Quatre Vents, 1988. Théâtre.

2724. Ghalem, Ali. *Une Femme pour mon fils*. Paris: Syros, 1979. Roman.

2725. ———. *Le Serpent à sept têtes*. Paris: Flammarion, 1984. Roman.

2726. Ghalem, Nadia (F). *Les Jardins de cristal*. Québec: Urtubise, 1981. Roman.

2727. ———. *L'Oiseau de fer*. Sherbrooke: Naaman, 1981. Nouvelles.

2728. ———. *La Villa désir*. Montréal: Guérin Littérature, 1988. Roman.

2729. Greki, Anna (F). *Algérie, capitale Alger*. Tunis: SNED, 1963. Ecrit en partie en arabe et en partie en français. Poésie.

2730. ———. *Temps forts*. Paris: Présence Africaine, 1966. (Publié à titre posthume). Poésie.

2731. Guendouz, Nadia (F). *Amal*. Alger: SNED, 1968. Poésie.

2732. ———. *La Corde*. Alger: SNED, 1974. Poésie.

2733. Haciane, Mustapha. *Les Orphelins de l'Empereur*. Alger: SNED, 1978. Théâtre.

2734. Haddad, Malek. *La Dernière impression*. Paris: Julliard, 1958. Roman.

2735. ———. *Les Femmes algériennes*. Alger: Ministère de l'Information, 1967. Album de photographies.

2736. ———. *Le Malheur en danger.* Paris: La Nef de Paris, 1956. (Nouvelle édition en 1988 chez Bouchène, Alger). Poésie.

2737. ———. *Le Quai aux fleurs ne répond plus.* Paris: Julliard, 1961. (Nouvelle édition dans la coll. 10/18). Roman.

2738. Hadj Hamou, Abdelkader. *Zohra, la femme du mineur.* Paris: Edition du Monde moderne, 1925. Roman.

2739. Hamoutene, Leïla (F). *Abîmes.* Alger: ENAG, 1992. Nouvelles.

2740. Houfani Berfas, Zahira (F). *L'Incomprise.* Alger: ENAL, 1989. Roman.

2741. Imache, Tassadit (F). *Une Fille sans histoire.* Paris: Calmann-Levy, 1989. Roman.

2742. Kacimi el Hassani, Mohammed. *Le Mouchoir.* Paris: L'Harmattan, 1987. Roman.

2743. Kadra-Hadjadji, Houria (F). *Oumelkheir.* Alger: ENAL, 1989. Roman.

2744. Kalouaz, Ahmed. *Celui qui regarde le soleil en face.* Alger: Laphomic, 1987. Nouvelles.

2745. Kateb, Yacine. *Le Cercle des représailles.* Paris: Seuil, 1959. Théâtre.

2746. ———. *L'Homme aux sandales de caoutchouc.* Paris: Seuil, 1970. Théâtre.

2747. ———. *Nedjma.* Paris: Seuil, 1956. (Nouvelle édition dans la coll. Point). Roman.

2748. ———. *L'Œuvre en fragments.* Paris: Sindbad, 1986. Inédits rassemblés et présentés par Jacqueline Arnaud. Poésie, théâtre et fragments divers.

2749. ———. *Le Polygone étoilé.* Paris: Seuil, 1966. Roman.

2750. ———. *Soliloques.* Bône: Imprimerie du Réveil bônois, 1946. Repris en partie dans Kateb, Yacine, *L'Œuvre en fragment,* 1991. Poésie.

2751. Abdoun, Mohammed-Ismaïl. *Kateb Yacine.* Paris; Alger: Nathan; SNED, 1983. (Coll. Classiques du monde).

2752. Arnaud, Jacqueline. *La Littérature maghrébine de langue française, v. 2: le cas de Kateb Yacine.* Paris: Publisud, 1986.

2753. Gafaiti, Hafid. *Kateb Yacine: un homme, une œuvre, un pays.* Alger: Laphomic, 1986. Entretien avec Kateb Yacine.

2754. Kerouani, Dalila (F). *Une Fille d'Algérie.* Paris et Bruxelles: Selection du Reader's Digest, 1992. Autobiographie.

2755. Kessas, Ferrudja (F). *Beur's story.* Paris: L'Harmattan, 1989. (Coll. Ecritures arabes, 55). Roman.

2756. Ketou, Safia (F). *Amie cithare.* Sherbrooke: Naaman, 1979. (Nouvelle édition en 1982). Poésie.

2757. ———. *La Planète mauve et autres nouvelles.* Sherbrooke: Naaman, 1983. Nouvelles.

2758. Kharbiche, Sakina (F). *La Suture.* Alger: Laphomic, 1993. Roman.

2759. Khodja, Chukri. *El Euldj, captif des Barbaresques.* Arras: INSAF, 1929. Roman.

2760. Koribaa, Nabhani. *Poèmes d'un enfant.* Alger: France-Afrique, 1935. Poésie.

2761. Korogli, Ammar. *Les Menottes du quotidien.* Paris: L'Harmattan, 1989. Nouvelles.

2762. Kréa, Henri. *Poèmes en forme de vestige.* Paris: Seghers, 1967. Poésie.

2763. ———. *Le Séisme.* Paris: P. J. Oswald, 1958. Théâtre.

2764. Lachmet, Djanet (F). *Le Cow-boy.* Paris: Belfond, 1983. Roman.

2765. Lallaoui, Mehdi. *Du Bidonville aux HLM.* Paris: Syros-Alternatives, 1993. (Coll. Au nom de la mémoire). Roman.

2766. Lamrani, Abdelaziz. *Piège à Tel Aviv.* Alger: SNED, 1980. Roman policier.

2767. Lebkiri, Moussa. *Il parlait à son balai.* Paris: L'Harmattan, 1992. Théâtre.

2768. ———. *Prince Trouduc en panach': théâtre conté.* Paris: L'Harmattan, 1993. Théâtre.

2769. Lemsine, Aïcha (F). *La Chrysalide.* Paris: Des Femmes, 1976. Roman.

2770. ———. *Ciel de porphyre.* Paris: Simoën, 1978. Roman.

2771. Achour, Christiane. *Entre le roman rose et le roman exotique: la Chrysalide de A. Lemsine. Essai de lecture critique.* Alger: ENAP, 1978.

2772. Lounès, Abderrahmane. *Chronique d'un couple ou la Birman-dreissienne.* Alger: SNED, 1982. Roman.

2773. ———. *Poèmes à coups de poing et à coups de pied.* Alger: SNED, 1981. Poésie.

2774. Mammeri, Farid. *La Pulpe et l'écorce.* Alger: ENAL, 1985. Poésie.

2775. Mammeri, Mouloud. *Le Banquet: la mort absurde des Aztèques.* Paris: Perrin, 1973. Théâtre.

2776. ———. *La Colline oubliée.* Paris: Plon, 1952. (Nouvelle édition en 1992 chez Gallimard, Folio 2353). Roman.

2777. ———. *Escales nouvelles*. Paris: La Découverte, 1992. Nouvelles.

2778. ———. *Le Fœhn*. Paris: Publisud, 1982. Théâtre.

2779. ———. *Les Isefra, poèmes de Si Mohand*. Paris: Maspero, 1969. Poésie.

2780. ———. *L'Opium* et *Le bâton*. Paris: Plon, 1965. Roman.

2781. ———. *Poèmes kabyles anciens*. Paris: Maspero, 1980. Poésie.

2782. ———. *Le Sommeil du juste*. Paris: Plon, 1955. Roman.

2783. ———. *La Traversée*. Paris: Plon, 1982. Roman.

2784. Djaout, Tahar. *Mouloud Mammeri*. Alger: Laphomic, 1987. Entretien avec Mouloud Mammeri.

2785. El Hassar-Zeghari, Latifa et Denise Louanchi. *Mouloud Mammeri*. Paris; Alger: Nathan; SNED, 1982. (Coll. Classiques du monde).

2786. Mortimer, Mildred. *Mouloud Mammeri, écrivain algérien*. Sherbrooke: Naaman, 1982.

2787. Mechakra, Yamina (F). *La Grotte éclatée*. Alger: SNED, 1979. Roman.

2788. Medjbeur, Tami. *Face au mur ou le journal d'un condamné à mort*. Alger: SNED, 1981. Autobiographie.

2789. Melouah, Ana (F). *Fleurs de pommier*. Alger: SNED, 1983. Poésie.

2790. Messali Hadj. *Les Mémoires de Messali Hadj*. Paris: Lattès, 1982. Mémoires.

2791. Messaoudi, Khalida (F) et Elisabeth Schemla (F). *Une Algérienne debout*. Paris: Flammarion, 1995. Entretiens.

2792. Mimouni, Rachid. *La Ceinture de l'ogresse*. Paris: Seghers, 1990. Nouvelles.

2793. ———. *De la Barbarie en général à l'Intégrisme en particulier*. Paris: Pré-aux-Clercs, 1992. Essai.

2794. ———. *Le Fleuve détourné*. Paris: Laffont, 1982. Roman.

2795. ———. *L'Honneur de la tribu*. Paris: Laffont, 1989. Roman.

2796. ———. *La Malédiction*. Paris: Stock, 1993. Roman.

2797. ———. *Une Peine à vivre*. Paris: Stock, 1991. (Nouvelle édition en 1993 chez Presse-Pocket, no 4589). Roman.

2798. ———. *Le Printemps n'en sera que plus beau*. Alger: SNED, 1978. Roman.

2799. ———. *Tombéza*. Paris: Laffont, 1984. Roman.

2800. Moati, Nine (F). *Rose d'Alger*. Paris: Fayard, 1991. Roman.

2801. Mokeddem, Malika (F). *Les Hommes qui marchent*. Paris: Ramsay, 1990. Roman.

2802. ———. *L'Interdite*. Paris: Grasset, 1993. Roman.

2803. ———. *Le Siècle des sauterelles*. Paris: Ramsay, 1992. Roman.

2804. Montera, Mahieddine. *Le Frison de la chair*. Alger: Soubiron, 1931. Théâtre et contes.

2805. Mouhoub, Hadjira (F). *Quand tourne le vent*. Alger: ENAP, 1988. Nouvelles.

2806. Nekachtali, Leïla (F). *Les Oies sauvages*. Alger: ENAL, 1986. Nouvelles.

2807. ———. *Petit brin d'herbe ciel d'espoir*. Alger: ENAL, 1985. Poésie.

2808. Nini, Soraya (F). *Ils disent que je suis une beurette*. Paris: Fixot, 1993. Roman.

2809. Ouahioune, Chabane. *Randonnées avec Aït Menguellet*. Alger: ENAP, 1992. Récit.

2810. Ouary, Malek. *La Montagne aux chacals*. Paris: Garnier, 1981. Roman.

2811. Ould Cheikh, Mohammed. *Chants pour Yasmina*. Oran: Fouque, 1930. (Nouvelle édition en 1937). Poésie.

2812. ———. *Myriem dans les palmes*. Oran: Plaza, 1936. Roman.

2813. Lanasri, Ahmed. *Mohammed Ould Cheikh: un romancier algérien des années trente*. Alger: Office de publications universitaires, 1986.

2814. Ouldamer, Mezioud. *Le Cauchemar immigré: dans la décomposition de la France*. Paris: Gérard Lébovici, 1986. Autobiographie.

2815. Oussedik, Tahar. *Des Héroïnes algériennes dans l'histoire*. Alger: Epigraphe/Dar el ljtihad, 1993. Témoignages romancés.

2816. ———. *Si Smaïl*. Alger: SNED, 1981. Autobiographie.

2817. Rech, Nacéra (F). *Plaidoyer d'une Algérienne*. Paris: La Pensée Universelle, 1991. Autobiographie.

2818. Rehamna, Nadjet (F). *A l'ombre d'une vie*. Paris: La Pensée Universelle, 1980. Poésie.

2819. Rezzoug, Leïla (F). *Apprivoiser l'insolence*. Paris: L'Harmattan, 1988. Roman.

2820. ———. *Douces errances*. Paris: L'Harmattan, 1992. (Coll. Ecritures arabes, 77). Roman.

2821. Sadjine, Taos (F). *Clair d'eau.* Alger: Laphomic, 1986. Poésie.

2822. Sassi, Salah (F). *Magie de mots.* Paris: Caractères, 1988. Poésie.

2823. Sebaa, Mohammed Nadhir. *Avis de recherches.* Aïn M'Iila: Numidia, 1988. Nouvelles.

2824. Sebbar, Leïla (F). *Les Carnets de Shérazade.* Paris: Stock, 1985. Roman.

2825. ———. *Le Chinois vert d'Afrique.* Paris: Stock, 1984. Roman.

2826. ———. *Fatima ou les Algériennes au square.* Paris: Stock, 1981. Roman.

2827. ———. *Le Fou de Shérazade.* Paris: Stock, 1991. Roman.

2828. ———. *J. H. cherche âme sœur.* Paris: Stock, 1987. Roman.

2829. ———. *Parle mon fils, parle à ta mère.* Paris: Stock, 1984. Roman.

2830. ———. *Shérazade, 17 ans, brune, frisée, les yeux verts.* Paris: Stock, 1982. Roman.

2831. ———. *Le Silence des rives.* Paris: Stock, 1993. Roman.

2832. ——— et Nancy Huston (F). *Lettres parisiennes.* Paris: Barrault, 1986. Correspondance.

2833. Sebti, Youcef. *L'Enfer et la folie.* Alger: SNED, 1981. Poésie.

2834. Sefouane, Fatiha (F). *L'Enfant de la haine.* Paris: L'Harmattan, 1990. (Coll. Ecritures arabes, 60). Roman.

2835. Sehaba, Mohammed. *Remparts.* Alger: ENAL, 1986. Poésie.

2836. Sénac, Jean. *Avant-corps*. Paris: Gallimard, 1968. Poésie.

2837. ———. *Citoyens de beauté*. Rodez: Subervie, 1967. Poésie.

2838. ———. *L'Ebauche du père*. Paris: Gallimard, 1989. Publié à titre posthume. Roman.

2839. ———. *Journal d'Alger: janvier-juillet 1954*. Pézenas: Le Haut Quartier, 1983. Publié à titre posthume. Journal.

2840. ———. *Poèmes*. Paris: Gallimard, 1954. Poésie.

2841. *Poésie au Sud: Jean Sénac et la nouvelle poésie algérienne d'expression française*. Marseille: Archives de la Ville, 1983.

2842. Skif, Hamid. *Poèmes d'El Asnam et d'autres lieux*. Alger: ENAL, 1986. Poésie.

2843. Smaïl, Saïd. *Les Barons de la pénurie*. Alger: ENAP, 1989. Roman.

2844. Tilikète, Fatma (F). *Les Déracinés*. Paris: Saint-Germain-des Prés, 1985. Poésie.

2845. Touabti, Hocine. *Dans la ville aux volets verts*. Paris: Challenges d'aujourd'hui, 1994. Roman.

2846. Touati, Fettouma (F). *Le Printemps désespéré: vies d'Algériennes*. Paris: L'Harmattan, 1984. (Coll. Encres noires, 10). Roman.

2847. Wakas, Safa (F). *La Grenade dégoupillée*. Ottawa: Myriade, 1984. (Nouvelle édition en 1986 chez ENAL, Alger). Roman.

2848. Yacine, Kateb *voir* Kateb, Yacine.

2849. Zehar, Aïssa (F). *Hind à l'âme pure ou l'histoire d'une mère*. Alger: Baconnier, 1942. Roman.

2850. Zehar, Hacène Farouk. *Miroir d'un fou*. Paris: Fayard, 1979. Roman.

2851. ———. *Peloton de tête*. Paris: Julliard, 1966. Nouvelles.

2852. Zenati, Rabah. *Bou-el-Nouar, le jeune Algérien*. Alger: La Maison des livres, 1945. Roman.

2853. Zenia, Salem. *Rêves de Yidir*. Paris: L'Harmattan, 1993. Bilingue berbère-français. Poésie.

2854. Zerari, Zhor (F). *Poèmes de prison*. Alger: Bouchène, 1988. Illustrations de Jeanne-Marie Francès. Poésie.

2855. Ziani, Rabia. *Le Déshérité*. Alger: SNED, 1981. Roman autobiographique.

2856. ———. *Et mourir à Ighil*. Alger: ENAP, 1992. Roman.

2857. ———. *La Main mutilée*. Alger: ENAL, 1986. Roman.

2858. Zinaï-Koudil, Hafsa (F). *La Fin d'un rêve*. Alger: ENAL, 1984. Roman.

2859. ———. *Le Pari perdu*. Alger: ENAL, 1986. Roman.

2860. ———. *Le Passé décomposé*. Alger: ENAL, 1993. Roman.

2861. Zitouni, Ahmed. *Aimez-vous Brahim?* Paris: Belfond, 1986. Roman.

2862. ———. *La Veuve et le pendu*. Paris: Manya, 1993. Roman.

MOROCCO/MAROC

Bibliographies

2863. Déjeux, Jean. *Dictionnaire des auteurs maghrébins de langue française.* Paris: Karthala, 1984. Maroc 1920-1982: pp. 215-265.

2864. ————. *Maghreb: littératures de langue française.* Paris: Arcantère, 1993. Maroc 1949-1989: pp. 459-497.

Anthology

2865. Ben Jelloun, Tahar. *La Mémoire future: anthologie de la nouvelle poésie du Maroc.* Paris: Maspero, 1976. (Coll. Voix).

General studies

2866. Akharbach, Latifa et Naijis Rerhaye. *Femmes et média.* Casablanca: Le Fennec, 1992. (Coll. Marocaines, citoyennes de demain).

2867. Gontard, Marc. *Le Moi étrange: littérature marocaine de langue française.* Paris: L'Harmattan, 1993.

2868. Ikken, Aïssa. *L'Animation par le théâtre au Maroc.* Rabat: Imprimerie Jeunesse et sport, 1982.

2869. "Littérature marocaine de langue française: récit et discours. Actes du colloque tenu à Marrakech les 9, 10 et 11 mars 1988." *Revue de la Faculté des lettres et des sciences humaines*, no. 33 (1989).

2870. Mernissi, Fatima. *Le Maroc raconté par ses femmes.* Rabat: SMER, 1986. Témoignages.

2871. Mouzouni, Lahcen. *Le Roman marocain de langue française.* Paris: Publisud, 1987.

2872. Tenkoul, Abderrahman. *Littérature marocaine d'écriture francaise: essais d'analyse sémiotique.* Casablanca: Afrique-Orient, 1985.

Authors

2873. Alaoui, Fatima (F). *L'Arbre sans racines ou je ne suis que journaliste*. Rabat: Editions de l'Ere nouvelle, 1982. Autobiographie.

2874. Baroudi, Abdallah. *Le Grain de la terre*. Rotterdam: Editions Hiwar, 1986. Théâtre.

2875. Bel Hachmy, Abdelkader. *La Dévoilée*. Tanger: Editions marocaines, 1952. En arabe et en français. Théâtre.

2876. Belhachmi, Ahmed. *Le Rempart de sable*. Rabat: ETNA, 1962. Publié sous le pseudonyme de Farid Faris. Théâtre.

2877. ———. *L'Oreille en écharpe*. Casablanca: Imprimeries réunies, 1956. Théâtre.

2878. Belrhiti, Mohammed Alaoui. *Fragments d'une mort parfumée*. Paris: Saint-Germain-des Prés, 1980. Poésie.

2879. ———. *Ruines d'un fusil orphelin*. Paris: L'Harmattan, 1984. Poésie.

2880. Ben Barka, Abdelkader. *El Mehdi Ben Barka, mon frère*. Paris: Laffont, 1966. Biographie.

2881. Ben Haddou, Halima (F). *Aïcha la rebelle*. Paris: Edition Jeune Afrique, 1982. Roman.

2882. Ben Jelloun, Tahar. *Les Amandiers sont morts de leurs blessures*. Paris: Maspero, 1976. Poésie et nouvelles.

2883. ———. *L'Ange aveugle*. Paris: Seuil, 1992. Nouvelles.

2884. ———. *L'Ecrivain public*. Paris: Seuil, 1983. Récit.

2885. ———. *L'Enfant de sable*. Paris: 1985, Seuil. Roman.

2886. ———. *La Fiancée de l'eau,* suivi de *Entretien avec M. Saïd Hammadi, ouvrier algérien.* Paris: Actes Sud, 1984. Théâtre.

2887. ———. *Harrounda.* Paris: Denoël, 1973. (Nouvelle édition dans la coll. Médianes). Roman.

2888. ———. *L'Homme rompu.* Paris: Seuil, 1994. Roman.

2889. ———. *Hommes sous linceul de silence.* Casablanca: Atlantes, 1971. Poésie.

2890. ———. *Jour de silence à Tanger.* Paris: Seuil, 1990. Récit.

2891. ———. *Moha le fou, Moha le sage.* Paris: Seuil, 1978. (Nouvelle édition dans la coll. Points). Roman.

2892. ———. *La Nuit sacrée.* Paris: Seuil, 1987. Roman.

2893. ———. *Le Pain nu.* Paris: Maspero, 1980. Traduction de l'arabe en français de l'autobiographie de Mohammed Choukri. Autobiographie.

2894. ———. *La Prière de l'absent.* Paris: Seuil, 1981. (Nouvelle édition dans la coll. Points). Roman.

2895. ———. *La Réclusion solitaire.* Paris: Denoël, 1976. Roman.

2896. ———. *La Remontée des cendres.* Paris: Seuil, 1991. Edition bilingue. Version arabe de Kadhim Jihad. Poésie.

2897. ———. *La Soudure fraternelle.* Paris: Arléa, 1994. Autobiographie.

2898. ———. *Les Yeux baissés.* Paris: Seuil, 1991. Roman.

2899. M'Henni, Mansour (dir.). *Tahar Ben Jelloun: stratégies d'écriture.* Paris: L'Harmattan, 1993.

2900. Ben Kerroum-Covlet, Antoinette (F). *Gardien du seuil.* Paris: L'Harmattan, 1988. (Coll. Ecritures arabes, 43). Roman.

2901. Bendahou, Noureddine. *Adhar ou l'aube des hirondelles.* Rabat: Institut d'études et recherches sur l'arabisation, 1988. Poésie.

2902. ———. *La Colère des épines.* Casablanca: Etablissement Benchara d'impression et d'édition Benimed, 1989. Poésie.

2903. Benhamza, Abderrahman. *D'un Sommeil à l'autre.* Rabat: Stouky, 1980. Récit.

2904. Berrada, Omar. *L'Encensoir.* Mohammedia: SODEN, 1987. Roman.

2905. Bouanani, Ahmed. *Les Persiennes.* Rabat: Stouky, 1980. Textes poétiques.

2906. Boucetta, Fatiha (F). *Anissa captive.* Casablanca: EDDIF, 1991. Roman.

2907. Boucheqif, Nasr-Eddine. *Témoignage pour ma mère.* Paris: Edition Epoque, 1984. Poésie.

2908. Bouissef Rekab, Driss. *A l'ombre de Lalla Chafia.* Paris: L'Harmattan, 1989. Autobiographie.

2909. Bounfour, Abdallah. *Atlassique.* Rabat: Stouky, 1980. Poésie.

2910. Bousfiha, Noureddine. *Juste avant l'Oubli.* Paris: Caractères, 1990. Poésie.

2911. ———. *Safari au sud d'une mémoire.* Paris: Caractères, 1980. Poésie.

2912. Chatt, Abdelkader *voir* Chatt, Benazous.

2913. Chatt, Benazous. *Mozaïques ternies.* Paris: Revue mondiale, 1932. Roman autobiographique.

2914. Chebab, Yamina (F). *L'Eau de mon puits.* Besançon: L'Amitié par le livre, 1987. Autobiographie.

2915. Chimenti, Elisa (F). *Au Cœur du harem: roman marocain.* Paris: Le Scorpion, 1958. Roman.

2916. ———. *Chants de femmes arabes.* Paris: Plon, 1942. Poésie.

2917. ———. *Eves marocaines.* Tanger: André, 1935. Contes et légendes.

2918. ———. *Légendes marocaines.* Paris: Le Scorpion, 1959. Légendes.

2919. Chniber, Mohammed Ghazi. *Les Murmures de la palmeraie.* Paris: L'Harmattan, 1988. Mémoires.

2920. Chraïbi, Driss. *Un Ami viendra vous voir.* Paris: Denoël, 1967. Roman.

2921. ———. *L'Ane.* Paris: Denoël, 1956. Roman.

2922. ———. *Les Boucs.* Paris: Denoël, 1955. (Nouvelle édition dans la coll. Relire). Roman.

2923. ———. *La Civilisation, ma mère!* Paris: Denoël, 1972. Roman.

2924. ———. *De tous les horizons.* Paris: Denoël, 1958. (Nouvelle édition en 1986 sous le titre *D'autres voix*). Roman.

2925. ———. *Une Enquête au pays.* Paris: Seuil, 1981. (Nouvelle édition dans la coll. Points). Roman.

2926. ———. *La Foule.* Paris: Denoël, 1961. Roman.

2927. ———. *L'Inspecteur Ali.* Paris: Denoël, 1991. (Nouvelle Edition en 1993 chez Gallimard dans la coll. Folio 2479). Roman.

2928. ———. *La Mère du printemps.* Paris: Denoël, 1982. Roman.

2929. ———. *Naissance à l'aube*. Paris: Seuil, 1986. Roman.

2930. ———. *Le Passé simple*. Paris: Denoël, 1954. (Nouvelle édition en 1986 chez Gallimard, Coll. Folio). Roman.

2931. ———. *Une Place au soleil*. Paris: Denoël, 1993. Roman.

2932. ———. *Succession ouverte*. Paris: Denoël, 1962. (Nouvelle édition dans la coll. Folio). Roman.

2933. Benchama, Lahcen. *L'Œuvre de Driss Chraïbi: réception critique des littératures maghrébines au Maroc.* Paris: L'Harmattan, 1994.

2934. El Berini, Mohammed. *Chaînes du passé.* Casablanca: Editions maghrébines, 1976. Nouvelles.

2935. El Maleh, Edmond Amran. *Mille ans un jour.* Grenoble: La Pensée Sauvage, 1986. Roman.

2936. ———. *Parcours immobile*. Paris: Maspero, 1980. Récit.

2937. El Malki, Omar. *Soundnyi*. Rabat: Pro-Culture, 1981. Poésie.

2938. El Moubaraki, Mohammed. *Zakaria, Premier voyage*. Paris: L'Harmattan, 1990. Roman.

2939. Elhany Mourad, Farida (F). *La Fille aux pieds nus.* Casablanca: Imprimerie Eddar el Beida, 1985. Roman.

2940. Faris, Farid *voir* Belhachmi, Ahmed.

2941. Fassi, Nouzha (F). *Le Ressac*. Paris: L'Harmattan, 1990. (Coll. Ecritures arabes, 55). Roman.

2942. Hadj Nasser, Badia (F). *Le Voile mis à nu*. Paris: Arcantère, 1984. Roman.

2943. Hamadi, M. *Une Corde sanglante autour du silence*. Bruxelles: Hajitkoum, 1983. Théâtre.

2944. Hassan II. *Le Défi*. Paris: Albin Michel, 1976. Mémoires.

2945. Himmich, Ben Salem. *Si la très grande mutation ne s'opère*. Casablanca: Editions Az-Zaman al-maghribi, 1980. Poésie.

2946. Houari, Leïla (F). *Les Cases basses*. Paris: L'Harmattan, 1993. (Coll. Ecritures arabes, 96). Théâtre.

2947. ———. *Quand tu verras la mer*. Paris: L'Harmattan, 1988. (Coll. Ecritures arabes, 37). Roman.

2948. ———. *Zeida de nulle part*. Paris: L'Harmattan, 1985. (Coll. Ecritures arabes, 17). Roman.

2949. Iahger, Mohammed. *Fou d'Israël fou de Dieu*. Paris: Nouvelles éditions Debresse, 1973. Roman.

2950. Jay, Salim. *Du Côté de Saint-Germain-des-Prés*. Paris: Bertoin, 1992. Mémoires.

2951. ———. *L'Oiseau vit de sa plume: essai d'autobiographie alimentaire*. Paris: Belfond, 1989. Récit.

2952. ———. *Portait du géniteur et poète officiel*. Paris: Denoël, 1985. Roman.

2953. ———. *La Semaine où Madame Simone eut cent ans*. Paris: La Différence, 1979. Roman.

2954. ———. *Tu seras nabab, mon fils*. Paris: Nouvelle Edition Rupture, 1982. Parodie du roman d'Irène Frain, *Le Nabab* (1982) publié sous le pseudonyme d'Irène Refrain. Roman.

2955. Khair-Eddine, Mohammed. *Agadir*. Paris: Seuil, 1967. Roman.

2956. ———. *Ce Maroc!* Paris: Seuil, 1975. Poésie.

2957. ———. *Corps négatif,* suivi de *Histoire d'un Bon Dieu.* Paris: Seuil, 1967. Roman.

2958. ———. *Le Déterreur.* Paris: Seuil, 1973. Roman.

2959. ———. *Légende et vie d'Agoun'chich.* Paris: Seuil, 1984. Roman.

2960. ———. *Moi, l'aigre.* Paris: Seuil, 1970. Théâtre.

2961. ———. *Nausée noire.* Londres: Siècle à mains, 1964. Poésie.

2962. ———. *Une Odeur de mantèque.* Paris: Seuil, 1976. Roman.

2963. ———. *Résurrection des fleurs sauvages.* Rabat: Stouky, 1981. Poésie.

2964. ———. *Une vie, un rêve, un peuple, toujours errants.* Paris: Seuil, 1978. Roman.

2965. Khatibi, Adbelkébir. *L'Amour bilingue.* Paris: Fata Morgana, 1983. (Nouvelle édition en 1992 chez Eddif, Casablanca). Roman.

2966. ———. *Un Eté à Stockholm.* Paris: Flammarion, 1990. Roman.

2967. ———. *Le Livre de sang.* Paris: Gallimard, 1979. Roman.

2968. ———. *Le Lutteur de classe à la manière taoïste.* Paris: Sindbad, 1976. Poésie.

2969. ———. *La Mémoire tatouée.* Paris: Denoël, 1971. (Nouvelles éditions dans les coll. 10/18 et Médianes). Roman.

2970. ———. *Penser le Maghreb.* Rabat: SMER, 1993. Essai.

2971. ———. *Le Prophète voilé.* Paris: L'Harmattan, 1979. Théâtre.

2972. Laâbi, Abdellatif. *Le Baptème chacaliste*. Paris: L'Harmattan, 1987. Théâtre.

2973. ———. *Le Chemin des Ordalies*. Paris: Denoël, 1982. Roman.

2974. ———. *L'Ecorché vif.* Paris: L'Harmattan, 1992. Poésie.

2975. ———. *L'Etreinte du monde*. Paris: La Différence, 1993. Poésie.

2976. ———. *Exercices de tolérance*. Paris: La Différence, 1993. Théâtre.

2977. ———. *L'Œil et la nuit*. Casablanca: Atlantes, 1969. (Nouvelle édition en 1982 chez la Société marocaine des éditeurs réunis). Roman.

2978. ———. *La Poésie palestinienne de combat*. Honfleur: P. J. Oswald, 1970. Anthologie.

2979. ———. *Le Règne de barbarie*. Paris: Seuil, 1980. (Réédition d'un recueil ronéotypé datant de 1976). Poésie.

2980. ———. *Les Rides du lion*. Paris: Messidor, 1989. Roman.

2981. ———. *Le Soleil se meurt*. Paris: La Différence, 1992. Poésie.

2982. ———. *Sous le bâillon, le poème, écrits de prison (1972-1980)*. Paris: L'Harmattan, 1981. Poésie.

2983. Alessandra, Jacques. *Laâbi, Abdellatif: la brûlure des interrogations*. Paris: L'Harmattan, 1985. Entretien avec Laâbi Abdellatif.

2984. *Pour Abdellatif Laâbi*. Paris; Cesson la Forêt: Nouvelles éditions ruptures; La Table rase, 1982.

2985. Ripault, Gislain. *Abdellatif Laâbi: un écrivain en Seine Saint-Denis.* Bobigny: Conseil Général de la Seine Saint-Denis, 1989. Entretien avec Abdellatif Laâbi.

2986. Lahbabi, Mohammed Aziz. *Adil.* Casablanca; Paris: Najah al-Jadila; L'Harmattan, 1983. Poésie.

2987. ———. *Chant d'espérance.* Le Puy: Cahiers du Nouvel Humanisme, 1952. Poésie.

2988. ———. *Espoir vagabon.* Blainville-sur-mer: L'Amitié par le livre, 1972. Traduit de l'arabe par l'auteur. (Nouvelle édition en 1982 chez l'Harmattan). Roman.

2989. ———. *Ivre d'innocence.* Paris: Saint-Germain-des-Prés, 1980. Poésie.

2990. ———. *Misères et lumières. Les Nouveaux chants d'espérance.* Paris: P. J. Oswald, 1958. (Nouvelle édition chez Dar el-Kitab, Casablanca). Poésie.

2991. ———. *Morsures sur le fer.* Casablanca: Dar el-Kitab, 1979. Traduit de l'arabe par Maurice Borrmans. Nouvelles.

2992. Comité de soutien. *Mohammed-Aziz Lahbabi. L'homme et l'œuvre.* Rabat: Najah al-jahida, 1987.

2993. Lahlou, Nabyl. "Ophélie n'est pas morte." *Pro-Culture,* no. 3-4 (1974): (Nouvelle édition en 1987 chez Le Fennec, Casablanca). Théâtre.

2994. Laokira, Mohammed. *Moments.* Rabat: Stouky, 1981. Illustré par Assa Ikken. Poésie.

2995. Lemlih, Saïd. *4 200 000 heures ou la griffe annulaire.* Casablanca: Imprimerie Benimed, 1981. Récit en partie autobiographique.

2996. Loakira, Mohammed. *L'Horizon est d'argile.* Honfleur: P. J. Oswald, 1972. Poésie.

2997. ———. *Marrakech.* Tanger: Editions marocaines et internationales, 1975. Poésie.

2998. ———. *L'Œil ébréché*. Rabat: Stouky, 1980. Poésie.

2999. Madani, Rachida (F). *Femme je suis*. Vitry: Inéditions Barbares, 1981. Poésie.

3000. Maleh, Edmond Amran. *Aïlen ou la nuit du récit*. Paris: Maspero, 1983. Roman.

3001. ———. *Mille ans un jour*. Grenoble: La Pensée sauvage, 1986. Roman.

3002. Mardi, Mohamed. *Mémoire futurible*. Tanger: Editions marocaines et internationales, 1993. Nouvelles.

3003. Menebhi, Saïda (F). *Poèmes, lettres et écrits de prison*. Paris: Comités de lutte contre la répression au Maroc, 1978. Ecrits autobiographiques.

3004. Morsy, Zaghloul. *Gués du temps*. Rabat: Imprimerie El Maaref el-Jadida, 1985. (Coll. Ecritures arabes, 14). Poésie.

3005. Mourad, Khireddine. *Le Chant d'Adapa*. Paris: Hatier, 1989. Poésie.

3006. ———. *Nadir ou la transhumance de l'être*. Casablanca: Le Fennec, 1992. Nouvelles.

3007. Nahon, Moïse. *Propos d'un vieux Marocain*. Paris: Leroux, 1939. Essai-témoignage.

3008. Nissaboury, Mostafa. *Plus haute mémoire*. Rabat: Atlantes, 1968. Poésie.

3009. Ouardighi, Abderrahim. *Les Moments d'amour*. Rabat: Imprimerie nouvelle, 1980. Poésie et nouvelles.

3010. Oussaïd, Brik. *Les Coquelicots de l'oriental: chronique d'une famille berbère marocaine*. Paris; Casablanca: La Découverte; Toubkal, 1984. (Nouvelle édition en 1988). Roman témoignage.

3011. Refrain, Irène *voir* Jay, Salim.

3012. Saaf, Abdallah. *Chroniques des jours de reflux.* Paris: L'Harmattan, 1993. Roman.

3013. Samie, Amale. *Cèdres et baleines de l'Atlas.* Paris: Picollec, 1991. Roman.

3014. Sbaï, Noufissa (F). *L'Enfant endormi.* Rabat: EDINO, 1987. Roman.

3015. Sefrioui, Ahmed. *La Boîte à merveilles.* Paris: Seuil, 1954. (Nouvelle édition en 1971). Roman.

3016. ———. *Le Chapelet d'ambre.* Paris: Julliard, 1949. (Nouvelle édition en 1964 chez Seuil). Contes et nouvelles.

3017. ———. *Le Jardin des sortilèges ou le parfum des légendes.* Paris: L'Harmattan, 1989. Contes.

3018. ———. *La Maison de servitude.* Alger: SNED, 1973. Roman.

3019. Serhane, Abdelhak. *Chant d'Ortie.* Paris: L'Harmattan, 1993. Poésie.

3020. ———. *Les Enfants des rues étroites.* Paris: Seuil, 1986. Roman.

3021. ———. *Messaouda.* Paris: Seuil, 1983. Roman.

3022. ———. *Le Soleil des obscurs.* Paris: Seuil, 1992. Roman.

3023. Souag, Moha. *L'Année de la chienne.* Tanger: Editions marocaines et internationales, 1979. Nouvelles.

3024. Zebdi, Kamel. *Echelle pour le futur.* Casablanca: Sochepresse, 1973. Poésie.

TUNISIA/TUNISIE

Bibliographies

3025. Déjeux, Jean. *Dictionnaire des auteurs maghrébins de langue française.* Paris: Karthala, 1984. Tunisie 1900-1982: pp. 267-331.

3026. ———. *Maghreb: littératures de langue française.* Paris: Arcantère, 1993. Tunisie 1946-1989: pp. 499-531.

Anthologies

3027. Fontaine, Jean. *Ecrivaines tunisiennes.* Tunis: Le Gai savoir, 1990.

3028. Garmadi, Salah. *Ecrivains de Tunisie.* Paris: Sindbad, 1981. (Anthologie de textes et poèmes traduits de l'arabe en français).

3029. Khadhar, Hedia. *Anthologie de la poésie tunisienne de langue française.* Paris: L'Harmattan, 1984.

General studies

3030. Bekri, Tahar. *Littératures de Tunisie et du Maghreb,* suivi de *Réflexions et propos sur la poésie et la littérature.* Paris: L'Harmattan, 1994.

3031. Fontaine, Jean. *Etudes de littérature tunisienne.* Tunis: Dar Annawras, 1989.

3032. ———. *Regards sur la littérature tunisienne.* Tunis: Cérès, 1991.

3033. Marzouki, Ihlem. *Le Mouvement des femmes en Tunisie au XXe siècle.* Tunis: Cérès Productions, 1993.

Authors

3034. Achour, Habib. *Ma vie politique et syndicale: enthousiasmes et déceptions, 1944-1951.* Tunis: Alif, 1989. Autobiographie.

3035. Arwy, Adel. *Josabeth et Mourad.* Sherbrooke: Naaman, 1981. Roman.

3036. Aslan, Mahmoud. *Entre deux mondes.* Tunis: La Kahena, 1932. Théâtre.

3037. ———. *Scènes de la vie du bled.* Tunis: La Kahena, 1932. Souvenirs d'enfance.

3038. ———. *Les Yeux noirs de Leila.* Tunis: Le Cénacle, 1940. Roman.

3039. Baccouche, Hachemi. *Baudruche.* Paris: Nouvelles éditions latines, 1959. Théâtre.

3040. ———. *La Dame de Carthage.* Paris: Nouvelles éditions latines, 1962. Roman historique.

3041. ———. *Ma foi demeure.* Paris: Nouvelles éditions latines, 1958. Roman autobiographique.

3042. Bécheur, Ali. *De Miel et d'aloès.* Tunis: Cérès-Productions, 1989. Roman.

3043. Béji, Hélé (F). *Itinéraire de Paris à Tunis.* Paris: Noël Blandin, 1992. Roman.

3044. ———. *L'Œil du jour.* Paris: Maurice Nadeau, 1985. Roman.

3045. Bekri, Tahar. *Le Chant du roi errant.* Paris: L'Harmattan, 1985. Poésie.

3046. ———. *Les Chapelets d'attache.* Troarn: Amiot Lenganey, 1993. Poésie.

3047. ———. *Le Cœur rompu aux océans.* Paris: L'Harmattan, 1988. Poésie.

3048. ———. *Le Laboureur du soleil,* suivi de *Grappes de la nuit.* Paris: Silex, 1983. Poésie.

3049. Bel Haj Yahia, Emma (F). *Chronique frontalière.* Paris: Noël Blandin, 1991. Roman.

3050. Ben Ali, Larbi. *Le Porteur d'eau.* Paris: Athanor, 1976. Poésie.

3051. Ben Salah, Rafik. *La Prophétie du chameau.* Genève: Rousseau, 1993. Roman.

3052. ———. *Retour d'exil ou sang femme.* Paris: Publisud, 1987. Roman.

3053. Ben Salem, M. *L'Antichambre de l'indépendance, 1947-1957.* Tunis: Cérès-Productions, 1988. Autobiographie.

3054. Benabdallah, Chadly. *Fantasia.* Paris: Janus, 1956. Poésie.

3055. ———. *Tunis au passé simple.* Tunis: Société tunisienne de diffusion, 1977. Souvenirs.

3056. Bénady, Claude. *Chanson du voile.* Tunis: Le Cénacle, 1941. Poésie.

3057. ———. *Les Etangs du soleil.* Paris: Les Cahiers de l'Oiseleur, 1981. Poésie.

3058. ———. *Un Eté qui vient de la mer.* Paris: Périples, 1972. Poésie.

3059. ———. *Hors de jeu, les morts.* Tunis: Périples, 1950. Poésie.

3060. ———. *Les Ramparts du bestiaire.* Paris: La Falaise, 1955. Roman.

3061. ———. *Recommencer l'amour.* Paris: Seghers, 1953. Poésie.

3062. Benattar, César. *Le Bled en lumière.* Paris: Taillandier, 1923. Contes.

3063. Bhiri, Slaheddine. *De Nulle part.* Paris: L'Harmattan, 1993. (Coll. Ecritures arabes, 88). Roman.

3064. ———. *Le Palestinien.* Lutry-Suisse: Bouchain, 1984. Roman.

3065. Boularès, Habib. *Le Temps d'El Boraq.* Tunis: Cérès-Productions, 1979. Texte bilingue arabe-français. Théâtre.

3066. Bouraoui, Hedi. *Arc-en-terre.* Paris: Albion Press, 1992. Poème.

3067. ———. *Echosmos.* Oakville: Mosaïc Press, 1986. Edition bilingue français-anglais. Poésie.

3068. ———. *Eclate module.* Montréal: Cosmos, 1972. Poésie.

3069. ———. *L'Icônaison.* Sherbrooke: Naaman, 1985. Roman-poème.

3070. ———. *Ignescent.* Paris: Silex, 1982. (Sous-titré 'prosèmes' par l'auteur). Poésie.

3071. ———. *Immensément croisé.* Paris: Saint-Germain-des-Prés, 1969. Théâtre.

3072. ———. *Musoktail.* Wheaton: Tower Associate, 1966. Poésie.

3073. ———. *Sans Frontières/Without Boundaries.* St-Louis du Missouri: Francité, 1979. Poésie.

3074. ———. *Tremblé.* Paris: Saint-Germain-des-Prés, 1969. Poésie.

3075. ———. *Vers et l'envers.* Downsview, York University: ECW Press, 1982. Poèsie et récits.

3076. Bourkhis, Ridha. *Chutes et blessures.* Ivry: Silex, 1987. Poésie.

3077. ———. *Un Retour au pays du bon Dieu.* Paris: L'Harmattan, 1989. (Coll. Ecritures arabes, 54). Roman.

3078. Chaïbi, Aïcha (F). *Rached.* Tunis: Maison tunisienne de l'édition, 1975. Roman.

3079. Chammam, Dorra (F). *Profanation.* Tunis: L'Or du temps, 1993.

3080. Danon, Vitalis. *La Hara conte.* Paris: Ivrit, 1929. (En collaboration avec Vehel et Ryvel). Nouvelles.

3081. ———. *Ninette de la rue du péché.* Tunis: La Kahena, 1938. Roman.

3082. Daoud, Jacqueline (F). *Traduit de l'abstrait.* Tunis: Cérès-Productions, 1968. Poésie.

3083. Djedidi, Hafedh. *Le Cimetière ou le souffle du Vénérable.* Paris: Présence Africaine, 1990. Roman.

3084. ———. *Rien que le fruit pour toute bouche.* Paris: Silex, 1986. Poésie.

3085. ——— et Guy Coissant. *Chassés-croisés.* Paris: L'Harmattan, 1988. Roman.

3086. Driss, Rachid. *A l'aube . . . la lanterne.* Tunis: Société tunisienne de diffusion, 1981. Autobiographie.

3087. El Abassy, Noureddine. *Les Heures brèves.* Tunis: Périples, 1950. Poésie.

3088. El Goulli, Sophie (F). *Les Mystères de Tunis.* Tunis: Editions Dar Ennawras, 1993. Roman.

3089. ———. *Nos Rêves.* Tunis: Union internationale des banques, 1974. Poésie.

3090. ———. *Signes.* Tunis: Société tunisienne d'édition, 1973. Poésie.

3091. ———. *Vertige solaire.* Tunis: Imprimerie Presses Graphic Industries, 1981. Poésie.

3092. El Houssi, Majid. *Ahmeta.* Abano Terme: Francisci, 1981. Poésie.

3093. ———. *Iris Ifriqiya.* Paris: Saint-Germain-des-Prés, 1981. Poésie.

3094. Essafi, Tahar. *La Sorcière d'émeraude.* Paris: Malfère, 1929. Contes.

3095. ———. *Les Toits d'émeraude.* Paris: Flammarion, 1924. Contes.

3096. Ferchiou, Naïdé (F). *Ombres carthaginoises.* Paris: L'Harmattan, 1993. (Coll. Ecritures arabes). Nouvelles.

3097. Ferhat, Salah. *Chant d'amour.* Inédit, 1918. Publié à Tunis, à compte d'auteur, en 1978. poésie.

3098. Garmadi, Salah. *Avec ou sans et Allahma alhaya.* Tunis: Cerès-Productions, 1970. Poèmes en arabe et en français. Poésie.

3099. ———. *Le Frigidaire.* Tunis: Alif, 1986. Publié à titre posthume en arabe et en français. Illustration de Juliette Garmadi. Nouvelles.

3100. ———. *Nos Ancêtres les Bédouins.* Paris: P. J. Oswald, 1975. Poésie.

3101. Gasmi, Mohammed. *Chronique des sans terre.* Paris: Publisud, 1986. Roman.

3102. Gellouz, Souad (F). *Les Jardins du nord.* Tunis: Salammbô, 1982. Roman autobiographique.

3103. Ghachem, Moncef. *Cap Africa.* Paris: L'Harmattan, 1989. Poésie.

3104. ———. *Car vivre est un pays.* Paris: Caractères, 1978. Poésie.

3105. ———. *Cent mille oiseaux.* Paris: Publié à compte d'auteur, 1975. Poésie.

3106. ———. *Gorges d'enclos.* Tunis: Maison de la culture Ibn Rachid, 1970. Poésie.

3107. Ghattas, Kamel. *Mystification à Beyrouth.* Tunis: Société des éditions nouvelles, 1978. Roman policier.

3108. ———. *Souris blanche à Madrid.* Tunis: Société des éditions nouvelles, 1977. Roman policier.

3109. Ghazi, M'Hamed Ferid. *Night, poésie nouvelle.* Tunis: Le Nord, 1949. Poèsie.

3110. Guellouze, Souad (F). *La Vie simple.* Tunis: Maison tunisienne de l'édition, 1975. Roman.

3111. Hachemi, Frida (F). *Ahlem.* Paris: La Pensée Universelle, 1981. Roman.

3112. Hafsia, Jalila (F). *Cendre à l'aube.* Tunis: Maison tunisienne de l'édition, 1975. Roman.

3113. Hamouda, Ali. *Etrange étranger.* Tunis: Salammbô, 1983. Nouvelles.

3114. Kacem, Abdelaziz. *Le Frontal.* Tunis: Maison tunisienne de l'édition, 1983. Poésie.

3115. Khouri-Dagher, Nadia (F). *Bleu marine.* Paris: L'Harmattan, 1993. Poésie.

3116. Loueslati, Chérif. *L'Entonnoir.* Paris: Imprimerie SEERCOP, 1983. Récit autobiographique.

3117. Mabrouk, Alia (F). *Hurlements.* Tunis: Alyssa, 1992. Roman.

3118. Mattera, Roland. *Retour en Tunisie après 30 ans d'absence.* Paris: L'Harmattan, 1993. Témoignage.

3119. Meddeb, Abdelwahab. *La Gazelle et l'enfant.* Marseille: Actes Sud, 1992. Roman.

3120. ———. *Phantasia.* Paris: Sindbad, 1986. Roman.

3121. ———. *Talismano.* Paris: Bourgeois, 1979. (Nouvelle édition en 1987 chez Sindbad, Paris). Roman.

3122. ———. *Tombeau d'Ibn Arabi.* Paris: Noël Blandin, 1987. Poésie.

3123. Mellah, Fawzi. *Néron ou les oiseaux de passage,* suivi de *Pourquoi jouer Néron?* Paris: P. J. Oswald, 1973. Théâtre.

3124. ———. *Le Palais du non-retour.* Paris: P. J. Oswald, 1975. Théâtre.

3125. ———. *La Reine vagabonde.* Paris: Seuil, 1988. Roman.

3126. Memmi, Albert. *Agar.* Paris: Buchet-Chastel, 1955. (Nouvelle édition en 1983 chez Gallimard, coll. Folio). Roman.

3127. ———. *Bonheurs.* Paris: Arléa, 1992.

3128. ———. *Le Désert ou la vie et les aventures de Jubaïr Ouali-el-Mammi.* Paris: Gallimard, 1977. (Nouvelle édition en 1986 dans la coll. Folio). Roman.

3129. ———. *Le Mirliton du ciel.* Paris: Julliard, 1990. Poésie.

3130. ———. *Le Pharaon.* Paris: Julliard, 1988. Roman.

3131. ———. *Le Scorpion ou la confession imaginaire.* Paris: Gallimard, 1969. (Nouvelle édition en 1989 dans la coll. Folio). Roman.

3132. ———. *La Statue de sel.* Paris: Buchet-Chastel, 1953. (Nouvelle édition en 1972 chez Gallimard, coll. Folio). Roman.

3133. Daviès, R. *Entretien.* Québec: L'Etincelle, 1975 (Entretien avec Albert Memmi, suivi d'une bibliographie de son œuvre).

3134. Dugas, Guy. *Albert Memmi, écrivain de la déchirure.* Sherbrooke: Naaman, 1984.

3135. Malka, Victor. *La Terre intérieure.* Paris: Gallimard, 1976. Entretiens avec Albert Memmi.

3136. Metoui, Moncef. *Messieurs . . . Je vous accuse.* Paris: Caractères, 1982. Théâtre.

3137. ———. *Où sont-ils?* Paris: Caractères, 1980. Poésie.

3138. ———. *Racisme, je te hais.* Paris: La Pensée Universelle, 1973. Roman.

3139. Mrabet, Aziza (F). *Grains de sable.* Tunis: L'Or du temps, 1992. Poésie.

3140. Mzali, Mohamed Salah. *Au fil de ma vie. Souvenirs d'un Tunisien.* Tunis: H. Mzali, 1972. Auto-biographie.

3141. Naccache, Gilbert. *Cristal.* Tunis: Salammbô, 1982. Roman.

3142. Nadir, Chams. *L'Astrobale de la mer.* Paris: Stock, 1980. De son vrai nom Mohammed Aziza. Roman.

3143. ———. *Le Livre des célébrations.* Paris: Publisud, 1983. Poésie.

3144. ———. *Les Portiques de la mer.* Paris: Editions MK, 1990. Contes.

3145. Nahum, André. *Partir en Kappara.* Paris: Piranas, 1977. Témoignage autobiographique.

3146. Nataf, Félix. *Juif tunisien: une vie au Maghreb racontée à ma fille.* Paris: Fayolle, 1978. Autobiographie.

3147. Ryvel. *L'Enfant de l'oukala et autres contes de la Hara.* Tunis: La Kahena, 1931.(Nouvelle édition en 1980 chez Lattès, Paris). Contes.

3148. ———. *Lumière sur la Hara.* Tunis: La Kahena, 1935. Nouvelles.

3149. ———. *Le Nebel du Galouth.* Tunis: Editions la cité des livres, 1946. Poésie.

3150. Saïd, Amina (F). *Marcher sur la terre.* Paris: La Différence, 1994. Poésie.

3151. ———. *Nul autre lieu.* Québec: Ecrits des forges, 1992. Poésie.

3152. ———. *Paysage, nuit friable.* Gap: Inéditions Barbare, 1980. Poésie.

3153. ———. *Le Secret.* Paris: Critérion, 1994. Contes.

3154. ———. *L'Une et l'autre nuit.* Chaillé: Le Dé bleu, 1993. Poésie.

3155. Sebag, Daisy (F). *Loin de la Terre rouge.* Paris: Figuière, 1929. Roman.

3156. Sfar, Tahar. *Journal d'un exilé. Zarzis 1935.* Tunis: Bouslama, 1960. Mémoires.

3157. Tlili, Mustapha. *Le Bruit dort.* Paris: Gallimard, 1978. Roman.

3158. ———. *Gloire des sables.* Paris: Alésia, 1982. Roman.

3159. ———. *La Montagne du lion.* Paris: Gallimard, 1988. Roman.

3160. ———. *La Rage aux tripes.* Paris: Gallimard, 1975. Roman.

3161. Valensi, Michel. *L'Empreinte.* Tunis: Salammbô, 1983. Roman.

3162. Valensi, Théodor. *Yasmina.* Paris: Méricant, 1922. (Nombreuses rééditions de 1926 à 1954). Roman.

3163. Zouari, Faouzia (F). *La Caravane des chimères.* Paris: Olivier Orban, 1990. Roman.

SOUTH OF THE SAHARA

OVERVIEW

Bibliographies

3164. "2500 Titres de littérature: Afrique subsaharienne" *Notre Librairie*, no. 94 (1988).

3165. Baratte-Eno Belinga, Thérèse, J. Chauveau-Rabut et Mukala Kadima-Nzuji. *Bibliographie des auteurs africains de langue française.* Paris: Nathan, 1979.

3166. Coulon, Virginie. *Bibliographie francophone de littérature africaine.* Vanves: EDICEF, 1994.

3167. Görög-Karady, Véronika. *Littérature orale d'Afrique noire: bibliographie annotée.* Paris: Conseil International de la langue française, 1992.

3168. Guyonneau, Christine M. "Auteurs féminins d'Afrique noire francophone et de sa diaspora." *Callaloo* 8, no. 2 & 3 (1985): 453-483 et 594-629.

3169. Kom, Ambroise. *Dictionnaire des œuvres littéraires négro-africaines de langue française: des origines à 1978.* Paris: ACCT, 1983.

3170. Lemaître, Henri (éd.). *Dictionnaire de la littérature française et francophone.* Paris: Bordas, 1981.

3171. *La Littérature africaine francophone: 200 suggestions de lecture.* Lausanne: Déclaration de Berne; Bibliothèque Cantonale et Universitaire, 1991.

3172. Magnier, Bernard. *Littératures africaines d'expression française: bibliographie selective: cent titres.* Yaoundé: CLE, 1983.

3173. Ngandu Nkashama, Pius. *Dictionnaire des œuvres littéraires africaines en langue française.* Paris: Nouvelles du sud, 1994.

3174. ————. *Les Années littéraires en Afrique (1897-1992).* Paris: L'Harmattan, 1994.

3175. *Répertoire des périodiques paraissant en Afrique au sud du Sahara.* Paris: Centre de Documentation en Sciences Humaines/CNRS, 1982.

3176. Waters, Harold. *Théâtre noir: encyclopédie des pièces en français par des auteurs noirs.* Washington, DC: Three Continents Press, 1988.

Anthologies

3177. Cendrars, Blaise. *Anthologie nègre.* Paris: Buchet/ Chastel, 1921. (Nouvelle édition en 1979).

3178. Chevrier, Jacques. *Littérature africaine: histoire et grands thèmes.* Paris: Hatier, 1990.

3179. Damas, Léon-Gontran. *Poètes d'expression française.* Paris: Seuil, 1947.

3180. Gey, Anne-Marie. *Anthologie de la poésie négro-africaine pour la jeunesse.* Dakar; Paris: Nouvelles Editions Africaines; EDICEF, 1984.

3181. Joubert, Jean-Louis (dir.). *Littérature francophone. Anthologie.* Paris: Nathan/ACCT, 1992.

3182. Kesteloot, Lilyan. *Anthologie négro-africaine: panorama critique des prosateurs, poètes et dramaturges noirs du XXᵉ siècle.* Paris: Marabout, 1967. (Nouvelle édition revue et augmentée en 1992).

3183. Lee, Sonia. *Les Romancières du Continent noir. Anthologie.* Paris: Hatier, 1994.

3184. Mateso, E. Locha. *Anthologie de la poésie d'Afrique d'expression française.* Paris: Hatier, 1987.

3185. Ngandu Nkashama, Pius. *Littératures africaines: 1930-1982. Anthologie.* Paris: Silex, 1984. (Nouvelle édition chez Silex en 1987).

3186. Ormerod, Beverley et Jean-Marie Volet. *Romancières africaines d'expression française: le sud du Sahara.* Paris: L'Harmattan, 1994.

3187. Scherer, Jacques. *Le Théâtre en Afrique noire francophone.* Paris: PUF, 1992.

3188. Senghor, Léopold Sédar. *Anthologie de la nouvelle poésie nègre et malgache de langue française.* Paris: Presses Universitaires de France, 1949. (Nouvelle édition en 1993 chez le même éditeur, coll. Quadridge, 66).

General studies

3189. Almeida, Irène Assiba d'. *Francophone African women writers: destroying the emptiness of silence.* Gainesville: University Press of Florida, 1994.

3190. Blair, Dorothy S. *African literature in French: a history of creative writing from West and Equatorial Africa.* Cambridge: CUP, 1981.

3191. Borgomano, Madeleine. *Voix et visages de femmes dans les livres écrits par des femmes en Afrique francophone.* Abidjan: CEDA, 1989.

3192. Breitinger, Eckhard et Sander Reinhard (éds.). *Interviews avec des écrivains africains francophones.* Bayreuth: Universität Bayreuth, 1988.

3193. Chemain-Degrange, Arlette. *Emancipation féminine et roman africain.* Dakar: Nouvelles Editions Africaines, 1981.

3194. *Colloque sur la négritude: Dakar, 1971.* Paris: Présence Africaine, 1972.

3195. Conteh-Morgan, John. *Theatre and drama in Francophone Africa: a critical introduction.* CUP, 1994.

3196. Coquery-Vidrovitch, Catherine. *Les Africaines: histoire des femmes d'Afrique noire du XIXe au XXe siècle.* Paris: Desjonquères, 1994.

3197. Cornaton, Michel. *Pouvoir et sexualité dans le roman africain: analyse du roman africain contemporain.* Paris: L'Harmattan, 1990.

3198. Grosskreutz, Béatrice. *Le Personnage de l'ancien dans le roman sénégalais et malien de l'époque coloniale.* Frankfurt: IKO, 1993.

3199. Hausser, Michel. *Pour une poétique de la négritude.* Paris: Silex, 1988. 2 v.

3200. Herzberger-Fofana, Pierrette. *Ecrivains africains et identités culturelles, entretiens.* Tübingen: Stauffenburg Verlag, 1989.

3201. Hourantier, Marie-José. *Du rituel au théâtre rituel: contribution à une esthétique théâtrale négro-africaine.* Paris: L'Harmattan, 1984.

3202. Joubert, Jean-Louis, et al. *Les Littératures francophones depuis 1945.* Paris: Bordas, 1986.

3203. Kesteloot, Lilyan. *Les Ecrivains noirs de langue française: naissance d'une littérature.* Bruxelles: Editions de l'Université de Bruxelles, 1963.

3204. Koné, Amadou, et al. *Des textes oraux au roman moderne.* Frankfurt: IKO, 1993.

3205. Mateso, Locha. *La littérature africaine et sa critique.* Paris: Karthala, 1986.

3206. Melone, Thomas (dir.). *La Littérature africaine à l'âge de la critique.* Paris: Gallimard, 1972.

3207. Milolo, Kembe. *L'Image de la femme chez les romanciers de l'Afrique noire francophone.* Fribourg: Editions universitaires de Fribourg, 1986.

3208. Monkasa-Bitumba et Jean-Pierre Jacquemin.
Forces littéraires d'Afrique: points de repères et témoignages.
Kinshasa: Afrique-Editions, 1987.

3209. Mouralis, Bernard. *Littérature et développement:
essai sur le statut, la fonction et la représentation de la
littérature négro-africaine.* Paris: Silex, 1984.

3210. N'Da, Pierre. *Le Conte africain et l'éducation.*
Paris: L'Harmattan, 1984.

3211. Ngandu Nkashama, Pius. *Les Années littéraires en
Afrique: 1912-1987.* Paris: L'Harmattan, 1993.

3212. "Nouvelles écritures féminines. 1. La Parole aux
femmes." *Notre Librairie,* no. 117 (1994).

3213. "Nouvelles écritures féminines. 2. Femmes d'ici et
d'ailleurs." *Notre Librairie,* no. 118 (1994).

3214. Paulme, Denise. *La Mère dévorante: essai sur la
morphologie des contes africains.* Paris: Gallimard, 1976.
(Nouvelle édition en 1986).

3215. Quaghebeur, Marc (éd.). *Papier blanc, encre
noire: cent ans de culture francophone en Afrique noire.*
Bruxelles: Labor, 1992. 2 v.

3216. *Quel théâtre pour le développement en Afrique?
Actes du stage-séminaire, Abidjan, 1978.* Dakar: Nouvelles
Editions Africaines, 1985. Mis sur pied par l'Institut Culturel
Africain.

3217. Ricard, Alain. *L'Invention du théâtre: le théâtre et
les comédiens en Afrique noire.* Lausanne: L'Age d'homme,
1986.

3218. ———. *Littératures d'Afrique noire: des langues
aux livres.* Paris: Kathala, 1994.

3219. Rouch, Alain et Gérard Clavreuil. *Littératures
nationales d'écriture française: Afrique noire, Caraïbes,
Océan indien: histoire littéraire et anthologie.* Paris: Bordas,
1986.

3220. Rugamba, Cyprian. *La Poésie face à l'histoire.* Butare: Institut national de recherche scientifique, 1987.

3221. Volet, Jean-Marie. *La Parole aux Africaines ou l'idée de pouvoir chez les romancières d'expression française de l'Afrique sub-saharienne.* Amsterdam: Rodopi, 1993.

BENIN/BÉNIN

General studies

3222. Houannou, Adrien. *La Littérature béninoise de langue française.* Paris: Karthala, 1984.

Authors

3223. Afoutou, Jean Marc-Aurèle. *Certitudes.* Dakar: Khoudia, 1991. (Coll. Ecrits des Forges: poésie, 3). Poésie.

3224. Agbossahessou. *Les Haleines sauvages.* Yaoundé: CLE, 1972. Poésie.

3225. Alapini, Julien. *Acteurs noirs.* Avignon: Les Presses Universelles, 1965. Théâtre.

3226. ———. *Les Initiés.* Avignon: Les Livres nouveaux, 1941. Roman.

3227. ———. *Le Petit Dahoméen.* Avignon: Les Presses Universelles, 1950. Roman.

3228. Almeida, Fernando d'. *L'Espace de la parole.* Paris: Silex, 1984. Poésie.

3229. Aplogan, Blaise. *La Kola brisée.* Paris: L'Harmattan, 1990. (Coll. Encres noires, 66). Roman.

3230. Bhêly-Quenum, Olympe. *Le Chant du lac.* Paris: Présence Africaine, 1965. Roman.

3231. ———. *L'Initié.* Paris: Présence Africaine, 1979. (Nouvelle édition en 1985). Roman.

3232. ———. *Un Piège sans fin.* Paris: Présence Africaine, 1960. (Nouvelle édition en 1985). Roman.

3233. Lecherbonnier, Bernard (éd.). *Olympe Bhely-Quenum par lui même.* Paris: Nathan, 1979. (Coll. Classiques du Monde).

3234. Carlos, Jérôme. *Cri de la liberté.* Cotonou: ABM, 1973. Poésie.

3235. ———. *Fleur du désert.* Abidjan: CEDA, 1990. Roman.

3236. Djinadou, Moudjib. *Mais que font donc les dieux de la neige?* Paris: L'Harmattan, 1993. (Coll. Encres noires, 119). Roman.

3237. ———. *Mo gbé le cri de mauvais augure.* Paris: L'Harmattan, 1991. (Coll. Encres noires, 84). Roman.

3238. Hazoumé, Paul. *Doguicimi.* Paris: Larose, 1938. Roman.

3239. Hessou, Henri D. *Les Vipères de Kétou.* Lomé: Nouvelles Editions Africaines, 1986. Nouvelles.

3240. Hountondji, Gisèle (F). *Une Citronnelle dans la neige.* Lomé: Nouvelles Editions Africaines, 1986. Autobiographie.

3241. Joachim, Paulin. *Oraison pour une re-naissance.* Paris: Silex, 1984. Poésie.

3242. Laleye, Barnabé. *Comme un singe dans la nuit.* Paris: L'Harmattan, 1986. (Coll. Encres noires, 34). Poésie.

3243. Laye, Barnabé. *Une Femme dans la lumière de l'aube.* Paris: Seghers, 1988. Roman.

3244. ———. *Mangalor.* Paris: Seghers, 1990. (Coll. Chemins d'Identité). Roman.

3245. Medetognon-Benissan, Tévi. *Tourbillons.* Lomé: Haho, 1985. Roman.

3246. Nouatin, Théophile. *L'Exil et la nuit.* Paris: L'Harmattan, 1993. (Coll. Encres noires, 114). Roman.

3247. Noutevi, Jonas. *Ombres et lumières.* Cotonou: Sonedis, 1991. Poésie.

3248. Ologoudou, Emile. *Prisonniers du Ponant.* Paris: L'Harmattan, 1986. (Coll. Encres noires, 35). Poésie.

3249. Pliya, Jean. *Le Chimpanzé amoureux.* Yaoundé: Saint-Paul, 1977. Nouvelles.

3250. ———. *Les Tresseurs de corde.* Paris: Hatier, 1987. (Coll. Monde noir poche, 44). Nouvelles.

3251. Prudencio, Eustache. *Vents du lac.* Cotonou: Editions du Bénin, 1967. Poésie.

3252. Tidjani Serpos, Abdou. *Le Dilemne.* Ouida: Imprimerie Souza, 1955. (Nouvelle édition en 1983 chez Silex, Paris). Nouvelles.

BURKINA FASO/BOURKINA

Bibliographies

3253. Benon, Baba. "Bibliographie." *Notre Librairie,* no. 101 (1990): 113-117.

3254. Zimmer, Wolfgang. *Répertoire du théâtre burkinabè.* Paris: L'Harmattan, 1992.

Anthologies

3255. *Anthologie de la jeune poésie burkinabè.* Ouagadougou: Presses africaines, 1984. (Sélection des œuvres présentées au Grand prix national des arts et des lettres 1983). Poésie.

3256. *Recueil théâtral de l'atelier théâtre burkinabè.* Ouagadougou: Presses africaines, 1986. Cinq pièces destinées au théâtre-forum. Théâtre.

General studies

3257. "Colloque de l'INSULLA." *Annales* série A, no. spécial (1988): la littérature orale burkinabè — le roman burkinabè — la poésie burkinabè — le théâtre burkinabè.

3258. Kabore, Oger. *Les Oiseaux s'ébattent. Chansons enfantines au Burkina Faso.* Paris: L'Harmattan, 1993.

3259. "Littérature du Burkina Faso." *Notre Librairie*, no. 101 (1990).

Authors

3260. Bamouni, Paulin Babou. *Luttes.* Paris: Silex, 1981. Poésie.

3261. Bazié, Jean-Hubert. *Champ d'août.* Ouagadougou: Imprimerie de la presse écrite, 1986. Nouvelles.

3262. ———. *Chronique du Burkina.* Ouagadougou: Imprimerie de la presse écrite, 1985. (La deuxième partie de cette chronique a été publiée en 1986). Roman.

3263. ———. *Lomboro de Bourasso.* Ouagadougou: Imprimerie nationale, 1988. Nouvelles.

3264. ———. *Sally-Alima.* Ouagadougou: Imprimerie de la presse écrite, 1985. Nouvelles.

3265. ———. *Zaka: la Maison.* Ouagadougou: Imprimerie Centrale, 1991. Roman.

3266. Boni, Nazi. *Crépuscule des temps anciens.* Paris: Présence Africaine, 1962. Chronique du Bwamu. Roman historique.

3267. Bonkian, Jean-Luc. *Le Fil des crevasses.* Ouagadougou: Socifa, 1991. Roman.

3268. Bonnet, Doris, Moussa Ouedraogo et Désiré Bonogo. *Proverbes et contes mossi.* Paris: EDICEF, 1982. (Coll. Fleuve et Flamme). Proverbes.

3269. Conombo, Joseph Issoufou. *Souvenirs de guerre d'un tirailleur sénégalais.* Paris: L'Harmattan, 1989. (Coll. Mémoires africaines). Autobiographie.

3270. Dabiré, Pierre. *Sansoa.* Paris: ORTF, 1969. Théâtre.

3271. Damiba, Geoffroy. *Patarbtaale le fils du pauvre.* Ouagadougou: Imprimerie Nouvelle du Centre, 1990. Roman.

3272. Damiba, Joseph et Barthélémy Sawadogo. *Poèmes-théâtre.* Ouagadougou: Presses africaines, 1983. Textes bilingues en mooré et français. Poésie et théâtre.

3273. Dao Sanou, Bernadette (F). *Poésie.* Ouagadougou: Presses africaines, 1986. L'ouvrage comprend aussi des poèmes de Jacques P. Bazié et de Prosper N. Bambara. Poésie.

3274. ———. *Poésie pour enfants.* Ouagadougou: Presses africaines, 1987. L'ouvrage comprend aussi des poèmes de Jean-Charles K. Kabré et de Théodore L. Kafando. Poésie.

3275. Diallo, Boubar. *Recueil de contes du Burkina-Faso.* Paris: L'Harmattan, 1993. Contes.

3276. Guingané, Jean-Pierre. *Le Fou.* Abidjan: CEDA, 1986. Théâtre.

3277. ———. *Papa, oublie-moi: pièce de théâtre-débat.* Ougadougou: UNICEF; Editions du Théâtre de la Fraternité, 1990. Théâtre.

3278. ———. *La Savane en transe.* Ouagadougou: Editions du Théâtre de la Fraternité, 1991. Théâtre.

3279. Hien, Ansomwin Ignace. *L'Enfer au paradis.* Ouagadougou: Presses africaines, 1988. Roman.

3280. ———. *Secrets d'alcôve.* Ouagadougou: Presses africaines, 1989. Nouvelle.

3281. Ilboudo, Monique (F). *Le Mal de la peau.* Ouagadougou: Imprimerie Nationale, 1992. Roman.

3282. Ilboudo, Patrick G. *Les Carnets secrets d'une fille de joie.* Ouagadougou: La Mante, 1988. Roman.

3283. ———. *Le Procès du muet.* Ouagadougou: La Mante, 1987. Roman.

3284. ———. *Les Vertiges du trône.* Ouagadougou: Editions INP, 1990. Roman.

3285. Ilboudo, Pierre Claver. *Adama ou la force des choses.* Paris: Présence Africaine, 1987. Roman.

3286. ———. *Le Fils aîné,* suivi de *Le Mariage de Tinga.* Paris: Silex, 1985. Roman et nouvelle.

3287. Kaboré Bila, Roger. *Indésirables.* Paris: L'Harmattan, 1990. (Coll. Encres noires, 68). Roman.

3288. Kanzié, Pierrette Sandra (F). *Les Tombes qui pleurent.* Ouagadougou: Imprimerie nouvelle du centre, 1987. Poésie.

3289. Nikiéma, Roger. *Dessein contraire.* Ouagadougou: Presses africaines, 1967. Roman.

3290. Ouattara, Vincent. *Aurore des accusés et des accusateurs.* Paris: L'Harmattan, 1994. Roman.

3291. Ouédraogo, Marc. *Gris bonbon.* Paris: Saint-Germain-des-Prés, 1984. Poésie.

3292. Ouédraogo, Yamba Elie. *On a giflé la montagne.* Paris: L'Harmattan, 1991. (Coll. Encres noires, 83). Roman.

3293. Sanon, Bowuroségé Jules. *Regard intérieur.* Paris: ARCAM, 1984. Poésie.

3294. Sawadogo, Etienne. *Contes de jadis, récits de naguère.* Dakar: Nouvelles Editions Africaines, 1982. Contes et récits.

3295. Seni, Lazoumou. *Makoé: poèmes.* Ouagadougou: Wotien et Fils, 1991. Poésie.

3296. Somdah, Marie Ange. *Demain sera beau.* Paris: Silex, 1989. Poésie.

3297. Somé, Jean-Baptiste. *Affaire de cœur.* Ouagadougou: Imprimerie Nationale, 1990. Roman.

3298. ———. *Le Miel amer.* Sherbrooke: Naaman, 1985. Roman.

3299. Tiendrébéogo, Yamba. *Contes du Larhallé.* Ouagadougou: Presses africaines, 1963. Suivi d'un recueil de proverbes et de devinettes du pays mossi.

3300. Titinga, Pacéré Frédéric. *Poème pour Koryo.* Ouagadougou: Imprimerie nouvelle du centre, 1987. Poésie.

3301. ———. *La Poésie des griots.* Paris: Silex, 1982. Poésie.

3302. Zongo, Daniel. *Charivaris.* Les Sables d'Olonnes: Imprimerie Pinson, 1977. Poésie.

3303. Zongo, Norbert. *Le Parachutage.* Ouagadougou: Editions ABC – Communication, 1988. Roman.

3304. ———. *Rougbêinga.* Ouagadougou: Editions INC, 1990. Roman.

BURUNDI

3305. Niyonsaba, Ambroise. *La Métamorphose.* Bujumbura: Régie des productions pédagogiques, 1989. Théâtre.

CAMEROON/CAMEROUN

Bibliographies

3306. Baratte, Thérèse. "Littérature camerounaise d'expression française: bibliographie." *Notre Librairie,* no. 100 (1990): 130-138. Suivi d'une bibliographie de la littérature camerounaise d'expression anglaise due à Bole Butake, pp. 139-141.

3307. Zimmer, Wolfgang. *Répertoire du théâtre camerounais*. Paris: L'Harmattan, 1986.

Anthologies

3308. Dakeyo, Paul. *Poèmes de demain: Anthologie de la poésie camerounaise de langue française*. Paris: Silex, 1982.

3309. Philombe, René. *Le Livre camerounais et ses auteurs*. Yaoundé: Semences Africaines, 1984.

General studies

3310. Ackad, Josette. *Le Roman camerounais et la critique*. Paris: Silex, 1985. (Coll. A3).

3311. Bjornson, Richard. *The African quest for freedom: Cameroonian writing and the national experience*. Bloomington: Indiana University Press, 1991.

3312. Brière, Eloïse A. *Le Roman camerounais et ses discours*. Paris: Nouvelles du sud, 1993.

3313. Butake, Bole et Gilbert Doho (éds.). *Théâtre camerounais/Cameroonian Theatre*. Yaoundé: Editions Bet & Co, 1988. Colloque de Yaoundé, novembre 1987.

3314. "Littérature camerounaise 1: l'éclosion de la parole." *Notre Librairie*, no. 99 (1989).

3315. "Littérature camerounaise 2: le livre dans tous ses états." *Notre Librairie*, no. 100 (1990).

Authors

3316. Abega, Séverin-Cécile. *Les Bimanes: sept nouvelles du village et du quartier*. Dakar: Nouvelles Editions Africaines, 1982. (Coll. Jeunesse). Nouvelles.

3317. ———. *La Latrine.* Dakar: Nouvelles Editions Africaines, 1988. Roman.

3318. ———. *Le Sein t'est pris.* Yaoundé: CLE, 1993. Théâtre.

3319. Abossolo Zoobo, Emile C. *Cameroun / Gabon: le D. A. S. S. monte à l'attaque.* Paris: L'Harmattan, 1985.

3320. Angui, Jean-Gaspard. *La Seconde épouse.* Sherbrooke: Naaman, 1985. Théâtre.

3321. Assiga-Ahanda, Marie-Thérèse (F). *Société africaine et High society: petite ethnologie de l'arrivisme.* Libreville: Lion, 1978. Roman.

3322. Ateba Yene, Théodore. *Cameroun: mémoire d'un colonisé.* Paris: L'Harmattan, 1988. (Coll. Mémoires africaines). Autobiographie.

3323. Awona, Stanislas. *Le Chômeur.* Yaoundé: Centre d'édition et de production de manuels et d'auxiliaires de l'enseignement, 1968. Théâtre.

3324. Awouma, Joseph-Marie et Jourdain Noah. *Contes et fables du Cameroun: initiation à la littérature orale.* Yaoundé: CLE, 1976. (Nouvelle édition en 1978). Contes.

3325. Bassek, Philomène M. (F). *La Tache de sang.* Paris: L'Harmattan, 1990. (Coll. Encres noires, 72). Roman.

3326. Bassek Ba Kobhio. *Les Eaux qui débordent.* Paris: L'Harmattan, 1984. (Coll. Encres noires, 26). Nouvelles.

3327. ———. *Sango Malo: Le maître du canton.* Paris: L'Harmattan. 1991. (Coll. Encres noires, 78). Nouvelles.

3328. Bebey, Francis. *Embarras et Cie.* Yaoundé: CLE, 1967. Nouvelles et poèmes.

3329. ———. *L'Enfant-Pluie.* Saint-Maur: Sépia, 1994. Roman.

3330. ———. *Le Fils d'Agatha Moudio.* Yaoundé: CLE, 1967. Roman.

3331. ———. *La Lune dans un seau tout rouge.* Paris: Hatier, 1989. Contes et nouvelles.

3332. ———. *Le Ministre et le griot.* Saint-Maur: Sépia, 1992. Roman.

3333. ———. *Nouvelle saison des fruits.* Dakar: Nouvelles Editions Africaines, 1980. Poésie.

3334. Bekombo, Firmin Alfred. *J'attends toujours.* Paris: L'Harmattan. 1989. Roman.

3335. Bélibi, Virginie (F). *Vers enivrants.* Yaoundé: CLE, 1987. Poésie.

3336. Benanga, Victor Béti. *Le Miroir bleu.* Yaoundé: Sopecam, 1990. Roman.

3337. Beti, Mongo. *Les Deux mères de Guillaume Ismaël Dzewatama, futur camionneur.* Paris: Buchet-Chastel, 1983. Roman.

3338. ———. *La France contre l'Afrique.* Paris: La Découverte, 1993. (Coll. Cahiers libres-essais). Récit autobiographique.

3339. ———. *L'Histoire du fou.* Paris: Julliard, 1994. Roman.

3340. ———. *Lettre ouverte aux camerounais ou la deuxième mort de Ruben Um Nyobé.* Rouen: Peuples noirs, 1986. Autobiographie.

3341. ———. *Mission terminée.* Paris: Buchet-Chastel, 1957. (Nouvelle édition en 1985 chez Hachette, Livre de poche 6089). Roman.

3342. ———. *Le Pauvre Christ de Bomba.* Paris: Laffont, 1956. (Nouvelle édition en 1993 chez Présence Africaine, Paris). Roman.

3343. ———. *Perpétue et l'habitude du malheur.* Paris: Buchet-Chastel, 1974. (Nouvelle édition en 1989). Roman.

3344. ———. *Remember Ruben.* Paris: Union Générale d'Editions, 1974. (Nouvelle édition en 1991 chez l'Harmattan, coll. Encres noires, 17). Roman.

3345. ———. *La Revanche de Guillaume Ismaël Dzewatama.* Paris: Buchet-Chastel, 1984. Roman.

3346. ———. *Le Roi miraculé.* Paris: Buchet-Chastel, 1958. (Nouvelle édition en 1972). Roman.

3347. ———. *La Ruine presque cocasse d'un polichinelle.* Rouen: Peuples noirs, 1979. Roman.

3348. ——— sous le pseudonyme d'Eza Boto. *Ville cruelle.* Paris: Présence Africaine, 1954. Roman.

3349. Mercier, R. et M. & S. Battestini. *Mongo Beti.* Paris: Nathan, 1984. (Coll. Littératures africaines, 5).

3350. Mouralis, Bernard. *Comprendre l'œuvre de Mongo Beti.* Issy-les-Moulineaux: Saint-Paul, 1981.

3351. Beyala, Calixthe (F). *Assèze l'Africaine.* Paris: Albin Michel, 1994. Roman.

3352. ———. *C'est le soleil qui m'a brûlée.* Paris: Stock, 1987. Roman.

3353. ———. *Maman a un amant.* Paris: Albin Michel, 1993. Roman.

3354. ———. *Le Petit Prince de Belleville.* Paris: Albin Michel, 1992. Roman.

3355. ———. *Seul le diable le savait.* Paris: Le Pré aux Clercs, 1990. Roman.

3356. ———. *Tu t'appelleras Tanga.* Paris: Stock, 1988. Roman.

3357. Bocquené, Henri. *Moi, un Mbororo*. Paris: Karthala, 1986. (Nouvelle édition en 1990). Autobiographie.

3358. Boto, Eza *voir* Beti, Mongo.

3359. Dakeyo, Paul. *Les Barbelés du matin*. Paris: Saint-Germain-des-Prés, 1973. Poésie.

3360. ———. *La Femme où j'ai mal*. Paris: Silex, 1989. Poésie.

3361. Dati, Marie Claire (F). *Les Ecarlates*. Yaoundé: Sopecam, 1992. Poésie.

3362. Dikolo, Jean-Pierre. *Athlètes à abattre: une aventure de Scorpion l'Africain*. Paris: Editions ABC, 1976. Roman.

3363. Dooh Bunya, Lydie (F). *La Brise du jour*. Yaoundé: CLE, 1977. Roman autobiographique.

3364. Effa, Gaston-Paul. *Quand le ciel se retire*. Paris: L'Harmattan, 1994. (Coll. Encres noires, 116). Roman.

3365. ———. *La Saveur de l'ombre*. Paris: L'Harmattan, 1993. (Coll. Encres noires, 108). Roman.

3366. Ekossono, Raymond. *Ainsi s'achève la vie d'un homme*. Yaoundé: Sopecam, 1989. Théâtre.

3367. Eno Belinga, Samuel-Martin. *Ballades et chansons africaines*. Bruxelles: Gnome, 1982. Poésie.

3368. Enobo Kosso, Martin. *Monologue d'une veuve angoissée*. Yaoundé: Semences Africaines, 1984. Roman.

3369. Essoumba, Joseph-Marie. *Manemba ou les souvenirs d'un enfant de brousse*. Yaoundé: Semences Africaines, 1987. Roman.

3370. Etoundi-Mballa, Patrice. *Une vie à l'envers*. Yaoundé: Sopecam, 1987. Roman.

3371. Etounga Manguelle, Daniel. *La Colline du fromager.* Yaoundé: CLE, 1979. Roman.

3372. Ewande, Daniel. *Vive le président! La fête africaine.* Paris: Albin Michel, 1968. (Nouvelle édition en 1984 chez l'Harmattan, coll. Encres noires, 23). Roman.

3373. Fogui, Jean-Pierre. *Demain . . . poèmes.* Yaoundé: Sopecam, 1991. Poésie.

3374. Kakpo, Martine (F) et Pierre. *La Feuille d'ordonnance d'un cordonnier immigré.* Paris: La Pensée Universelle, 1986. Témoignage.

3375. Karone, Yodi. *A la recherche du cannibale-amour.* Paris: Nathan, 1988. (Coll. Espace sud). Roman.

3376. ———. *Le Bal des caïmans.* Paris: Karthala, 1980. (Coll. Lettres noires, 1). Roman.

3377. ———. *Les Beaux gosses.* Paris: Publisud, 1988. Roman.

3378. ———. *Nègre de paille,* suivi de *Nouvelles.* Paris: Silex, 1982. Roman et nouvelles.

3379. Kayo, Patrice. *Chansons populaires bamiléké,* suivi de *Déchirements.* Paris: Silex, 1984. Poésie.

3380. ———. *Les Sauterelles.* Yaoundé: CLE, 1986. Nouvelles.

3381. Kengni, Joseph. *Dans le pétrin.* Yaoundé: Semences Africaines, 1983. (Nouvelle édition en 1989). Théâtre.

3382. Kum'a N'Dumbe III, Alexandre. *Amilcar Cabral ou la tempête en Guinée Bissau.* Paris: P. J. Oswald, 1973. Théâtre.

3383. Kuoh-Moukouri, Jacques. *Doigts noirs: je fus écrivain-interprète au Cameroun.* Montréal: Edition à la page, 1963. Autobiographie.

3384. Kuoh-Moukoury, Thérèse (F). *Rencontres essentielles*. Paris: Adamawa, 1968. Roman.

3385. Lenou, Jean Mba. *L'Enfant bamileke*. Lausanne: Edition Clarté, 1971. Autobiographie.

3386. Manga Mado, Henri-Richard. *Complaintes d'un forçat*. Yaoundé: CLE, 1970. Roman.

3387. Matip, Benjamin. *Afrique, nous t'ignorons*. Paris: Renée Lacoste, 1956. Roman.

3388. ———. *Laisse-nous bâtir une Afrique debout*. Paris: Africascope, 1979. Théâtre.

3389. Matip, Marie-Claire (F). *Ngonda*. Yaoundé: Au Messager, 1958. Autobiographie.

3390. Mbarga Kouma, Marie-Charlotte (F). *Les Insatiables*. Yaoundé: Sopecam, 1989. Pièce écrite et jouée en 1967 sous le titre *La Famille africaine*. Théâtre.

3391. Mbock, Charly Gabriel. *La Croix du cœur*. Yaoundé: CLE, 1984. Roman.

3392. Medou Mvomo, Rémy-Gilbert. *Afrika ba'a*. Yaoundé: CLE, 1969. (Nouvelle édition en 1979). Roman.

3393. ———. *Les Enchaînés*. Yaoundé: CLE, 1979. Théâtre.

3394. ———. *Le Journal de Faliou*. Yaoundé: CLE, 1972. Roman.

3395. Mendo Ze, Gervais. *La Forêt illuminée,* suivi de *Boule de chagrin*. Paris: Editions ABC, 1987. Théâtre.

3396. Mfomo, Gabriel Evouna. *Au pays des initiés. Contes ewondo du Cameroun*. Traduction française. Paris: Karthala, 1982. Contes.

3397. Mokto, Joseph-Jules. *Ramitou, mon étrangère*. Yaoundé: CLE, 1971. Roman.

3398. Motaze Akam. *Le Circuit de la mort*. Paris: Editions Actuelles, 1984. Roman.

3399. Mpoudi Ngolle, Evelyne (F). *Sous la cendre le feu*. Paris: L'Harmattan, 1990. (Coll. Encres noires, 67). Roman.

3400. Mveng, Engelbert. *Balafon*. Yaoundé: CLE, 1972. Poésie.

3401. Mvolo, Samuel. *Les Fiancés du grand fleuve*. Yaoundé: CLE, 1973. Roman.

3402. Mvotto-Bina, Jeanne Irène (F). *Les Fleurs du passé*. Yaoundé: Semences Africaines, 1977. Poésie.

3403. Naha, Désiré. *Sur le chemin du suicide: l'autobiographie d'un jeune noir à la vie difficile*. Yaoundé: Edition du Demi-lettré, 1977. Autobiographie.

3404. Nanga, Bernard. *Les Chauves-souris*. Paris: Présence Africaine, 1980. Roman.

3405. ———. *Poèmes sans frontières,* suivi de *Poèmes pour sourire*. Yaoundé: Agence littéraire africaine, 1987. Poésie.

3406. ———. *La Trahison de Marianne*. Dakar: Nouvelles Editions Africaines, 1984. Roman.

3407. Ndachi Tagne, David. *Mr. Handlock ou le boulanger poétique*. Yaoundé: CLE, 1985. Théâtre.

3408. ———. *La Reine captive*. Paris: L'Harmattan, 1986. (Coll. Encres noires, 39). Roman.

3409. ———. *Sangs mêlés, sang péché*. Paris: l'Harmattan, 1992. (Coll. Poètes des cinq continents). Poésie.

3410. Ndedi-Penda, Patrice. *La Nasse*. Yaoundé: CLE, 1971. Roman.

3411. Ndjehoya, Blaise. *Le Nègre Potemkine*. Paris: Lieu Commun, 1988. Roman.

3412. Ndzagaap, Timothée. *La Fille du roi a menti.* Yaoundé: Semences Africaines, 1972. Théâtre.

3413. ———. *Le Mariage d'un jour.* Bafoussam: Librairie populaire, 1981. Théâtre.

3414. Nga Ndongo, Valentin. *Les Puces.* Paris: Editions ABC, 1984. Roman.

3415. Ngo Mai, Jeanne (F). *Poèmes sauvages et lamentations.* Monte-Carlo: Palais Miami, 1967. Poésie.

3416. Nguedam, Christophe. *Murmure et soupir.* Honfleur: J. P. Oswald, 1972. Poésie.

3417. Njami, Simon. *African Gigolo.* Paris: Seghers, 1989. Roman.

3418. ———. *Les Enfants de la cité.* Paris: Gallimard, 1987. (Coll. Folio junior). Roman.

3419. Njoya, Rabiatou (F). *Ange noir ange blanc.* Yaoundé: CLE, 1968. Théâtre.

3420. ———. *La Dernière aimée.* Yaoundé: CLE, 1974. Théâtre.

3421. ———. *Haute trahison.* Yaoundé: Sopecam, 1990. Théâtre.

3422. ———. "La Porteuse d'eau." dans *L'Exilé de l'eau.* Douala: AfricAvenir, 1991. Nouvelle.

3423. ———. *Raison de royaume.* Yaoundé: Sopecam, 1990. Théâtre.

3424. ———. *Toute la rente y passe.* Yaoundé: CLE, 1967. Théâtre.

3425. Nkamgnia, Samuel. *Jeunesse et patrie: poèmes.* Yaoundé: Saint-Paul, 1968. Poésie.

3426. ———. *Si mon mari s'en rend compte.* Buéa: Belafrique, 1983. Roman.

3427. Nkamgnia, Samuel et Justine Nankam (F). *Celle que l'on croyait loin.* Buéa: Belafrique, 1985. Nouvelles.

3428. Nkollo, Jean-Jacques. *Boris et Pavlone.* Paris: L'Harmattan, 1993. (Coll. Poètes des cinq continents). Roman et poésie.

3429. ———. *Brouillard.* Paris: L'Harmattan, 1990. (Coll. Encres noires, 73). Roman.

3430. ———. *La Joyeuse déraison.* Paris: L'Harmattan, 1992. (Coll. Encres noires, 91). Roman.

3431. Nkou, Joseph. *Le Détenteur.* Abidjan: Nouvelles Editions Africaines, 1984. Roman.

3432. Nyunaï, Jean-Paul. *La Nuit de ma vie.* Paris: Debresse, 1961. Poésie.

3433. Nzodom, Pierre Epato. *Sur les pistes d'aventure.* Yaoundé: Semences Africaines, 1980. Roman.

3434. Nzouankeu, Jacques-Muriel. *Le Souffle des ancêtres.* Yaoundé: CLE, 1965. Nouvelles.

3435. Obama, Jean-Baptiste. *Assimilados.* Paris: ORTF, 1972. Théâtre.

3436. Ongoum, Louis-Marie. *Pondah.* Yaoundé: Sopecam, 1989. Roman.

3437. Ouoham Tchidjo, Stanislas. *Par Décret présidentiel . . .* Paris: L'Harmattan, 1993. (Coll. Encres noires, 100). Roman.

3438. Owono, Joseph. *Tante Bella.* Yaoundé: Au Messager, 1959. Roman.

3439. Oyono, Ferdinand. *Chemin d'Europe.* Paris: Julliard, 1960. (Nouvelle édition en 1973 chez U.G.E., Paris). Paris.

3440. ———. *Une Vie de boy*. Paris: Julliard, 1956. (Nouvelle édition en 1970 chez Presses Pocket, Paris). Roman.

3441. ———. *Le Vieux nègre et la médaille*. Paris: Julliard, 1956. (Nouvelles éditions en 1972 chez U.E.G., Paris et en 1980 chez CLE, Yaoundé). Roman.

3442. Chevrier, Jacques. *Une Vie de Boy*. Paris: Hatier, 1977. (Coll. Profil d'une œuvre, 54).

3443. Delmas, Philippe. *Le Vieux nègre et la médaille de Ferdinand Oyono: étude critique*. Paris: Nathan, 1986. (Coll. Une œuvre, un auteur).

3444. Mendo Ze, Gervais. *La Prose romanesque de Ferdinand Oyono*. Yaoundé: Université de Yaoundé, 1984.

3445. Mercier, Roger et S. Battestini. *Ferdinand Oyono: écrivain camerounais*. Paris: Nathan, 1964. (Coll. Littérature africaine, 8).

3446. Minyono-Nkodo, M. *Comprendre Le Vieux nègre et la médaille*. Issy-les-Moulineaux: Saint-Paul, 1978. (Coll. Classiques africains).

3447. Oyono Mbia, Guillaume. *Jusqu'à nouvel avis*. Yaoundé: CLE, 1970. Théâtre.

3448. ———. *Notre fille ne se mariera pas*. Paris: ORTF, 1971. Théâtre.

3449. ———. *Le Train spécial de son Excellence*. Yaoundé: CLE, 1979. Théâtre.

3450. ———. *Trois prétendants ... un mari*. Yaoundé: CLE, 1964. Théâtre.

3451. Mupini, Ongom. *Comprendre Trois prétendants ... un mari de Guillaume Oyono Mbia*. Issy-les-Moulineaux: Saint-Paul, 1985. (Coll. Classiques africains).

3452. Pabé, Mongo. *Un Enfant comme les autres*. Yaoundé: CLE, 1972. Nouvelle.

3453. ———. *L'Homme de la rue.* Paris: Hatier, 1987. Roman.

3454. ———. *Innocente Assimba.* Yaoundé: CLE, 1971. Théâtre.

3455. ———. *Nos Ancêtres les baobabs.* Paris: L'Harmattan, 1994. (Coll. Encres noires, 122). Roman.

3456. ———. *Père inconnu.* Paris: EDICEF, 1985. Roman.

3457. ———. *Le Philosophe et le sorcier.* Yaoundé: Edition Le Flambeau, 1983. Théâtre.

3458. Philombe, René. *Choc anti choc.* Yaoundé: Semences Africaines, 1978. Roman & Poésie.

3459. ———. *Les Epoux célibataires.* Yaoundé: APEC, 1971. Théâtre.

3460. ———. *N'Krumah n'est pas mort.* Yaoundé: Semences Africaines, 1972. Poésie.

3461. ———. *La Passerelle divine.* Yaoundé: APEC, 1959. Légende.

3462. ———. *Sola ma chérie.* Yaoundé: CLE, 1966. Roman.

3463. ———. *Un Sorcier blanc à Zangali.* Yaoundé: CLE, 1969. Roman.

3464. Rifoe, Simon. *Le Tour du Cameroun en 59 jours.* Yaoundé: Abbia, 1965. Autobiographie.

3465. Sanduo, Lazarre. *Une Dure vie scolaire.* Yaoundé: CLE, 1972. Autobiographie.

3466. Sengat-Kuo, François. *Fleurs de laterite.* Monte-Carlo: Regain, 1954. Poésie.

3467. Tchakoute, Paul. *Les Dieux trancheront ou la farce inhumaine.* Paris: Edition P. J. Oswald, 1973. Théâtre.

3468. ———. *Les Femmes en cage.* Bafoussam: Librairie Populaire, 1980. Théâtre.

3469. ———. *Samba.* Yaoundé: CLE, 1980. (Nouvelle édition en 1988). Théâtre.

3470. Tchoumba Ngouankeu. *Autour du lac Tchad.* Yaoundé: CLE, 1969. Contes.

3471. Thiam, Abdul Karim. *Ramsès II, le nègre.* Abidjan: Editions Livre Sud (EDILIS), 1993. Théâtre.

3472. Um Nyobe, Ruben. *Ecrits sous maquis.* Paris: L'Harmattan, 1989. Présenté par J. A. Mbembe. Biographie.

3473. Werewere Liking (F). *L'Amour-cent-vies.* Paris: Publisud, 1988. Roman.

3474. ———. *Elle sera de jaspe et de corail: journal d'une misovire.* Paris: L'Harmattan, 1983. (Coll. Encres noires, 21). Chant-roman.

3475. ———. *On ne raisonne pas avec le venin.* Paris: Saint-Germain-des-Prés, 1977. Poésie.

3476. ———. *Orphée-dafric.* Paris: L'Harmattan, 1981. (Suivi de Manuna Ma Njock (F), *Orphée d'Afrique*, théâtre rituel). Roman.

3477. ———. *Singue Mura.* Abidjan: Ki-Yi, 1990. Théâtre.

3478. ———. *Spectacles rituels.* Abidjan: Nouvelles éditions africaines, 1987. Théâtre.

3479. ———. *Un Touareg s'est marié à un Pygmée: épopée m'vet pour une Afrique présente.* Carnières, Belgique: Lansman, 1992. Théâtre.

3480. ——— et Manuna Ma Njock (F). *A la rencontre de . . .* Dakar: Nouvelles Editions Africaines, 1980. Récit.

3481. ——— et Marie-José Hourantier (F). *Liboy li Nkundung.* Issy les Moulineaux: Saint-Paul, 1980. Conte.

3482. Yanou, Etienne. *L'Homme-dieu de Bisso.* Yaoundé: CLE, 1974. Roman.

3483. Zanga Tsogo, Delphine (F). *L'Oiseau en cage.* Dakar; Paris: Nouvelles Editions Africaines; EDICEF, 1983. (Coll. Jeunesse). Roman.

3484. ———. *Vies de femmes.* Yaoundé: CLE, 1983. Roman.

CENTRAL AFRICAN REPUBLIC/ CENTRAFRIQUE

Bibliography

3485. Penel, Jean-Dominique. "Repères bibliographiques." *Notre Librairie*, no. 97 (1989): 110-112.

Anthologies

3486. Penel, Jean-Dominique. *Anthologie de la poésie centrafricaine.* Paris: L'Harmattan, 1990. (Coll. Poètes des cinq continents).

3487. Saulnier, Pierre. *A tene ti be–Africa ou les contes de la République centrafricaine.* Le Poire-sur-vie: Imprimerie graphique de l'Ouest, 1982-1985. 3 fascicules.

General studies

3488. "Littérature centrafricaine." *Notre Librairie*, no. 97 (1989).

Authors

3489. Ananissoh, Théo. *Territoires du nord.* Paris: L'Harmattan, 1992. (Coll. Encres noires, 94). Roman.

3490. Bamboté, Makombo Pierre. *Coup d'état nègre.* Montréal: Humanitas, 1987. Roman.

3491. ———. *Nouvelles de Bangui*. Montréal: Presses de l'Université, 1980. Nouvelles.

3492. ———. *La Poésie est dans l'histoire*. Paris: P. J. Oswald, 1960. Poésie.

3493. ———. *Princesse Mandapu*. Paris: Présence Africaine, 1972. (Nouvelle édition en 1988 chez Nathan; Présence Africaine, Paris). Roman.

3494. Danzi, Gabriel. *Un Soleil au bout de la nuit*. Dakar: Nouvelles Editions Africaines, 1985. Roman.

3495. Gallo, Therry-Jacques. *N'garagba, la maison des morts: un prisonnier sous Bokassa*. Paris: L'Harmattan, 1988. Autobiographie.

3496. Goyémidé, Etienne. *Le Dernier survivant de la caravane*. Paris: Hatier, 1985. (Coll. Monde noir poche, 32). Roman.

3497. ———. *Le Silence de la forêt*. Paris: Hatier, 1984. (Coll. Monde noir poche, 26). Roman.

3498. Ipeko-Etomane, Faustin Albert. *L'Ombre des interdits*. Yaoundé: CLE, 1970. Théâtre.

3499. ———. *Poèmes du renouveau*. Bagdad: Imprimerie al Arruya, 1978. Poésie.

3500. ———. *Le Téléphone*. Yaoundé: CLE, 1976. Théâtre.

3501. Kazangba, G. *Le Mariage Yokoma*. s.l.: s.n., 1955. Théâtre.

3502. Maran, René. *Batouala*. Paris: Albin Michel, 1921. Roman.

3503. Sammy, Pierre. *L'Odissée de Mongou*. Paris: Hatier, 1977. (Coll. Monde noir poche, 22). Roman.

3504. Siango, Benoît Basile. *Prière à Notre Dame de L'Oubangui*. s.l.: s.n., 1955. Poésie.

3505. Yavoucko, Cyriaque. *Crépuscule et défi.* Paris: L'Harmattan, 1979. (Coll. Encres noires, 1). Roman.

3506. Zomboui, Ganga. *Invasion au cœur de l'Afrique.* Paris: L'Harmattan, 1989. (Coll. Encres noires, 58). Roman.

CONGO

Bibliographies

3507. "Bibliographie." *Notre Librairie,* no. 92-93 (1988): 210-217.

3508. Mamonsono-Pindi, Léopold et Bemba, Sylvain. *Bio-Bibliographie des écrivains congolais.* Brazzaville: Editions congolaises littéraires, 1979.

Anthology

3509. Tati-Loutard, Jean-Baptiste. *Anthologie de la littérature congolaise d'expression française.* Yaoundé: CLE, 1976

General studies

3510. Anyinefa, Koffi. *Littérature et politique en Afrique noire: socialisme et dictature comme thèmes du roman congolais d'expression française.* Bayreuth: Eckhard Breitinger, 1990.

3511. Devesa, Jean-Michel (dir.). *Magie et écriture au Congo.* Paris: L'Harmattan, 1994. (Coll. Critiques littéraires).

3512. "Littérature congolaise." *Notre Librairie,* no. 92-93 (1988).

3513. Piniau, Bernard. *Congo-Zaïre, 1874-1981: La perception du lointain.* Paris: L'Harmattan, 1992.

Authors

3514. Baker, Léandre-Alain. *Ici s'achève le voyage.* Paris: L'Harmattan, 1989. (Coll. Encres noires, 60). Roman.

3515. Balou-Tchichelle, Jeannette (F). *Cœur en exil.* Paris: La Pensée Universelle, 1989. Roman.

3516. Banana, Alphonse. *Cœur sur la braise.* Paris: Saint-Germain-des-Prés, 1983. Poésie.

3517. Bemba, Sylvain. *Le Dernier des cargonautes.* Paris: L'Harmattan, 1984. (Coll. Encres noires, 22). Roman.

3518. ———. *Un Foutu monde pour un blanchisseur trop honnête.* Yaoundé: CLE, 1979. Théâtre.

3519. ———. *Léopolis.* Paris: Hatier, 1985. (Coll. Monde noir poche, 31). Roman.

3520. ———. *Rêves portatifs.* Dakar: Nouvelles Editions Africaines, 1979. Roman.

3521. ———. *Le Soleil est parti à M'Pemba.* Paris: Présence Africaine, 1982. Roman.

3522. ———, (sous le pseudonyme de Martial Malinda). *L'Enfer c'est Orféo.* Paris: ORTF, 1970. Théâtre.

3523. Biniakounou, Pierre. *Chômeur à Brazzaville.* Dakar: Nouvelles Editions Africaines, 1977. Roman.

3524. Blouin, Andrée (F). *My Country Africa: Autobiography of a black passionaria.* New York: Praeger, 1983. In collaboration with Jean MacKellar. Autobiography.

3525. Bokoko, Sylvie (F). *Mafouaou.* Dakar: Nouvelles Editions Africaines, 1982. Publié dans un ouvrage intitulé *Trois Nouvelles.* Nouvelle.

3526. Bokyiendze, Fulbert. *Une Epine dans le cœur, du sable dans le cerveau.* Kinshasa: Editions ILLUCTHCECO, 1983. Théâtre.

3527. Dadié, Bernard Binlin. *Béatrice du Congo.* Paris: Présence Africaine, 1970. (Nouvelle édition en 1988). Théâtre.

3528. Diamoneka, Cécile Ivelyse (F). *Voix des cascades.* Paris: Présence Africaine, 1982. Poésie.

3529. Dongala, Emmanuel. *Le Feu des origines.* Paris: Albin Michel, 1987. Roman.

3530. ———. *Un Fusil dans la main, un poème dans la poche.* Paris: Albin Michel, 1973. Roman.

3531. ———. *Jazz et vin de palme.* Paris: Hatier, 1982. (Coll. Monde noir poche, 13). Nouvelles.

3532. Dabla, Séwanou Jean-Jacques. *Jazz et vin de palme de Dongala: étude critique.* Paris: Nathan, 1986. (Coll. Une œuvre, un auteur).

3533. Etoumba, Paule (F). *Un Mot fracasse un avenir.* Honfleur: J. P. Oswald, 1971. Poésie.

3534. Kimbidima, Julien Omer. *Les Filles du président.* Paris: L'Harmattan, 1987. (Coll. Encres noires, 41). Roman.

3535. ———. *Kriste est une gonzesse.* Paris: L'Harmattan, 1990. (Coll. Encres noires, 71). Roman.

3536. Laurans, Francine (F). *Tourmente sous les tropiques.* Paris: La Pensée Universelle, 1989. Roman.

3537. Letembet-Ambily, Antoine. *L'Epopée de la rénovation.* Brazzaville: Imprimerie des Armées, 1988. Théâtre.

3538. Lissouba, Binéka (F). *Les Libres propos de Binéka.* Saint Maur: Sépia, 1994. Chroniques radio-phoniques.

3539. Loango, Dominique. *La Cité flamboyante.* Paris: Edition du Scorpion, 1959. (Coll. Alternance). Poésie.

3540. Lopes, Henri. *Le Chercheur d'Afriques.* Paris: Seuil, 1990. Roman.

3541. ———. *La Nouvelle romance.* Yaoundé: CLE, 1976. Roman.

3542. ———. *Le Pleurer-rire*. Paris: Présence Africaine, 1982. Roman.

3543. ———. *Sans Tam-tam*. Yaoundé: CLE, 1977. Roman.

3544. ———. *Sur l'autre rive*. Paris: Seuil, 1992. Roman.

3545. ———. *Tribaliques*. Yaoundé: CLE, 1971. (Nouvelle édition en 1983 aux Presses Pocket). Nouvelles.

3546. Daninos, Guy. *Comprendre Tribaliques*. Issy-les-Moulineaux: Saint-Paul, 1987. (Coll. Classiques africains).

3547. Malanda, Ange-Séverin. *Henri Lopes et l'impératif romanesque*. Paris: Silex, 1987.

3548. Rouch, Alain. *Tribaliques d'Henri Lopes: étude critique*. Dakar; Paris: Nouvelles Editions Africaines; Nathan, 1984. (Coll. Une œuvre, un auteur).

3549. Makey, Auguy. *Francofole*. Paris: L'Harmattan, 1993. (Coll. Encres noires, 95). Nouvelles.

3550. Makhele, Caya. *Le Cercle des vertiges*. Paris: L'Harmattan, 1992. (Coll. Encres noires, 90). Roman.

3551. ———. *L'Homme au landau*. Paris: L'Harmattan, 1988. (Coll. Encres noires, 46). Roman.

3552. Makouta-Mboukou, Jean-Pierre. *L'Ame bleue*. Yaoundé: CLE, 1971. Poésie.

3553. ———. *Le Contestant*. Paris: La Pensée Universelle, 1973. Roman.

3554. ———. *Les Dents du destin*. Dakar: Nouvelles Editions Africaines, 1984. Roman.

3555. ———. *En quête de liberté ou une vie d'espoir*. Yaoundé: CLE, 1970. Roman.

3556. ———. *. . . et l'homme triompha*. Paris: Fondation du prix mondial de la paix, 1983. Récit.

3557. ———. *Les Exilés de la forêt vierge ou le grand complot.* Paris: P. J. Oswald, 1974. (Nouvelle édition en 1981 chez l'Harmattan, coll. Encres noires, 10). Roman.

3558. ———. *L'Homme-aux-pataugas.* Paris: L'Harmattan, 1992. (Coll. Encres noires, 99). Roman.

3559. Malinda, Martial *voir* Bemba, Sylvain.

3560. Malonga, Jean. *Cœur d'Ayrenne.* Paris: Présence Africaine, 1954. Roman.

3561. Mamonsono, Léopold Pindy. *Héros dans l'ombre.* Brazzaville: Editions Littératures congolaises, 1979. Poésie.

3562. Menga, Guy. *Case de Gaulle.* Paris: Karthala, 1985. (Coll. Lettres du Sud). Roman.

3563. ———. *Le Cicérone de la Médina.* Paris: ACCT; RFI, 1973. (Coll. 10 nouvelles de . . .). Nouvelle.

3564. ———. *Kotawali.* Dakar: Nouvelles Editions Africaines, 1977. Roman.

3565. ———. *Moni-Mambou, retrouvailles.* Saint-Maur: Sépia, 1991. Nouvelles.

3566. ———. *L'Oracle, La Marmite de Koka-M'Bala.* Monte Carlo: Regain, 1966. Théâtre.

3567. ———. *La Palabre stérile.* Yaoundé: CLE, 1968. Roman.

3568. M'Fouilou, Dominique. *La Soumission.* Paris: L'Harmattan, 1977. Roman.

3569. ———. *Vent d'espoir sur Brazzaville.* Paris: L'Harmattan, 1991. (Coll. Encres noires, 75). Roman.

3570. N'Debeka, Maxime. *Equatorium.* Paris: Présence Africaine, 1987. Théâtre.

3571. ———. *Les Lendemains qui chantent.* Paris: Présence Africaine, 1982. Théâtre.

3572. ———. *Le Président*. Paris: P. J. Oswald, 1970. (Nouvelle édition en 1982 chez l'Harmattan, Paris). Théâtre.

3573. ———. *Soleils neufs*. Yaoundé: CLE, 1969. Poésie.

3574. ———. *Vécus au miroir*. Paris: Publisud, 1991. Nouvelles.

3575. Néné, Amélia (F). *Fleurs de vie*. Paris: Présence Africaine, 1980. Poésie.

3576. Nkouka, Alphonse. *Deuxième bureau*. Yaoundé: CLE, 1980. Roman.

3577. N'Zalabacka, Placide. *Le Tipoye doré*. Brazzaville: Imprimerie nationale, 1968. (Nouvelle édition en 1976 chez P. J. Oswald, Paris). Roman.

3578. Safou-Safouesse, Félicité (F). *Pensées pour votre album*. Chez l'auteur, 1985. Poésie.

3579. Sathoud, Ghislaine Nelly (F). *L'Ombre de Banda*. [Congo]: ADELF, 1990. Poésie.

3580. Sinda, Martial. *Premier chant du départ*. Paris: Seghers, 1955. Poésie.

3581. Sony Labou Tansi. *L'Anté-peuple*. Paris: Seuil, 1983. Roman.

3582. ———. "Antoine m'a vendu son destin." *Equateur*, no. 1 (1986). Théâtre.

3583. ———. *Une Chouette petite vie bien osée*. Carnières, Belgique: Lansman, 1992. Théâtre.

3584. ———. *Conscience de tracteur*. Dakar: Nouvelles Editions Africaines, 1979. Théâtre.

3585. ———. *L'Etat honteux*. Paris: Seuil, 1981. Roman.

3586. ———. *Le Malentendu*. Paris: ACCT; RFI, 1978. (Coll. 10 nouvelles de . . .). Nouvelle.

3587. ———. *La Parenthèse de sang,* suivi de *Je soussigné cardiaque.* Paris: Hatier, 1981. (Coll. Monde noir poche 11). Théâtre.

3588. ———. *Les Sept solitudes de Lorsa Lopez.* Paris: Seuil, 1985. (Nouvelle édition en 1994, coll. Points). Roman.

3589. ———. *La Vie et demie.* Paris: Seuil, 1979. (Nouvelle édition en 1988, coll. Points roman, 309). Roman.

3590. ———. *Les Yeux du volcan.* Paris: Seuil, 1988. Roman.

3591. Fettweiss, Nadine. *Lecture sémiotique de l'Antépeuple de Sony Labou Tansi.* Bruxelles: Cahiers du CEDAF-ASDOC, no 1, série 4 (1989).

3592. Tati-Loutard, Jean-Baptiste. *Chroniques congolaises.* Paris: P.J. Oswald, 1974. (Nouvelle édition en 1978 chez l'Harmattan, Paris). Nouvelles.

3593. ———. *Les Normes du Temps.* Lubumbashi: Mont Noir, 1974. Poésie.

3594. ———. *Nouvelles chroniques congolaises.* Paris: Présence Africaine, 1980. Nouvelles.

3595. ———. *Poèmes de la mer.* Yaoundé: CLE, 1968. Poésie.

3596. ———. *Le Récit de la mort.* Paris: Présence Africaine, 1987. Roman.

3597. ———. *Le Serpent austral: poèmes.* Paris: Présence Africaine, 1992. Poésie.

3598. ———. *La Tradition du songe,* suivi de *Eléments de la vie poétique.* Paris: Présence Africaine, 1985. Poésie.

3599. Tchicaya U Tam'Si. *Les Cancrelats.* Paris: Albin Michel, 1980. Roman.

3600. ———. *Ces Fruits si doux de l'arbre à pain.* Paris: Seghers, 1987. Roman.

3601. ———. *La Main sèche*. Paris: Laffont, 1980. (Coll. Chemins d'identité). Nouvelles.

3602. ———. *Le Mauvais sang*. Paris: P. J. Oswald, 1955. (Nouvelle édition en 1978 chez l'Harmattan). Poésie.

3603. ———. *Les Méduses ou les orties de mer*. Paris: Albin Michel, 1982. Roman.

3604. ———. *Les Phalènes*. Paris: Albin Michel, 1984. Roman.

3605. ———. *La Veste d'intérieur,* suivi de *Notes de veille*. Paris: Nubia, 1977. Poésie.

3606. ———. *Le Zulu,* suivi de *Vwéné le fondateur*. Paris: Nubia, 1977. Théâtre.

3607. "Tchicaya U Tam'Si." *Europe*, no. 750 (1991). Numéro spécial.

3608. Vincent, Michel. *Le Monde romanesque de Tchicaya U Tam'si*. Paris: L'Harmattan, 1994.

3609. Tchicaya Unti B'Kune. *Soleil sans lendemain*. Paris: L'Harmattan, 1981. Roman.

3610. Tchichelle Tchivela. *L'Exil ou la tombe*. Paris: Présence Africaine, 1986. Nouvelles.

3611. ———. *Longue est la nuit*. Paris: Hatier, 1981. (Coll. Monde noire poche, 4). Nouvelles.

3612. Tsibinda, Marie-Léontine (F). *Demain un autre jour*. Paris: Silex, 1987. Poésie.

3613. ———. *Une Lèvre naissant d'une autre*. Heidelberg: Editions bantoues, 1984. Poésie.

3614. ———. *Mayombé*. Paris: Saint-Germain-des-Prés, 1980. Poésie.

3615. ———. *Poèmes de la terre*. Brazzaville: Editions littéraires congolaises, 1980. Poésie.

DJIBOUTI

Authors

3616. Erouart-Siad, Patrick. *Océanie*. Paris: Seuil, 1992. Roman.

3617. Farah, Daher Ahmed. *Splendeur éphémère*. Paris: L'Harmattan, 1993. (Coll. Encres noires, 93). Roman.

3618. Rabeh, Omar Osman. *Le Cercle et la spirale*. Paris: Les Lettres libres, 1984. Autobiographie.

3619. Waberi, Abdourahman A. *Le Pays sans ombre*. Paris: Le Serpent à plumes, 1994. Nouvelles.

ETHIOPIA/ETHIOPIE

Author

3620. Kifle, Sélassié Béséat et Alfâdio. *Nuit et grêle*. Paris: Nubia, 1981. Poésie.

GABON

Bibliography

3621. "Bibliographie de la littérature gabonaise écrite." *Notre Librairie,* no. 105 (1991): 150-151.

Anthologies

3622. Abessolo, Jean-Baptiste, et al. *Contes du Gabon*. Paris: CLE International, 1981. Contes.

3623. Adam, Jean-Jérôme. *Fables, proverbes et devinettes du Haut-Ogooué*. Paris: Classiques africains, 1977.

3624. *Anthologie de la littérature gabonaise*. Libreville; Montréal: Ministère de l'Education; Beauchemin, 1976.

3625. Merlet, Annie. *Légendes et histoires des Myéné de l'Ogooué.* Libreville; Paris: Centre Culturel Saint-Exupéry; Sépia, 1989. Contes.

3626. Raponda-Walker. *Contes gabonais.* Paris: Présence Africaine, 1987.

General studies

3627. "Littérature gabonaise." *Notre Librairie,* no. 105 (1991).

Authors

3628. Allogho-Oke, Ferdinand. *Biboubouah.* Paris: L'Harmattan, 1985. Nouvelles.

3629. Emoane Mintsa-Mi-Okong. *Le Temps tue.* Libreville: Multipress, 1989. Théâtre.

3630. Kama-Bongo, Joséphine (F). *Obali.* Libreville: s.n., 1974. Théâtre.

3631. Lima, Josette (F). *Poèmes.* Dakar: Florilège, 1966. Poésie.

3632. Mbou Yembi, Léon. *Les Affinités affectives.* Paris: Silex, 1986. Récit.

3633. Mongaryas, Ben Quentin Jean-Claude. *Voyage au cœur de la plèbe.* Paris: Silex, 1986. Poésie.

3634. Moubouyi, Richard. *La Voix des ancêtres.* Libreville: Multipress, 1986. Proverbes et légendes.

3635. Moundjegou, Pierre-Edgar alias Magang-Ma-Mbuju Wisi. *Ainsi parlaient les anciens.* Paris: Silex, 1987. Poésie.

3636. Moussirou-Mouyama, Auguste. *Parole de vivant.* Paris: L'Harmattan, 1992. (Coll. Encres noires, 101). Roman.

3637. Ndaot, Séraphin. *Le Dissident.* Paris: Silex, 1986. Roman.

3638. Ndong Mbeng, Hubert Freddy. *Les Matitis.* Paris: Sépia, 1992. Roman.

3639. Ndong Ndoutoume, Tsira. *Le M'vet: l'homme, la mort et l'immortalité.* Paris: L'Harmattan, 1993. Récit.

3640. Nyonda, Vincent de Paul. *Le Combat de Mbombi,* suivi de *Emergence d'une nouvelle société et de Bonjour Bessieux!* Paris: Edition François-Réder, 1987. Théâtre.

3641. ———. *Epopée Mulombi.* Libreville: Editions Multipress, 1987. Théâtre.

3642. ———. *La Mort de Guykafi,* suivi de *Deux albinos à la M'Passa et de Le Soûlard.* Paris: L'Harmattan, 1981. (Coll. Encres noires 11). Théâtre.

3643. ———. *Le Roi Mouanga.* Libreville: Editions Multipress, 1988. Théâtre.

3644. Odounga. *Poèmes.* Libreville: Multipress, 1989. Poésie.

3645. Okoumba-Nkoghe. *Adia: La honte progressive.* Paris: Akpagnon, 1985. Roman.

3646. ———. *La Mouche et la glu.* Paris: Présence Africaine, 1984. Roman.

3647. ———. *Paroles vives écorchées.* Paris: Arcam, 1979. Poésie.

3648. ———. *Rhône-Ogooué.* Paris: Arcam, 1980. Poésie.

3649. ———. *Siana: aube éternelle.* Paris: Arcam, 1982. (Nouvelle édition en 1986 chez Silex, Paris). Roman.

3650. Owondo, Laurent. *Au bout du silence.* Paris: Hatier; CEDA, 1985. (Coll. Monde noir poche, 37). Roman.

3651. ———. *La Folle du gouverneur.* Carnières, Belgique: Lansman, 1990. (Coll. Théâtre à vif, 4). Théâtre.

3652. Godard, Roger. *Pour une lecture du roman «Au bout du silence» de Laurent Owondo.* Sainte-Geneviève-des-Bois: Maison Rhodanienne, 1988.

3653. Rawiri, Georges. *Chants du Gabon.* Paris: EDICEF, 1975. Poésie.

3654. Rawiri, Ntyugwetondo Angèle (F). *Elonga.* Paris: Silex, 1986. Première parution en 1980. Roman.

3655. ———. *Fureurs et cris de femme.* Paris: L'Harmattan, 1989. (Coll. Encres noires, 55). Roman.

3656. ———. *G'amèrakano au carrefour.* Paris: Silex, 1988. Première parution en 1983. Roman.

GUINEA/GUINÉE

Bibliography

3657. "Bibliographie sélective: littérature guinéenne d'expression française." *Notre Librairie,* no. 88-89 (1987): 156-163.

Anthologies

3658. Diadite, Hadji Koutino. *Proverbes, maximes, sentences et citations.* Conakry: INPL, 1986. Proverbes et maximes.

3659. Sow, Alpha Ibrahima. *La Femme, la vache, la foi: écrivains et poètes du Fouta-Djallon.* Paris: A. Colin, 1966. Anthologie.

General studies

3660. Camara, Sory. *Gens de la parole: essai sur la condition et le rôle des griots dans la société malinké.* Conakry; Paris: ACCT, SAEC; Karthala, 1992.

3661. "Littérature guinéenne d'expression française." *Notre Librairie,* no. 88-89 (1987).

Authors

3662. Baldé de Labé, Sirah (F). *D'un Fouta-Djalloo à l'autre.* Paris: La Pensée Universelle, 1985. Roman.

3663. Bangoura, Kiri Di. *La Source d'ébène.* Paris: L'Harmattan, 1991. (Coll. Encres noires, 86). Roman.

3664. Barry, Kesso (F). *Kesso par Kesso Barry, Princesse peuhle.* Paris: Seghers, 1988. Autobiographie.

3665. Camara, Kaba 41. *Sois et lutte.* Conakry: INPL, 1983. Poésie.

3666. Camara, Laye. *Dramouss.* Paris: Plon, 1966. Roman.

3667. ———. *L'Enfant noir.* Paris: Plon, 1953. Roman.

3668. ———. *Le Maître de la parole.* Paris: Plon, 1968. Roman.

3669. ———. *Le Regard du roi.* Paris: Plon, 1954. Roman.

3670. Charrier, Monique. *L'Enfant noir de Camara Laye.* Paris: Hachette, 1980.

3671. Mercier, R. et M. & S. Battestini. *Camara Laye, écrivain guinéen.* Paris: Nathan, 1984. (Coll. Littérature africaine).

3672. Yepri, S. L. *Relire «L'Enfant noir».* Abidjan: Nouvelles Éditions Africaines, 1987.

3673. Camara, Moyamed Mounir. *Le Flambeau incendiaire.* Conakry: IDEC, 1983. Poésie.

3674. Camara, Sikhé. *Clairière dans le ciel.* Paris: Présence Africaine, 1973. Poésie.

3675. Cissé, Ahmed-Tidjani. *Au nom du peuple.* Paris: Nubia, 1991. Théâtre.

3676. ———. *Quand les graines éclosent*. Paris: Nubia, 1983. Poésie.

3677. Cissé, Emile. *Faralako: roman d'un petit village africain*. Rennes: Imprimerie commerciale, 1959. Roman.

3678. Doré, Ansoumane. *Ce sera à l'ombre des cocotiers*. Malakoff: Nouvelles Editions Bayardère, 1987. Roman.

3679. Fantouré, Mohamed Alioum. *Le Cercle des tropiques*. Paris: Présence Africaine, 1972. Roman.

3680. ———. *Le Récit du cirque: de la vallée des morts*. Paris: Buchet-Chastel, 1975. Roman.

3681. ———. *Le Voile ténébreux*. Paris: Présence Africaine, 1985. Roman.

3682. Fodeba, Keïta. *Aube africaine*. Paris: Seghers, 1965. Poésie.

3683. ———. *Poèmes africains*. Paris: Seghers, 1950.

3684. Fodekara, Cherif Aïdra. Le Royaume de Sinaban. Yaoundé: CLE, 1973. Roman.

3685. Kamara, Lamine. *Safrin ou le duel au fouet*. Paris: Présence Africaine & ACCT, 1991. Roman.

3686. Kante, Cheick Oumar. *Après les nuits, les années blanches*. Paris: L'Harmattan, 1993. (Coll. Encres noires, 113). Roman.

3687. ———. *Douze pour une coupe*. Paris: Présence Africaine, 1987. Roman.

3688. ———. *Fatoba, l'archipel mutant*. Paris: L'Harmattan, 1992. (Coll. Encres noires, 85). Roman.

3689. Monénembo, Tierno. *Un Attiéké pour Elgass*. Paris: Seuil, 1992. Roman.

3690. ———. *Les Crapauds-brousse*. Paris: Seuil, 1979. Roman.

3691. ———. *Les Ecailles du ciel*. Paris: Seuil, 1986. Roman.

3692. ———. *Un Rêve utile*. Paris: Seuil, 1991. Roman.

3693. Niane, Djibril Tamsir. *Méry*. Dakar: Nouvelles Editions Africaines, 1975. Nouvelles.

3694. ———. *Soundjata ou l'épopée mandingue*. Paris: Présence Africaine, 1960. Roman.

3695. Sassine, Williams. *L'Alphabète*. Paris: Présence Africaine, 1985. Contes.

3696. ———. *Le Jeune homme de sable*. Paris: Présence Africaine, 1979. Roman.

3697. ———. *Saint Monsieur Baly*. Paris: Présence Africaine, 1973. Roman.

3698. ———. *Wirriyamu*. Paris: Présence Africaine, 1976. Roman.

3699. ———. *Le Zéhéros n'est pas n'importe qui*. Paris: Présence Africaine, 1985. Roman.

3700. Touré, Ahmed Sékou. *Poèmes militants*. Conakry: Imprimerie Nationale Patrice Lumumba, 1972. Poésie.

3701. Traoré, Mamadou Ray Autra. *Vers la liberté*. Pékin: Librairie du Nouveau Monde, 1961. Poésie.

3702. Zoumou, Roger-Goto. *Témoignages éloquents*. Beyrouth: OLP, 1978. Poésie.

GUINEA–BISSAU/GUINÉE–BISSAO

Authors

3703. Nyangoma, Nadine (F). *Le Chant des fusillés*. Dakar: Nouvelles Editions Africaines, 1981. Roman.

3704. ———. *Mourir debout*. Dakar: Nouvelles Editions Africaines, 1983. Roman.

IVORY COAST/CÔTE D'IVOIRE

Bibliography

3705. Rouch, Alain et Michèle Nardi. "Bibliographie (Littérature ivoirienne)." *Notre Librairie*, no. 87 (1987): 159-165.

Anthology

3706. Bandaman, Maurice, et al. *Portrait des siècles meurtris: anthologie de la poésie de Côte-d'Ivoire*. Paris: Nouvelles du Sud, 1993.

General studies

3707. Amon d'Aby, François-Joseph. *Le Théâtre en Côte d'Ivoire: des origines à 1960*. Abidjan: CEDA, 1988.

3708. Krol, Pierre-André. *Avoir 20 ans en Afrique: reportage*. Paris: L'Harmattan, 1994.

3709. "Littérature de Côte d'Ivoire 1: la mémoire et les mots." *Notre Librairie*, no. 86 (1987).

3710. "Littérature de Côte d'Ivoire 2: écrire aujourd' hui." *Notre Librairie*, no. 87 (1987).

Authors

3711. Abondio, Josette D. (F). *Kouassi Koko . . . ma mère*. Abidjan: EDILIS, 1993. Roman.

3712. Adiaffi, Anne Marie (F). *La Ligne brisée*. Abidjan: Nouvelles Editions Africaines, 1989. Roman.

3713. ———. *Une Vie hypothéquée*. Abidjan: Nouvelles Editions Africaines, 1984. Roman.

3714. Adiaffi, Jean-Marie. *La Carte d'identité*. Paris: Hatier, 1980. (Coll. Monde noir poche, 7). Roman.

3715. ———. *Galerie infernale*. Abidjan: CEDA, 1984. Poésie.

3716. ———. *Silence, on développe*. Paris: Nouvelles du Sud, 1992. Roman.

3717. ———. *Yalé Sonan*. Paris: Edition et Promotion, 1969. Poésie.

3718. Aka, Marie-Gisèle (F). *Les Haillons de l'amour*. Abidjan: CEDA, 1994. Roman.

3719. Ake Loba, Gérard. *Kocoumbo, l'étudiant noir*. Paris: Flammarion, 1960. (Nouvelle édition en 1983, coll. J'ai lu). Roman.

3720. ———. *Le Sas des parvenus*. Paris: Flammarion, 1990. Roman.

3721. Akoto, Paul Yaho. *L'Envol des tisserins*. Abidjan: CEDA, 1986. Roman.

3722. Amoi, Assamala (F). *Impasse*. Abidjan: CEDA, 1987. Nouvelles.

3723. Amon d'Aby, François-Joseph. *Entraves*. Abidjan: s.n., 1955. Théâtre.

3724. ———. *Kwao Adjoba*. Paris: Les Paragraphes littéraires, 1956. Théâtre.

3725. ———. *Le Murmure du roi*. Abidjan: Nouvelles Editions Africaines, 1984. Contes.

3726. ———. *Proverbes populaires de Côte-d'Ivoire*. Abidjan: CEDA, 1984. Proverbes.

3727. Anouma, Joseph. *L'Enfer géosynclinal*. Abidjan: CEDA, Nouvelles Editions Africaines; Fraternité Matin, 1985. Poésie.

3728. Assamoua, Michèle (F). *Le Défi.* Abidjan: Nouvelles Editions Africaines, 1984. Nouvelles.

3729. Atta Koffi, Raphaël. *Les Dernières paroles de Koimé.* Paris: Debresse, 1961. Roman.

3730. Bandaman, Maurice. *Une femme pour une médaille.* Abidjan: CEDA, 1987. Nouvelles.

3731. ———. *Le Fils de-la-femme-mâle.* Paris: L'Harmattan, 1993. (Coll. Encres noires, 109). Conte romanesque.

3732. Bassori, Timité. *Les Eaux claires de ma source.* Paris: ORTF; ACCT, 1973. Nouvelle.

3733. Bolli, Fatou (F). *Djigbô.* Abidjan: CEDA, 1977. Roman.

3734. Boni, Tanella Suzanne (F). *De l'autre côté du soleil.* Dakar; Paris: Nouvelles Editions Africaines du Sénégal; EDICEF, 1991. (Coll. NEA-EDICEF Jeunesse). Roman.

3735. ———. *La Fugue d'Ozone.* Dakar; Paris: Nouvelles Editions Africaines du Sénégal; EDICEF, 1992. (Coll. NEA-EDICEF Jeunesse). Roman.

3736. ———. *Labyrinthe.* Dakar: Nouvelles Editions Africaines, 1984. Poésie.

3737. ———. *Une Vie de crabe.* Dakar: Nouvelles Editions Africaines du Sénégal, 1990. Roman.

3738. Bonny, Michel Aka. *Chants et pleurs avant l'aurore.* Nice: Imprimerie la victoire, 1951. Poésie.

3739. Cavally, Jeanne de (F). *Le Réveillon de Boubacar.* Abidjan: Nouvelles Editions Africaines, 1981. Livre pour les enfants. Conte.

3740. Coulibaly, Micheline (F). *Embouteillage.* Abidjan: EDILIS, 1992. (Coll. Ardeurs tropicales). Nouvelles.

3741. Dadié, Bernard Binlin. *Afrique debout!* Paris: Seghers, 1950. Poésie.

3742. ———. *Béatrice du Congo.* Paris: Présence Africaine, 1970. (Nouvelle édition en 1988). Théâtre.

3743. ———. *Carnet de prison.* Abidjan: CEDA, 1981. Autobiographie.

3744. ———. *Climbié.* Paris: Seghers, 1956. Roman.

3745. ———. *Commandant Taureault et ses nègres.* Abidjan: CEDA, 1980. Roman.

3746. ———. *Les Jambes du fils de Dieu.* Paris: Hatier, 1980. (Coll. Monde noir poche, 8). Nouvelles.

3747. ———. *Légendes africaines; Afrique debout (poésie); Climbié (roman); La Ronde des jours (poésie).* Paris: Presses Pocket, 1962. Poésie et roman.

3748. ———. *Un Nègre à Paris.* Paris: Présence Africaine, 1959. (Nouvelle édition en 1984). Roman.

3749. ———. *Patron de New York.* Paris: Présence Africaine, 1964. Roman.

3750. Edebiri, Uniomwan (éd.). *Bernard Dadié: hommages et études.* Ivry-sur-Seine: Nouvelles du Sud; ACCT, 1992.

3751. Kotchy, Barthélémy. *La Critique sociale dans l'œuvre théâtrale de Bernard Dadié.* Paris: L'Harmattan, 1984.

3752. Mercier, Roger et Simon Battestini. *Bernard Dadié.* Paris: Nathan, 1964. (Coll. Littérature africaine, 7).

3753. Quillateau, C. *Bernard Dadié: l'homme et l'œuvre.* Paris: Présence Africaine, 1967.

3754. Vincileoni, Nicole. *Comprendre l'œuvre de Bernard B. Dadié.* Issy-les-Moulineaux: Saint-Paul, 1987.

3755. Dem, Tidiane. *Mariama.* Abidjan: Nouvelles Editions Africaines, 1987. Roman.

3756. ———. *Masseni.* Abidjan: Nouvelles Editions Africaines, 1977. (Nouvelle édition en 1987). Roman.

3757. Deniel, Raymond. *Oui, patron!: boys cuisiniers en Abidjan.* Abidjan; Paris: INADES; Karthala, 1991. Témoignages.

3758. Dervain, Eugène. *Saran ou la Reine scélérate.* Yaoundé: CLE, 1968. Théâtre.

3759. ———. *Termites.* Paris: P. J. Oswald, 1976. Théâtre.

3760. Dodo, Jean Digben. *Le Médiateur.* Abidjan: Nouvelles Editions Africaines, 1984. Roman.

3761. ———. *Wazzi la mousso du forestier.* Abidjan: Nouvelles Editions Africaines, 1977. Roman.

3762. Douteo, Bertin. *La Maison isolée.* Monte-Carlo: Palais Miami, 1963. Poésie.

3763. Duprey de la Ruffinière, Pierre. *CF8Bli, homme pensant.* Paris: Nouvelles Editions Latines, 1948. Roman.

3764. ———. *Le Coupeur de bois.* Paris: Nouvelles Editions Latines, 1946. Roman.

3765. ———. *Le Pyromane apaisé.* Abidjan: Nouvelles Editions Africaines, 1979. Roman.

3766. Fatho-Amoy. *Chaque aurore est une chance.* Abidjan: CEDA, 1980. Poésie.

3767. Hazoumé, Flore (F). *Cauchemars.* Abidjan: EDILIS, 1994. (Coll. Découvertes). Nouvelles.

3768. ———. *Rencontres.* Abidjan: Nouvelles Editions Africaines, 1984. Nouvelles.

3769. Kakou Oklomin (F). *Okouossai ou le mal de mère.* Abidjan: CEDA, 1984. Roman.

3770. Kaya, Simone (F). *Les Danseuses d'impé-eya, jeunes filles à Abidjan.* Abidjan: INADES, 1976. Autobiographie.

3771. ———. *Le Prix d'une vie.* Abidjan: CEDA, 1984. Roman.

3772. Koné, Amadou. *Les Canaris sont vides.* Abidjan: Nouvelles Editions Africaines, 1984. Théâtre.

3773. ———. *Les Frasques d'Ebinto.* Paris: La Pensée Universelle, 1975. (Nouvelle édition en 1980 chez Hatier, Coll. Monde noir poche, 3). Roman.

3774. ———. *Liens.* Abidjan: CEDA, 1980. Nouvelles.

3775. ———. *Sous le pouvoir de Blakoros I: Traites.* Abidjan: Nouvelles Editions Africaines, 1980. Roman.

3776. ———. *Sous le pouvoir de Blakoros II: Courses.* Abidjan: Nouvelles Editions Africaines, 1981. Roman.

3777. Koné, Maurice. *La Guirlande des verbes.* Paris: Edition Jean Grassin, 1961. Poésie.

3778. ———. *Le Jeune homme de Bouaké.* Paris: Edition Jean Grassin, 1962. Roman.

3779. Kouadio, Akissi (F). *Un Impossible amour: une Ivoirienne raconte.* Abidjan: INADES, 1983. Autobiographie.

3780. Kouame Koffi, Eugène Pacelli. *Empreintes, griffes poétiques.* Abidjan: Imprimerie Commerciale, 1971. Poésie.

3781. Koulibaly, Isaïe Biton. *Ah! les femmes.* Lomé: Haho, 1987. Nouvelles.

3782. ———. *Ah! les hommes . . .* Lomé: Haho, 1991. Nouvelles.

3783. ———. *Les Deux amis*. Abidjan: Nouvelles Editions Africaines, 1978. Nouvelles.

3784. ———. *Le Domestique du président*. Abidjan: CEDA, 1981. Roman.

3785. ———. *Les Leçons d'amour de ma meilleure amie*. Abidjan: Bognini, 1991. Nouvelles.

3786. Kourouma, Ahmadou. *Monnè: outrages et défis*. Paris: Seuil, 1990. (Nouvelle édition en 1992 dans la coll. Points roman, 513). Roman.

3787. ———. *Les Soleils des indépendances*. Montréal: Presses Universitaires, 1968. (Nouvelle édition en 1990 chez Seuil, coll. Points, R 419). Roman.

3788. *Essai sur Les Soleils des indépendances d'Ahmadou Kourouma*. Abidjan: Nouvelles Éditions Africaines, 1985. Séminaire de l'ILENA, 1978.

3789. Jeusse, Marie-Paule. *Les Soleils des indépendances d'Ahmadou Kourouma*. Abidjan; Paris: Nouvelles Editions Africaines; Nathan, 1984. (Coll. Une œuvre, un auteur).

3790. Ngandu Nkashama, Pius. *Kourouma et le mythe: une lecture de Le Soleil des indépendances*. Paris: Silex, 1985.

3791. Nicolas, Jean-Claude. *Comprendre Les Soleils des indépendances d'Ahmadou Kourouma*. Issy-les-Moulineaux: Saint-Paul, 1986. (Coll. Classiques africains).

3792. Kumassi Brou, Grégoire. *Tiziu*. Abidjan: Imprimerie Nationale, 1983. Poésie.

3793. Nokan, Zégoua Gbessi Charles. *Le Matin sera rouge*. Yaoundé: CLE, 1984. Roman.

3794. ———. *Mon chemin débouche sur la grand' route*. Abidjan: CEDA, 1985. Roman.

3795. ———. *Les Petites rivières*. Abidjan: CEDA, 1983. Roman.

3796. ———. *Le Soleil noir point.* Paris: Présence Africaine, 1962. Théâtre.

3797. ———. *Violent était le vent.* Paris: Présence Africaine, 1966. Roman.

3798. Otitro. *Un Douloureux plaisir.* Abidjan: CEDA, 1984. Roman.

3799. Ouassenan, Gaston Koné. *L'Empire du gouffre.* Abidjan: CEDA, 1990. (Coll. CEDA Fiction). Roman.

3800. ———. *L'Homme qui vécut trois vies.* Issy-les-Moulineaux: Saint-Paul, 1976. Roman.

3801. Oussou-Essui, Denis. *Les Saisons sèches.* Paris: l'Harmattan, 1979. (Coll. Encres noires, 2). Roman.

3802. ———. *La Souche calcinée.* Yaoundé: CLE, 1973. Roman.

3803. ———. *Vers de nouveaux horizons.* Paris: Le Scorpion, 1965. Roman.

3804. Tadjo, Véronique (F). *A vol d'oiseau.* Paris: Nathan, 1986. (Nouvelle édition en 1992 chez l'Harmattan, coll. Encres noires, 105). Roman.

3805. ———. *La Chanson de la vie.* Paris: Hatier, 1989. (Coll. Monde noir jeunesse). Histoires pour les enfants et poésie.

3806. ———. *Latérite.* Paris: Hatier, 1984. (Coll. Monde noir poche, 24). Poésie.

3807. ———. *Le Royaume aveugle.* Paris: L'Harmattan, 1990. (Coll. Encres noires, 80). Roman.

3808. Tiémélé, Jean-Baptiste. *Aoyu,* suivi de *Yaley.* Paris: Silex, 1987. Poésie.

3809. Yaou, Regina (F). *Aihui Anka.* Abidjan: Nouvelles Editions Africaines, 1988. Roman.

3810. ———. *Lezou Marie ou les écueils de la vie.*
Dakar; Abidjan: Nouvelles Editions Africaines; EDICEF,
1982. (Coll. Jeunesse). Roman.

3811. ———. *La Révolte d'Affiba.* Abidjan: Nouvelles
Editions Africaines, 1985. Roman.

3812. Zadi Zaourou, Bernard. *Césarienne.* Abidjan:
CEDA, 1984. Poésie.

3813. Zirignon, Grobli. *Dispersions.* Paris: Silex, 1982.
Poésie.

MALI

Bibliographies

3814. Ba Konaré, Adame. *Dictionnaire des femmes
célèbres du Mali des temps mytico-légendaires au 26 mars
1991.* Bamako: Jamana, 1993. Le prénom de Madame Ba
Konaré est orthographié Adam sur la page de couverture.

3815. "Bibliographie." *Notre Librairie,* no. 75-76
(1989): 229-242.

Anthologies

3816. *Le Théâtre populaire en Côte-d'Ivoire: œuvres
choisies.* Abidjan: Centre culturel et folklorique de Côte-
d'Ivoire, 1965.

3817. Traoré, Issa Falaba. *Contes et récits du terroir.*
Bamako: Editions populaires, 1970.

3818. Travele, Moussa. *Proverbes et contes bambara.*
Paris: Geuthner, 1923. Bilingue bambara-français. Nouvelle
édition en 1977.

General studies

3819. *La Geste de Ségou racontée par les griots
bambara.* Paris: Armand Colin, 1971. Edition bilingue,
traduite en français et éditée par Gérard Dumestre. Récit.

3820. *Initiation à la linguistique africaine par les langues du Mali.* Paris: Karthala, 1980.

3821. Kesteloot, Lilyan. *L'Epopée bambara de Ségou.* Paris: L'Harmattan, 1993. 2 v. Avec la collaboration de Amadou Traoré, Jean-Baptiste Traoré et Amadou Hampâté Bâ. Reprend en partie des épisodes de L'Epopée bambara publiées chez A. Colin, 1975 et Nathan, 1972.

3822. "Littérature malienne." *Notre Librairie,* no. 75-76 (1989).

Authors

3823. Ascofare, Abdoulaye. *Domestiquer les rêves.* Bamako: Editions populaires, 1976. Poésie.

3824. Bâ, Amadou Hampâté. *Amkoullel, l'enfant peul.* Paris: Actes Sud, 1991. Mémoires.

3825. ———. *L'Eclat de la grande étoile.* Paris: A. Colin, 1974. (Coll. Classiques Africains, 15). Roman.

3826. ———. *L'Etrange destin de Wangrin.* Paris: Union Générale d'Editions, 1973. (Coll. 10/18. Nouveau tirage en 1991 contenant la postface livrée par l'auteur en 1986). Biographie.

3827. ———. *Kaïdara: récit initiatique peul.* Paris: Julliard, 1968. (Coll. Classiques africains, 7, en collaboration avec Lilyan Kesteloot). Sous le titre *Kaydara* nouvelle édition en 1978 d'une version légèrement modifiée chez les Nouvelles Editions Africaines, Dakar. Récit.

3828. ———. *Koumen: texte initiatique des pasteurs peuls.* s.l.: Mouton, 1961. En collaboration avec G. Dieterlen. Récit.

3829. ———. *Njeddo Dewal: mère de la calamité.* Dakar: Nouvelles Editions Africaines, 1985. Récit.

3830. ———. *Petit Bodiel et autres contes de la savane.* Paris: Stock, 1994. Nouvelles.

3831. ——. *La Poignée de poussière: contes et récits du Mali.* Dakar: Nouvelles Éditions Africaines, 1987. Contes.

3832. Devey, Muriel. *Hampâté Bâ: l'homme de la tradition.* Lomé, Dakar; Paris: Nouvelles Editions Africaines du Togo, du Sénégal; Livre Sud, 1993. Biographie.

3833. Jouanny, Robert (éd.). *Lectures de l'œuvre de Hampâté Bâ.* Paris: L'Harmattan, 1992. (Coll. Critiques littéraires). Actes de la journée d'études organisée à la Sorbonne le 6 décembre 1991.

3834. Ngorwanubusa, Juvénal. *Boubou Hama et Amadou Hampâté Bâ: la négritude des sources.* Paris: Publisud; ACCT, 1993. (Coll. Littératures; Traverses des espaces francophones).

3835. Werewere Liking (F). *Une vision de Kaydara d'Hamadou-Hampaté-Ba.* Abidjan: Nouvelles Editions Africaines, 1984.

3836. Badian, Seydou. *Les Dirigeants d'Afrique noire face à leur peuple.* Paris: F. Maspéro, 1964. (Coll. Cahiers libres, 65). Essai.

3837. ——. *Noces sacrées: les Dieux de Kouroulamini.* Paris: Présence Africaine, 1977. Roman.

3838. ——. *Le Sang des masques.* Paris: Laffont, 1976. Roman.

3839. ——. *Sous l'orage.* Avignon: Les Presses Universelles, 1957. (Nouvelle édition en 1973, suivi de La Mort de Chaka (théâtre) chez Présence Africaine, Paris). Roman et théâtre.

3840. Battestini, M. et S. *Seydou Badian.* Paris: Nathan, 1968. (Coll. Classiques du monde. Littérature africaine, 10).

3841. Tsoungui, Françoise. *Comprendre 'Sous l'orage' de Seydou Badian.* Issy-les-Moulineaux: Saint-Paul, 1985. (Coll. Classiques africains).

3842. Bokoum, Saïdou. *Chaîne: une descente aux enfers.* Paris: Denoël, 1974. Témoignage.

3843. Cissé, Youssouf Tata et Wâ Kamissoko. *Soundjata: la gloire du Mali.* Paris: Karthala; Arsan, 1991. Fait suite à *La Grande geste du Mali* transmise par Wâ Kamissoko. Biographie.

3844. Cissoko, Siriman. *Ressac de nous-mêmes.* Paris: Présence Africaine, 1967. Poésie.

3845. Dembele, Nagognimé Urbain. *L'Inceste et le parricide.* Bamako: Imprimeries du Mali, 1982. Roman.

3846. ———. *Tchagoua, né d'un défunt.* Bamako: Editions populaires du Mali, 1978. Roman.

3847. Dembele, Sidiki. *Les Inutiles.* Monte-Carlo: Regain, 1960. (Nouvelle édition en 1985 chez Les Nouvelles Editions Africaines, Dakar). Roman.

3848. Diabaté, Massa Makan. *L'Assemblée des Djinns.* Paris: Présence Africaine, 1985. Roman.

3849. ———. *Le Boucher de Kouta.* Paris: Hatier, 1982. (Coll. Monde noir poche, 15). Roman.

3850. ———. *Le Coiffeur de Kouta.* Paris: Hatier, 1980. (Coll. Monde noir poche, 2). Roman.

3851. ———. *Comme une piqure de guêpe.* Paris: Présence Africaine, 1980. Roman.

3852. ———. *Le Lieutenant de Kouta.* Paris: Hatier, 1979. (Coll. Monde noir poche, 23). Roman.

3853. Diallo, Georges. *La Nuit du destin: le cheminement d'un jeune Africain et d'une Européenne.* Paris: Casterman, 1969. Récit.

3854. Diawara, Gaoussou. *L'Aube des béliers.* Paris: Radio France Internationale, 1975. Théâtre.

3855 Fofana, Aïcha. (F) *Mariage, on copie.* Bamako: Jamana, 1994. Roman.

3856. Gologo, Mamadou. *Le Rescapé de l'Ethylos.* Paris: Présence Africaine, 1963. Roman.

3857. Issébéré, Hamadoun Ibrahima. *Clameurs d'antan et soleils présents.* Dakar: Nouvelles Editions Africaines, 1980. Poésie.

3858. Kaba, Alkaly. *Nègres, qu'avez-vous fait?* Bamako: Editions populaires du Mali, 1972. Théâtre.

3859. ———. *Walenda; la leçon.* Paris: Saint-Germain-des Prés, 1976. Récit.

3860. Kéita, Aoua (F). *Femme d'Afrique: la vie d'Aoua Kéita racontée par elle-même.* Paris: Présence Africaine, 1975. Autobiographie.

3861. Keita, Modibo S. *L'Archer bassari.* Paris: Karthala, 1984. Roman.

3862. Konaté, Moussa. *Une Aube incertaine.* Paris: Présence Africaine, 1985. Roman.

3863. ———. *Chronique d'une journée de répression.* Paris: L'Harmattan, 1988. (Coll. Encres noires, 47). Roman.

3864. ———. *Fils du chaos.* Paris: L'Harmattan, 1986. (Coll. Encres noires, 37). Roman.

3865. ———. *Le Prix de l'âme.* Paris: Présence Africaine, 1981. Roman.

3866. Ly, Ibrahima. *Les Noctuelles vivent de larmes: 1. ténèbres blanches.* Paris: L'Harmattan, 1988. (Coll. Encres noires, 50). Roman.

3867. ———. *Toiles d'araignées.* Paris: L'Harmattan, 1982. (Coll. Encres noires, 16). Roman.

3868. *Paroles pour un continent: la vie et l'œuvre d'Ibrahima Ly.* Paris: L'Harmattam, 1990. Extraits du brouillon du second volume des *Noctuelles vivent de larmes* et témoignages de ses amis et de ses proches.

3869. Ouane, Ibrahima Mamadou. *L'Enigme du Macina.* Monte-Carlo: Regain, 1952. Roman.

3870. ———. *Fâdimâtâ la princesse du désert,* suivi de *Drame de Déguembéré.* Avignon: Les Presses Universelles, 1955. Roman.

3871. ———. *Les Filles de la reine Cléopâtre.* Paris: Les Paragraphes littéraires, 1961.

3872. ———. *Lettres d'un Africain.* Monte-Carlo: Regain, 1955. Récit.

3873. ———. *Pérégrinations soudanaises.* Lyon: Editions du Capricorne et du Lion, 1960. Poésie.

3874. Ouologuem, Yambo. *Le Devoir de violence.* Paris: Seuil, 1968. Roman.

3875. ———. *Les Mille et une bibles du sexe.* Paris: Edition du dauphin, 1969. (Publié sous le pseudonyme d'Utto Rodolph). Roman.

3876. Sagara, A. *Légendes du Mali.* Bamako: Jamana, 1990. Légendes.

3877. Sangare, Yadji. *Naïssa.* Bamako: Editions populaires, 1972. Roman.

3878. Sidibe, Mamby. *Contes populaires du Mali.* Paris: Présence Africaine, 1982. (2 v). Contes et légendes.

3879. Sissoko, Fily Dabo. *Les Jeux du destin.* Paris: J. Grassin, 1970. Poésie.

3880. ———. *Sagesse noire: sentences et proverbes malinkés.* Paris: La Tour du Guet, 1955. Proverbes.

3881. Traoré, Ismaïla Samba. *Les Ruchers de la capitale.* Paris: L'Harmattan, 1982. (Coll. Encre noires, 19). Roman.

3882. Traoré, Issa Baba. *L'Ombre du passé*. Bamako: Editions populaires, 1972. Roman.

3883. Traoré, Seydou. *Vingt-cinq ans d'escaliers ou la vie d'un planton*. Dakar: Nouvelles Editions Africaines, 1975. (Coll. Vies africaines). Témoignage.

MAURITANIA/MAURITANIE

Anthology

3884. Martin Granel, Nicolas, Idoumou Ould Mohamed Lemine et Georges Voisset. *Guide de la littérature mauritanienne: une anthologie méthodique*. Paris: L'Harmattan, 1993.

General studies

3885. Belvaude, Catherine. *Ouverture sur la littérature en Mauritanie: tradition orale, écriture, témoignages*. Paris: L'Harmattan, 1989.

Authors

3886. Bâ, Amadou Oumar. *Les Mystères du Bani, roman soudanais*. Monte-Carlo: Regain, 1960. Roman.

3887. ———. *Presque griffonnages sur la francophonie*. Dakar: IFAN, 1966. Poésie.

3888. Diagana, Ousmane Moussa. "La Légende du Wagandu vue par Sia Yatabere (théâtre)." *Théâtre Sud*, no. 1 (1990).

3889. Gueye, Téné Youssouf. *A l'Orée du Sahel*. Dakar: Nouvelles Editions Africaines, 1975. Nouvelles.

3890. ———. *Rellâ ou les voies de l'honneur*. Dakar: Nouvelles Editions Africaines, 1983. Nouvelles.

3891. Ould Ebnou, Moussa. *L'Amour impossible*. Paris: L'Harmattan, 1990. (Coll. Encres noires, 63). Roman.

3892. ———. *Barzakh.* Paris: L'Harmattan, 1994. Conte.

3893. Sall, Djibril. *Cimetière rectiligne.* Nouakchott: Société Nationale de Presse et d'Edition, 1978. Poésie.

NIGER

Bibliographies

3894. "Auteurs nigériens." *Notre Librairie,* no. 107 (1991): 186-190.

3895. Dan-Inna, Chaïbou et Jean-Dominique Penel. *Bibliographie de la littérature nigérienne.* Niamey: Imprimerie nationale du Niger, 1988.

General studies

3896. "Littérature nigérienne." *Notre Librairie,* no. 107 (1991).

3897. Penel, Jean-Dominique et Amadou Mailele. *Rencontre: littérature nigérienne.* Niamey: Editions du Ténéré, 1990. 3 v.

Authors

3898. Ada, Boureima. *Le Baiser amer de la faim.* Niamey: Imprimerie nationale du Niger, n.d. Roman.

3899. Adamou, Idé. *La Camisole de paille.* Niamey: Imprimerie nationale du Niger, 1987. Roman.

3900. ———. *Cri inachevé.* Niamey: Imprimerie nationale du Niger, 1984. Poésie.

3901. Amadou, Ousmane. *Chroniques judiciaires.* Niamey: Imprimerie nationale du Niger, 1987. Nouvelles.

3902. ———. *Le Nouveau juge.* Dakar: Nouvelles Editions Africaines, 1981. Roman.

3903. ———. *Quinze ans ça suffit.* Dakar: Nouvelles Editions Africaines, 1977. Roman.

3904. Diado, Amadou. *Maïmou ou le drame de l'amour.* Niamey: Editions du Niger, 1972. Roman suivi de poésie.

3905. Diallo, Amadou Hassana. *Moisson de ma jeunesse.* Niamey: Imprimerie nationale du Niger, 1981. Récit.

3906. Ebokea, Marie-Félicité (F). *Femmes fragmentées.* Paris: L'Harmattan, 1994. (Inclue, la nouvelle «Baby rose»). Nouvelles.

3907. Halilou Sabbo, Mahamadou. *Abboki ou L'Appel de la côte.* Dakar: Nouvelles Editions Africaines, 1978. Roman.

3908. ———. *Caprices du destin.* Niamey: Imprimerie nationale du Niger, 1981. Roman.

3909. ———. *Gomma, adorable Gomma.* Niamey: Sahel Hebdo, 1990. Nouvelle.

3910. Hama, Boubou. *Bagouma et Tiégouma.* Paris: Présence Africaine, 1973. 2 v. Récit.

3911. ———. *Contes et légendes du Niger.* Paris: Présence Africaine, 1976. 6 v. Contes.

3912. ———. *Le Double d'hier rencontre demain.* Paris: Union Générale d'Editions, 1973. (Coll. 10/18). Récit.

3913. ———. *La Force du lait.* Niamey: Imprimerie nationale du Niger, 1971. Théâtre.

3914. ———. *Izé-Ghani.* Paris: Présence Africaine, 1985. (2 v. coll. Jeunesse). Contes.

3915. ———. *Kotia-Nima.* Paris: Présence Africaine, 1969. 3 v. Mémoires.

3916. ———. *Taabi-Too: contes et légendes du Niger.* Abidjan: Nouvelles Editions Africaines, 1989. Contes.

3917. Ngorwanubusa, Juvénal. *Boubou Hama et Amadou Hampâté Bâ: la négritude des sources.* Paris: Publisud; ACCT, 1993. (Coll. Littératures; Traverses des espaces francophones).

3918. Hamani, Alassane Fatouma (F). *Fleurs confisquées et autres nouvelles.* Niamey: CCFN, 1992. Nouvelles.

3919. Hawad. *Caravane de la soif.* Aix-en-Provence: Edisud, 1985. (Traduit du touareg en français). Poésie.

3920. ———. *Chants de la soif et de l'égarement.* Aix-en-Provence: Edisud, 1987. Traduit du touareg en français. Poésie.

3921. ———. *Froissevent.* Paris: Noël Blandin, 1991. (Traduit du touareg en français). Roman.

3922. ———. *Testament nomade.* Paris: Sillages, 1988. (Traduit du touareg en français. Nouvelle édition en 1991 chez Blandin, Paris). Poésie.

3923. ———. *Yasida.* Paris: Noël Blandin, 1991. Traduit du touareg en français par Hélène Claudot. Roman.

3924. Idé, Oumarou. *Gros plan.* Dakar: Nouvelles Editions Africaines, 1977. Roman.

3925. ———. *Le Représentant.* Abidjan: Nouvelles Editions Africaines, 1984. Roman.

3926. Kanta, Abdoua. *Le Déraciné.* Paris: UNESCO 1972. Nouvelle.

3927. ———. *Halimatou.* Paris: Hatier, 1987. (Coll. Jeunesse). Repris d'une nouvelle du même auteur publiée en 1973 sous le titre L'Aînée de la famille par Radio-France. Nouvelle.

3928. Maïga, Kangaï Seyni, Moussa Mahamadou et Salif Dago. *La Calebasse renversée.* Paris: L'Harmattan, 1992. (Coll. Encres noires, 102). Nouvelles.

3929. Mamani, Abdoulaye. *Le Balai*. Paris: Radio-France, 1973. Théâtre.

3930. ———. *Œuvres poétiques*. Paris: L'Harmattan, 1993. (Coll. Poètes des cinq continents). Poésie.

3931. ———. *Poémérides*. Paris: P. J. Oswald, 1972. Poésie.

3932. ———. *Sarraounia*. Paris: L'Harmattan, 1980. (Coll. Encres noires, 4). Roman.

3933. Mariko, Kélétégui Abdourahmane. *Souvenirs de la boucle du Niger*. Dakar: Nouvelles Editions Africaines, 1980. Roman.

3934. ———. *Sur les rives du fleuve Niger, contes sahéliens*. Paris: Kathala, 1984. Contes.

3935. Mayaki, Djibo. *Aoua*. s.l.: s.n., 1965. Théâtre.

3936. ———. *L'option*. s.l.: s.n., 1985. Scénario.

3937. ———. *La Paille*. s.l.: s.n., 1983. Théâtre.

3938. Naybis Waali, Mohammadou. *Kaara karaatu*. Niamey: Centre d'études linguistiques et historiques par tradition orale, 1970.

3939. Ousmane, Amadou. *L'Honneur perdu*. Niamey: Nouvelles Imprimeries du Niger, 1993. Roman.

3940. Salifou, André. *Le Fils de Sogolon*. Niamey: Edition Issa Béri, 1985. Théâtre.

3941. Say, Bania Mahamadou. *Le Voyage d'Hamado*. Dakar; Paris: Nouvelles Editions Africaines; EDICEF, 1982. (Coll. Jeunesse). Roman.

3942. Soli, Abdourahamane. *Le Chemin du pélerin*. Niamey: Imprimeries du Niger, 1988. Récit.

3943. Yacou, Soumaïla Karanta. *Harandan*. Niamey: INDRAP, 1980. Poésie.

3944. Zoumé, Boubé. *Les Souffles du cœur.* Yaoundé: CLE, 1977. Poésie.

NIGERIA

Author

3945. Ugochukwu, Françoise (F). *Une Poussière d'or.* Paris: EDICEF 1987. Roman pour les jeunes.

RWANDA

Anthologies

3946. Gasarabwe, Edouard. *Contes du Rwanda: soirée au pays des mille collines.* Paris: L'Harmattan, 1988. (Coll. La Légende des mondes). Contes.

3947. ———. *Kibiribiri: l'oiseau de pluie.* Paris: L'Harmattan, 1991. Contes.

Authors

3948. Muamini, Thérèse (F) et Nadine Bitner (F). *Mon Fils mon amour.* Paris: Ramsay, 1995. Témoignage.

3949. Naigiziki, J. Saverio. *Mes Transes à trente ans: tome 1: de mal en pis.* Butare: Astrida, groupe scolaire, 1955. Roman.

3950. ———. *Mes Transes à trente ans: tome 2: de pis en mieux.* Butare: Astrida, groupe scolaire, 1955. Roman.

3951. ———. *L'Optimiste.* Butare: Astrida, groupe scolaire, 1954. (Nouvelle édition chez Kraus Reprint, 1977). Théâtre.

3952. Ntirushwa, Joseph. *Légitime vengeance.* Paris: La Pensée Universelle, 1983. Théâtre.

3953. ———. *Raison d'Etat.* Kigali: chez l'auteur, 1975. Roman.

3954. Rugamba, Cyprian. *La Bataille de frontière.* Butare: Institut national de recherche scientifique, 1985. Théâtre.

3955. ———. *La Nativité.* Butare: Institut national de recherche scientifique, 1987. Théâtre.

SENEGAL/SÉNÉGAL

Bibliography

3956. Ndiaye, Raphaël. "Bibliographie de la littérature sénégalaise écrite." *Notre Librairie,* no. 81 (1989): 171-179.

Anthologies

3957. Bonn, Gisela. *Le Sénégal écrit: anthologie de la littérature sénégalaise d'expression française.* Tübingen: Erdmann, 1976.

3958. Kesteloot, Lilyan et Cherif Mbodj. *Contes et mythes wolof.* Dakar: Nouvelles Editions Africaines, 1983. (Tome 2 Kesteloot et Bassirou Dieng, en 1989).

General studies

3959. Blair, Dorothy S. *Senegalese literature: a critical history.* Boston: Twayne, 1984.

3960. Coulon, Christian. *Le Marabout et le prince: Islam et pouvoir au Sénégal.* Paris: Pedone, 1981.

3961. Diop, Alioune. *Le Théâtre traditionnel au Sénégal.* Dakar: Nouvelles Editions Africaines du Sénégal, 1990.

3962. Dumont, Pierre. *Le Français et les langues africaines au Sénégal.* Paris: Karthala, 1983.

3963. Glinga, Werner. *Literatur in Senegal: Geschichte, Mythos und gesellschaftliches Ideal in der oralen und schriftlichen Literatur.* Berlin: Dietrich Reimer Verlag, 1990.

3964. "Littérature sénégalaise." *Notre Librairie,* no. 81 (1989).

3965. Sall, Babacar. *Poésie du Sénégal.* Paris: Silex 1988.

Authors

3966. Bâ, Mariama (F). *Un Chant écarlate.* Dakar: Nouvelles Editions Africaines, 1981. Roman.

3967. ———. *Une si longue lettre.* Dakar: Nouvelles Editions Africaines, 1979. Roman.

3968. Grésillon, Marie. *Une si longue lettre de Mariama Bâ: étude.* Issy-les Moulineaux: Saint-Paul, 1986. (Coll. Classiques africains, 831).

3969. Badiane, Cheikh. *Aïda-Mbène ou les fantasmes de Mor Diop.* Dakar: Nouvelles Editions Africaines, 1982. Roman.

3970. Benga, Sokhna (F). *Le Dard du secret.* Dakar: Khoudia, 1990. (Coll. Roman, 1). Roman.

3971. Boilat, Abbé David. *Esquisses sénégalaises.* Karthala: Paris, 1984. (Première édition: Paris: s.n., 1853). Témoignage.

3972. Cornevin, R. et Y. Bouquillon. *David Boilat le précurseur.* Dakar: Nouvelles Editions Africaines, 1981.

3973. Carrère, Charles. *Mémoires de la pluie.* Luxembourg: Euro-Editor, 1983. Poésie.

3974. Cissokho, Aïssatou (F). *Dakar, la touriste autochtone.* Paris: L'Harmattan, 1986. (Coll. Encres noires, 42). Roman.

3975. Dia, Amadou Cissé. *La Mort du Damel.* Paris: 1947. (Nouvelle édition en 1965 et 1978, précédé de *Les Derniers jours de Lat-Dior*, chez Présence Africaine Paris). Théâtre.

3976. Diagne, Amadou Mapaté. *Les Trois volontés de Malick*. Paris: Larose, 1920. Conte.

3977. Diakhaté, Lamine. *Chalys d'Harlem*. Dakar: Nouvelles Editions Africaines, 1978. Roman.

3978. ———. *Le Sahélien de Lagos*. Dakar: Nouvelles Editions Africaines, 1984. Roman.

3979. ———. *Terres médianes*. Paris: Saint-Germain-des-Prés, 1984. Poésie.

3980. Diallo, Bakary. *Force-bonté*. Paris: Rieder, 1926. (Nouvelle édition en 1985 chez les Nouvelles Editions Africaines, Dakar). Roman.

3981. Diallo, Nafissatou (F). *Awa la petite marchande*. Dakar; Paris: Nouvelles Editions Africaines; EDICEF, 1981. (Coll. Jeunesse). Roman.

3982. ———. *De Tilène au Plateau: une enfance dakaroise*. Dakar: Nouvelles Editions Africaines, 1975. Autobiographie.

3983. ———. *Le Fort maudit*. Paris: Hatier, 1980. (Coll. Monde noir poche, 6). Roman.

3984. ———. *La Princesse de Tiali*. Dakar: Nouvelles Editions Africaines, 1987. Roman. (Publié sous le nom de Nafissatou Niang Diallo).

3985. Diam, Aïssatou (F). *Mélissa mon amour*. Paris: Edition Africa, 1991. (Coll. Plaisir d'Afrique, 1). Roman.

3986. Diaw, Mohamed Lamine. *Foudre noire: poèmes*. Dakar: Khoudia, 1990. (Coll. Poésie, 2). Poésie.

3987. Diop, Birago. *A Rebrousse-gens: épissures, entrelacs et reliefs: mémoires 3*. Paris: Présence Africaine, 1982. Mémoires.

3988. ———. *A Rebrousse-temps: mémoires 2*. Paris: Présence Africaine, 1982. Mémoires.

3989. ———. *Les Contes d'Amadou Koumba*. Paris: Fasquelle, 1947. (Nouvelle édition en 1961 chez Présence Africaine, Paris). Contes.

3990. ———. *Les Contes d'Awa*. Dakar: Nouvelles Editions Africaines, 1977. Contes.

3991. ———. *Contes et lavanes*. Paris: Présence Africaine, 1963. (Nouvelle édition en 1980 chez les Nouvelles Editions Africaines, Dakar).

3992. ———. *De mon temps: mémoires 4*. Paris: Présence Africaine, 1982. Mémoires.

3993. ———. *Et les yeux pour me dire: mémoires 5*. Paris: L'Harmattan, 1989. (Coll. Mémoires africaines: Sénégal). Mémoires.

3994. ———. *La Plume raboutée: mémoires 1*. Paris: Présence Africaine, 1978. Mémoires.

3995. Kane, Mohamadou. *Birago Diop: l'homme et l'œuvre*. Paris: Présence Africaine, 1971.

3996. Mercier, Roger et Simon Battestini. *Birago Diop, écrivain sénégalais*. Paris: Nathan, 1964. (Coll. Littérature africaine, 6).

3997. Mouralis, Bernard. *Les Contes d'Amadou Koumba de Birago Diop*. Paris: Bertrand Lacoste, 1991. (Coll. Parcours de lecture, 24).

3998. Diop, Boubacar Boris. *Les Tambours de la mémoire*. Paris: Nathan, 1988. (Coll. Espace sud). Roman.

3999. ———. *Le Temps de Tamango* (roman), suivi de *Thiaroye terre rouge (théâtre)*. Paris: L'Harmattan, 1981. (Coll. Encres noires, 13). Roman et Théâtre.

4000. ———. *Les Traces de la meute*. Paris: L'Harmattan, 1994. (Coll. Encres noires, 120). Roman.

4001. Diop, David Mandessi. *Coups de pilon*. Paris: Présence Africaine, 1956. (Nouvelle édition en 1980). Poésie.

4002. Diop, Massyla. *Les Chemins du salut*. Paris: s.n., 1923. Récit.

4003. ———. *Le Réprouvé*. Paris: s.n., 1912. Récit.

4004. Diop, Meissa (F) et Guy Franquet. *Pa'gauloises*. Paris: Flammarion, 1991.

4005. Diop, Mouhamadou Moukhtar. *La Prédiction*. Dakar: Khoudia, 1991. (Coll. Roman, 3). Roman.

4006. Diop, Ousmane Socé. *Contes et légendes d'Afrique noire*. Dakar: Gensul et Garcin, 1942. Contes.

4007. ———. *Karim: roman sénégalais*. Paris: Nouvelles Editions Latines, 1935. Roman.

4008. ———. *Mirages de Paris*. Paris: Nouvelles Editions Latines, 1937. Roman.

4009. Diouri, Aïcha (F). *La Mauvaise passe*. Dakar: Khoudia, 1990. (Coll. Fruits verts, 1). Roman.

4010. Doumbi-Fakoly. *Certificat de contrôle anti-sida*. Paris: Publisud, 1988. (Coll. L'Espace de la parole). Roman.

4011. ———. *Morts pour la France*. Paris: Karthala, 1983. (Coll. Lettres du Sud). Roman.

4012. ———. *La Retraite anticipée du Guide suprême*. Paris: L'Harmattan, 1984. (Coll. Encres noires, 27). Roman.

4013. ———. *La Révolte des Galsénésiennes*. Paris: Publisud, 1991. (Coll. Littératures). Roman.

4014. Fall, Khadi (F). *Mademba*. Paris: L'Harmattan, 1989. (Coll. Encres noires, 59). Roman.

4015. ———. *Senteurs d'hivernage*. Paris: L'Harmattan, 1992. (Coll. Encres noires, 98). Roman.

4016. Fall, Kiné Kirama (F). *Chant de la rivière fraîche*. Dakar: Nouvelles Editions Africaines, 1975. Poésie.

4017. Fall, Malick. *Reliefs*. Paris: Présence Africaine, 1964. Poésie.

4018. Kane, Abdoulaye Elimane. *La Maison du figuier*. Dakar: Nouvelles Editions Africaines du Sénégal, 1992. Roman.

4019. Kane, Cheikh Hamidou. *L'Aventure ambiguë*. Paris: Julliard, 1961. (Nouvelle édition en 1972 chez UEG dans la coll. 10/18). Roman.

4020. Getrey, Jean. *Comprendre L'Aventure ambiguë*. Issy-les-Moulineaux: Saint-Paul, 1982. (Coll. Classiques africains).

4021. Mercier, Roger et Simon Battestini. *Cheikh Amidou Kane, écrivain sénégalais*. Paris: Nathan, 1964. (Coll. Littérature africaine, 1).

4022. Kébé, M'baye Gana. *Ebéniques*. Dakar: Nouvelles Editions Africaines, 1975. Poésie.

4023. Ken Bugul (F). *Le Baobab fou*. Dakar: Nouvelles Editions Africaines, 1982. Autobiographie.

4024. ———. *Cendres et braises*. Paris: L'Harmattan, 1994. (Coll. Encres noires, 126). Roman.

4025. Lam, Aboubacry Moussa. *La Fièvre de la terre*. Paris: L'Harmattan, 1990. (Coll. Encres noires, 81). Roman.

4026. Lemoine, Lucien. *Douta Seck ou la tragédie du roi Christophe*. Paris: Présence Africaine, 1993. Biographie.

4027. Maïga Ka, Aminata (F). *En votre nom et au mien*. Abidjan: Nouvelles Editions Africaines C.I., 1989. Roman.

4028 ———. *La Voie du salut,* suivi de *Le Miroir de la vie*. Paris: Présence Africaine, 1985. Nouvelles.

4029. Mandeleau, Tita (F). *Signare Anna*. Dakar: Nouvelles Editions Africaines du Sénégal, 1991. Roman.

4030. Mayoro Diop, Abd'el Aziz. *Prisonniers de la vie.* Dakar: Nouvelles Editions Africaines du Sénégal, 1993. Roman.

4031. M'Baye, Jonas Younousse. *L'Ultime issue.* s.l.: Editions de l'Académie européenne du livre, 1992. Roman.

4032. Mbaye d'Erneville, Annette (F). *La Bague de cuivre et d'argent.* Dakar: Nouvelles Editions Africaines, 1983. Nouvelle pour les enfants primée au Concours Jeune Afrique en 1961. Nouvelle.

4033. ———. *Kaddu.* Dakar: Imprimerie A. Diop, 1966. Poésie.

4034. ———. *Poèmes africains.* Dakar: Centre national d'art français, 1965. Poésie.

4035. Mbengue Diakhate, Ndèye Coumba (F). *Filles du soleil.* Abidjan: Nouvelles Editions Africaines, 1980. Poésie.

4036. Mordasini, Diana (F). *Le Botillon perdu.* Dakar: Nouvelles Editions Africaines du Sénégal, 1991. Roman.

4037. Ndao, Cheikh Aliou. *Un Bouquet d'épines pour elle.* Paris: Présence Africaine, 1988. Roman.

4038. ———. *Burr Tillen roi de la Médina.* Paris: Présence Africaine, 1972. (Nouvelle édition en 1988). Roman.

4039. ———. *Excellence, vos épouses!* Dakar: Nouvelles Editions Africaines, 1983. Roman.

4040. ———. *Kaïrée.* Grenoble: Imprimerie Eymond, 1962. Poésie.

4041. ———. *Le Marabout de la sécheresse.* Dakar: Nouvelles Editions Africaines, 1979. Nouvelles.

4042. N'Diaye, Catherine (F). *Gens de sable.* Paris: POL, 1984. Autobiographie.

4043. NDiaye, Marie (F). *Comédie classique*. Paris: POL, 1987. Roman.

4044. ———. *En famille*. Paris: Editions de Minuit, 1990. Roman.

4045. ———. *La Femme changée en bûche*. Paris: Editions de Minuit, 1989. Roman.

4046. ———. *Quant au riche avenir*. Paris: Editions de Minuit, 1985. Roman.

4047. ———. *Un Temps de saison*. Paris: Editions de Minuit, 1994. Roman.

4048. Ndiaye, Ndèye Boury (F). *Collier de cheville*. Dakar: Nouvelles Editions Africaines, 1983. Roman.

4049. Ndiaye Sow, Fatou (F). *Fleurs du Sahel*. Dakar: Nouvelles Editions Africaines du Sénégal, 1990. Poésie.

4050. Ndoye, Mariama (F). *De vous à moi*. Paris: Présence Africaine, 1990. Nouvelles.

4051. ———. *Sur des chemins pavoisés*. Abidjan: CEDA, 1993. Roman.

4052. Ngom, Mbissane. *La Voix des champs*. Dakar: Nouvelles Editions Africaines du Sénégal, n.d. Roman.

4053. Niane, Anne-Marie (F). *L'Etrangère*. Paris: Hatier, 1985. Recueil des nouvelles primées dans le cadre du 9e concours radiophonique de la meilleure nouvelle de langue française. Nouvelle.

4054. Sadji, Abdoulaye. *Maïmouna*. Paris: Présence Africaine, 1958. (Nouvelle édition en 1980). Roman.

4055. ———. *Nini*. Paris: Présence Africaine, 1955. Roman.

4056. ———. *Tounka une légende de la mer*. Dakar: Imprimerie A. Diop, 1952. Conte.

4057. Diouf, Madior. *Nini, mulâtresse du Sénégal d'Abdoulaye Sadji*. Dakar: Khoudia, 1990. (Coll. CAEC-Université 1).

4058. Grésillon, Marie. *Maïmouna d'Abdoulaye Sadji*. Issy-les-Moulineaux: Saint-Paul, 1985. (Coll. Classiques africains).

4059. Sall, Amadou Lamine. *Comme un iceberg en flammes*. Dakar: Nouvelles Editions Africaines du Sénégal, 1982. Poésie.

4060. Seck, Alioune Badara. *La Mare aux grenouilles*. Paris: L'Harmattan, 1990. (Coll. Encres noires, 64). Roman.

4061. ———. *Le Monde des grands*. Paris: L'Harmattan, 1988. Roman.

4062. Seck Mbacké, Mame (F). *Le Froid et le piment*. Dakar: Nouvelles Editions Africaines, 1983. Témoignages.

4063. Seck, Papa Ibrahima. *Sangomar: stèles pour un nouvel humanisme*. Paris: L'Harmattan, 1993. (Coll. Poètes des cinq continents). Poésie.

4064. Sembene, Ousmane. *Les Bouts de bois de Dieu*. Paris: Le Livre contemporain, 1960. (Nouvelle publication en 1971 dans les Presses Pocket, Paris). Roman.

4065. ———. *Le Dernier de l'empire*. Paris: L'Harmattan, 1981. Roman.

4066. ———. *Le Docker noir*. Paris: Debresse, 1956. (Nouvelle édition en 1973 chez Présence Africaine, Paris). Roman.

4067. ———. *Niiwam,* suivi de *Taaw*. Paris: Présence Africaine, 1987. Nouvelles.

4068. ———. *Ô Pays mon beau peuple*. Paris: Amiot-Dumont, 1957. (Nouvelle édition en 1975 dans les Presses Pocket, Paris). Roman.

4069. ———. *Vehi-Ciosane,* suivi de *Le Mandat.* Paris: Présence Africaine, 1965. Nouvelles.

4070. ———. *Voltaïque, la noire de* . . . Paris: Présence Africaine, 1962. Nouvelles.

4071. ———. *Xala.* Paris: Présence Africaine, 1973. Roman.

4072. Gadjigo, Samba, et al. *Ousmane Sembène: dialogues with critics and writers.* Amherst: University of Massachusetts Press, 1993.

4073. Vieyra, Paulin Soumanou. *Sembène Ousmane cinéaste.* Paris: Présence Africaine, 1972. (Coll. Approches).

4074. Sene, Nar. *Walu! (au secours!).* Paris: L'Harmattan, 1990. (Coll. Encres noires, 69). Roman.

4075. Senghor, Léopold Sédar. *Ce que je crois: négritude, francité et civilisation de l'universel.* Paris: Grasset, 1988.

4076 ———. *Liberté 5: le dialogue des cultures.* Paris: Seuil, 1993.

4077. ———. *Œuvre poétique.* Paris: Seuil, 1990. (Coll. Points, 210). Comprend Chants d'ombre [1945], Hosties noires [1948], Ethiopiques [1956], Nocturnes [1961], Lettres d'hivernage [1972], Elégies majeures et Poèmes perdus.

4078. ———. *Poèmes.* Paris: Seuil, 1985. (Œuvre intégrale. Coll. Points, 30). Poésie.

4079. ———. *La Poésie de l'Action.* Paris: Stock, 1980. Conversations avec Mohamed Aziza.

4080. Biondi, Jean-Pierre. *Senghor ou la tentation de l'universel.* Paris: Denoël, 1993. (Coll. Destins croisés). Biographie.

4081. Kesteloot, Lilyan. *Comprendre les Poèmes de Léopold Sédar Senghor*. Issy-les-Moulineaux: Saint-Paul, 1986. (Coll. Classiques africains).

4082. Malraux, André. *Hôtes de passage*. Paris: Gallimard, 1975.

4083. Mercier, Roger et Simon Battestini. *Léopold Sédar Senghor, poète sénégalais*. Paris: Nathan, 1964. (Nouvelle édition en 1985. Coll. Classiques du monde).

4084. Nespoulous-Neuville, Josiane. *Léopold Sédar Senghor: de la tradition à l'universalisme*. Paris: Seuil, 1988.

4085. Ngandu Nkashama, Pius. *Négritude et poétique: une lecture de l'œuvre critique de Léopold Sédar Senghor*. Paris: L'Harmattan, 1993. (Coll. Littératures: Traverses des espaces francophones).

4086. Signaté, Ibrahima. *Une Aube si fragile*. Dakar: Nouvelles Editions Africaines, 1977. Roman.

4087. Sougoufara Cheikh. *Baol – Baol, mon ami*. Paris: L'Harmattan, 1992. (Coll. Encres noires, 96). Roman.

4088. Sow Fall, Aminata (F). *L'Appel des arènes*. Dakar: Nouvelles Editions Africaines, 1982. Roman.

4089. ———. *L'Ex-père de la nation*. Paris: L'Harmattan, 1987. (Coll. Encres noires, 43). Roman.

4090. ———. *La Grève des Bàttu*. Dakar: Nouvelles Editions Africaines, 1979. Roman.

4091. ———. *Le Jujubier du patriarche*. Dakar: Khoudia, 1993. Roman.

4092. ———. *Le Revenant*. Dakar: Nouvelles Editions Africaines, 1976. Roman.

4093. Borgomano, Madeleine. *L'Appel des arènes d'Aminata Sow Fall*. Dakar: Nouvelles Editions Africaines, 1984.

4094. Sow, Mamadou. *Les Cinq nuits de Gnilane*. Paris: L'Harmattan, 1992. (Coll. Encres noires, 89). Roman.

4095. ———. *Su Suuf Seddee: l'échec*. Dakar: ENDA, 1984. Roman.

4096. Sow Mbaye, Amina (F). *Mademoiselle*. Dakar; Paris: Nouvelles Editions Africaines; EDICEF, 1984. (Coll. Jeunesse). Autobiographie.

4097. Sylla, Khady (F). *Le Jeu de la mer*. Paris: L'Harmattan, 1992. (Coll. Encres noires, 106). Roman.

4098. Wane, Abdoulaye Baïla. *Les Habitués du Paradis*. Dakar: Nouvelles Editions Africaines, 1978. Roman.

4099. Warner-Vieyra, Myriam (F). *Femmes échouées*. Paris: Présence Africaine, 1988. Nouvelles.

4100. ———. *Juletane*. Paris: Présence Africaine, 1982. Roman.

4101. ———. *Le Quimboiseur l'avait dit*. Paris: Présence Africaine, 1980. Roman.

4102. Wone, Amadou Tidiane. *Lorsque la nuit se déchire*. Paris: L'Harmattan, 1990. (Coll. Encres noires, 74). Roman.

SOMALIA/SOMALIE

Authors

4103. Erouart-Siad, Patrick. *Cahiers de la mort colibri*. Paris: Seuil, 1987. Roman.

4104. Syad, William Joseph Farah. *Khamsine*. Paris: Présence Africaine, 1959. Poésie.

4105. ———. *Naufragés du destin*. Paris: Présence Africaine, 1978. Poésie.

SUDAN/SOUDAN

Anthology

4106. Yagi, Viviane Amina. *Contes du Soudan.* Paris: Publisud, 1989. Contes.

Authors

4107. El Mahdi, El Tayeb. *L'Ephémère,* suivi de *Le Sonneur de cor et de Que les murs tombent.* Paris: L'Harmattan, 1991. (Trois pièces de théâtre publiées dans la coll. Encres noires, 82). Théâtre

4108. ———. *Le Jeu des maîtres.* Paris: L'Harmattan, 1988. Théâtre.

TCHAD/CHAD

Anthology

4109. Tchazabe Louafaya, Madi. *Contes moundang du Tchad.* Paris: Karthala; ACCT, 1990. (Coll. Contes et légendes). Contes.

Authors

4110 Bangui, Antoine. *Les Ombres de Kôh.* Paris: Hatier, 1984. (Coll. Monde noir poche, 21). Roman.

4111. Bruneau, Xavier. *Roboa-Nat, le sorcier malgré lui.* Yaoundé: CLE, 1972. Théâtre.

4112. Hassan Abbakar, Mahamat. *Un Tchadien à l'aventure.* Paris: L'Harmattan, 1992. Autobiographie.

4113. Khidir, Zakaria Fadoul. *Loin de moi-même.* Paris: L'Harmattan, 1990. Mémoires.

4114. Kotoko, Ahmed. *Le Destin de Hamaï ou le long chemin vers l'indépendance du Tchad.* Paris: L'Harmattan, 1989. (Coll. Mémoires africaines). Biographie.

4115. Moustapha, Baba. *Le Commandant Chaka*. Paris: Hatier, 1983. (Coll. Monde noir poche). Théâtre.

4116 Naindouba, Maoundoé. *L'Etudiant de Soweto*. Paris: Hatier, 1981. (Suivi de *Trop c'est trop* du Camerounais Protais Asseng. Coll. Monde noir poche, 12). Théâtre.

4117. Tchoumba Ngouankeu. *Autour du lac Tchad*. Yaoundé: CLE, 1969. Contes.

TOGO

General studies

4118. *En savoir plus sur la littérature togolaise*. Lomé: Institut National des Sciences de l'Education, 1987. (Coll. Didactiques Série B, 20).

4119. Riesz, Janos et Alain Ricard (éds.). *Le Champ littéraire togolais*. Bayreuth: E. Breitinger, 1991. (Bayreuth African Studies, 23).

Authors

4120. Adotevi, Adovi John Bosco. *Sacrilège à Mandali*. Yaoundé: CLE, 1980. Roman.

4121. Akakpo-Ahianyo, Anani. *Au hasard de la vie*. Dakar: Nouvelles Editions Africaines, 1983. Poésie.

4122. Aladji, Victor. *La Voix de l'ombre*. Lomé: Haho, 1985. Roman.

4123. Alemdrodjo, Kagni. *Chemins de croix ou chronique d'une mise à mort symbolique*. Lomé: Nouvelles Edition Africaines du Togo, 1991. Théâtre.

4124. ———. *La Saga des rois*. Lomé: Nouvelles Edition Africaines du Togo, 1992. Théâtre.

4125. Amela, Hilla-Laobé. *Odes lyriques*. Lomé: Akpagnon, 1983. Poésie.

4126. Amenyedzi, Anane Sename. *La Calebasse empoisonnée*. Dakar: Nouvelles Editions Africaines, 1982. Théâtre.

4127. Ananou, David. *Le Fils du fétiche*. Paris: Nouvelles éditions latines, 1955. Roman.

4128. Apedo-Ameh, Moorhouse. *Le Mariage d'Isaac et de Rebecca: pièce de Kantata*. Lomé: Haho, 1990. Traduction en français d'une pièce écrite en éwé par Apedo-Ameh en 1943. Théâtre.

4129. Ayache, Georges. *Si la maison de votre voisin brûle*. Paris: Editions ABC, 1983. Roman.

4130. Couchoro, Félix. *Amour de féticheuse*. Ouidah: Imprimerie d'Almeida, 1941. Roman.

4131. ———. *L'Esclave*. Lomé: Akpagnon, 1983. (Première publication dans La Dépêche africaine, 1929). Roman.

4132. ———. *L'Héritage, cette peste*. Lomé: Editogo, 1963. Roman.

4133. Dabla, Séwanou Jean-Jacques. *Catharsis*. Amiens: Edition Corps Puce, 1990. Poésie.

4134. Dogbé, Yves-Emmanuel. *Flamme blême*. Lomé: Akpagnon, 1980. Nouvelle édition de vers publiés en 1969. Poésie.

4135. ———. *L'Incarcéré*. Lomé: Akpagnon, 1980. Roman.

4136. Ekué, Christiane Tchotcho Akoua (F). *Le Crime de la rue des notables*. Lomé: Nouvelles Editions Africaines, 1989. Roman.

4137. Gad Ami (F). *Etrange héritage*. Lomé: Nouvelles Editions Africaines, 1985. Roman.

4138. Gomez, Koffi. *Gagio ou l'argent, cette peste.* Lomé: Etablissement National des Editions du Togo, 1983. Théâtre.

4139. ———. *Opération marigot.* Dakar: Nouvelles Editions Africaines, 1982. Roman.

4140. Inawisi, Nayé Théophile. *Les Grands jours.* Lomé: Apkagnon, 1983. Poésie.

4141. Koffi Koffi. *Expériences de ma jeunesse.* Lomé: Editogo, 1982. Autobiographie.

4142. Kossi Efoui, Josué. "Le Carrefour." *Théâtre sud,* no. 2 (1990).

4143. ———. *Récupérations.* Carnières, Belgique: Lansman, 1992. (Coll. Théâtre à vif). Théâtre.

4144. Kpomassié, Tété Michel. *L'Africain du Groënland.* Paris: Flammarion, 1981. Autobiographie.

4145. Pinto, Komlavi Jean-Marie. *Les Mémoires d'Emilienne.* Paris: L'Harmattan, 1990. (Coll. Encres noires, 60). Roman.

4146. Sedzro-Komlan, Kokou. *Nos vertes années.* Lomé: Haho, 1987. Roman.

4147. Senah, K. *Les Vautours et autres nouvelles.* Lomé: Haho, 1990. Nouvelles.

4148. Towaly. *Leur figure-là.* Paris: L'Harmattan, 1985. (Coll. Encres noires, 31). Nouvelles.

4149. Typamm, Paul Akakpo. *Rythmes et cadences.* Lomé: Akpagnon, 1981. Poésie.

4150. Wezin, Kris. *La Puissance et l'éternité.* Lomé: Akpagnon, 1985. Poésie.

4151. Yamgnane, Koffi. *Droits, devoirs et crocodile.* Paris: Laffont, 1992. Autobiographie.

4152. Zinsou, Senouvo Agbota. *Le Club.* Lomé: Haho, 1984. Théâtre.

4153. ———. *On joue la comédie.* Lomé; Haarlem: Haho; In de Knipscheer, 1984. Nouvelle édition d'une pièce publiée par Radio France Internationale en 1975. Théâtre.

4154. ———. *La Tortue qui chante,* suivi de *La Femme du blanchisseur et de Les Aventures de Yévi au pays des monstres.* Paris: Hatier, 1987. (Coll. Monde noir poche, 49). Théâtre.

ZAÏRE

Bibliography

4155. Ngandu Nkashama, Pius. *Le Livre littéraire: bibliographie de la littérature du Congo (Kinshasa).* Paris: L'Harmattan, 1994.

Anthologies

4156. Babudaa, Malibato. *Anthologie: textes choisis d'auteurs zaïrois.* Kinshasa: ECA, 1988.

4157. Ngandu Nkashama, Pius. *La Terre à vivre: anthologie de la poésie du Congo-Kinshasa.* Paris: L'Harmattan, 1994.

General studies

4158. Ikupasa O'mos. *Tradition, mythe et art romanesque au Zaïre: littérature cyclique et roman zaïrois.* Kinshasa: Centre de recherches pédagogiques, 1988.

4159. Kapalanga Gazungil Sang Amin. *Les Spectacles d'animation politique en République du Zaïre.* Louvain: Cahiers du théâtre de Louvain, 1989.

4160. Mbuyamba Kankolongo, Alphonse. *Guide de la littérature zaïroise de langue française 1974-1992.* Kinshasa: Editions universitaires africaines, 1993.

4161. Mukala Kadima-Nzuji. *La Littérature zaïroise de langue française (1945-1965)*. Paris: Karthala, 1984.

4162. Yamaina Mandala. *La Femme zaïroise et la littérature*. Kinshasa: La Grue Couronnée, 1974.

Authors

4163. Abongo-E-Manzeku. *Flamme noire*. Kinshasa: Union des écrivains zaïrois, 1984. Poésie.

4164. Basembe, Désiré-Joseph. *Les Aventures de Mobaron*. Elisabethville: Editions du progrès, 1947. Récit.

4165. Bolamba, J'ongungu Lokolé Antoine-Roger. *Esanzo, chants pour mon pays*. Paris: Présence Africaine, 1955. (Nouvelle éditions en 1977 chez Naaman, Sherbrooke). Poésie.

4166. ———. *Premiers essais*. Paris: Présence Africaine, 1955. (Nouvelle édition bilingue français-anglais en 1977 chez Naaman, Sherbrooke). Poésie.

4167. Bolya, Baenga. *Cannibale*. Lausanne: Pierre-Marcel Favre, 1986. Roman.

4168. Bosek'ilolo, Lima-Baleka (F). *Les Marais brûlés*. Kinshasa: Centre Africain de littérature, 1973. Poésie.

4169. Buabua Wa Kayembe Mubadiate. *Combat pour l'Azanie*. Dakar: Nouvelles Editions Africaines, 1984. Roman.

4170. ———. *Le Délégué général*. Paris: Silex, 1982. Théâtre.

4171. ———. *Les Flammes de Soweto*. Kinshasa: La Grue Couronnée, 1979. Théâtre.

4172. Diangitukwa, Fweley. *Couronne d'épines*. Paris: Saint-Germain-des-Prés, 1985. Poésie.

4173. Diur, Ntumb (F). *Zaïna qui hurle dans la nuit*. Paris: Hatier, 1986. Théâtre.

4174. Djungu-Simba, Kamatenda Charles. *On a échoué.* Kinshasa: Editions du Trottoir, 1991. Roman.

4175. ——. *Turbulences.* Kinshasa: Editions du Trottoir, 1992. Poésie.

4176. Elebe, Lisembe Philippe. *Les Cailloux de l'espoir.* Genève: Poésie Vivante, 1987. Poésie.

4177. ——. *Chant de la terre, chant de l'eau.* Paris: Oswald, 1973. Théâtre.

4178. ——. *La Joconde d'ébène.* Paris: Saint-Germain-des-Prés, 1977. Poésie.

4179. ——. *Mélodie africaine.* Paris: Saint-Germain-des-Prés, 1970. Poésie.

4180. ——. *Rythmes.* Kinshasa: Mont Noir, 1972. Poésie.

4181. ——. *Stations du monde: poèmes.* Paris: Les Paragraphes littéraires de Paris, 1979. Poésie.

4182. Elebe Ma Ekonzo. *Un Echo dans la nuit.* Kinshasa: Union des Ecrivains Zaïrois, 1983. Roman.

4183. Intiomale Mbonino. *Les Ondes.* Lubumbashi: Imprimerie I.S.P., 1986. Poésie.

4184. Kabagema-Mirindi, Tharcisse. *Muko ou la trahison d'un héros,* suivi de *Le Disciple.* Paris: L'Harmattan, 1992. (Coll. Encres noires, 92). Récits.

4185. Kabongo Kongo Kola. *Le Pouvoir.* Kinshasa: Presses Universitaires du Zaïre, 1984. Roman.

4186. Kabwasa, Nsang O'Khan. *Les Fleurs de Maskaram.* Paris: L'Harmattan, 1993. (Coll. Encres noires, 111). Roman.

4187. Kadima-Nzuji, Mukala Dieudonné. *Les Ressacs.* Kinshasa: Lettres congolaises, 1966. Poésie.

4188. Kalanda, Makiba. *Tabalayi*. Léopoldville: Imprimerie Concordia, 1963. Nouvelle.

4189. Kalonji, Christine (F). *Dernière genèse*. Paris: Saint-Germain-des-Prés, 1975. Nouvelle.

4190. Kama Kamanda. *Chants de brumes*. Liège: Dricot, 1986. Poésie.

4191. ———. *Eclipse*. Paris: Saint-Germain-des-Prés, 1987. (Coll. A l'écoute des sources). Poésie.

4192. ———. *L'Exil des songes*. Paris: L'Harmattan, 1992. (Coll. Poètes des cinq continents). Poésie.

4193. ———. *Lointaines sont les rives du destin*. Paris: L'Harmattan, 1994. (Coll. Encres noires, 125).

4194. ———. *Les Myriades des temps vécus*. Paris: L'Harmattan, 1992. (Coll. Poètes des cinq continents). Poésie.

4195. ———. *Les Résignations*. Paris: Présence Africaine, 1986. Poésie.

4196. Sartin, Pierette. *Kama Kamanda poète de l'exil*. Paris: L'Harmattan, 1994.

4197. Kanza, Thomas. *Sans rancune*. Londres: Editions Scotland, 1965. Roman.

4198. Kawata Ashem Tem. *Des Cendres et des flammes*. Kinshasa: Edition Lokole, 1980. Roman.

4199. Kiswa, Claude. *Le Fleuve Zaïre*. Paris: Athanor, 1977. Poésie.

4200. Kitende, M. M., et al. *Un Voyage comme tant d'autres*. Abidjan; Paris: CEDA; Hatier, 1984. Suivi de 11 autres nouvelles d'auteurs différents. Nouvelle. (Coll. Monde noir poche, 29).

4201. Kompany Wa Kompany. *Les Tortures d'Eyenga*. Kinshasa: Union des écrivains zaïrois, 1985. Roman.

4202. Lomami-Tshibamba, Paul. *Ngando (Le Crocodile)*. Bruxelles: Edition Gearges-Deny, n.d. Prix littéraire de la foire de Bruxelles, 1948. Nouvelle édition en 1982 chez Présence Africaine et Lokole. Roman.

4203. ———. *Ngemena*. Paris: CLE, 1981. Roman.

4204. ———. *La Récompense de la cruauté*, suivi de *N'Gobila des M'swata*. Kinshasa: Mont Noir, 1972. Nouvelles.

4205. Lumuna-Sando, C. K. *Lovanium. La Kasala du 4 juin*. Bruxelles: A.F.R.I.C.A., 1982. Récit.

4206. Luya Laye Kelaka. *Station d'adieu*. Kinshasa: Union des écrivains zaïrois, 1984. Poésie.

4207. Makulo, Akambu. *La Vie de Disasi Makulo, ancien esclave de Tippo Tim et catéchiste de Grenfell*. Kinshasa: Saint-Paul Afrique, 1983. Biographie.

4208. Malembe, Timothée. *Le Mystère de l'enfant disparu*. Léopoldville: Editions de l'Etoile, 1962. (Nouvelle édition en 1970 chez Kraus Reprints). Roman.

4209. Masegabio Nzanzu, Philippe. *La Cendre demeure*. Kinshasa: Lokole, 1983. Poésie.

4210. Matala Mukadi Tshiakatumba. *Réveil dans un nid de flammes*. Paris: Seghers, 1969. Poésie.

4211. Mikanza Mobyem M. K. *Notre sang*. Kinshasa: AS Editions, 1991. Théâtre.

4212. Mobiala, Louis (pseudonyme du RP Albert Leysbeth). *Je ne te haïrai pas*. Kinshasa: Bibliothèque de l'Etoile, 1953. Roman.

4213. Mudimbe, Vumbi-Yoka Valentin Yves. *Le Bel immonde*. Paris: Présence Africaine, 1976. Roman.

4214. ———. *Entrailles, précédé de Fulgurances d'une lézarde*. Paris: Saint-Germain-des-Prés, 1973. Poésie.

4215. ———. *Entre les eaux: Dieu, un prêtre, la révolution.* Paris: Nathan, 1973. (Nouvelle édition en 1986 chez les Nouvelles Editions Africaines). Roman.

4216. ———. *Réflexions sur la vie quotidienne.* Kinshasa: Mont Noir, 1972. Roman.

4217. ———. *Shaba Deux: les carnets de mère Marie-Gertrude.* Paris: Présence Africaine, 1990. Roman.

4218. Mouralis, Bernard. *V.Y. Mudimbe ou le discours, l'écart et l'écriture.* Paris: Présence Africaine, 1988.

4219. Mukulumania Wa Ngate. *L'Envers d'une amitié.* Kinshasa: Zenda, 1987. Nouvelles.

4220. Musangi Mtemo. *Sabu, un enfant de chez nous,* suivi de *Village en sursis.* Kinshasa-Gombe: Union des écrivains zaïrois, 1983. Nouvelles.

4221. Mutombo, Dieudonné. *Victoire de l'amour.* Léopoldville: Bibliothèque de l'Etoile, 1954. (Nouvelle édition en 1970 chez Kraus Reprints). Roman.

4222 Mwamb'a Musa, Mangol. *Visages d'homme.* Paris: Silex, 1982. Poésie.

4223. Mweya, Tol'ande Elisabeth Françoise (F). *Ahata,* suivi de *Récit de la damnée.* Kinshasa: Bobiso, 1977. Nouvelles.

4224. ———. *Remous de feuilles.* Kinshasa: Mont noir, 1972. (Série jeune littérature, 9). Poésie.

4225. Ndoki Kitekutu. *J'ai épousé une vierge!* Kinshasa: Saint-Paul Afrique, 1984. Roman.

4226. Ngandu Nkashama, Pius. *Les Etoiles écrasées.* Paris: Publisud, 1988. (Coll. L'Espace de la parole). Roman.

4227. ———. *Le Fils de la tribu,* suivi de *La Mulatresse Anna.* Dakar: Nouvelles Editions Africaines, 1983. (Coll. Créativité 10-7). Roman.

4228. ———. *Un Jour de grand soleil sur les montagnes de l'Ethiopie.* Paris: L'Harmattan, 1991. (Coll. Encres noires, 87). Roman.

4229. ———. *La Malédiction.* Paris: Silex; ACCT, 1983. Nouvelle.

4230. ———. *Des Mangroves en terre haute.* Paris: L'Harmattan, 1990. (Coll. Encres noires, 78 bis). Roman.

4231. ———. *May Britt de Santa Cruz.* Paris: L'Harmattan, 1993. (Coll. Encres noires). Théâtre.

4232. ———. *La Mort faite homme.* Paris: L'Harmattan, 1986. (Coll. Encres noires, 38). Roman.

4233. ———. *Le Pacte de sang.* Paris: L'Harmattan, 1984. (Coll. Encres noires, 25). Roman.

4234. ———. *Vie et mœurs d'un primitif en Essonne 91000.* Paris: L'Harmattan, 1987. (Coll. Encres noires, 44). Roman.

4235. Kalonji, Zezeze M. *Une Ecriture de la passion chez Pius Ngandu Nkashama.* Paris: L'Harmattan, 1992.

4236. Ngenzi Lonta Mwene Malomba, Charles. *La Fille du forgeron.* Kinshasa: Bobiso, 1969. Théâtre.

4237. Ngombo, Mbala. *Deux vies, un temps nouveau.* Kinshasa: Okapi, 1973. Roman.

4238. Ngoye, Achille. *Kin-la-joie, Kin-la folie.* Paris: L'Harmattan, 1993. (Coll. Encres noires, 112). Roman.

4239. N'landu, Kavidi Wivine. *Leurres et lueurs.* Bruxelles: André de Roche, 1984. Poésie.

4240. Nsimba Mumbamuna. *Lettres kinoises.* Kinshasa: Centre Africain de Littérature, 1974. Roman épistolaire.

4241. Nzau, Antonio Junior. *Traite au Zaïre.* Paris: L'Harmattan, 1984. (Coll. Polars noirs, 1). Roman.

4242. Nzuji, Madiya Clémentine (F). *Gestes interrompus.* Lubumbashi: Mandore, 1976. Poésie.

4243. ———. *Kasalà.* Kinshasa: Mandore, 1969. Poésie.

4244. ———. *Lenga et autres contes d'inspiration traditionnelle.* Lubumbashi: Saint-Paul Afrique, 1976. Contes.

4245. ———. *Lianes.* Kinshasa: Mont noir, 1971. Poésie.

4246. ———. *Le Temps des amants.* Kinshasa: Mandore, 1969. Poésie.

4247. Pika Pia. *La Détresse et l'adieu.* Kinshasa: Pipia, 1983. Poésie.

4248. Ruti, Antoine M. *Affamez-les, ils vous adoreront.* Paris: L'Harmattan, 1992. (Coll. Encres noires, 88). Conte.

4249. Tshibanda Wamuela Bujitu. *Un Cauchemar.* Lubumbashi: Saint-Paul Afrique, 1993. Récit.

4250. ———. *De Kolwesi à Kasaji: souvenirs du lieutenant Nzinga.* Kinshasa: Saint-Paul Afrique, 1980. Roman.

4251. ———. *Je ne suis pas un sorcier.* Kinshasa: Saint-Paul Afrique, 1981. Roman.

4252. ———. *Londola ou le cercueil volant,* suivi de *Le Malade mental.* Kinshasa: Saint-Paul Afrique, 1984. Nouvelles.

4253. Tshilolo Kabika (F). *Le Pilier du chef et autres contes.* Lubumbashi: Pavillon des Ecrivains zaïrois, 1986. Contes.

4254. Tshisungu Wa Tshisungu, J. *Le Croissant des larmes.* Paris: L'Harmattan, 1990. Roman.

4255. Wenu Bekare. *Les Entrelacs ou les tribulations de l'intellectuel africain.* Lubumbashi: Union des écrivains zaïrois-shaba, 1986. Théâtre.

4256. Yisuku Gafudzi, Tito. *La Rosée du ciel*. Kinshasa: Propoza, 1982. Roman.

4257. Yoka Lye Mudaba. *Tshira ou la danse des ombres et des masques*. Kinshasa-Limete: Lokole, 1984. Théâtre.

4258. ———, et al. *Le Fossoyeur*. Paris: Hatier, 1986. (Monde noir poche, 42. Comprend huit nouvelles d'auteurs différents). Nouvelles.

4259. Zamenga Batukezanga. *Bandoki*. Kinshasa: Saint-Paul Afrique, 1972. (Nouvelle édition en 1983). Roman.

4260. ———. *Un Boy à Prétoria*. Kinshasa: Saint-Paul Afrique, 1990. Roman.

4261. ———. *Carte postale*. Kinshasa: Basenzi, 1974. (Nouvelle édition en 1977 chez les Editions Saint-Paul). Roman.

4262. ———. *Chérie Basso*. Kinshasa: Saint-Paul Afrique, 1983. Roman.

4263. ———. *Un Croco à Luozi*. Kinshasa: Saint-Paul Afrique, 1982. Roman.

4264. ———. *Les Hauts et les bas*. Kinshasa: Saint-Paul Afrique, 1971. (Nouvelle édition en 1984). Nouvelle.

4265. ———. *Lettres d'Amérique*. Kinshasa: Zabat, 1982. Roman.

4266. ———. *Mille kilomètres à pied*. Kinshasa: Saint-Paul Afrique, 1979. Roman.

4267. ———. *Mon mari en grève*. Kinshasa: Zabat, 1986. Roman.

4268. ———. *Le Réfugié*. Kinshasa: EDICVA, 1984. Roman.

4269. ———. *Sept frères et une sœur*. Kinshasa: Saint-Paul Afrique, 1975. (Nouvelle édition en 1983). Roman.

4270. ———. *Souvenirs d'un village*. Kinshasa: Saint-Paul Afrique, 1971. (Nouvelle éditions en 1983).

4271. ———. *Terre des ancêtres*. Kinshasa: Basenzi, 1974. Roman.

4272. Ngoma Binda. *Zamenga Batukezanga: vie et œuvre*. Kinshasa: Saint-Paul Afrique, 1990.

MADAGASCAR

Bibliography

4273. "2000 titres de littérature: Océan indien." *Notre Librairie*, no. 116 (1994): 24-44. (Madagascar).

Anthologies

4274. Rajemisa-Raolison, Régis. *Les Poètes malgaches d'expression française*. Tananarive: Imprimerie catholique, 1983.

4275. Ramarosoa, Liliane (dir.). *Anthologie de la littérature malgache d'expression française dans les années 1980*. Paris: L'Harmattan, 1994.

4276. Renel, C. *Contes de Madagascar*. Paris: Ernest Leroux, 1910. 2 v. Contes.

4277. Schrive, Maurice (dir.). *Contes Betsimiraraka*. Tamatave; Antananario: Alliance française; Foi et Justice, 1992. Contes du nord est de Madagascar. Dessins de Max Razafindrainibe. Edition bilingue malgache - français. Contes.

4278. Vally-Samat, Renée. *Contes et légendes de Madagascar*. Paris: Nathan, 1962. Contes.

General studies

4279. Domenichini-Ramiaramanana, Bakoly. *Du ohabolana au hainteny: langue, littérature and politique à Magadascar*. Paris: Karthala, 1983.

4280. "Madagascar. 2. La littérature d'expression française." *Notre Librairie*, no. 110 (1992).

4281. "Poésie et nouvelle." *Recherches et Cultures*, no. 5 (1990).

Authors

4282. Abraham, Elie-Charles. *Pétales*. Tananarive: Imprimerie catholique, 1977. Poésie.

4283. ———. *Les Saisons de mon cœur*. Tananarive: 1940. Poésie.

4284. Andria, Aimée (F). *L'Année en fleurs*. Paris: Editions de la Revue Moderne, 1973. Poésie.

4285. ———. *Les Anticorps ou le déclin d'une vie*. Paris: Dany Thibaud, 1981. Roman.

4286. ———. *Brouillard*. Paris: Louis Soulanges, 1967. Roman.

4287. ———. *L'Esquif*. Paris: Louis Soulanges, 1968. Roman.

4288. Andrianarahinjaka, Lucien Michel. *Terre promise*. Tananarive: Editions Revue de l'Océan Indien, 1988. Poésie.

4289. Bezoro, Edouard. *La Sœur inconnue*. Paris: Figuières, 1932. Roman.

4290. Dox. *Chants capricorniens*. Antananarivo: Centre d'information et de documentation scientifique et technique, 1991. De son vrai nom Jean Verdi Salomon Razakandraina. Poésie.

4291. Dréo, Pelandrova (F). *Pelandrova*. Montvilliers: CEDS, 1976. Roman autobiographique.

4292. Jaomanoro, David. *La Retraite*. Carnières: Promotion Théâtre, 1990. (Coll. Théâtre en tête). Théâtre.

4293. Nirina, Esther. *Lente spirale*. Tananarive: Editions Revue de l'Océan Indien, 1990. Poésie.

4294. ———. *Silencieuse respiration*. Orléans: Serjent, 1978. Poésie.

4295. ———. *Simple voyelle*. Orléans: Serjent, 1980. Poésie.

4296. Rabearivelo, Jean-Joseph. *Aux Portes de la ville*. Tananarive: Imprimerie officielle, 1936. Musique de Benoît Rakotomanga sur des paroles et airs anciens. (Nouvelle édition en 1991). Théâtre.

4297. ———. *Chants pour Abéone*. Tananarive: Imprimerie Henri Vidalie, 1936. (Nouvelle édition en 1991 chez CIDST, Tananarive). Poésie.

4298. ———. *La Coupe de cendres*. Tananarive: Pitot de la Beaujardière, 1924. Poésie.

4299. ———. *Des Stances oubliées*. Tananarive: Imprimerie Liva, 1959. Poésie.

4300. ———. *Imaitsoanala fille d'oiseau: cantate*. Tananarive: Imprimerie officielle, 1935. Théâtre.

4301. ———. *L'Interférence*. Paris: Hatier, 1988. Suivi de la nouvelle *Un Conte de la nuit*. En 1987, Charlotte Rafenomanjato a écrit une adaptation pour la scène du roman, inédite à ce jour. Roman.

4302. ———. *Poèmes, presque-songes. Traduit de la nuit. Chants pour Abéone*. Paris: Hatier, 1990. Nouvelle édition de poèmes publiés antérieurement. Poésie.

4303. ———. *Sylves*. Tananarive: Imprimerie de l'Imerina, 1927. (Nouvelle édition en 1991 chez CIDST, Tananarive). Poésie.

4304. ———. *Volumes*. Tananarive: Imprimerie de l'Iimerina, 1928. Poésie.

4305. *Jean-Joseph Rabearivelo, cet inconnu?* Paris: Editions du Sud, 1990. Actes du colloque international de Madagascar: Antananarivo, 1987.

4306. Rabemananjara, Jacques. *Agape des dieux. Tritriva.* Paris: Présence Africaine, 1962. (Nouvelle édition en 1988). Théâtre.

4307. ———. *Antidote.* Paris: Présence Africaine, 1961. Poésie.

4308. ———. *Antsa.* Paris: Présence Africaine, 1956. Edition antérieure: Imprimerie R. Drivon, 1948. Poésie.

4309. ———. *Les Boutriers de l'aurore.* Paris: Présence Africaine, 1957. Théâtre.

4310. ———. *Les Dieux malgaches.* Gap: Orphys, 1947. Version destinée à la scène. Nouvelle édition en 1988 chez Présence Africaine, Paris. Théâtre.

4311. ———. *Lamba.* Paris: Présence Africaine, 1956. (Préface d'Aimé Césaire). Poésie.

4312. ———. *Les Ordalies: sonnets d'outre-temps.* Paris: Présence Africaine, 1972. Poésie.

4313. ———. *Poésie. Œuvres complètes.* Paris: Présence Africaine, 1978. Poésie.

4314. ———. *Rien qu'encens et filigrane.* Paris: Présence Africaine, 1987. Poésie.

4315. ———. *Rites millénaires.* Paris: Seghers, 1955. (Préface de Senghor). Poésie.

4316. ———. *Sur les marches du soir.* Gap: Orphys, 1942. Poésie.

4317. ———. *Thrènes d'avant l'aurore: Madagascar.* Paris: Présence Africaine, 1985. Poésie.

4318. Ravelonanosky, G. *Jacques Rabemananjara: textes commentés.* Paris: Nathan, 1970. (Coll. Classiques du monde).

4319. Rabemananjara, Raymond William. *Chronique d'une saison carcérale en Lémurie*. Tananarive: Editions Revue de l'Océan Indien, 1990. Roman.

4320. ———. *Rendez-vous au capricorne*. Paris: L'Harmattan, 1990. Roman.

4321. Rabezanahary, Dominique. *Tout part en fumée . . . sauf l'amitié*. Inédit, 1991. Théâtre.

4322. Rafenomanjato, Charlotte (F). *L'Oiseau de proie*. Inédit, 1989. Théâtre.

4323. ———. *Le Pétale écarlate*. Tananarive: Société malgache d'édition, 1990. Roman.

4324. ———. *Le Troupeau*. Inédit, 1990. Théâtre.

4325. Raharimanana, Jean-Luc. *Lépreux! et dix-neuf autres nouvelles. 12e concours de la meilleure nouvelle RFI*. Paris: Hatier, 1992. Nouvelle.

4326. ———. *Le Prophète et le président*. Inédit, 1990. Théâtre.

4327. Rajemisa-Raolison, Régis. *Les Fleurs de l'Ile rouge*. Tananarive: Imprimerie tananarivienne, 1948. (Nouvelle édition en 1983 chez l'Imprimerie catholique, Tananarive). Poésie.

4328. Rakonoiref, François (dir.). *Le Mythe d'Ibonia*. Antananarivo: Foi et justice, 1993. Bilingue malgache-français. Contes.

4329. Rakotoson, Michèle (F). *Le Bain des reliques*. Paris: Karthala, 1988. Roman.

4330. ———. *Dadabé*, suivi de *Le Voyage et la complainte d'un naufrage*. Paris: Karthala, 1984. Nouvelles.

4331. ———. *La Maison morte: un jour ma mémoire*. Paris: L'Harmattan, 1991. (Coll. Théâtre sud, 3). Théâtre.

4332. Rakotovao Cohen-Bessy, Annick (F). *Journal d'un Malgache du XIXe siècle.* Paris: L'Harmattan, 1991. Présentation, traduction et annotations du manuscrit de Rakotovao, 1843-1906. Mémoires.

4333. Rakotozafy, Nivoarisoa Mathilde (F). *Les Chaînes de la liberté.* Antananarivo: Chez l'auteur, 1990. Poésie.

4334. Ramboa, Adrien. *El Mozo ou le gamin d'Espagne.* Tananarive: 1963. Roman.

4335. Ramboa, Eugénie (F). *Lys noirs de l'Ile rouge.* La Chapelle Montligeon: Imprimerie de Montligeon, 1931. Récit autobiographique.

4336. Ranaivo, Flavien. *L'Ombre et le vent.* Tananarive: Imprimerie officielle, 1947. (Nouvelle édition en 1970 chez Kraus Reprint, Nendeln). Poésie.

4337. Valette, Jean. *Flavien Ranaivo. Textes commentés.* Paris: Nathan, 1968. (Coll. Classiques du monde).

4338. Randriamirado, Narcisse. *Allons'omelette.* Inédit, 1991. Théâtre.

4339. Randrianasolo-Ravony, Pierre. *Serments de prisonniers.* Tananarive: Trano printy loterana, 1973. Poésie.

4340. Rasaloarijao, Perle (F). *Plein-Songe.* Inédit. (Poèmes écrit entre 1979 et 1991). Poésie.

4341. Rasamoelina, Robert. *Mon Séjour chez les Vazimba Baosy de Bemaraha.* Tananarive: Imprimerie Tatsinana, 1988. Récit.

4342. Ratoejanahary, Maxime. *Chante ma lire.* Tananarive: Trano printy loterana, 1990. Poésie.

4343. Ravoaja, Suzanne (F). *Fanano.* Créteil: Centre d'Etudes et de Recherches sur les Civilisations, Langues et Littérature d'Expression Française, 1989. Théâtre.

4344. Razafindramady-Cerezo, Suzy (F). *Madagascar mon pays.* s.l.: Imprimerie Deval, 1981.

PORTUGUESE
AND OTHER LITERATURES

PORTUGUESE

OVERVIEW

Bibliographies

4345. Chamberlain, Bobby J. *Portuguese language and Luso-Brazilian literature: an annotated guide to selected reference works.* New York: Modern Language Association, 1989.

4346. Ferreira, Manuel, and Gerald Moser. *Bibliografia das literaturas africanas de expressão portuguesa.* Lisbon: Ed. Imprensa Nacional/Casa da Moeda, 1983.

4347. Moser, Gerald, and Manuel Ferreira. *A New bibliography of the Lusophone literatures of Africa=Nova bibliografia das literaturas africanas de expressão portuguesa.* London: H. Zell, 1993. 2nd rev. ed. Sequel to 4346.

Anthologies

4348. Andrade, Mário de. *La poésie africaine d'expression portugaise.* Paris: Oswald, 1969. Tr. de Jean Todrani. (Les poètes contemporains en poche; 9). Poetry.

4349. ———. *Literatura africana de expressão portuguesa.* Nendeln: Kraus, 1970. 2 v. Reprint of: Algiers, 1968.

4350. Burness, Don (ed. and tr.). *Echoes of the sunbird: an anthology of contemporary African poetry.* Athens, Ohio: Ohio University, Center for International Studies, 1993. (Monographs in international studies. African series; 62).

4351. ———. (ed.). *A Horse of white clouds: poems from Lusophone Africa.* Athens, Ohio: Center for International Studies, Ohio University, 1989. Parallel Portuguese-English text. (Monographs in international studies. Africa series; 55).

4352. César, Amândio. *Antologia do conto ultramarino.* Lisbon: Ed. Verbo, 1972. (Biblioteca Básixa Verbo; 85).

4353. ———. *Contos portugueses do ultramar.* Porto: Portucalense Ed., 1969. 2 v.

4354. Chipasula, Frank (ed.). *When my brothers come home: poems from Central and Southern Africa.* Middletown, CT: Wesleyan University Press, 1985.

4355. Dickinson, Margaret (ed. and tr.). *When bullets begin to flower: poems of resistance from Angola, Mozambique and Guiné.* Nairobi: EAPH, 1972. Also pub: Nairobi: Heinemann Kenya, 1989.

4356. Ferreira, Serafim (ed.). *Resistência Africana.* Lisbon: Dabril, 1975. (Universidade de Povo; 2). Poetry.

4357. Medina, Cremilda de Araújo. *Sonha mamana Africa.* São Paulo: Epopeia, 1987. Poetry and prose.

4358. Tavani, Giuseppe (ed.). *Poesia africana di rivolta: Angola, Mozambico, Guinea, Capo Verde, São Tomé.* Bari, Italy: Laterza, 1969. (Tempi Nuovi; 31).

General studies

4359. Burness, Don. *Critical perspectives on Lusophone literature from Africa.* Washington: Three Continents Press, 1981. English and Portuguese.

4360. Ferreira, Manuel. *Literaturas africanas de expressão portuguesa.* Lisbon: Instituto de Cultura Portuguesa, 1977. 2 v. (Biblioteca Breve; 6-7).

4361. ———. *Literaturas africanas de língua portuguesa.* Lisbon: Fundação Calouste Gulbenkian, 1987.

4362. ———. *No reino de Caliban: antologia panorâmica da poesia africana de expressão portuguesa.* Lisbon: Seara Nova, 1975. 3 v.

4363. ———. *O discurso no percurso africano* Lisbon: Plátano, 1989.

4364. Gérard, Albert S. (ed.). *European-language writing in sub-Saharan Africa.* Budapest: Akadémiai Kiadó, 1986. 2 v. (A Comparative history of literatures in European languages; 6).

4365. Hamilton, Russell G. *Voices from an empire: a history of Afro-Portuguese literature.* Minneapolis: University of Minnesota Press, 1975.

4366. Margarido, Alfredo. *Estudos sobre literatura das nações africanas de lingua portuguesa.* Lisbon: Regra do Jogo, 1980.

4367. Massa, Jean Michel. *Dix études sur la langue portugaise en Afrique.* Rennes: Presses universitaires, 1990.

4368. ———, Manuel Ferreira, and José Augusto França (eds.). *Les littératures africaines de langue portugaise: à la recherche de l'identité individuelle et nationale: actes du Colloque International, Paris, 1984.* Paris: Fondation Calouste Gulbenkian/Centre Culturel Portugais, 1985.

4369. Moser, Gerald. *Essays in Portuguese-African literature.* University Park: Pennsylvania State University, 1969.

4370. Nwezeh, E. C. *Literature and colonialism in Lusophone Africa.* Lagos: Centre for Black African Studies and Civilization, 1986.

4371. Oliveira, Mário, and H. G. Teixeira (eds.). *Reler Africa.* Coimbra: Coimbra University Press, 1990.

4372. Preto-Rodas, Richard A. *Negritude as a theme in the poetry of the Portuguese-speaking world.* Gainesville: University of Florida Press, 1970.

4373. Rosário, Lourenço. *A narrativa africana de expressão oral.* Lisbon: ICALP & Angolé, 1989.

4374. Santilli, Maria Aparecida. *Estórias africanas: história e antologia.* São Paulo: Atica, 1985.

4375. Santos, Eduardo dos. *A negritude e a luta pelas independências na Africa portuguesa.* Lisbon: Minerva, 1975. (Minerva de Bolso; 40).

4376. Trigo, Salvato. *Introduçao à literatura angolana de expressão portuguesa.* Porto: Brasília Editora, 1977.

4377. Venâncio, José Carlos. *Literatura e poder na Africa lusófona.* Lisbon: Instituto de Cultura e Língua Portuguesa, Ministéria da Eduçao, 1992. (Diálogo).

ANGOLA

Bibliographies

4378. Chamberlain, Bobby J. *Portuguese language and Luso-Brazilian literature: an annotated guide to selected reference works.* New York: Modern Language Association, 1989.

4379. Moser, Gerald, and Manuel Ferreira. *A New bibliography of the Lusophone literatures of Africa=Nova bibliografia das literaturas africanas de expressão portuguesa.* London: H. Zell, 1993. 2nd rev. ed., pp. 59-161.

4380. Mourão, Fernando, et al. *Contribuiçao a uma bio-bibliografia sobre Fernando Monteiro de Castro Soromenho.* São Paulo: Centro de Estudos Africanos, 1977.

Anthologies

4381. Burness, Don. *Fire: six writers from Angola, Mozambique and Cape Verde.* Washington: Three Continents Press, 1977.

4382. Dickinson, Margaret (ed. and tr.). *When bullets begin to flower: poems of resistance from Angola,*

Mozambique and Guiné. Nairobi: EAPH, 1972. Also pub: Nairobi: Heinemann Kenya, 1989.

4383. Wolfers, Michael (ed. and tr.). *Poems from Angola.* London: Heinemann, 1979. (AWS; 215).

General studies

4384. Andrade, Costa. *Literatura angolana (opiniões).* Lisbon; Luanda: Edições 70; UEA, 1980. (Autores Angolanos 5).

4385. António, Mário. *A sociedade angolana do fim do século XIX e um seu escritor.* Luanda: Nós, 1961.

4386. Ervedosa, Carlos. *A literatura Angolana: Resenha historica.* Lisbon: Casa dos Estudantes do Império, 1963. Rev. ed.: *Roteiro da Literatura angolana.* Luanda: Sociedade Cultural de Angola, 1975.

4387. Laban, Michel. *Angola: encontro com escritores.* Porto: Fundação António de Almeida, 1991. 2 v. Interviews.

4388. Mourão, Fernando. *A Sociedade Angolana através da Literatura.* São Paulo: Editora Atica, 1978. (Ensaios; 381).

4389. Neto, Agostinho. *On Literature and national culture.* Luanda: Angolan Writers Union, 1979. (Cadernos lavra e oficina; 20). Essays.

4390. Ryáuzova, Helena A. *Dez anos de literatura angolana: ensaio sobre e moderna literatura angolana 1975-1985.* Lisbon; Luanda: Edições 70; UEA, 1987. (Estudos; 11).

Authors

4391. Abranches, Henrique. *Cântico barroco.* Lisbon; Luanda: Edições 70; UEA, 1988. (Contemporâneos). Poetry.

4392. ———. *Kissoko de guerra.* Luanda; Porto: UEA; Asa, 1989. 2 v. Novel.

4393. ———. *A konkhava de Feti*. Lisbon: Edições 70, 1981. (Coll. Autores Angolanos; 36). Novel.

4394. ———. *O clã de Novembrino*. Luanda; Porto: UEA; Asa, 1989. 3 v. Novel.

4395. Abreu, Antero. *Permanência*. Lisbon; Luanda: Edições 70; UEA, 1979 (Autores Angolanos; 18). Poetry.

4396. ———. *Poesia intermitente*. Lisbon; Luanda: Edições 70; UEA, 1988. (Contemporâneos). Poetry.

4397. ———. *A Tua voz Angola*. Luanda: UEA, 1978. (Cadernos Lavra e oficina; 11). Poetry.

4398. Agualusa, José Eduardo. *A conjura*. Lisbon: Caminho, 1989. (Coll. Uma Terra Sem Amos). Novel.

4399. ———. *A Feira dos assombrados*. Lisbon: Vega, 1992. Novel.

4400. Albuquerque, Orlando de. *Histórias do diablo: contos*. Braga: Capricórnio & Pax, 1979. Stories.

4401. ———. *O Homem que tinha a chuva*. Lisbon: Agência-Geral do Ultramar, 1968. Novel.

4402. ———. *Ovimbanda*. Sá da Bandeira: Imbondeiro, 1967. (Coll. Circulo; 2/3). Drama.

4403. Andrade, Costa. *No velho ninguém toca*. Lisbon: Sá da Costa, 1979. (Vozes do Mundo; 12). Drama.

4404. ———. *Poesia com armas*. Lisbon: Sá da Costa, 1975. (Vozes do Mundo; 4). Also pub.: Luanda: UEA, 1978.

4405. António, Mario. *Rosto de Europa*. Braga: Editora Pax, 1968. (Metropole e Ultramar; 40). Poetry.

4406. Antunes, Antonio Lobo. *South of nowhere: a novel*. New York: Random House, 1983. Tr. of: *Os cus de Judas*.

4407. Assis Junior, António. *O Segredo da Morta: romance de costumes angolenses.* Luanda: Luzitana, 1934. Novel.

4408. Barbeitos, Arlindo. *Angola Angolê Angolema.* Lisbon: Sá da Costa, 1976. (Vozes do mundo; 6). Poetry.

4409. ———. *Fiapos de sonho.* Lisbon: Vega, 1992. Poetry.

4410. Bessa Victor, Geraldo. *Monandengue.* Lisbon: Livraria Portugal, 1973. Poetry.

4411. Cardoso, António. *Baixa e musseques.* Lisbon; Luanda: Edições 70; UEA, 1980 (Autores Angola; 30). Stories.

4412. ———. *Chão de exilio.* Lisbon: Africa Editores, 1980. (Cantico Geral). Poetry.

4413. Cardoso, Boaventura. *Dizanga Dia Muenhu.* Lisbon: Edições 70, 1977. (Autores Angolanos; 12). Stories.

4414. Carvalho, Ruy. *Lavra paralela.* Luanda: UEA, 1987. (Cadernos Lavra & Oficina; 70). Poetry.

4415. Cosme, Leonel. *A revolta.* Sá da Bandeira: Imbondeiro, 1963. 3 v. Trilogy. v. 2: *A Terra da promissnao.* (Porto: Afrontamento, 1988). Novel.

4416. Cruz, Tomaz Vieira da. *Quissange.* Luanda: Lello, 1971. Poetry.

4417. David, Raúl. *Narrativas ao acaso.* Luanda: UEA, 1988. 2 v. (Cadernos Lavra & Oficina; 32, 77). Stories.

4418. Ervedosa, Carlos. *Era no tempo das acácias floridas.* Linda-a-Velha: ALAC, 1991. (Varia Angola). Poetry and stories.

4419. Feijoó k, J. A. S. Lopito. *Cartas de amor.* Pontevedera, Spain; Braga: Minho, 1990. (Cadernos do Povo. Poesia). Poetry.

4420. Ferreira, Carlos. *Começar de novo*. Luanda: UEA, 1986. (Cadernos Lavra & Oficina; 61). Poetry.

4421. Figueira, Luís. *Miragem africana*. Porto: Companhia Portuguesa, 1935. Novel.

4422. Jacinto, António. *Poemas*. Lisbon: Casa dos Estudantes do Império, 1961. (Autores Ultramarinos; 9). Poetry.

4423. ———. *Sobreviver em Tarrafal de Santiago*. Lisbon; Luanda: Ulisseia; UEA, 1984. Poetry.

4424. Lara, Alda (F). *Poemas*. Sá da Bandeira: Edicoes Imbondeiro, 1966. Poetry.

4425. ———. *Poesia*. Luanda: Caderinos Lavra & Oficina, 1979. Poetry.

4426. ———. *Tempo de chuva*. Lobito: Capricórnio, 1973. Short stories.

4427. César, Amândio. *Alda Lara: na moderna poesia de Angola*. Lisboa: Edições do Tempo, 1978.

4428. Lara Filho, Ernesto. *O Canto do matrindinde*. Lobito: Capricórnio, 1974. (Cadernos Capricórnio; 21/22). Poetry.

4429. Lima, Manuel dos Santos. *As Lágrimas e o vento: romance*. [Lisboa]: Africa editora, 1975. Novel.

4430. ———. *A pele do diabo: drama em III actos*. Lisboa: Africa editora, 1977. (Colecçáo Tempo africano; 4). Drama.

4431. Macedo, Jorge. *Clima do Povo*. Lisbon: Edições 70, 1977. (Autores Angolanos; 5). Poetry.

4432. ———. *Voz de tambarino*. Lisbon; Luanda: Edições 70; UEA, 1980. (Autores Angolanos; 28). Poetry.

4433. Maimona, João. *As abelhas do dia*. Luanda: UEA, 1988. (Contemporâneos). Poetry.

4434. Melo, Jão. *Tanto amor (1983-1988)*. Luanda: UEA, 1989. (Contemporâneos). Poetry.

4435. Neto, Agostinho. *A renúncia impossível*. Luanda: INALD, 1983. Poetry.

4436. ———. *Sagrada esperança*. Lisbon: Sá da Costa, 1974. (Vozes do Mundo; 1). Pub. in English as: *Sacred hope*. Dar es Salaam: Tanzania Publishing House, 1974. Poetry.

4437. Neto, Eugénia. *Foi esperança e foi certeza*. Lisbon; Luanda: Edições 70; UEA, 1979. (Autores angolanos; 22). Poetry.

4438. Pepetela. *Mayombe*. Lisbon; Luanda: Edições 70; UEA, 1980. Pub. in English: London: Heinemann, 1983, Harare: ZPH, 1983. Novel.

4439. ———. *Muana Puó*. Lisbon; Luanda: Edições 70; UEA, 1978. (Autores Angolanos; 14). Novel.

4440. ———. *O Cão e os caluandas: estórias de um cão pastor na cidade de Luanda*. Lisbon; Luanda: Pub. Dom Quixote; UEA, 1985. (Autores de lingua Portuguesa). Novel.

4441. Pimentel, Carlos. *Tijolo a Tijolo*. Luanda: Instituto Nacional do Livro e do Disco, 1980. Poetry.

4442. Ribas, Oscar. *Tudo isto aconteceu*. Luanda: Ediçao do Autor, 1975. Autobiographical novel.

4443. Rocha, Jofre. *Assim se fez madrugada*. Lisbon: Edições 70, 1977. (Autores angolanos; 9). Poetry.

4444. Rui, Manuel. *Regresso adiado*. Lisbon: Ediçoes 70, 1978. 2nd ed. (Autores Angolanos; 7). Short stories.

4445. ———. *Yes, comrade!* Minneapolis: University of Minnesota Press, 1993. Orig. pub. as: *Sim, camarada!* Lisboa: Edições 70, 1977. Tr. by R. W. Sousa. Short stories.

4446. Santos, Amaldo. *O cesto de Katandu e outros contos*. Luanda; Lisbon: UEA; Edições 70, 1987. (Autores Angolanos; 42). Short stories.

4447. Soromenho, Castro. *Terra morta*. Rio de Janeiro: Livraria-Editôra da Casa do Estudante do Brasil, 1949. Novel.

4448. Bastide, Roger. *L'Afrique dans l'oeuvre de Castro Soromenho*. Paris: Oswald, 1960.

4449. Van-Dúnem, Domingos. *O Panfleto*. Luanda: UEA, 1988. Drama.

4450. Vieira, José Luandino. *João Vêncio: os seus amores*. Lisbon; Luanda: Edições 70; UEA, 1979. Novella.

4451. ————. *Luuanda*. London: Heinemann, 1980. Tr. by T. L. Bender and D. S. Hill. (AWS; 222). First pub. in Portuguese: Lisbon: ABC, 1963. Short stories.

4452. ————. *No Antigamente na Vida*. Lisbon: Edições 70, 1974. Autobiographical stories.

4453. ————. *Nós, os do Makulusu*. Lisbon: Sá da Costa, 1974. (Vozes do Mundo; 2). Novel.

4454. ————. *A Vida verdadeira de Domingos Xavier*. Lisbon: Edições 70, 1974. Written in 1961. First pub. in French: Paris: Présence Africaine, 1971. Pub. in English as: *The Real life of Domingos Xavier*. London: Heinemann, 1978. Novel.

4455. ————. *Vidas novas*. Porto: Afrotamento, 1975. Stories.

4456. Laban, Michel, et al. *Luandino: José Luandino Vieira e a sua obra: estudos, testemunhos, entrevistas*. Lisboa: Edições 70, 1980.

4457. Xitu, Uanhenga. *Manana*. Lisbon: Edições 70, 1978. (Autores angolanos; 11). Novel.

4458. ————. *The World of mestre Tamoda*. London: Readers International, 1988. Orig. pub. as: *Os discursos de "Mestre" Tamoda*. Lisbon; Luanda: Ulisseia; UEA, 1984. Stories.

CAPE VERDE/ILHAS de CABO VERDE

Bibliographies

4459. Chamberlain, Bobby J. *Portuguese language and Luso-Brazilian literature: an annotated guide to selected reference works.* New York: Modern Language Association, 1989.

4460. McCarthy, Joseph M. *Guinea-Bissau and Cape Verde Islands: a comprehensive bibliography.* New York: Garland, 1977.

4461. Moser, Gerald, and Manuel Ferreira. *A New bibliography of the Lusophone literatures of Africa=Nova bibliografia das literaturas africanas de expressão portuguesa.* London: H. Zell, 1993. 2nd rev. ed., pp. 162-219.

Anthologies

4462. Burness, Don. *Fire: six writers from Angola, Mozambique and Cape Verde.* Washington: Three Continents Press, 1977.

4463. Ellen, Maria M. *Across the Atlantic: an anthology of Cape Verdean literature.* North Dartmouth, MA: Centre for the Portuguese Speaking World, 1988.

4464. Figueiredo, Jaime de. *Modernos poetas cabo-verdianos.* Praia: Henriquinas do Achamento de Cabo Verde, 1961. Poetry.

4465. Mariano, Gabriel. *Ladeira grande: antologia poética.* Lisbon: Vega, 1993. Poetry.

4466. Romano, Luís. *Contravento: antologia bilinge de poetas caboverdianos.* Taunton, MA: Atlantis, 1982.

4467. ———. *Ilha: contos lusoverdianos de temática europáfrica & brasilamérica.* Mindelo, Cape Verde: Ilhéu, 1991. Short stories.

General studies

4468. Araujo, Norman. *A Study of Cape Verdean literature.* Boston: Boston College, 1966.

4469. Ferreira, Manuel. *A aventura crioula, ou Cabo Verde, uma sintese étnica e cultural.* Lisbon: Ulisseia, 1976. Enlarged ed. pub.: Lisbon: Plátano, 1973.

4470. Laban, Michel (entrevistas de). *Cabo Verde: encontro com escritores.* Porto: Fundaçáo Eng. António de Almeida, 1992. 2 v. Interviews.

4471. Moser, Gerald. *Changing Africa: the first literary generation of independent Cape Verde.* Philadelphia: American Philosophical Society, 1992. (Transactions; v. 82 pt. 4).

4472. Romano, Luís. *Evocação de Portugal e presença do Brasil na literatura caboverdeana.* Mossoró, Brazil: Prefeitura Municipal, 1966.

4473. Silveira, Onésimo. *Consciencializaçao na literatura caboverdiana.* Lisbon: Casa dos Estudantes do Império, 1963.

Authors

4474. Almada, José Luís Hopfer. *A Sombra do sol.* Praia, Cape Verde: Ed. Voz di Povo & Movimento Pró-Cultura, 1990. 2 v. Poetry.

4475. Amarilis, Orlanda (F). *Cais-do-Sodré té Salamansa.* Coimbra, Portugal: Centelha, 1974. Short stories.

4476. Barbosa, Jorge. *Arquipélago.* S. Vicente: Ed. Claridade, 1935. Poetry.

4477. ———. *Poesias.* Praia, Cape Verde: ICL, 1989. (Coll. Poesia). Poetry.

4478. Duarte, Vera. *Amanhã amadrugada.* Lisbon: Vega, 1983. "Tomorrow the dawn." Poetry.

4479. Fortes, Corsino. *Arvore e tambor.* Praia; Lisbon: ICL; Ed. Pub. Dom Quixote, 1986. Poetry.

4480. Frusoni, Sérgio. *Vangêle contód d'nôs móda.* S. Filipe (Fogo Island): Ed. Terra Nova, 1979. Poetry.

4481. Lopes, Baltasar. *A Cademata – Le Carnet.* Praia, Cape Verde: ICL & Centre Culturel Français, 1986. Short story.

4482. ———. *Chiquinho.* São Vicente; Lisbon: Claridade, 1947. Novel.

4483. Lopes, José. *Braits (Sonnets): The nurses of Hong-Kong, President Roosevelt, Saudoso adeus, Inscriptio.* Lisbon: Ed. Império, 1945. Poems in English, Portuguese, and Latin.

4484. ———. *Poesias escolhidas.* Praia, Cape Verde: Comissão para as Comemorações do I. Centenario do Nascimento do Poeta, 1972. Poetry.

4485. Lopes, Manuel. *Chuva braba.* Lisbon: Instituto de Cultura e Fomento de Cabo Verde, 1956. Novel.

4486. ———. *Os flagelados do vento leste.* Lisbon: Ed. Ulisseia, 1960. Also pub.: Lisbon: Vega, 1991. Novel.

4487. Martins, Ovidio. *Caminnhada.* Lisbon: Casa dos Estudantes do Império, 1962. (Autores ultramarinos; 13). Poetry.

4488. ———. *Gritarie. Berrarrei. Matarei. Não vou para Pasárgada.* Rotterdam: Cabo-Verdianidade, 1973. (Coll. Antievasão). Poetry in Creole and Portuguese.

4489. ———. *Tchutchinha.* Praia, Cape Verde: ICL, 1983. (Coll. Dragoeiro). Tales.

4490. Miranda, Nuno. *40 poemas escolhidos.* Lisbon: Agência-Geral do Ultramar, 1974. (Coll. Unidade. Poesia; 12).

4491. ———. *Cais de pedra.* Praia, Cape Verde: ICL, 1989. Novel.

4492. Os'orio, Oswaldo (ed.). *Emergência da poesia em Amílcar Cabral: 30 poemas.* Praia: ICL, 1983. (Dragoeiro). Poetry and essays.

4493. Rodrigues, João. *O casamento de Juquim Dadana.* São Vicente: Pub. Gráfia do Mindelo, 1979. Novella.

4494. Varela, João Manuel. *O primeiro livro de Notcha.* São Vicente: Gráfica Mindelo, 1975. (Discursos; 4). Poetry.

4495. Vieira, Arménio. *Cabo Verde.* Praia: CIDAC, 1979. Poetry.

4496. ———. *O eleito do sol.* Praia: Sonacor, 1989. Novel.

4497. Vieira, Artur. *Matilde: viage di distino.* Rio de Janiero: Privately printed, 1991. Creole and Portuguese. Drama.

GUINEA-BISSAU/GUINÉ-BISSAU

Bibliographies

4498. Chamberlain, Bobby J. *Portuguese language and Luso-Brazilian literature: an annotated guide to selected reference works.* New York: Modern Language Association, 1989.

4499. McCarthy, Joseph M. *Guinea-Bissau and Cape Verde Islands: a comprehensive bibliography.* New York: Garland, 1977.

4500. Moser, Gerald, and Manuel Ferreira. *A New bibliography of the Lusophone literatures of Africa=Nova bibliografia das literaturas africanas de expressão portuguesa.* London: H. Zell, 1993. 2nd rev. ed., pp. 220-226.

Anthologies

4501. *Antologia poética da Guinéa-Bissau.* Bissau; Lisbon: União Nacional dos Artistas e Escritores de Guiné-Bissau; Inquérito, 1990.

4502. Dickinson, Margaret (ed. and tr.). *When bullets begin to flower: poems of resistance from Angola, Mozambique and Guiné.* Nairobi: EAPH, 1972. Also pub: Nairobi: Heinemann Kenya, 1989.

General studies

4503. Ferreira, Manuel. *Literaturas africanas de expressão portuguesa.* Lisbon: Instituto de Cultura Portuguesa, 1977. v. 1.

Authors

4504. Cabral, Vasco. *A Luta é a minha primavera: poemas.* Linda-a-Velha, Portugal: Africa Ed., 1981. Poetry.

4505. Ferreira, João. *Uaná.* São Paulo: Global, 1986. Novel.

4506. Proença, Hélder. *Não posso adiar a palavra.* Lisbon: Sá da Costa, 1982. (Vozes do mundo). Poetry.

MOZAMBIQUE/MOÇAMBIQUE

Bibliographies

4507. Chamberlain, Bobby J. *Portuguese language and Luso-Brazilian literature: an annotated guide to selected reference works.* New York: Modern Language Association, 1989.

4508. Moser, Gerald, and Manuel Ferreira. *A New bibliography of the Lusophone literatures of Africa=Nova bibliografia das literaturas africanas de expressão portuguesa.* London: H. Zell, 1993. 2nd rev. ed., pp. 227-274.

Anthologies

4509. Burness, Don. *Fire: six writers from Angola, Mozambique and Cape Verde.* Washington: Three Continents Press, 1977.

4510. ———— (ed.). *A Horse of white clouds: poems from Lusophone Africa.* Athens, Ohio: Center for International Studies, Ohio University, 1989. Parallel Portuguese-English text. (Monographs in international studies. Africa series; 55).

4511. Carlos, Papiniano (ed.). *As Armas estão acesas nas nossas Mãos: antologia breve da poesia revolucionária de Moçambique.* Porto: Edições a Pesar de Tudo, 1976. Poetry.

4512. Dickinson, Margaret (ed. and tr.). *When bullets begin to flower: poems of resistance from Angola, Mozambique and Guiné.* Nairobi: EAPH, 1972. Also pub: Nairobi: Heinemann Kenya, 1989.

4513. García, Xosé Lois. *Poesia mozambicana del siglo XX.* Saragossa: Olifante-Poesia, 1987. Spanish and Portuguese.

4514. Mendes, Orlando, et al. *Sobre literatura moçambicana.* Maputo: Instituto Nacional do Livro e do Disco, 1982. Critical anthology of poetry, essays, and stories.

4515. Searle, Chris (comp.). *The Sunflower of hope: poems from the Mozambican revolution.* London: Allison & Busby, 1982.

General studies

4516. Ferreira, Manuel. *Literaturas africanas de expressão portuguesa.* Lisbon: Instituto de Cultura Portuguesa, 1977. v. 2.

4517. Mendonça, Fátima. *Literatura moçambicana: a história e as escritas.* Maputo: Faculdade de Letras & Núcleo Editorial da Universidade Eduardo Mondlane, 1988.

Authors

4518. Azevdo, Alexandre P. *Minkulungwane*. Maputo: Associação dos Combatentes da Lutade Libertação Nacional, 1988. Fiction.

4519. Azevdo, Mario J. *The Returning hunter*. Thompson, CT: Inter Culture, 1978. (African sketches). Novella.

4520. Bucuane, Juvenal. *Segredos da alma*. Maputo: Associação dos Escritores Moçambicanos, 1989. (Colecção Timbila; 9). Poetry.

4521. Cardoso, Carlos. *Directo ao assunto*. Maputo: Tempográfica, 1985 (Colecção "Gostar de Ler"; 8). Poetry.

4522. Chiziane, Paulina. *Balada de amor ao vento*. [Maputo]: Associaçao dos Escritores Moçambicanos, 1990. (Karingana; 12). Fiction.

4523. Couto, Fernando. *Feições para um retrato*. Beira: Automóvel e Touring Clube de Moçambique, 1973. (Vozes ce Moçambique; 1). Poetry.

4524. Couto, Mia. *Cada homem é uma raça: estórias*. Lisbon: Caminho, 1990. (Uma Terra sem amos; 52). Stories.

4525. ———. *Cronicando*. Lisboa: Caminho, 1991. Fiction.

4526. ———. *Every man is a race*. Oxford: Heinemann, 1994. (AWS). Tr. of: *Cada homem é uma raça*, and *Cronicando*, by David Brookshaw. Fiction.

4527. ———. *Raíz de orvalho*. Maputo: Ed. Caderns Tempo, 1983. Poetry.

4528. ———. *Terra sonámbula: romance*. Lisboa: Caminho, 1992. (Uma Terra sem amos; 62). Novel.

4529. ———. *Voices made night*. Oxford: Heinemann, 1990. Tr. by David Brookshaw. Orig. pub. as: *Vozes anoitecidas*. Maputo: AEMO, 1986. Short stories.

4530. Craveirinha, José. *Chigubo*. Lisbon: Casa dos Estudantes de Império, 1964. (Autores ultramarinos; 14). Poetry.

4531. ———. *Karingana ua karingana*. Lourenço Marques: Académica, 1974. 2nd ed.: Lisbon: Edições 70, 1982. Poetry.

4532. ———. *Maria*. Linda-a-Velha, Portugal: Africa, Literatura, Arte e Cultura, 1988. (Collecçao Africana). Poetry.

4533. Leite, Ana Mafalda. *A poética de J. Craveirinha*. Lisbon: Vega, 1991. (Palavra africana).

4534. Dias, João Pedro Grabato ["Quadros, António"]. *O povo é nos*. Porto: Afrontamento, 1991. Poetry.

4535. Ferreira, Reinaldo. *Poemas*. Lourenço Marques [Maputo]: Imprensa Nacional, 1960. Poetry.

4536. Guerra, Ruy Pereira, Rui. *Calabar, o elógio da traição*. Rio de Janiero: Civilização Brasileira, 1973. Drama.

4537. Honwana, Luis Bernardo. *We killed Mangy-Dog and other Mozambique stories*. London: Heinemann, 1969. Tr. by D. Guedes. (AWS; 60). First pub. as: *Nós matamos o cão tinhoso!* Lourenço Marques: Sociedade de Imprensa de Moçambique, 1964. Short stories.

4538. Khan, Gulamo. *Moçambicano*. Maputo: AEMO, 1990. (Colecção Timbila; 8). Poetry.

4539. Knopfli, Rui. *Memória consentida: 20 anos de poesia 1959/1979*. Lisbon: Imprensa Nacional/Casa da Moeda, 1984.

4540. ———. *O escriba acocorado*. Lisbon: Liv. Moraes, 1978. Poetry.

4541. Magaia, Lina. *Dumba nengue: run for your life: peasant tales of tragedy in Mozambique*. Trenton: Africa World Press, 1988. Orig. pub.: Maputo: Cadernos Tempo, 1987.

4542. Melo, Guilherme. *As raizes do ódio*. Lisbon: Arcádia, 1965. 2nd ed.: Beira: Notícias da Beira, 1991. Novel.

4543. ———. *A estranha aventura*. Beira: Notícias da Beira, 1961. (Prosadores de Moçambique). Stories.

4544. ———. *A sombra dos dias*. Lisbon: Bertrand & Circulo de Leitores, 1981. Autobiographical novel.

4545. Mendes, Orlando. *Adeus de gutucúmbui*. Lourenço Marques [Maputo]: Académica, 1974. Poetry.

4546. ———. *Lume florindo na forja*. Lisbon; Maputo: Edições 70; INLD, 1980. (Autores Moçambicanos; 3). Poetry.

4547. ———. *Portagem*. Beira: Notícias da Beira, 1965. 2nd ed.: Maputo: INLD, 1982. Novel.

4548. Nogar, Rui. *Silêncio escancarado*. Maputo: INLD, 1982. (Autores Moçambicanos; 7). Poetry.

4549. Pitta, Eduardo. *A linguagem da desordem*. Lisbon: Imprensa Nacional/Casa da Moeda, 1983. Poetry.

4550. Polanah, Luis. *The Saga of a cotton capulana*. Madison: African Studies Center, University of Wisconsin, 1981. Tr. by Tamara Bender. (Occasional paper). Fiction.

4551. Santos, Marcelino dos. *Canto do amor natural*. Maputo: AEMO, 1985. Poetry.

4552. Saúte, Nelson, and António Sopa (eds.). *A Ilha de Moçambique pela voz dos poetas*. Lisbon: Edições 70, 1992. Poetry and prose.

4553. Sousa, Noémia de (F). *Poemas*. Lourenço Marques [Maputo]: Privately printed, 1951. Poetry.

4554. Viegas, Jorge. *Novelo de chamas*. Linda-a-Velha, Portugal: ALAC, 1989. (A preto & branco; 2). Poetry.

4555. White, Eduardo. *O País de mim*. Maputo: AEMO, 1989. (Coleçcão Timbila; 10). Poetry.

SÃO TOMÉ and PRÍNCIPE ISLANDS/ILHAS de SÃO TOMÉ e PRÍNCIPE

Bibliographies

4556. Chamberlain, Bobby J. *Portuguese language and Luso-Brazilian literature: an annotated guide to selected reference works.* New York: Modern Language Association, 1989.

4557. Moser, Gerald, and Manuel Ferreira. *A New bibliography of the Lusophone literatures of Africa=Nova bibliografia das literaturas africanas de expressão portuguesa.* London: H. Zell, 1993. 2nd rev. ed., pp. 275-285.

4558. Santos, Issú. *Síntese bibliográfica das ilhas de S. Tomé e Príncipe.* São Tomé: Ed. Imprensa Nacional, 1973.

Anthologies

4559. César, Amândio (ed.). *Presença do arquipélago de S. Tomé e Príncipe na moderna cultura portuguesa.* Lisboa: Clamara Municipal, 1968. Poetry and stories.

4560. Massa, Françoise et Jean-Michel Massa (eds.). *Fablier de São Tomé=Fabulário São-Tomense.* Paris: Conseil international de la langue française, 1984. (Fleuve et flamme). Tr. par E. Giusti. In Creole and French. Tales.

4561. Neves, Carlos Agostinho das. *Antologia poética de S. Tomé e Príncipe.* São Tomé: Arquivo Histórico, 1977.

General studies

4562. Ferreira, Manuel. *Literaturas africanas de expressão portuguesa.* Lisbon: Instituto de Cultura Portuguesa, 1977. v. 1.

Authors

4563. Alegre, Costa. *Versos.* Lisbon: Liv. Ferin, 1916. Poetry.

4564. Anjos, Gustavo dos. *Bandeira para um cadáver.* São Tomé: Direcção Nacional da Cultura, 1984. (Gravana nova; 1). Short story.

4565. Cinatti, Ruy. *Lemranças para S. Tomé e Príncipe.* Evora, Portugal: Instituto Universitário, 1979. Poetry.

4566. Costa Alegre, Caetano da. *Verses.* Lisbon: Livraria, 1916. Poetry.

4567. De Almeida, José Maria. *Maiá Póçon, contos africanos.* Lisbon: Momento, 1937. Short stories.

4568. Espírito Santo, Aldo (F). *E nosso o solo sagrado da terra.* Lisbon: Ulmeiro, 1978. (Vozes das Ilhas; 1). Poetry.

4569. ———. *O Jorgal das Ilhas.* São Tomé: [s.n.], 1976. Poetry.

4570. ———. *Rio seco, água molhada.* São Tomé: [s.n.], 1984. Poetry.

4571. Marky, Sum. *As mulatinhas.* Rio de Janeiro: Record Ed., 1973. Novel.

4572. Reis, Fernando. *Roça.* Lisbon: Adastra, 1960. Novel.

4573. Tenreiro, Francisco José. *Coração em Africa.* Linda-a-Velha, Portugal: Africa Ed., 1982. (Para e história das literaturas africanas de expressão portuguesa; 1). Poetry.

4574. ———. *Ilha de Nome Santo.* Coimbra, Portugal: Colecção Novo Cancioneiro, 1942. Poetry.

4575. Veiga, Marcelo da Mata, Marcelo Francisco Veiga da. *O canto do ossôbo.* Linda-a-Velha, Portugal: ALAC, 1989. (Para e história das literaturas africanas de expressão portuguesa; 8). Poetry.

AFRIKAANS

(South Africa, Namibia)

Bibliography

4576. Toerien, Barend J. *Afrikaans literature in translation: a bibliography.* Cape Town: Carrefour Press, 1993.

Anthologies

4577. Aucamp, Hennie (ed.). *Vuurslag: kortkortverhale.* Cape Town: Tafelberg, 1991.

4578. Brink, André, and J. M. Coetzee (eds.). *A Land apart: a contemporary South African reader.* London: Faber, 1986.

4579. Fourie, Corlia (ed.). *Vrou--mens: verhale deur vroue oor vroue.* Cape Town: Human & Rousseau, 1992.

4580. Grove, Alewyn Petrus (ed.). *Hoogtepunte in die Afrikaanse verhaalkuns.* Cape Town: Tafelberg, 1985. 6th ed.

4581. ———— and C. J. D. Harvey (eds.). *Afrikaans poems.* Cape Town: OUP, 1969.

4582. Krige, Uys, and Jack Cope (eds.). *The Penguin book of South African verse.* London: Penguin, 1968.

4583. Trump, Martin. *Armed vision: Afrikaans writers in English.* Craighall: Ad. Donker, 1987. Short stories.

General studies

4584. Brink, André. *Aspekte van die nuwe prosa.* Pretoria: Academica, 1967.

4585. ————. *Literatur in die strydperk.* Kaapstad: Human & Rousseau, 1985.

4586. Coetzee, A. *Marxisme en die Afrikaanse letterkunde*. Belleville: University of the Western Cape, 1988. (Taal-en-politiekreeks; 2).

4587. Cope, Jack. *The Adversary within: dissident writers in Afrikaans*. Cape Town; Atlantic Highlands: D. Philip; Humanities Press, 1982.

4588. De Waal, J. H. H. *Johannes Van Wyk: 'n historiese roman in Afrikaans*. Pretoria: de Bussy, 1921.

4589. Gardner, Judy H. *Impaired vision: portraits of black women in the Afrikaans novel, 1948-1988*. Utrecht; Amsterdam: Kairos; VU University Press, 1991.

4590. Haarhoff, Dorian. *The Wild South-West: frontier myths and metaphors in literature set in Namibia, 1760-1988*. Johannesburg: Witwatersrand University Press, 1991.

4591. Johl, Ronèl. *Kritiek in krisis: vryheid vir die teks*. Durban: Butterworth, 1986.

4592. Kannemeyer, J. C. *A History of Afrikaans literature*. Pietermaritzburg: Shuter & Shooter, 1993.

4593. Louw, Nicolaas Petrus Van Wyk. *Deurskouende verband*. Cape Town: Human & Rousseau, 1977.

4594. ————. *Vernuwing in die prosa: grepe uit ons Afrikaanse ervaring*. Pretoria: Academica, 1970.

4595. Nienaber, Petrus Johannes. *Perspektief en profiel: 'n geskiedenis van die Afrikaanse letterkunde*. Johannesburg: Afrikaanse Pers-Boekhandel, 1980. 3rd. verb. uitgawe.

4596. Senekal, Jan. *Bronne by die studie van Afrikaanse prosawerke*. Johannesburg: Perskor, 1984.

4597. Smith, Julian. *Toneel en politiek*. Belleville: University of Western Cape, 1990. (Taal-en-politiekreeks; 3).

4598. Van der Merwe, C. N. *Breaking barriers: stereotypes and the changing of values in Afrikaans writing, 1875-1990*. Amsterdam; Atlanta: Rodopi, 1993.

4599. Wiehahn, Rialette. *Die Afrikaanse poesiekritiek: 'n historiesteoretise beskouing.* Cape Town: Academica, 1965.

Authors

4600. Behr, Mark. *Die reuk van appels.* Strand, South Africa: Queillerie, 1993. Novel.

4601. Blignaut, Audrey (F). *Die Rooi granaat.* Cape Town: Tafelberg, 1964. Essays.

4602. Botha, Elize (F). *Prosakroniek.* Cape Town: Tafelberg, 1987.

4603. Breytenbach, Breyten. *And Death white as words: an anthology of the poetry of Breyten Breytenbach.* London: Collings, 1978. Ed. by J. M. Coetzee.

4604. ———. *Eklips: die derde bundel van die ongedantse dans.* Emmarentia, South Africa: Taurus, 1983. Poetry.

4605. ———. *In Africa even the flies are happy: selected poems, 1964-1977.* London: Calder, 1978. Tr. by D. Hirson.

4606. ———. *Judas eye, and, Self-portrait/ deathwatch.* London: Faber, 1988. Tr. from Afrikaans. Poetry/essays.

4607. ———. *Lewendood: kantlynkarteling by 'n digbundel.* Emmarentia, South Africa: Taurus, 1985. Poetry.

4608. ———. *Nege landskappe van ons tye bemaak aan 'n beminde.* Johannesburg: Hond/Intaka, 1993. Poetry.

4609. ———. *A Season in paradise.* London: Cape, 1980. Orig. pub. as: *'N Seison in die paradys.* Johannesburg: Perskor, 1976. Tr. by Rike Vaughan. Biography.

4610. Ferreira, Jeanette (F). *Breyten, die Simbool daar.* Cape Town: Saayman & Weber, 1985.

4611. Galloway, Francis. *Breyten Breytenbach as openbare figuur.* Pretoria: Haum-Literêr, 1990.

4612. Viviers, Jack. *Breyten: 'n verslag oor Breyten Breytenbach.* Cape Town: Tafelberg, 1978.

4613. Brink, André. *The Ambassador.* London: Faber, 1985. Pub. in Afrikaans as: *Die Ambassadeur.* Cape Town: Human & Rousseau, 1963. Novel. See also English section.

4614. ———. *A Dry white season.* London: W. H. Allen, 1979. Pub. in Afrikaans as: *'n Droë wit seisoen.* Johannesburg: Taurus, 1979. Novel.

4615. ———. *An Instant in the wind.* London: W. H. Allen, 1976. Pub. in Afrikaans as: *'n Oomblik in die wind.* Johannesburg: Taurus, 1975. Novel.

4616. ———. *Inteendeel: Synde die lewe van 'n beroemde rebel, soldaat, reisiger, ontdekker, bouer, skribent, Latinis, leser, minaar en leuenaar.* Cape Town: Human & Rousseau, 1993. Pub. in English as: *On the contrary.* London: Secker, 1993.

4617. ———. *Looking on darkness: a novel.* London; New York: W. H. Allen; Morrow, 1974. Tr. of: *Kennis van die Aand.*

4618. ———. *Mapmakers: writing in a state of siege.* London: Faber, 1983.

4619. ———. *Rumours of rain.* London: W. H. Allen, 1978. Pub. in Afrikaans as: *Gerugte van reën.* Cape Town: Human & Rousseau, 1978. Novel.

4620. Senekal, Jan (ed.). *Donker weerlig: literêre opstelle oor die werke von André P. Brink.* Kenwyn: Jutalit, 1988.

4621. Cussons, Sheila (F). *Die Heilige modder.* Cape Town: Tafelberg, 1988. Poetry.

4622. Deacon, Thomas. *Die predikasies van Jacob Oerson.* Cape Town: Tafelberg, 1993. Poetry.

4623. Du Plessis, Phil. *Openbaringe en Johannes.* Cape Town: Carrefour, 1992. Poetry.

4624. Eybers, Elizabeth (F). *Noodluik*. Cape Town: Human & Rousseau, 1990. Poetry.

4625. ———. *Versamelde gedigte*. Cape Town: Human & Rousseau, 1990. Collected poetry.

4626. Lindenberg, Ester, Hans, and Ernst (eds.). *Uit liefde en ironie: liber amicorum Elisabeth Eybers*. Amsterdam: Querido, 1990.

4627. Goosen, Jeanne (F). *Not all of us*. Strand, South Africa: Queillerie, 1992. Tr. by André Brink. Orig. pub. as: *Ons is nie almal so nie*. Novel.

4628. Huismans, Emma (F). *Berigte van weerstand*. Johannesburg: Taurus, 1990. Short stories.

4629. Jonker, Ingrid (F). *Selected poems*. London: Cape, 1968. Tr. from Afrikaans by Jack Cope and William Plomer.

4630. Joubert, Elsa (F). *Dansmaat*. Cape Town: Tafelberg, 1993. Short stories.

4631. ———. *Missionaris*. Cape Town: Tafelberg, 1988. Novel.

4632. ———. *Poppie Nongena*. Johannesburg; London: J. Ball; Hodder, 1980. Orig. pub. as: *Die Swerfjare van Poppie Nongena*. Tafelberg, 1978. Novel.

4633. Krige, Uys. *Die Grone kring*. Kaapstad: Human & Rousseau, 1976. Orig. pub. in 1956. Poetry.

4634. ———. *Versamelde gedigte*. Pretoria: Van Schaik, 1985. Ed. by J. C. Kannemeyer. Poetry.

4635. Kannemeyer, J. C. (ed.). *Die Veelsydige Krige: vyf studies oor die skrywer en die mens*. Cape Town: Human & Rousseau, 1988.

4636. Krog, Antjie (F). *Lady Anne*. Johannesburg: Taurus, 1989. Poetry.

4637. Leroux, Etienne. *Seven days at the Silbersteins.* London: W. H. Allen, 1968. Tr. of: *Sewe dae by die Silbersteins.* Novel.

4538. Liebenberg, Wilhelm. *As die nood hoog is.* Groenkloof, South Africa: Hond, 1993.

4639. Prinsloo, Koos. *Weifeling.* Johannesburg: Hond/Intaka, 1993. Short stories.

4640. Rousseau, Ina (F). *Grotwater.* Cape Town: Human & Rousseau, 1989. Poetry.

4641. Schoeman, Karel. *Another country.* London: Sinclair-Stevenson, 1991. Also pub.: Picador, 1994. Fiction.

4642. ———. *Promised land.* London: Futura, 1979. Tr. of: *Na die geliefde land.* Fiction.

4643. ———. *Take leave and go.* London: Sinclair-Stevenson, 1992. Tr. from Afrikaans. Fiction.

4644. Small, Adam. *Kanna Hy Kô Hystoe.* Cape Town: Tafelberg, 1965. Drama. See also English section.

4645. ———. *Kitaar my kruis.* Cape Town: Haum De Jager Publishers, 1974. Poetry.

4646. Smit, Berta (F). *Juffrou Sophia vlug vorentoe.* Strand, South Africa: Queillerie, 1993. Novel.

4647. Snyders, Peter. *'n Waarskynlike mens.* Greenhaven, South Africa: Unison, 1992. Poetry.

4648. Stockenström, Wilma (F). *Die Heengaanrefrein.* Cape Town: Human and Rousseau, 1988. Poetry.

4649. Van Heerden, Etienne. *Ancestral voices.* London: Allison & Busby, 1994. Tr. by Michael Hacksley. Novel.

4650. ———. *Casspirs en Campari's.* Cape Town: Tafelberg, 1991. Novel.

GERMAN

(Cameroon, Namibia)

Bibliography

4651. Dippold, Max F. *Une bibliographie de Cameroun: les écrits en langue Allemande.* Yaoundé; Freiburg: CLE; Instituts für Soziale Zusammenarbeit, 1971.

General studies

4652. Haarhoff, Dorian. *The Wild South-West: frontier myths and metaphors in literature set in Namibia, 1760-1988.* Johannesburg: Witwatersrand University Press, 1991.

4653. Nwezeh, E. C. *Africa in French and German fiction, 1911-1938.* Ile-Ife: University of Ife Press, 1979.

Authors

4654. Angula, Helmut Pau Kangulohi. *The Two thousand days of Haimbodi ya Haufiku.* Windhoek: Gamsberg Macmillan, 1990. First pub. in German as: *Die Zweitausend Tage des Haimbooi ya Haufika.* Bremen: University of Bremen, 1986. Autobiographical fiction.

4655. Timm, Uwe. *Morenga: Roman.* München: Verlagsgruppe Bertselmann, 1978. Historical novel.

SPANISH

(Equatorial Guinea, Western Sahara)

Bibliography

4656. Liniger-Goumaz, M. *Historical Dictionary of Equatorial Guinea.* Metuchen, NJ: Scarecrow Press, 1988. (African historical dictionaries; 21). 2nd ed.

Anthology

4657. Farès, Nabile. *Chants d'histoire et de vie des roses de sable: texte bilingue pour un peuple sahrawi=Escuchando tu historia.* Paris: L'Harmattan, 1978. Poetry.

Authors

4658. Evita, Leoncio. *Cuando los Combes luchaban: novela de costumbres de Guinea española.* Madrid: Instituo de Estudios Africanos, 1950. Novel.

4659. Manfredi Cano, D. *Tierra negra.* Barcelona: Luis de Caralt, 1957. Novel.

4660. Nsué Angüe, María. *Ekomo.* Madrid: Universidad Nacional de Educación a Distancisa, 1985. Novel.

AUTHORS INDEX

Numbers following author's name refer to entries.

FEMALE LITERARY AUTHORS INDEX

First item listed only.
Consult previous main *Authors Index* for full details.
Critics not included.

COUNTRIES INDEX

759 (Akamba); 823 (Luo); 1207-1269 (English)

Lesotho: 352-386 (Sesotho); 754 (oral literature); 1383-1386 (English)

Liberia: 18; 2056-2065 (English)

Libya: 1033-1062 (Arabic)

Madagascar: 18; 278-333 (Malagasy); 480 (Swahili); 4273-4344 (French)

Malawi: 727, 780 (oral literature); 788, 819-820, 833 (Chewa); 1387-1427 (English)

Mali: 741, 779, 783 (oral literature); 750, 770 (Bambara); 767 (Peul); 784 (Maninka); 3814-3883 (French)

Mauritania: 776 (oral literature); 1063-1068 (Arabic); 3884-3893 (French)

Morocco: 563 (Tamazight); 1069-1092 (Arabic); 2863-3024 (French)

Mozambique: 18; 527 (Swahili); 733 (Tsonga); 825-826 (Shangaan); 1668 (English); 4358, 4507-4555 (Portuguese)

Namibia: 739, 755 (oral literature); 744, 806 (Oshikwanyama); 758 (San);

790 (Herero); 793, 831 (Oshindonga); 794 (Oshiwambo); 809 (Gciriku); 1428-1445 (English); 4590 (Afrikaans); 4652-4655 (German)

Niger: 555, 568 (Tamazight); 767 (Peul); 220-250 (Hausa); 3894-3944 (French)

Nigeria: 18; 220-250 (Hausa); 251-277 (Igbo); 641-669 (Yoruba); 730 (Fulani); 766 (Ogoni); 769 (Edo); 798 (Ijo); 1139 (Arabic); 2066-2350 (English); 3945 (French)

Rwanda: 728, 737, 745, 747, 771, 782, 808 (Kinyarwanda); 3946-3955 (French)

São Tomé & Príncipe: 4556-4575 (Portuguese)

Senegal: 18; 732 (Peul); 735; 3965 (Wolof); 736 (Manding); 760, 774 (Fulani/Fulbe); 1140 (Arabic); 3956-4102 (French)

Sierra Leone: 18; 743 (Limba); 772 (Woi); 2351-2367 (English)

Somalia: 448-474 (Somali); 1270-1278 (English); 4103-4105 (French)

South Africa: 18, 154; 334-351 (Ndebele); 352-386 (Sesotho); 585-606

ABOUT THE AUTHORS

Peter Limb has published on many aspects of African studies, including history, literature, and bibliography. His works include *The ANC and Black Workers in South Africa, 1912-1992: An Annotated Bibliography* (London: H. Zell, 1993). His reviews have appeared in *Journal of Modern African Studies, African Book Publishing Record,* and *Australian Library Review.* He compiles a regular bibliographical column for the *Southern African Review of Books.* In 1995 he was a visiting fellow at the Mayibuye Centre, University of the Western Cape, and his catalog of the *Papers of Yusuf Dadoo* will be published by that Centre in 1996. He is a librarian at the Reid Library, University of Western Australia, where he has completed postgraduate studies in African studies. He is coeditor of H-Africa, the Internet scholarly discussion group on African studies. [plimb@library.uwa.edu.au].

Jean-Marie Volet is a research fellow at the University of Western Australia. He has taught and researched Francophone African literatures for many years. His literary interests include the fictionalization of contemporary issues, the process of canonization of literary texts and the emergence of women novelists in African literatures. He has published numerous articles and reviews on Francophone African literatures in international journals. His last two books are: *La Parole aux Africaines* (Amsterdam: Rodopi, 1993) and, with Beverley Ormerod, *Romancières d'Afrique Noire: Le Sud du Sahara* (Paris: L'Harmattan, 1994). He is currently working on *l'effet-personnage,* and in particular on the nature and function of secondary characters in African as well as other literatures. [jvolet@uniwa.uwa.edu.au].